THE
SPANISH LABYRINTH

THE
SPANISH LABYRINTH

An Account of the
Social and Political Background of
the Civil War

BY

GERALD BRENAN

CAMBRIDGE
At the University Press
1967

PUBLISHED BY

THE SYNDICS OF THE CAMBRIDGE UNIVERSITY PRESS

Bentley House, 200 Euston Road, London, N.W. 1
American Branch: 32 East 57th Street, New York 22, N.Y.

First edition	1943
Second edition	1950
First paperback edition	1960
Reprinted	1962
	1964
	1967

Printed in the U.S.A.

CONTENTS

Part I

THE ANCIEN RÉGIME, 1874–1931

Part II

THE CONDITION OF THE WORKING CLASSES

Part III

THE REPUBLIC

PREFACE TO THE SECOND EDITION

This book was written during and immediately after the Civil War. It was often difficult to get the material I needed and still more difficult, in the heated atmosphere of Spanish politics, to rely upon what I got. I had, too, to contend in my own mind with strong feelings and prejudices, for I had taken sides in the war in support of the Republic against the Nationalist Movement. Those who remember the intense passions aroused all over the world by this conflict will understand how difficult it was to see Spanish affairs objectively. Yet I tried to do so, for my object in writing this book was not to justify the side I supported, but rather to explain to myself and to others how things had turned out as they did. I especially wished to make clear the mistakes and illusions of the Spanish Left, for they were the people who, on the whole, seemed to me to have the greatest amount of justice and decency on their side and, since most persons of good will in other countries supported them and their cause was also that of the Democracies, the lessons to be learned from their failure might find a wide audience. Not of course that I claimed to see further at the time than the actors in these events, but that in the course of writing about them, the mistakes stood out and demanded to be taken notice of.

On rereading this book to-day, nine years after it was finished, I naturally find some things in it that I would like to change. Errors of fact have been corrected, but passages which require rewriting or amplifying have had to be left as they are. The chapter I am least satisfied with is that which deals with the struggle between the Liberals and the Church. A national Church, even when it has fallen far below what is expected of it, has resources of a different kind from those of a political party. It is not to be judged, as we Anglo-Saxons are apt to suppose, as a sort of divinely appointed ethical society, whose health and vigour depend solely upon the religious spirit of its members. At its lowest it occupies a key position in the social pattern of the country, from which, especially in agricultural communities, it cannot easily be displaced. Then, if it is a Catholic Church, it has a certain unsuspected power of rising and expanding, because it provides something for which there is an increasing demand in times of stress. This is especially true in Spain, where a destructive and sceptical frame of mind is accompanied, often in the same person, by a deep longing for faith and certainty.

My mistake in this chapter was to take up a too exclusively moral and political attitude. The Spanish Church has a vitality which its conduct does not suggest. When one has finished pointing out its narrowness, its obstinacy, its talent for making enemies, as well as its incapacity for adapting itself to modern times, there is still a good deal left to be said. At all events it is the power which remains in the field when wars and revolutions are over, when everything else has failed, the parent to whom the Prodigal, not entirely willingly, returns.

It is true that a Church as rigid and uncompromising as the Spanish Church is not conceivable in France or Italy. But is not that the case with almost every other Spanish body and institution? The Spaniards who most strongly object to it—the intellectuals and the Liberals—are precisely those who wish to see their country more European. That, no doubt, if one has been born a Spaniard, is a sensible ideal, yet, seen from this side of the Pyrenees, the chief virtue of Spain may be thought to lie in its intractability. Death by monotony, by sameness, by loss of identity is—if we are spared destruction in another war—the fate held out by the brave new world of universal control and amalgamation. Against that death Spain will put up a long drawn out resistance.

As regards the rest of the book, I have little to say. So far as I am aware, no new material has appeared to affect the account I have given of the events which led up to the Civil War. Nor have my opinions upon these events changed in any important particular. I feel more sympathetic than I did to General Primo de Rivera, though it is certain that, as I have pointed out, his brief age of gold was a consequence of the American boom; and I feel less patient with the folly of the Republicans in attacking the Church, neglecting the land question and generally overestimating their own strength. But these are matters of degree and if I were to rewrite this book to-morrow, I should not do so very differently. Of the folly and wickedness of the Military rising, dependent as it was upon foreign assistance, there can to-day be no two opinions. With a little patience the Right would have gained much of what it sought without a war, for the Popular Front was breaking up rapidly through its inner discords, and a revolution from the Left had already been tried and had failed. But the Nationalist leaders had had their heads turned by Nazi Germany: they wanted nothing less than a complete victory with the annihilation of their enemies; and their followers, who in any case had no choice, were frightened. The result was a civil war which has ruined Spain for half a century.

PREFACE TO THE FIRST EDITION

Nearly ninety years ago Karl Marx observed that the knowledge of Spanish history in his time was altogether inadequate. 'There is perhaps', he wrote, 'no country except Turkey, so little known to and so falsely judged by Europe as Spain.' And he went on to explain that this was because historians 'instead of viewing the strength and resources of these peoples in their provincial and local organization have drawn at the source of their court histories'. These remarks still have a good deal of truth in them. The standard histories of the Peninsula give a false impression of the events they describe. And this is due chiefly to one thing. Spain, both economically and psychologically, differs so greatly from the other countries of Western Europe that the words of which most history is made—feudalism, autocracy, liberalism, Church, Army, Parliament, trade union and so forth—have quite other meanings there to what they have in France or England. Only if this is made clear, only if each piece of the political and economic machine is separately described, only if the provincial questions are fully gone into and the interactions of all the local and sectional organizations on one another are brought to light will anything like a true impression be arrived at.

The first point to be noticed is the strength of provincial and municipal feeling. Spain is the land of the *patria chica*. Every village, every town is the centre of an intense social and political life. As in classical times, a man's allegiance is first of all to his native place, or to his family or social group in it, and only secondly to his country and government. In what one may call its normal condition Spain is a collection of small, mutually hostile or indifferent republics held together in a loose federation. At certain great periods (the Caliphate, the Reconquista, the Siglo de Oro) these small centres have become infected by a common feeling or idea and have moved in unison: then when the impetus given by this idea declined, they have fallen apart and resumed their separate and egoistic existence. It is this that has given its spectacular character to Spanish history. Instead of a slow building up of forces such as one sees in other European nations, there has been an alternation between the petty quarrels of tribal life and great upsurges of energy that come, economically speaking, from nowhere.

The main political problem has therefore always been how to strike a balance between an effective central government and the needs of local autonomy. If too much force is applied at the centre, the provinces revolt and proclaim their independence: if too little, they withdraw into themselves and practise passive resistance. At the best of times Spain is a difficult country to govern. And it happens that this difficulty has been accentuated, if it has not been caused, by one thing. Castile, which by its geographical position and its history represents the centralizing tradition, is a barren tableland, poor in agriculture, in minerals and in industry. The provinces of the sea border are all much richer and more industrious. Thus though Spain can only be held together by Castile—for a Spain governed from Barcelona, Bilbao or Seville is unthinkable—the Castilians lack the industrial and commercial dynamism to provide an effective economic organization. Their outlook is military and authoritarian, and the richer and more industrious provinces have been quick to realize that, so long as they are governed by Castile, not only their local liberties but also their economic interests will be sacrificed. There have no doubt been partial exceptions to this—the reign of Carlos III (who was brought up in Italy) and the Dictatorship of Primo de Rivera (an Andalusian) stand out—but in general one may say that the principal cause of Spanish separatism has been the industrial and commercial apathy of the Castilians. How else can one explain the fact that at a time when modern methods of production and communication were welding together the European nations and when the small states of Germany and Italy were uniting, the separatist tendencies in Spain were becoming more acute?

There is often however something to be said for living out of one's age. The concentration of the social forces of a country into small local groups brings compensations. By their failure to form a politically homogeneous nation Spaniards have preserved a kind of life which was common in the Middle Ages and in antiquity, but which modern men, the children of small families and diffuse societies, have lost. Most of the qualities we admire them for come from this. Their vigour and independence of character, the quickness and completeness of their response to any social situation, their emotional integrity, their gift of words—and, one should add, their chronic indiscipline—are all due to the fact that they have gone on living the intense life of the Greek city-state or Arab tribe or medieval commune. Instead of the agora, there is the club and café. Politics are municipal or tribal and in this sense real—that the man on the losing side pays a forfeit. Hence the political acuteness which strikes even the most superficial observer of the Spaniards, but hence too the ineffectuality. Even the best minds among them rarely escape sufficiently from the web of personal relations to dominate the scene around them. The same causes that have made Spaniards the most vigorous and human people in Europe have condemned them to long eras of political stagnation and futility.

It goes without saying that the tendency of the country to divide up its life into small local compartments has not excluded other lines of cleavage. There has also been a class stratification and a class struggle. But even this has been deeply affected by the provincial question. Thus, to take only the simplest case, one finds in those provinces where there were autonomist leanings among the bourgeoisie, that the working classes adopted a wildly expansive and liberty-loving form of socialism known as anarchism, whereas in Castile they preferred a severely authoritarian and centralizing Marxism. Even the Marxist heretics (the 'Trotskyist' P.O.U.M.) hailed from Catalonia. It might be thought that the rise of Liberalism in Castile in the last century was an exception to this. But Liberalism reached Madrid from Andalusia and was accepted by the Castilians when they saw what use they could make of it. They found it not only strengthened the Castilian bourgeoisie by handing over to them the Church lands and common lands free of all feudal embarrassments, but that it provided them with an instrument of government of strongly centralizing tendencies. The one element in the Constitution which gave some measure of local autonomy, the provision for the free election of the Municipal councils, was suppressed as soon as the Carlists had been safely defeated, whilst the difficulty presented by the clause in the constitution requiring general elections to the Cortes was got over by the organization of local bosses or caciques, who saw to it that only the Government nominees got in. Thus the triumph of the Liberal Party failed to bring any of the characteristic features of parliamentary Liberalism. Spain continued to be ruled by the landlords, who alone held all the political power. The real Liberals, the petite bourgeoisie of the South and East, found themselves left out in the cold and condemned to a sterile ferment of radical and federal propaganda, with occasional revolutions, till the end of the century. The seed they had sown was then reaped by the Anarchists.

It is thus clear that the pattern of political forces in Spain has been determined throughout by geography. In the East and South there was Catalan nationalism among the middle classes and anarcho-syndicalism among the factory workers and agricultural labourers—both movements that lay stress on liberty. In Castile there was an authoritarian Catholic conservatism based on land tenure and an equally authoritarian Marxism that drew its strength from land hunger. In the North there were autonomist movements linked to an ultra-Catholic, agrarian creed known as Carlism. Even such widely felt movements as Republicanism had a regional background, because, however centrally minded its leaders might be, however Castilian in their outlook, they could only reach and hold power with the aid of Catalonia. Just as the Carlists, for all their autocratic ways, had been forced to promise the Basques and Navarrese their historic *fueros*, so the Republicans and Socialists of 1931, Castilians to the marrow almost all of them, were obliged to grant the Catalans a very high degree of autonomy. Indeed, as their enemies increased their pressure against them, they were compelled to go farther and to hand out autonomy statutes to the Basques and Galicians as well—an example of the fact that every popular movement, every Republican régime in Spain, tends under pressure of events to become federal and that the farther it carries its federal programme, the weaker it becomes, because it has parted with power to the provinces. Military revolts, on the contrary, which also (unless they have foreign aid) require the Catalan spring-board, are able to go back on their promises as soon as they are established in power, because they rule by force and not by consent.

But what was it that made these various parties into which Spain was divided so incapable of coming to terms with one another? As well explain why it is that the nations of Europe find it so difficult to live in harmony. Spain is a miniature Europe and the Spaniards are great power lovers. This comparison, however, must not lead one to exaggerate the separatist sentiments of the different provinces. Even Catalans feel themselves to be Spaniards. The force behind every autonomist movement in the Peninsula is the discontent of the petite bourgeoisie at the narrow and impecunious groove in which they live. The root of their local jingoism is economic. But the peculiar inter-twining of provincial and social issues and the balance of power tactics adopted by the Governments at Madrid have helped very greatly to increase the tension. One may see this best in the case of Barcelona, where Conservative Governments systematically built up the power of the revolutionary working classes in order to keep in check the middle classes, who were clamouring for autonomy, and even, on one occasion,

when the Anarchists had failed to do their job, laid bombs at the doors
of the capitalists themselves. A régime given over to wretched shifts
and petty politics of this kind does not contribute to the peaceful
development of a country. On the contrary it is a source of perpetual
irritation. More than anything else it has been the failure of the ruling
classes to provide honest government, or to show the least regard for
the complaints that cried to Heaven against them from the provinces,
that has made Spain the classic land of insurrections.

There is perhaps one more factor in the political scene that needs
to be taken account of—the influence of religion. To understand this
one must go back some way in history. Modern Spain owes her
existence as a nation to the Reconquista. For eight centuries the work
of driving out the Moslems was her peculiar vocation, and her unity
was the reward of its successful conclusion. The crusading impulse
had by this time become so much a part of the national character that
till complete exhaustion set in in the seventeenth century the holy
war was continued without any regard for self-interest against the
Protestants. The Church had naturally taken a leading part in these
events. The clergy were the guardians of the great idea that Spaniards
were fighting for, and under their influence Spaniards became accustomed to thinking that all differences of opinion were crimes and all
wars were ideological. Then, in 1812, the Church became engaged in
a political struggle with the Liberals. This struggle led to a civil war
that lasted seven years and, though the Church lost, politics and
religion were left so fatally entwined that they could never afterwards
be separated. This became clear when it was seen that the defeat of the
Church had thrown it into the arms of the landowners, so that from
now on an attack on the one would inevitably mean an attack on the
other. The harmonizing role which religion had played in the social
disputes of the sixteenth and seventeenth centuries had changed to
one of exacerbation.

Then, at the beginning of this century, a general decay of religious
faith set in. The middle classes fell off first and after them the working
classes, but religion had meant so much to the poor that they were left
with the hunger for something to replace it. And this something could
only be one of the political doctrines, anarchism or socialism, that they
found waiting for them. They adopted them therefore in the same
spirit, with the same crusading ardour and singleness of mind with
which in previous ages they had adopted Catholicism. For a time it
seemed that a compromise might be possible because the Socialist

leaders desired reform rather than revolution, but the intransigeance of the governing classes combined with the decline of the economic situation and the rise of fascism in Austria and of Nazism in Germany made this impossible.

In other countries respect for the State might have acted as a moderating influence. But this was a feeling that not a single party in Spain ever showed. A succession of disreputable sovereigns had discredited the Monarchy. Military *pronunciamientos* had compromised the Army and corrupt elections had destroyed faith in the Cortes. The Church, which had initiated the most terrible civil war of the century, was a permanent focus of disaffection. To most Spaniards the Government meant simply the clique of politicians which had managed to get into power, and none had any moral authority outside its own circle of supporters. One may say that the only thing that delayed the outbreak of civil war was that no party felt strong enough to begin.

Under these political and social alignments there lay of course an economic question. In raw materials and in foodstuffs, as well as in manufactures, Spain was in 1931 more self-sufficient than any other European country. But to make it a working concern the earnings of the peasants and agricultural labourers needed to be raised to enable them to buy more in the towns. This however, under the system of private ownership of land, was not easy. The soil through the greater part of the country is poor and the rainfall deficient: the land has to support a far larger population than modern farming technique will allow. With even the best organization only a low standard of living would have been possible. But in most parts of the country the level of farming was backward, the credit system unhelpful and the marketing system worse, whilst the number of middle-class families (many of them extremely poor and others just drones) was greater than the wealth of the country could support. The result for more than half the population was therefore chronic undernourishment, amounting in bad years to semi-starvation. This provided a permanent incitement to revolution. And yet so accustomed are the Spanish poor to privation that without the loss of hold of the Church and the introduction of new creeds to replace it, this factor would not have been sufficient. The revolutionary forces in Spain had to be moral and ideological ones and the working classes aspired rather to freedom and control of their own affairs than to a higher standard of living. Where there was envy of the rich (and Spaniards are a very envious race) it took the form of desiring to bring them down almost as much as of raising themselves.

The Civil War was the explosion in the powder magazine that had been slowly accumulating. The Popular Front elections had temporarily aligned the political forces in Spain on two opposite, though by no means well assorted, sides. The Army then rose, expecting with its usual over-confidence to overwhelm the population of the large towns within a few days. But the heroism of the working classes defeated this project and the revolution they had so long waited for, but would probably never have been able to launch themselves, began. It is in the nature of revolutions to throw up moments when all the more brilliant dreams of the human race seem about to be realized, and the Catalans with their expansive and self-dramatizing character were not behind other peoples in this respect. Visitors to Barcelona in the autumn of 1936 will never forget the moving and uplifting experience[1] and, as the resistance to the military rebellion stiffened, the impressions they brought back with them spread to wider and wider circles. Spain became the scene of a drama in which it seemed as if the fortunes of the civilized world were being played out in miniature. As in a crystal, those people who had eyes for the future looked, expecting to read there their own fate.

Spain, the symbol, was however rather a different thing from Spain, the actuality. The war had begun as a straightforward class struggle between the reactionary landowners on one side and the revolutionary peasants and factory workers on the other. The Church, the Army officers and the majority of the middle classes supported the former, and the petite bourgeoisie and the intellectuals the latter. Such is the broad outline, though the fact that the Republicans had bought over by the grant of an autonomy statute two of the most solidly Catholic and anti-liberal provinces in the country introduces a complication. But this apparently simple setting concealed, on the anti-fascist side, a fatal dilemma. Was the revolution to be carried out according to the ideas of the anarchists, or to the very different and much less radical ones of the Socialists? And what was to be the position of the Catalan peasants and petite bourgeoisie, caught between the Scylla of the C.N.T. and the Charybdis of the centralizing Madrid Government?

[1] Perhaps it is not too cynical to recall the similar scenes that attended the inauguration of the short-lived Federal Republic of 1873. This is how Alexandre Dumas *fils*, a cold and unemotional Frenchman, who professed to despise popular movements and in politics belonged more to the Right than to the Left, reacted to a street demonstration in Barcelona in November 1868: 'Hier, ivre de bonheur, il me fut impossible de retenir les larmes qui par instants coulaient sur mes joues; il me semblait que je voyais les yeux ouverts le plus beau rêve de ma vie—la République Universelle.'

No answer to these questions other than a second civil war seemed possible, when suddenly they were solved, or at least postponed, by fresh events. For the Spaniards, it turned out, were not to be left to fight out the war by themselves. Two totalitarian nations, Germany and Russia, intervened and their intervention led to the growth almost overnight of the small Falangist and Communist parties to positions of overriding influence. The Falangists absorbed the popular, more or less Left Wing elements on their side, and the Communists absorbed or worked in with the Right Wing of the Republicans. The C.N.T., deprived of its hopes of social revolution, adopted a more and more passive attitude. The Carlists submitted. For a time the success of the new parties seemed to show how strong was the desire in Spain for an efficient central party that would make a clean sweep of the futile struggles of the past hundred and fifty years and impose a final solution, but in the end their totalitarian ideals and methods and their dependence upon foreign nations led to a reaction against them. Receptive as Spaniards are on the surface to ideas that come from abroad, they are at bottom extremely tenacious of their own clannish ways of life, and it soon became evident that, except by foreign domination, these all-embracing parties would not be able to establish themselves. Since the termination of the war, the colossal failure of the Falange to produce tolerable conditions for anyone not a member of their own party, and their peculiar combination of graft, apathy and terrorism, have put the final touch to their unpopularity.

And what of the future? The Civil War was an appalling calamity in which every class and every party lost. In addition to the million or two dead, the health of the people has been sapped by the famine and disease that have followed it. Hundreds of thousands are still in prison. Both physically and morally Spain is the wreck of what it was. The hope of a resurrection lies in the indomitable vitality of the Spanish race and in the fulfilment, when the war is over, of the promises of lease-lend assistance that have been held out to all European nations by the Allies. Among other things, this help should include the provision of the hydraulic machinery needed for doubling the irrigated areas of the country, of machine tools for manufacturing tractors and other farm implements, and of research stations where the best technique for farming the dry areas can be worked out. The setting up of tolerable social and economic conditions in the Peninsula is a measure indispensable to the peace and prosperity of Europe.

It may be asked, what interest can a detailed account of recent
Spanish history have for the English-speaking peoples? In one sense
very little, for the problems of Spain are not ours. Living under the
shadow of European events and reflecting superficially and belatedly
the political trends of the great industrialized nations, Spaniards are in
reality obliged to cope all the time with very different social and
economic situations. This means that in all their affairs nothing is
ever quite what it seems. We grope in a sort of fog when we try to
understand them, and if we are politicians rather than historians or
psychologists, if what we are out for are confirmations of our own
theories and opinions or illustrations of general political trends, we
shall come away disappointed. Everything to be found in Spain is *sui
generis*.

And yet no one who cares for European culture can close his eyes
to the potentialities of this remarkable people. In recent years they
have produced in art Picasso, in mechanics the auto-giro, in medicine
at least one new and surprising invention. In literature and in music
their output has been characteristic and original. What then has been
their contribution to social and political ideas? Here it must at once
be said that, if we search books for the answer, we shall find nothing
very definite. And yet I believe that under all the folly and frenzy of
Spanish politics a consistent attitude emerges. Take, for example,
those two entirely indigenous products of the country, Spanish
Anarchism and Carlism. As political systems neither need be regarded
seriously: the one seeks to realize a dream of the remote future, the
other to recapture an idealized past. But as criticisms of society both
canalize a feeling that is very deep-seated among Spaniards. One may
describe this as a hatred of political shams, a craving for a richer and
deeper social life, an acceptance of a low material standard of living
and a belief that the ideal of human dignity and brotherhood can never
be obtained by political means alone, but must be sought in a moral
reformation (compulsory, it is needless to say) of society. That is what
one might call the characteristic Spanish attitude. Contrary to the
Liberal doctrine which separates Church from State and society from
government, it aims at an integration of political and social life. But
it is not totalitarian. Far from asserting the moral supremacy of the
State, it holds the Christian view that every human being, whatever his
capacity or intelligence, is an end in himself, and that the State exists
solely to advance these ends. And it goes further. The long and bitter
experience which Spaniards have had of the workings of bureaucracy

has led them to stress the superiority of society to government, of custom to law, of the judgement of neighbours to legal forms of justice and to insist on the need for an inner faith or ideology, since this alone will enable men to act as they should, in mutual harmony, without the need for compulsion. It is a religious ideal, and if it has struck so much deeper roots in Spain than in other European countries, that is no doubt due largely to the influence of Moslem ideas upon a Christian community. The deeper layers of Spanish political thought and feeling are Oriental.

I must thank my friends, Don Luis Araquistáin and Mr Arthur Lehning, for reading and criticizing my MSS.: the International Institute of Social History of Amsterdam (now at Oxford) and Mr J. Langdon Davies for lending me otherwise unobtainable books and periodicals: Don Enrique Moreno, Dr Max Nettlau, Mr E. H. G. Dobby and many Spanish friends for valuable suggestions and information: Miss Alyse Gregory for kindly correcting the proofs, and finally Dr Franz Borkenau without whose advice and encouragement this book would probably never have been written. To express here what I owe to the Spanish people for the kindness and hospitality I received from them during the years I spent among them would be impossible. This book, which I began in order to distract my mind from the horrors and suspense of the Civil War, is simply one more proof of the deep and lasting impression which Spain makes on those who know her.

G. B.

December 1942

CHRONOLOGICAL TABLE

[*Events concerning working-class organizations are in italic*]

Sept.	1868	Fall of Isabella II
Oct.	1868	*Fanelli, Bakunin's emissary, arrives in Spain*
June	1870	*Spanish Regional Federation of International founded at Barcelona*
Dec.	1870	Amadeo of Savoy becomes King
April	1872	Carlist War begins
Sept.	1872	Congress of International at the Hague and final breach between Bakunin and Marx
Dec.	1872	*Congress of Regional Federation of International at Cordova*
Feb.	1873	Abdication of Amadeo
Feb.	1873	Proclamation of Democratic Federal Republic
June	1873	Cantonalist insurrections begin
Jan.	1874	General Pavía dissolves Cortes. *International declared illegal*
Dec.	1874	Proclamation of Alfonso XII at Sagunto
Feb.	1876	End of Carlist War
May	1879	*Socialist Party founded*
Feb.	1881	Liberal Government of Sagasta. Trade unions legalised. *Regional Federation of International refounded*
	1883	*Mano Negra*
Nov.	1885	Death of Alfonso XII. Regency of María Cristina. Pact of Pardo between politicians
May	1886	Birth of Alfonso XIII
	1888	*Regional Federation of International breaks up. Foundation of Socialist trade union, the U.G.T.*
Mar.	1892	Catalan Nationalists draw up the *Bases de Manresa*
	1892–1897	Epidemic of bomb-throwing in Barcelona
Aug.	1897	Assassination of Cánovas
	1898	War with U.S.A. and loss of colonies
Feb.	1902	*General strike in Barcelona*
May	1902	Alfonso XIII comes of age
Jan.	1903	Death of Sagasta
	1903–1905	*Wave of Anarchist strikes in Andalusia*
Feb.	1906	Law of Jurisdictions. *Solidaridad Catalana founded*
Jan. 1907–Oct. 1909		Maura Government
July	1909	*Semana Trágica. Ferrer shot. Pablo Iglesias elected to Cortes*
Oct.	1910	*Anarcho-Syndicalist trade union, the C.N.T., founded*
Feb. 1910–Nov. 1912		Canalejas Government
Nov.	1912	Canalejas assassinated
	1913	Law of Mancomunidades
	1917	*Juntas de Defensa in army.* Renovation Movement
Aug.	1917	*General strike of U.G.T. and C.N.T.* Collapse of Renovation Movement
	1917–1919	*Wave of Anarchist strikes in Andalusia and the Levante*
Feb.	1919	*Strike at the Canadiense (Barcelona)*
	1919–1923	*War of pistoleros in Barcelona*
June	1921	Destruction of Spanish Army at Annual. *Communist Party founded*
Sept.	1923	Military Dictatorship of Primo de Rivera
	1925	Moroccan War concluded. Civil Dictatorship set up
	1927	*Federación Anarquista Ibérica or F.A.I. founded*

Jan. 1930	Fall of Primo de Rivera
Apr. 14, 1931	Proclamation of Republic
July 1931	Constituent Cortes meets
Dec. 1931	*Left Communist Party founded by Nin and Maurín*
Jan. 1932	*Rising of F.A.I. and Left Communists in Llobregat Valley*
Aug. 1932	General Sanjurjo's rising at Seville
Sept. 1932	Passage of Catalan Autonomy Statute
Jan. 1933	*Rising of F.A.I. in Barcelona. Casas Viejas*
April 1933	Municipal elections to the *burgos podridos*
Nov. 1933	Second Cortes of Republic elected
Dec. 1933	*Rising of the C.N.T. in Aragon*
Jan. 1934	Esquerra defeat Lliga in elections to Generalidad. *Alianza Obrera founded by Largo Caballero and Maurín*
April 1934	Generalidad passes *Ley de Cultivos*
June 1934	*Campesinos' strike*
Oct. 1934	Rising of Generalidad in Barcelona and of miners in Asturias
Dec. 1935	*Straperlo* scandal. Portela Valladares forms Government
Feb. 1936	*P.O.U.M. founded by reunion of Left Communists and Bloque Obrero y Campesino*
Feb. 1936	Popular Front victory at elections
May 1936	Azaña becomes President of Republic
July 12, 1936	Calvo Sotelo murdered
July 16, 1936	Rising of Army in Morocco. Civil War begins

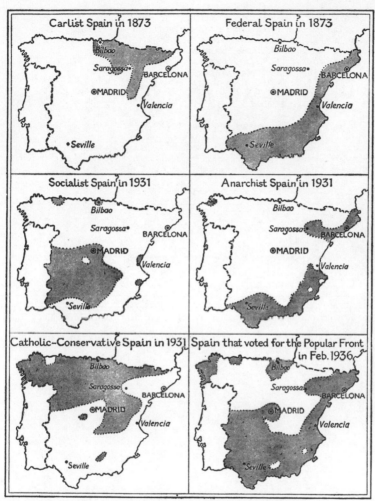

Six Maps to show the Fundamental Political Divisions of Spain
from 1873 to 1936

Part I

THE *ANCIEN RÉGIME*

1874–1931

I do not know where we are going, but I do know
this — that wherever it is we shall lose our way. SAGASTA.

~~~

Chapter I

THE RESTORATION, 1874–1898

Finally I would say that though the Spaniards have wit, industry and means sufficient for the restoration of their kingdom, they will not restore it: and though
entirely capable of saving the State, they will not save it—because they do not want to.
SELASTIANO FOSCARINI, Venetian Ambassador at Madrid in 1682–1686.

On Christmas Eve 1874 a Spanish general, Martínez Campos, halted
the handful of troops that he commanded by an olive grove under the
hill of Saguntum and made a speech at the end of which he proclaimed Alfonso XII king of Spain. The ragged conscripts, led by
their sergeants, cheered. A few officers, who remembered they had
sworn loyalty to the Republic, fell out. The rest, with shining eyes,
dreaming of new uniforms and of promotion, remounted their horses
and the column continued its march to Valencia. The last sixty years
had seen a great many *pronunciamientos* of this sort on an average
one every twenty months—but none that was more successful. The
First Republic fell without a shot being fired to defend it and a few
weeks later the young king, then a cadet at Sandhurst, landed at
Barcelona.

The man to whom the Restoration was due was not, however, a
general. The *coup d'état* had been premature—the result of a competition between Army commanders to obtain the honour. The real
architect of the new order was a Conservative politician, Don Antonio
Cánovas del Castillo, who, ever since it had become clear that the
revolution of 1868 would fail, had been carefully preparing it. He at
once assumed the leadership of the provisional government and
began the difficult work of drawing up the new Constitution—the

sixth of that century—which was to last until Primo de Rivera overthrew it.

Cánovas was an unusually cultured and intelligent man, and he was
under no illusions as to the moral and material condition of Spain at
that time. He had spent the last four years studying in the archives of
Simancas the causes of the rapid decline of Spain in the seventeenth
century and in particular during the catastrophic ministry of the
Conde de Olivares, whose situation, he observed, had in many respects been similar to his own. A man of exceptional talent, Olivares
had come into power at a critical moment with the mission of saving
and rebuilding the country—and he had failed. His mistake, as
Cánovas saw it, had been the usual Spanish one—of attempting to
carry out ambitious projects without sufficiently considering the economic and material means by which they were to be achieved. The
Spanish national vice had always been over-confidence and optimism.
Cánovas, who hated optimists, determined to take exactly the opposite path: to give the country a rest from civil wars and politics: to
encourage it to build up its industries and enrich itself, and to hope
that, as the ruling classes became by this process more European, they
would lose some of their native sloth and egoism and acquire a greater
sense of their responsibilities.

There was nothing in the temper of Spain at this time to make these
views unacceptable. A cloud of pessimism and inertia hung over
everything. Patriotic Spaniards felt despair when they thought of the
recent history of their country. The glorious national rising against
Napoleon had been followed by twenty-six years of savage reaction
and civil war: this had been succeeded by the anarchic rule of the
generals which, under a delightful but scandalously unchaste queen, in
a Ruritanian atmosphere of railway speculation and uniforms, had
lasted for another twenty-eight. Then there had come a revolution and
Isabella was turned out. The middle classes had risen because her
camarilla governments had taken away their liberties, the generals had
risen because she had chosen a lover who was not in the Guards, the
people had risen because they had lost their common lands and because they disliked being sent to die in remote unhealthy climates in
incomprehensible wars. But, when Isabella had gone, no agreement
could be come to as to the best form of government: a king of the anti-
clerical house of Savoy was tried and rejected: then came the federal
republic, which ended in disaster. The Carlists had overrun the
northern provinces: there had been a 'Cantonalist' rising in the south

which had to be suppressed by force. And now a Bourbon, a young insignificant-looking man, with none of the good looks of his reputed father, the Catalan guardsman, was on the throne again. Political feeling had never been lower, and though there was general relief that the form of government had been settled, no one felt any hope or enthusiasm as to the future.

It was in this not uncongenial atmosphere that Cánovas set out to build the new state. He was guided by two main principles—one to exclude the Army from political power—the other on no account to trust to free elections.

As to the Army—everyone now blamed it for the troubles and up-heavals of the last thirty years. In the twenties and thirties it had been the champion of the weak middle classes who were more or less Liberal, and had saved the country from the dreaded Carlists. After winning the Carlist War, it had ruled the country itself, mainly for its own profit but also, to a certain extent, with the sanction of the middle and lower-middle classes. Now that Carlism, as it was thought, was finally crushed, its function was gone, and Cánovas determined that it should be reduced for ever to the normal role of armies—the defence of the country against outside enemies.

Cánovas' second principle is more difficult to explain. He greatly admired the English parliamentary system—to the point, it is said, of knowing many of the chief speeches of Gladstone and Disraeli by heart—and in his Constitution he imitated its outward form carefully. He also introduced a property qualification by which the (mostly illiterate) working classes were excluded from the vote. One would have supposed therefore that the middle and lower-middle classes could have been allowed to express their opinion freely and to choose their candidates at elections. But this is what he deliberately set him-self to prevent. Although the press was free—that was one thing he insisted upon—there was not a single honest or genuine election to the Cortes during his life or indeed (since the system he set up continued after him) until the disappearance of the Monarchy in 1931.

The explanation of this anomaly is a simple one. Cánovas, as a politician, saw that Spain must be governed for a time by the upper classes, who alone could be counted on to support the new regime. But the country (that is to say those who had the right to vote) was mainly Radical with a strong admixture of Republicans, and under free elections they would have returned a Radical majority to the Cortes. This was the reason why the elections had at first, until the

Monarchy should gain strength and prestige, to be controlled. Besides, there were more general and permanent reasons. Since the beginning of the civil wars distrust of public opinion had become endemic among Spaniards. The old happy sense of unity under King and Church had gone and left a crowd of suspicions behind it. Now Spaniards are by nature a suspicious and exclusive race: they live habitually in small compartments and like to settle their affairs through little sets or groups. Everything for their family, their friends, their dependants, their class, is their rule, and nothing for outsiders. Had the general voter been allowed in, no pact between the Liberal and Conservative parties could have been made, since they would not have trusted one another. The exclusion of that dangerous and unpredictable factor, public opinion, was essential.

Cánovas shared all this pessimism as to the reasonableness and ductibility of the people: indeed he extended it to his own class as well. *Son españoles los que no pueden ser otra cosa*, he once said, when asked to define, for the purposes of some clause of the Constitution, the limits of Spanish nationality—'Spaniards are those people who can't be anything else'. And out of this pessimism came his belief that the affairs of the country must be conducted by a small, select class of politicians, the most intelligent, the most eloquent, the best educated, who could be trusted to do what was necessary. Thus, gradually, he hoped, serious currents of political opinion would be formed and the upper and middle classes—at present so inert and so egoistic—would wake up to their responsibilities. 'I come to galvanize', he used to say, 'the political corpse of Spain.' But in fact, like his predecessor Olivares, though for exactly opposite reasons, he merely caused it to decay more rapidly.

The middle years of the nineteenth century had seen Army dictatorships or reactionary governments interrupted every few years by military revolutions. Since 1814 no Liberal government had come in except by violence. Cánovas was too intelligent not to see the inconvenience and the danger of that. He therefore arranged that Conservative governments should be succeeded regularly by Liberal governments. The plan he followed was, whenever an economic crisis or a serious strike came along, to resign and let the Liberals deal with it. This explains why most of the repressive legislation passed during the rest of the century was passed by them. But in fact there was no longer any difference whatever between Liberals and Conservatives, except that the Liberals were anti-clerical and interested themselves in education, whilst the Conservatives professed a mild concern for agriculture and for social conditions.

In 1885 the King died of consumption and a few months later the Queen Regent gave birth to a posthumous child—Alfonso XIII. As the King lay on his death-bed the politicians met at the Palace of the Pardo and signed a pact by which the practice they had already initiated of taking turns at government was formally consecrated. So risks to the dynasty were avoided. Cánovas, who was then in power, resigned and his Liberal opponent Sagasta formed a government. To keep the Radicals quiet an act of Universal Suffrage was passed with a great blare of trumpets, but it made no difference at all. The rule remained that whatever government made the elections won them. This was so much a matter of course that the election results were sometimes published in the official newspaper before they took place. It was rare for even a single candidate who was not nominated by the Government to get in.

But perhaps it would be as well to explain how these results were obtained. The electioneering machine had its apex in the Home Office. From there orders were issued to the Civil Governors of the provinces giving them the names of the Government candidates and sometimes even the approximate majorities by which they must appear to win. Not all belonged to the same party. If a Conservative government was conducting the election, a fair number of Liberals and sometimes even an inoffensive Republican or two would be let in. The Government deputies did not wish, like the members of Fascist states, to talk in the void—they were cultivated, reasonable men, and to develop their ideas properly and to score points they needed an opposition. They were also artists of the spoken word and anyone who had a fine style of oratory, even if his views were somewhat heterodox, was given a seat.

The first task then of the Civil Governor, as soon as he had his orders from the Home Office, was to prepare the municipalities. If by some chance the right men had not been elected to these, an irregularity would be discovered in the accounts of the Council and others substituted in their place. The municipalities then drew up the lists of the voters. Naturally only those who could be trusted to support the official candidate were placed on the lists, and whenever the numbers of these were insufficient, the same persons would be put down several times. Even the dead could be called upon: on one occasion a whole cemetery, seven hundred strong, gave their vote, and it was edifying to see that though they had been illiterate in their lifetime, they had all learned to write in the grave.[1]

For some time these measures were sufficient: as, however, years passed and people began to show a real desire to elect their own candidates, further falsifications of the ballot became necessary. The simplest way of doing this was by *actas en blanco*. The members of the ballot committee would certify that they had counted the votes, but would leave the column of results blank for the Civil Governor to fill in as he pleased later. If for any reason this was impossible, the police would exclude voters, ballot papers would be accidentally destroyed or gangs of toughs hired to break the ballot-boxes. And since the official candidates neither visited their constituencies nor made election declarations, it goes without saying that unofficial ones were not allowed to do so either.[2]

[1] This trick was called *pucherazo*. Speaking of the 'saturnalia' which took place when elections were to be held, Antonio Maura said: 'A swarm of high and low agents of the Government falls on villages and towns and unfolds the whole repertory of its overbearing acts, puts in practice all the arts of abuse, and realizes the most outrageous falsifications and manipulations and tries on the most ingenious tricks and deceits.'

He goes on: 'Then have you ever reflected upon a thing which has become to us axiomatic, but which is nevertheless strange? That after an election all the provincial governors have to be removed.... This signifies anyhow a lesser evil—the fact that the governor who has put pressure on the alcaldes, who has bargained for their electoral support in exchange for his closing his eyes to all their immoralities and illegal actions...who has menaced and fined alcaldes who would not *servir al gobierno*, serve the Government, as the phrase goes, and has made a thousand enemies by these acts, finds the province too hot to hold him any longer.'

From a speech made in the Congress, 8 April 1891. *35 años de vida publica*, vol. II, pp. 227–231.

[2] See Madariaga, *Spain*, p. 104. A. Posada, *Estudios sobre el Régimen Parlamentario en España*, p. 29, and J. Chamberlain, *El Atraso de España*, p. 97–169.

Another method was to issue to supporters ballot papers with secret identification marks. It could then be known before the counting began what the result of the election would be. If unfavourable to the Government, a sufficient number of false papers were secretly added to ensure the requisite majority. In 1905 the Socialist candidates, Pablo Iglesias and Largo Caballero, secured their election to the Madrid Municipal Council by faking these private identification marks, so that till the counting began the Government believed that its supporters had secured a majority.

Señor Cambó, the distinguished banker and industrialist and leader of the Catalan Conservatives, has summed up what he describes as the 'immense fiction of the constitutional regime in Spain from Ferdinand VII to September 1923'.

'During a whole century, Spain has lived under the appearance of a constitutional democratic regime, without the people having ever, directly or indirectly, had the least share in the Government. The same men who gave them their political rights took good care to prevent their ever using them. "It is the people's own fault that they do not exercise those rights" said and still say those who usurp them, but the fact is that when in Catalonia in 1907 popular suffrage came to be regarded as the key to political rights, the governing classes of all parties.... took care to stifle and corrupt it. Who does not remember elections in which the Civil Governors used the

These methods sufficed for the large towns where the Governor could keep an eye on what was happening; in the small towns and country districts, however, another kind of person was required—the *cacique*. The cacique—the term is derived from an Indian word meaning chief—is a man, generally a large landowner, who in exchange for certain unwritten privileges organizes the district politically on the Government's behalf.

There have probably always been caciques in Spain: no doubt the Romans found them useful when they broke up the Celt-Iberian tribes. At all events writers of the seventeenth century complain of them and in the eighteenth they are spoken of as the scourge of the country. But it was constitutional governments and the popular vote that gave them their real power. Their palmiest days were from 1840 to 1917, after which, with the rise of a real public opinion and of a genuine body of voters, they began to lose their influence. The obligations of a cacique to the Government were to see that the right candidates were elected, in exchange for which they were given the protection of the Civil Governors and of the judges and magistrates and of course the active assistance of the police. In most parts of Spain (the Basque provinces alone excepted) they were practically omnipotent. They appointed the mayors in the small towns and villages, controlled the local judges and public functionaries and through them distributed the taxation. Their fiscal principle was a simple one: to excuse themselves and their friends from paying taxes and to charge their enemies double or treble. They also usurped common lands, pastured their cattle on other people's arable and diverted their neighbours' irrigation water to their own fields. If anyone tried to stand up against them, lawsuits were brought against him and he was ruined.

Their particular mode of operation varied with the form of land tenure: in the north, where the properties are much divided and the small farmers are usually in debt, the cacique would be a local worthy, a lawyer or perhaps even a priest, representing some conservative interest or association, who lent money on mortgage. The man who had borrowed from him had to vote as he was told. In other parts of

police to steal the voting urns or in which the counts of votes were falsified in the very rooms in which justice is administered? Who does not remember that vote of the elected deputies to the Cortes declaring valid a gross and obvious falsification, as a result of which we saw a number of respectable people accepting as their colleague in Parliament an individual whom they would never permit to enter their private houses?' (*Por la Concordia*, p. 189.)

Spain the caciques were usually large landowners. They used the
threat of unemployment. In Andalusia their behaviour was often
particularly outrageous and violent. In the first half of the last century
they were leagued with the bandits and down to the beginning of this
one they kept bands of roughs who beat up anyone who disagreed
with them. At election times their party was called the *Partido de la
Porra*, or Cudgel party, and all through the revolutionary elections
of 1868, in spite of the opposition of the Government and of the whole
country, they kept their hold on the municipalities. Even so late as
1920, in a small village where the author was living, the cacique had
a man murdered on the main road in full daylight in sight of a dozen
or more people, and though the affair cost him a good deal of money
neither he nor his accomplices were punished.

The principal caciques were rich men who controlled dozens of
villages, and under them lived other lesser caciques and others perhaps under them. Sometimes in one town or village there would be
two of them, one 'Liberal' and one 'Conservative', who, far from
keeping the gentleman's agreement of the politicians in Madrid, would
be on terms of bitter enmity with one another. Then one had 'village
politics' with all its *odios* and *venganzas*. As a distinguished historian, Gumersindo de Azcárate, said: 'Caciquism is simply a feudalism of a new kind, a hundred times more repugnant than the military
feudalism of the Middle Ages.'

It is not surprising therefore that the majority of Spaniards—in
country districts the immense majority—preferred to keep clear of
politics. It was better to put up with wrongs and injustices of every
kind than to risk worse things by protesting. For the law courts gave
no protection. The separation of the powers is a thing that has never
existed in Spain and judges and magistrates were simply Government employees who took their orders from above.[1] They condemned
and acquitted at the word of the Civil Governor. And still worse
were the village tribunals under the direct orders of the alcalde and
of the cacique who had appointed him. Even in serious cases that lay
beyond their jurisdiction they were generally able, by withholding
evidence, corrupting witnesses and so on, to obtain the result they
wished for. Only a patient and fatalistic race such as the Spaniards
could have put up for so long with conditions that lacked even the
most elementary justice.

But this injustice was merely one symptom of a much more general

[1] See Note A on p. 15 at end of chapter.

evil—the corruption of all the upper layers of society. In politics everyone except a few leading politicians, who in any case had no hesitation in living by the venality of others, was tarred with the same brush. Cánovas himself gave, in the space of five years, more than twelve hundred titles and orders. His lieutenant, Romero Robledo (who as Minister for Home Affairs was the organizer of the cacique system), on one occasion granted himself 282,000 pesetas for irrigating his own estates.[1] Not only was there a prodigious amount of graft in the municipalities, but it was considered treason to denounce it. Thus when an honest and disinterested man, the Marqués de Cabriñana, exposed the notorious scandals of the Madrid Urban Council, he was not only condemned for libel, but the whole of the aristocracy, some of whom participated in these frauds, cut him.

The rich, too, evaded almost all their taxes. In 1902 the Minister of Agriculture stated in the Senate that the drawing up of the new land survey had shown that in four provinces the yearly concealment in taxation returns amounted to over three million acres, on which the tax due to the State would be at least three million pesetas. It was variously estimated that the fiscal fraud in property for all Spain reached from 50 to 80 per cent of the total due.[2] But the poor did not benefit by this—on the contrary, they had to pay far more. In 1909 M. Marvaud, a competent and impartial witness, found small landowners paying from 30 to 40 pesetas tax per acre whilst large estates close by paid nothing at all.[3] And on top of this one finds the President of the Supreme Court declaring in 1876 that one-third of the taxes that were raised remained in the hands of the agents and never reached the Government.

But one must, I think, be careful what inferences one draws from this state of things. Spain is not the only country to have gone through periods of political and social corruption. At some time or other every nation in Europe has had similar experiences. It may therefore be useful to take as a point of comparison the case of England towards the end of the eighteenth century. England then, like Spain in 1880, was an agricultural country ruled by a parliament of landlords whose principal requirement was a high tariff on foreign wheat. An industrial and mining movement, disregarded by Parliament, was just beginning to grow up. In the large towns starvation wages were pro-

[1] See Fernández Almagro, *Historia del Reinado de Alfonso XIII*, p. 60.
[2] See Note B on p. 15 at end of chapter.
[3] A. Marvaud, *L'Espagne au XXième Siècle*, pp. 247–248.

ducing an unruly and ignorant population whose existence was felt to be a continual danger to society. There was also an impoverished lower-middle class, whose hold on life was precarious.

In both countries, too, the large landowners were busy enclosing the common lands: in England, by means of private bills brought in with a complete disregard for the rights of the villagers: in Spain, as the result of a general policy due not so much to the pressure of eager landlords as to Liberal ideas. There was great political corruption and the Church, lost to all sense of its religious obligations, had ceased to be anything more than a prop for the rich.

Yet here the resemblance ends. In England there were no caciques. The large landlords spent the greater part of the year on their estates where, in spite of the enclosures of the common lands and of the ferocious laws against poachers, they remained popular figures and impartial administrators of justice on the bench. In England, too, there was a generous system of poor law relief and no police. In Spain, on the other hand, there was a police force armed with rifles and no poor law. The Spanish nobility lived in the large towns and rarely visited their estates, and the administration of justice, though milder than in England, was corrupt and partial.[1]

Then in England trade was flourishing. English capital and English energy were busy developing the new industries. In Spain most of the capital was foreign, whilst the greater part of the trade and industry of the country (just as it had been in the seventeenth century) was in the hands of the English and French. In short, England in 1750 was a healthy and energetic if somewhat heartless and brutal country, and her vices were those of a growing and rapidly changing organism, whilst Spain, passing through the same economic phase a hundred and fifty years later, was one of the sick men of Europe.

How is one to explain this fatal lethargy? It certainly could not be put down to any falling off in the intrinsic energies of the Spanish people. *Todo decae con frecuencia en España, menos la raza*—as Cánovas said. 'Everything decays in Spain except the race.' No one who has been south of the Pyrenees would disagree with that. Spaniards in Cánovas' time were what they have always been—a race of immense, even of excessive vitality. But they suffered from a disease which

---

[1] The surprising mildness and, on paper, excellence of the Spanish penal system is due to Jeremy Bentham who in 1820, at the request of the Spanish Cortes, drew up a reformed penal code. But till the reign of Ferdinand VII Spanish public opinion had never tolerated severe punishments except for heresy, and the brutality of the old English penal system would never have been possible there.

radiated from above downwards. And the chief symptom of that disease was the dissociation of their political system and of the class of landowners which operated it from the social and economic needs of the country.

The defects of the Spanish upper classes are sometimes put down to their having a feudal mentality. I do not think this word has been well chosen: feudalism implies a sense of mutual obligations that has long been entirely lacking in Spain, besides which, historically speaking, there has never (except in Aragon) been any true feudal age in the Peninsula. The prototype of modern Spanish society is to be found in the seventeenth century, in the period that followed that immense expansion which transformed a rude, uncultured, poverty-stricken but virile country (if one excepts Catalonia and those parts of the south-east where Mediterranean influences prevailed) in the course of a few years into a vast Empire. Spain came too easily and too quickly into her heritage, without sufficient economic or cultural preparation, and it acted on her like an intoxicant. Spanish pride, Spanish belief in miracles, Spanish contempt for work, Spanish impatience and destructiveness, though they had existed before in Castile, now received a powerful impetus. Especially Spanish contempt for work. After 1580 the few cloth industries that had grown up in Castile declined and Spaniards became a rentier race, a nation of gentlemen, living in parasitic dependence upon the gold and silver of the Indies and the industry of the Low Countries.

This is, after all, the common fate of hardy and primitive races that conquer advanced civilizations. The history of the East (where pastoral races alternately conquer and are absorbed by agricultural ones) is full of such rapid rises and declines. Spanish history in the seventeenth century shows the decay of a ruling class that had dominated but never sufficiently understood nor absorbed European civilization. And since they lived on their own soil and not on that of the countries they exploited, Spain simply reverted to its primitive, poverty-stricken condition. But meanwhile the gentlemanly ideal with its hall-mark of leisure had become part of the national character. Work had become the degrading thing. To avoid it, it was thought better to live by one's wits or, if one had influence, to swell the vast number of scribblers and sinecure holders in Government offices. There lies the root of all successive political institutions in the Peninsula. Yet one should remember the ascetic side to this ideal of the leisured life, which redeems it from baseness and vulgarity. The hidalgo was ready to give up comfort, to suffer cold and hunger if he could live with honour. Putting this in other words, one may say that Spaniards became accustomed to living for great and spectacular ends, and declined when the bourgeois ideal of work, perseverance and duty, became the only one which could create or hold together society.

This leads one to ask what precisely is required if Spain is to play her part once more in European civilization. She has, as I think history clearly shows, only existed as a nation when under the influence of some powerful idea or impulse: as soon as that idea has declined, the atoms of the molecule have separated and have begun to vibrate and to collide on their own account. We see that first in the time of Augustus, when Roman civilization subdued the warlike Iberian tribes. Hardly was the military domination complete when Spain absorbed the Roman idea as Gaul never could and produced generals, emperors, philosophers and poets till Italy seemed scarcely more than a Spanish province. But the decline in the following centuries was so complete that even the Pyrenees could not protect the Peninsula against the Germanic hordes that swept over it. The last of these, the Visigoths, founded a settled kingdom out of the broken pieces of the Empire, but failed to give it new life, so that in 710 a few thousand Arabs were able to conquer and to convert within a few years the greater part of the country. Islam brought with it a great egalitarian idea—the brotherhood of all classes and races under one banner—which Christianity with its priestly hierarchy and its indifference to civic virtues had failed to provide, and this idea and the breaking-up of estates and reduction of taxes which was its immediate consequence made possible an economic revival in those parts of Spain which, till they were finally ruined by Castile, had always been more cultured and more industrious. This revival produced a brilliant but politically unstable civilization, breaking down with the first weak government into a number of small but highly civilized states, which in the struggle to maintain themselves against the Christians of the north, allowed themselves to be absorbed in the new and barbarous Moroccan empires which had been founded on the fringe of the desert by fanatical dervishes.

The Reconquista began when the small barbarian kingdoms, into which Christian Spain had divided, came—chiefly through the influence of the French monks of Cluny—to feel a new consciousness of their historical role, but the idea underlying the Reconquest was not at this time religious so much as social and political. These early crusaders brought a new form of liberty—that of the self-governing communes which with extraordinary force and vigour had sprung up as if by magic all over the northern and central parts of the country. The *raison d'être* of these communes was that the kings and nobles, wishing to repopulate the abandoned plains and to defend them against the Moors, had been obliged to free their serfs and to grant them extensive privileges. This movement was brought to a halt in the thirteenth century by the chronic inability of the Castilians to think in economic and agricultural terms instead of in military and pastoral ones. They ruined by their incompetence and lack of commercial instinct the new, immensely rich territories they had conquered, and Christian Spain broke up again for more than two centuries, its task half finished, into hopeless civil war and anarchy.

The union of Castile and Aragon, the capture of Granada and the focusing of popular hatred on the Jews provided with almost miraculous suddenness[1] the motive force of the third great age—a military, religious, colonizing enterprise—but it declined so rapidly that by 1640 four provinces of Spain were attempting to separate and to declare their independence: Portugal broke away and a long civil war was necessary to prevent Catalonia from seceding to France.

Again in 1890, in the period which we are discussing, there were separatist movements in various provinces—but what was far more serious, far more corrosive, were the separatist tendencies of the various corporations, such as the Church and the Army, and of the horizontal layers of society, the classes.[2] Cánovas' work had been to patch up provisionally the differences that in the previous century had separated Church and Army and politicians by allowing them all to enrich themselves together, with the result not only of demoralizing *en masse* the upper and middle classes to which they belonged, but of separating them by an immense gulf from the rest of the country. The system of 'elections from above' made the whole position irremediable. The vote, since modern Europe is not in fact, however

---

[1] The Spanish Empire of the sixteenth century had no economic basis in Spain. But for the accidental discovery of America by Columbus, it would have collapsed in 1570 with the revolt of the Netherlands for lack of money to sustain the war.

[2] This is the chief theme of Ortega y Gasset's *España Invertebrada*, a book essential to the understanding of modern Spain. One may put beside it a quotation from the economist Martínez de la Mata, who wrote in the middle of the seventeenth century: 'The most obvious defect which one finds in the body of this republic is that there does not exist in any one of its parts any love or regard for the conservation of the whole; for every man thinks solely of present utility and not at all of the future.' (*Discurso VIII*, s. 103.)

much some people may desire it, organized like the Middle Ages in close corporations, is the only method of rooting the political system and the class that administers it in society. By refusing to allow it to be exercised, not only did the politicians lose all influence, but the upper classes became detached from the lower layers to which they were in any case too weakly anchored. Already by 1900 they appear in the eyes of a great many Spaniards as a class of parasites, getting everything, giving nothing and revolving, under a thin coating of foreign varnish, among the stale feelings and aspirations of the seventeenth century.

'To speak of the idleness of the Spaniard without explaining it is to say nothing. The system of work in any society is surely determined much less by the proletariat than by the directing classes. Everywhere where the middle classes are industrious, the people knows how to work. If we can get the privileged classes to work, that is the whole problem.'[1]

Such was the opinion of Joaquín Aguilera, Secretary of the Fomento, the great association of Catalan industrialists; and indeed there is scarcely a traveller to Spain since 1600 who has not thought it his duty to preach a sermon on the theme of the 'lazy Spaniards'. I will at present merely say this—that if a race of such magnificent natural energies as the Spanish has continued generation after generation to live in this way, it is only because they have been waiting for an idea—a plan of work—that will move their imaginations. We need not blame them for having found little to inspire them in the dreary capitalist frenzy of the last century. Capitalism for us in England has been simply a normal development from a previous state of things, but to Spaniards it has always represented something foreign which had therefore to be imitated (Spain is the country *par excellence* of foreign imitations), but could not be made to work. Nor are historical growth and development Spanish processes: the economic foundation which these require is lacking. As we shall see later the poverty of the soil and the unevenness of the rainfall has given a violent rhythm to Spanish history, inhibiting the normal accumulation of raw resources, but creating a psychological disposition which is sometimes capable of producing great and striking effects.

It is for this reason, no doubt, that Spain, since the loss of its Catholic faith, has been above everything else a country in search of an ideology. A new idea, an incitement to common action, might, it

[1] See Aguilera's article in *El Trabajo Nacional*, 16 March 1910.

was felt, release those energies that hitherto had been directed inwards so that, instead of pullulating aimlessly by itself, Spain would be able to send out rays of light and energy upon the world. This was the force behind the Republic, behind the Socialist and Anarcho-Syndicalist movements—behind even those patriotic and military ideas which prepared the way for Fascism. The following chapters will describe the growth of these ideologies and how by the very fact of their diversity they ended by producing a situation which was insoluble.

FURTHER NOTES ON CHAPTER I

A (p. 8). That well-known authority on Spanish life and letters, A. Morel-Fatio, writes as follows in his essay *L'Espagne de Don Quichotte*: 'The conviction that the governor and the magistrate are the born enemies of the feeble and the poor, that they belong body and soul to the first person who takes the trouble to suborn them and that their acts have no other motive but self-interest: the conviction that posts are given only to favour and money and that one only accepts one in order to enrich oneself—this conviction was firmly established in Cervantes' mind, as indeed in that of most of his compatriots. A just judge or a disinterested administration exist only by way of exception. The rule is venality, corruption and also incapacity, for what need is there for merit, when everything is obtained without it.' (*Études sur l'Espagne*, I, 1890).

One may compare with this an extract from the statement of Antonio Maura, the eminent Conservative statesman, which he contributed to Joaquín Costa's *Oligarquía y Caciquismo*: 'It is a tradition in our country that the public authorities should not attempt to act so as to enforce the law, to secure justice, to further culture, to increase prosperity or to direct the life of the people towards the destinies that its peculiar genius and vocation point to. Anyone who speaks merely of what he has seen will confess that such desires as have been shown by governments to employ in this way their constitutional functions have been ephemeral, incidental and quickly suffocated. The variety of programmes, hymns, forms of organization and methods for obtaining power... have broken the uninterrupted and systematic propensity to replace right with arbitrariness or justice and good example with the sordid domination of the hand which has been able to impose itself.'

These no doubt have been the opinions of most Spaniards in all ages and from whatever class they have come. Yet one ought not to take such opinions quite at their face value, but should make some allowance for the idealism of Spaniards in political matters and for their abnormal sensitiveness to injustice. No race is more severe in its judgements upon these things. Favouritism and commission-taking show as blackly in their eyes as embezzlement. Spaniards, as a race, are neither just nor fair, but they are honest. Indeed I am inclined to think that if we had in England the temptations to dishonesty that there are in Spain, we should not come nearly so well out of it.

B (p. 9). In an official report by the Land Survey Department in 1900 the total occultation in land tax returns for Spain was estimated at 38 million acres. The total amount of cultivated land in Spain at this time was 43 million acres and 63 million acres were pasturage. See Torrez Muñoz, *Catastro General Parcelario*, Madrid, 1903, p. 333, quoted by A. Marvaud, *L'Espagne au XXième Siècle*, p. 248, Note. Also Fernando de los Ríos, 'Agrarian Problem in Spain', *International Labour Review*, June 1925.

Primo de Rivera's finance minister, Calvo Sotelo, describes the scenes that followed when in October 1923, immediately after seizing power, the Dictator issued a decree giving a special moratorium during which all concealers of revenue must declare their true incomes. For several days on end there were long queues of landowners and industrialists anxious to make their peace with the State. 'Among them', he adds, 'were to be found many people who were extremely well-known: a very high percentage consisted of influential and powerful Spaniards.' (*Mis Servicios al Estado*, 1931, p. 124.)

Chapter II

THE PARLIAMENTARY REGIME AND
THE CATALAN QUESTION, 1898–1909

The Government of Spain is the most perfect that ancient legislators could devise, but the corruption of the times has filled it with abuses. From the poor to the rich everyone consumes and devours the estate of the king, some taking little bites, the nobility large ones and the grandees enormous portions.... Many think it a miracle that the Monarchy is still in existence.

GIOVANNI CORNARO, Venetian Ambassador at Madrid in 1681–1682.

The end of the Restoration Period came in 1898 with the war with the United States. In a few months Spain lost the last of its colonial possessions—the Philippines, Cuba and Puerto Rico. The disaster had for many years been predictable. Unless the Cubans, who had risen in arms against the shameful misgovernment of the mother country, could be granted autonomy, it was certain that the United States would interfere. Cánovas, who had before him the fatal example of Olivares, seems to have understood this, but the jingoistic mood in Spain, the insistence of the upper classes and of the Army upon firm measures, made concessions impossible.[1] General Weyler was sent out to subdue the islanders by fire and by sword and the horrors of his concentration camps created a feeling in America which led to intervention. Cánovas died from the bullet of an Italian anarchist a few months before war broke out.

The loss of the last relics of the once immense colonial empire produced consternation in the country, but so little reflection as to its causes and so little change of heart that Silvela, the Conservative

---

[1] Olivares' refusal to renew the twelve years' truce with the Dutch and the fatal war with France which followed from this led to the same results as Cánovas' obstinacy over Cuba—that is, to a movement for independence in Catalonia. Thus, after more than twenty years of caution and premeditation, Cánovas fell into that very error which he had determined to avoid. There is an explanation for this. In his old age he had married a young and fascinating wife, with whom he was much in love. A desire for honour, power and glory, things which he had previously despised, came over him and he began to take up a more intransigeant line on all political questions. This was the easier for him because his temperament was naturally impatient and authoritarian. When therefore the upper classes and the Army officers began to clamour for war to the death against the Cuban insurgents, Cánovas, though in his clearer moments he must have foreseen the inevitable result, did not lag behind them.

Prime Minister, remarked with despair that he 'could scarcely feel the pulse of Spain'. Yet this in fact was the lowest moment and the end of an era. From now on a new Spain begins.

Between 1898 and 1931—the date of the advent of the Republic—a double process is apparent in Spanish history. The main movement, the one that is most visible to the eye, is the continued disintegration of the various elements that make up the older Spain—administration, Army, Church, the social classes, the links between the provinces, which in the absence of any common plan of life turn on one another and attempt to destroy one another. The other process, scarcely noticeable at first and never very strong, is a recuperative one, which ends, however, by raising the moral and intellectual level of the country and for almost the first time since 1680 gives Spain the right to be considered as a part (and a valuable part) of modern Europe.

I will take first of all what is most obvious—the politicians and their struggle with the Army, on which two other factors, the King and the Catalan question, impinge.

From 1900 to 1923, the date on which Primo de Rivera overthrew it, the political regime set up by Cánovas was functioning every year with greater difficulty. There are two main reasons for this—the first, that by the mere process of time and by the gradual reawakening of public opinion, it was becoming discredited. The second reason was the undermining action of the King, which prevented the movement for restoring the prestige of the Cortes by free elections from coming to a head and so prepared the way for a victory of the Army.

The politicians were ceasing to be popular. On the deaths of Cánovas and Sagasta (1897 and 1903) the Conservative and Liberal parties both split, and though they closed their ranks soon afterwards it was not long before they were again in difficulties. Maura, the new Conservative leader, had to be eliminated for his ultra-clerical leanings, and Canalejas, the hope of the Liberal party, was shot, as Cánovas had been, by an anarchist. Elections still continued to be conducted in the old way, though with ever-increasing disgust and resentment throughout the country. After 1910 Republicans and Socialists were beginning to get elected in small numbers in the large towns in spite of the immense odds against them, though in the country districts the cacique was still unassailable. But one notices as time goes on the ever-increasing amount of force that was needed to produce the desired results. More and more frequently police and bands of roughs had to be called in to keep away hostile voters, whilst landlords were obliged to make it clear to their hitherto docile tenants or labourers that failure to vote for the right man would bring eviction and dismissal. After 1917 it actually became necessary in most provinces to *buy* votes—a clear proof that the old practices were breaking down.

Another disturbing feature of the political machine was the army of *cesantes* or Government employees who lost their posts whenever their party went out of office. There was nothing particularly new about this: it had been the normal practice in the seventeenth century whenever the King dismissed his chief minister, but in the struggle between the Army chiefs after the Carlist Wars it was revived on an immense scale and became the rule in all succeeding changes of government.[1] In an era of *coups d'état* and petty revolutions such general dismissals might have some justification—but as those times had now passed and the difference between Liberals and Conservatives had become much more one of men than of principle, it was obvious that they served another purpose.

For the Spanish parliamentary system was simply one more proof of how little the ideas of the governing classes had altered since the seventeenth century. Under new names, the method was the same. The machine that had supported great ministers like Lerma and Uceda was little different from that which now supported Dato and Romanones. The object in both cases was the private enrichment and support of factions, which did not consist merely of a few highly placed individuals but penetrated down through modest clerks and functionaries to the poorest layers of the people. Spain after all is the country where history (and how monotonously!) repeats itself. The parasitical condition of Spanish economy since 1580, when Spaniards ceased to live by their own enterprise and industry and crowded into the offices of the State, has stamped an indelible character on the upper and middle classes.[2]

To understand better this immense extension and chronic instability of the bureaucracy one must remember that since the middle of the last century, in spite of its strong local and provincial feelings, Spain has had one of the most centralized governments in Europe and that every country postman, village schoolmaster and customs official has owed his appointment to the minister in Madrid. All these petty functionaries, together with a host of Government clerks and officials, down to the humblest hall porters and hangers-on, have obtained their

---

[1] See J. Tanski, *L'Espagne en 1842 et 1843.*
[2] See note A on p. 35 at end of chapter.

posts through being the retainers of some political person.[1] There was practically no civil service and, except for one or two technical branches, candidates for the Government service were not troubled with competitive examinations. The budget of the State, as Lerroux said, was the civil list of a party.

The result of this state of affairs was an enormous increase in the number of Government employees: a decrease in their efficiency, since they were not chosen on a competitive basis, and in their honesty, since the budget could not provide them with a sufficient salary to live on.[2] Every clerkship or secretaryship would be duplicated—each party having its own nominee—and on every change of government a large number of these would be thrown out of work without a salary. If the opposition party remained too long in power, these poor men would be reduced to great distress and their clamour, reaching the ears of humane ministers, would sometimes be sufficient to produce a change of government. *Quítate tu para ponerme yo,* 'You get out and let me in', became the main principle of party politics.

But it was not only Government posts that were in the party patronage. The chief industrial concerns in Spain, especially the banks and the railways, were closely linked to politics: they depended on the politicians to get favourable consideration for their interests, whilst the politicians depended on them to get well-paid jobs for themselves and their families. As a result most Spanish industries, and in particular the railways, were, like the State itself, obliged to

---

[1] Romanones in his *Notas de Una Vida* (p. 71) remarks that elections in Spain are won by offering jobs and by possessing friends. In explanation of this he gives the following extract from one of the daily papers: 'To-day the Alcalde of Madrid, the Conde de Romanones, has resigned. To-morrow a special train will leave for Guadalajara [Romanones' home town] with the employees of the municipality who were appointed by him and are now being replaced.' This notice, which was published to annoy him, in fact did him, he says, a great deal of good.

Romanones was a master of electioneering tactics. His successful manipulation of the municipal elections in 1910, when the Socialists and Republicans were with great difficulty kept out, earned him his grandeeship and the Grand Cross of Carlos III. About the deeds of another great faker of elections, the Conservative La Cierva, the proverb grew up *Mata al rey y vete a Murcia*: 'Kill the King and go to Murcia.' For Murcia was La Cierva's constituency and, so it was said, the worst criminals found safe refuge there. One should remember that, till the Republic frightened the richer classes into contributing to the Ceda, there were no party funds in Spain, so that in one way or another the Government had to pay all electioneering expenses.

[2] Not all were badly paid. According to Posada the 114 ministers and permanent secretaries to the Cortes received 1,469,840 pesetas (about £60,000) a year in salaries between them. See A. Posada, *Estudios sobre el Régimen Parlamentario en España,* p. 105. Quoted from *El Imparcial,* 7 and 8 March 1890.

support large numbers of superfluous directors and lesser employees who were certainly not chosen for their efficiency. The Cortes itself was no longer what it had been in the last century. The debates were duller, now that the great speakers of the past were dead. Agriculture, finance and industry were scarcely represented— most of the deputies being journalists or lawyers, versed only in the subtle intricacies and manœuvres of the game. They formed a small and compact class: in 1922, for example, in the last Cortes elected before the Dictatorship, 113 deputies were near relations of political leaders.[1] The greater part of their time was spent in intrigues destined to favour this or that interest or to secure patronage for this or that person. One example of this will suffice. A well-known deputy has related that every politician kept a little book containing particulars of the irregularities and secret abuses committed by the different Government departments. When he wanted something from one of these and was not attended to, he would consult his little book and put down a question upon an embarrassing subject. The minister concerned would meet him afterwards in the lobbies and they would come to an understanding.[2]

That such parliaments did little legislation goes without saying; for one thing the ministers had no time for preparing it: except for two or three permanent officials at the Treasury there were no technical advisers to assist them, for their subordinates, who changed with every government, were untrained and incompetent. They themselves spent twelve hours a day on routine work, signing thousands of papers and receiving hundreds of people.[3] Custom obliged them to

[1] See Ciges Aparicio, *España bajo la Dinastía de los Borbones*, p. 433.
[2] See A. Posada, *op. cit.* p. 91.
[3] Some idea of the prodigious amount of *paperasserie* required in Spanish administration will be gathered from the fact that every village with a population of more than a thousand had its municipal clerk, a salaried official who usually had as much work as he could get through in a ten-hour day. Yet these villages had scarcely any municipal services whatever: such questions as roads, drainage, housing, electric light, telephones did not exist for them. These clerks or *secretarios*, I should add, played an important role in the cacique system. As they were miserably underpaid, they could only live by taking bribes. They therefore became the servants of the cacique and since, in small villages, they were the only people who understood the complicated system of administration, they had all the other municipal officers in their power. The most upright alcaldes would find, when a change of government brought their term of office to an end, that they had unwittingly broken the law in many respects and would now be made to pay the penalty for it. These persecutions were part of the ordinary routine of village *venganzas*. See on this Zugasti, *El Bandolerismo*, Part I, Vol. III, pp. 115–238. Although bandits ceased to exist after 1880, his remarks upon Andalusian caciques and village politics remained largely true down to the Dictatorship.

receive all applicants and their antechambers were crowded from morning to night like a panel doctor's waiting room. Had it not been for an autonomous and unpolitical body, the *Comisión de Reformas Sociales* set up in 1883 by Moret and reorganized in 1903 as the *Instituto de Reformas Sociales*, whose business it was to study social conditions and prepare laws for remedying them, no legislation of a social character would have been passed at all. As it was, the opposition of the industrialists blocked nearly all attempts at reform: the first timid factory acts giving compensation for workmen injured by machinery and limiting the hours of work for children were passed in 1900—1902, but not observed.[1] Some protection was given to pregnant women at the same time, and in 1911 factory inspectors were appointed, though in such conditions as to make them almost useless. This is the sum total of social legislation passed in Spain before 1918. A housing act brought in to compel landlords to keep their houses in decent repair has never to this day been enforced. The only administrative act of any importance passed during the first quarter of the century was a decree giving a mild amount of devolution to the Catalans.

And yet it would be a mistake to suppose that every Spanish politician accepted without protest the state of corruption and stagnation to which politics had been reduced. Above the swarm of nonentities who only attended the Cortes in order to fish for favours for their relations or friends, there were always a number of men, among whom must be included the leaders of the different parties, who were both honest and capable. But in the tangle of conflicting interests in which they had to work, with no pressure of an electorate behind them to give them authority, they were powerless. The only effective support they could look for was from the King: with his good will the legislation which was blocked by the Chamber could be passed by decree and ministries could be stabilized. But the King, unfortunately, was the last person to be relied upon.

Alfonso XIII had begun to rule in 1902 on his sixteenth birthday. He was a precocious and lively boy who took a keen enjoyment in the exercise of his functions, but he had had the disadvantage of a bad upbringing and of an insufficient education.[2] The Conde de Romanones

---

[1] By the act of March 1900 children under 10 were forbidden to work in factories *unless they could already read.* None under 16 could work in mines. See A. Marvaud, *La Question Sociale en Espagne,* pp. 235-240.

[2] The King was brought up by a doting mother in an intensely clerical atmosphere. His tutor, Father Montaña, was a violent reactionary. He was never sent to

has given a vivid account of his first cabinet meeting, held after the ceremony of taking the oath to the Constitution. It was a very hot day and the ministers returned to the Palace exhausted and hungry after the long session in the Cortes. But the King, instead of dismissing them, intimated that he wished to hold at once a cabinet council. Then, with the air of a man who has been presiding over cabinet councils all his life, he made one or two peremptory enquiries as to the state of the Army and, following this up, pointed out that, according to such and such an article in the Constitution, he had the sole and absolute right of granting honours and titles. 'I therefore warn you that I reserve for myself alone this right.' The Duke of Veragua politely replied that, by another article, this was not the case, and after a tactful concession by the Prime Minister the cabinet meeting ended. But the impression was left of a man who, whatever his other qualities might be, was not indifferent to power.

And unfortunately for Spain, the whole political machine was dependent on him. To obtain a majority in the Chamber, the ministers had to be able to *make* the elections. They could only do this if they could secure a decree of dissolution from the King. The King therefore, instead of the electorate, became the sole arbiter of governments and made them and remade them as he pleased.

'The Conservative party', wrote the Conde de Romanones in his Memoirs, 'in order to remain in power a little over two years (from December 1902 to July 1905) passed through five total crises with five prime ministers and sixty-six new ministers.' The cause of this, he went on to say, lay in the weakness of the parties and in the intrigues of the King, 'who seemed to enjoy changing frequently the persons to whom, more or less completely, he gave his confidence'.

The two and a half years that followed saw seven different cabinets, due to the same cause.[1] It is unlikely that the King had at this time any definite plan for discrediting the parliamentary regime or for moving towards a more personal rule. It was merely that he had

---

finish his education abroad. As he was a spirited boy he reacted against the stuffy atmosphere of this court and found encouragement in the only other people with whom he had any contact—his military attachés. Thus the Army came to stand in his eyes for everything that was manly and heroic. Probably these simple romantic feelings played as large a part in bringing about his downfall as the political intrigues for which he developed a sort of mania or the absorption in purely dynastic interests of which he is so often accused.

[1] The first twenty-one years of Alfonso's reign—from 1902 to 1923—saw thirty-three entirely different governments. In the sixteen years of the Queen Regent's administration there were only eleven.

power and that he enjoyed using it. The strain of frivolity and un-reliability that came into the Spanish Bourbon family from María Luisa, the queen painted by Goya, was evident in his character. ·But the results were the same as though he had deliberately tried to sabotage the Constitution. Any hopes that the more honest and in-telligent politicians conceived of restoring some decency to politics or even of passing the most obvious and necessary legislation were thwarted by the King. Whether from love of power, instability of character or sheer ignorance of the social conditions in his country, he regularly and unfailingly wrecked them.

Perhaps the political machine could have gone on running quietly for some time longer, scattering its benefits upon a small ruling caste and their retainers, if a problem had not appeared, too urgent to be put aside, yet far too serious to be solved by such a discredited body. This was the Catalan question. For more than twenty years it poisoned the political atmosphere in Spain much as the Irish question had poisoned that in England—with the difference, however, that Catalonia is not a backward and impoverished island, but the chief industrial district of the Peninsula.

The Catalan question is, to begin with, merely one rather special instance of the general problem of Spanish regionalism. The Iberian Peninsula, as everyone knows, is divided by mountain ranges and by variations of altitude into regions which are climatically and geogra-phically very different from one another. At Valencia, for example, rice is grown and dates ripen, whilst Burgos, a bare 200 miles away, has a climate resembling that of Poland. These regional variations have led to the growth of strong local patriotisms, which whenever the power of the central government is relaxed, come to a head. During the Peninsular War, for example, some twenty or so provincial juntas declared themselves independent and one, the Junta of Murcia, having occasion to treat with the British Government, wrote that their province desired to treat with it 'not as one shopkeeper with another, but as one court with another court and as one sovereign nation with another sovereign nation'. Again in 1873, during the brief rule of the Federal Republic, all except one of the cities of the south-east from Seville to Valencia remembered their origins as Mediterranean city-states and declared themselves free ports and in-dependent cantons, acknowledging no central authority. And there has scarcely been a peasant rising since 1840 when some village or other has not called a full assembly of all its inhabitants and declared itself a free and independent state. Yet I think it would be a mistake to take these movements as showing a real and fixed desire for independence of Madrid. The economic unity of Spain has long been recognized by every educated person. They are to a great extent simply protests against bad government.

The Catalan question however is somewhat different. Both linguistically and culturally Catalonia was originally an extension of the south of France rather than a part of Spain and, under the rich merchant class which ruled it during the Middle Ages, it acquired an active, enterprising character and a European outlook very different from that of its semi-pastoral neighbours on the interior plateaux. The thirteenth and fourteenth centuries were its period of greatest prosperity. First under the Counts of Barcelona and then incorporated in the Crown of Aragon it monopolized the carrying trade of the Western Mediterranean and extended its rule over Naples and Sicily, but the discovery of America and the ruin of the Mediterranean trade by the Turks led to a decline. It was not however till the seventeenth century, 150 years after its union with Castile, when the prestige of the Crown had begun to decline, that there was any question of a separatist movement.

Spain then was still the same confederation of loosely connected states which it had been in 1500. The provinces which belonged to the Crown of Castile had some cohesion, though the Basque provinces might be regarded as semi-independent republics, and the Asturians and Galicians retained their local laws and privileges, but of the four kingdoms and one county incorporated in the Crown of Aragon (Valencia, Majorca, Aragon and Barcelona) each had its own laws and parliament and the King could neither raise money nor send foreign (i.e. Castilian) troops into their territory without obtaining their permission. So foreign indeed was Castile to a member of the Aragonese Confederation that the Catalans maintained consuls in Andalusia and were not permitted to trade with America.[1] Neither

---

[1] In 1596 Philip II gave permission to subjects of the Crown of Aragon to reside in America, but in fact obstacles were put in their way and they could not do business there till much later. And until 1717 Seville held a monopoly in all colonial trade.

It is interesting to speculate on what would have happened had it been Ferdinand and not Isabella who put down the money for Columbus' voyage. It would then have fallen to the Catalans and the Valencians to open up America, and Castile would have been excluded. One can hardly doubt that the whole course and character of Spanish history would have been different: the decline in the seventeenth century would not have occurred because the development of trade, industry and

Philip II nor his successors made any attempt to build up a more centralized state. The unity of Spain was held to lie not in its political ties but in its ideology—that is, in its religion—and the guardian of this unity was the Inquisition.

When Olivares, however, became chief minister in 1623 two things were becoming apparent: the economic decline of Spain was proceeding at a tremendous pace and the wars in Holland and Germany, which had no connection with Spanish interests but were undertaken in support of religion, were hastening it. The Catalans were naturally the first Spaniards to grasp this and to draw the obvious deductions from it. On the other hand Olivares perceived, what was also true, that in the inevitable duel which was approaching with France, France would win because she was a centralized country.[1] He therefore drew up secret plans for modifying the jealously guarded privileges of the Catalans and of the other autonomous regions. The Catalans got wind of this and on Corpus Christi Day 1640, in the middle of a war with France, they rose and placed themselves under the protection of the French king. Their rebellion was the signal for a successful rising in Portugal and for unsuccessful movements in Andalusia and in Aragon. (There had been a previous rebellion of the Basques a few years earlier.) Barcelona did not submit till 1652, and the war continued in the mountains till 1659, when it was ended by the Peace of the Pyrenees, by which Spain surrendered the northernmost province of Catalonia, Roussillon, and the district of the Cerdagne, to France. The Government was too weak to impose any penalties on the Catalans.

agriculture in Spain would have prevented it. On the other hand the work of colonization would have suffered. The energy with which the Castilians explored, conquered and settled America was beyond the power of any other nation at that time. It has something of the sweep and magnificence of the conquests made by the Arab tribes after the death of Mohammed. Both were the work of men who were very lightly attached to the soil and who were born hungry.

[1] When Olivares asked the Catalans how, in their opinion, the ills of Spain could be remedied: 'Stay at home', was the answer. 'Repopulate the country, cultivate our fields, fortify our cities, open our ports to commerce and re-establish our factories...the treasure from America should be spent on this and not on senseless and disgraceful wars.' Quoted by Manuel Pugés, *Como triunfó el Proteccionismo en España*, p. 43, from a German economist, Scherer.

The Catalan question was therefore the same in 1640 as it was in 1900. But Olivares' view is also comprehensible: 'Foreign politicians say that the Monarchy of Spain is merely a fantastical body defended by general opinion but not by substance.' (See *Nicandro*—a book written or inspired by Olivares to justify him after his disgrace.) For Spain was then, as Britain in 1938, a lazy and satisfied world power, whose authority was menaced by the rise of a new state far better organized for war than she was.

Less than forty years later, in the War of the Spanish Succession, the Catalans again rose against Madrid and offered their support to the Allies. But when they failed and Barcelona was stormed after a dreadful siege, they found that they no longer had the mild descendants of Philip II to make their peace with, but Bourbon princes who had learned autocracy at the court of Louis XIV. The Castle of Montjuich was built to dominate Barcelona, the six Catalan universities were suppressed and a new foundation made under the eye of the King at Cervera, whilst the Catalan *fueros* or liberties were abolished.[1] In exchange they obtained encouragement for their new industries and later on in the century some rights in trading with America, and with this they were for a while contented.

The centralizing policy of the Bourbons was continued in the next century by their political heirs, the Liberals. The only question between Catalonia and Madrid was now that of tariffs. The Catalans demanded sufficiently high tariffs on manufactured articles to keep out all English and French competition, and the Liberals, though they yielded in fact to most of these demands, were nominally free-traders.[2] In the forties the Catalan manufacturers organized themselves in an *Instituto Industrial de Cataluña*, chiefly to defend high tariffs, and in 1869, when the revolution had brought in a genuinely free-trade government, this body was reorganized as the famous *Fomento de Trabajo Nacional*. A protectionist policy returned in 1874 with Cánovas, but every commercial treaty with France or England raised protests in Barcelona.

Meanwhile the modern Catalan movement was beginning. Catalonia had lost between 1822 and 1837 her penal law, her commercial law, her coinage, her special tribunals, even her right to use Catalan in the schools without any protest. But very soon after that a revival of Catalan national feeling began. At first it was purely literary. In the fifties there were competitions between Catalan poets, and mediaeval festivals such as the *Jocs Florals* were revived. The sixties saw a revival of the language (which had ceased to be spoken except in the

[1] Yet more than seventy years later Arthur Young was shocked to see that the Catalans were still treated as a subject race and that their nobility were forbidden to wear swords.

[2] The fall of the Liberal dictatorship of Espartero in 1843, in spite of the immense position he had obtained as victor in the Carlist War, was largely due to the opposition of the Catalan factory owners to the commercial treaty he was preparing with England, which would have allowed Manchester cottons to compete with Catalan manufactures. On the question of tariffs Madrid has always given way to Barcelona.

villages) and the foundation of the first newspaper in Catalan and of a theatre for Catalan plays. The federal movement of 1868—1873 was welcomed by intellectuals in Barcelona, and it is scarcely an accident that three of the leading figures of the revolutionary period—Prim, Pi y Margall and Figueras—were Catalans. But it was the final defeat of the Carlists in 1876 that turned Catalan Nationalism into a serious movement.

The countryside in Catalonia had always been Carlist: the small landowners and farmers had fought fanatically for the first Don Carlos, and though they had shown less enthusiasm for his grandson, they had not abandoned their opinions. Carlism in the last century implied not merely extreme clericalism, but devolution and local liberties. By associating itself with the demand for these the Church had found champions for its cause both among the Basques and in Catalonia. When therefore Carlism was defeated for the second time and its cause was seen to be irretrievably lost, it was natural for the Church, both in the Basque provinces and in Catalonia, to throw its influence on to the side of the rising autonomous movements. In Catalonia the Bishop of Vich became one of the leaders of the nationalist party, and not only the specifically Carlist families, but practically the whole of the rich upper-middle classes of Barcelona, who as a matter of course had clerical leanings, joined it. Till 1900 therefore and indeed, except for a short interlude, down to 1923 Catalan Nationalism was a predominantly Right-wing movement.

There existed also, however, a Left wing, which, though numerically weak, was important because it included most of the intellectuals and had a strong influence in the drawing up of the combined Catalan programme. It too had sprung from the defeat of one of the extreme revolutionary parties by the oligarchy of the Restoration: in this case the federals of Pi y Margall, to which its leader, Almirall, had originally belonged. In 1886 he published his famous book *Lo Catalanisme*, which summed up the aims and history of Catalan Nationalism and indicated the course along which it was to develop. The culmination of this stage of the movement came with the drawing up in 1892 of the *Bases de Manresa*—a far-reaching political programme, incompatible either with economic facts or with Spanish unity, but subscribed to enthusiastically by both the Right and the Left wing Catalan parties. The cultural campaign started by Prat de la Riba in the *Renaixensa* a couple of years later was a parallel development.

The next stage came with the entry on the scenes of economic factors. The loss of Cuba, in which the Catalan industrialists had large interests, provoked a feeling of anger against Madrid, to whose intransigeance it was held to have been due. This was not altogether just, for the opposition of the Catalan mill-owners to Cuban autonomy had been one of the factors that had led to the disaster, but their complaints of the incompetent way in which the affairs of the country were managed by Madrid, of the scandals of the administration, of the huge sums spent upon an army which was always defeated when it took the field and of the general indifference of the Government to trade and commerce were better founded. It was the old complaint of Catalonia against Castile, based upon fundamentally different conceptions of government, and reinforced by special grievances. 'We in Catalonia must sweat and toil so that ten thousand drones in the Madrid Government offices may live', the Catalans would say. And they would go on to point out that, although their population was only one-eighth of that of Spain, they paid one-quarter of the State taxes and that only one-tenth of the total budget came back to their province. These were much the same complaints that their ancestors had expressed in 1640. It was a point of view natural to a trading and manufacturing community which finds itself under the rule of an oligarchy that, though in many respects more cultured than themselves,[1] had no serious urge towards money making and asked only to be allowed to continue its own torpid, agreeable existence. And it was when this feeling came to a head among the Catalan manufacturers and merged with the clerical sentiments of the *clases acomodadas* or 'comfortable classes' of the large towns and with the Carlist traditions of the country districts, that Catalan Nationalism became for the first time a powerful and disintegrating force in Spanish politics. A party was formed, the *Lliga Regionalista* or 'Regionalist League', comprising all the various Right-wing elements and in Francisco Cambó, the President of the *Fomento* (later also the President of the *Chade*, the principal electrical company in Spain, and director of various banking houses), it had the good luck to find an intelligent and active leader.

---

[1] Visitors to Barcelona must often have noticed with amazement the architecture in which the *nouveau-riche*, ultra-Catholic bourgeoisie of this period expressed at the same time their ardent nationalism and their pride in their money. The villas of the Tibidabo are built so as to avoid right angles even in the doors or windows, because the right angle is 'not found in Nature'. That vast, unfinished, neo-gothic church, the Sagrada Familia, is decorated with stone friezes and mouldings representing the fauna and flora, the gastropods and lepidoptera of Catalonia, enlarged mechanically from nature so as to obtain absolute accuracy. Not even in the European architecture of the period can one discover anything quite so vulgar or pretentious.

In 1901 this party, usually known simply as the Lliga, won a famous and unexpected victory at the polls and the struggle for Catalan autonomy commenced in earnest.

Barcelona now and for the next twenty years became the scene of extraordinarily complicated and unscrupulous manœuvres: radical Republicans contested elections with the secret support of Conservative Madrid: gangsters were taken into the pay of the Government, the anarchists were provoked or egged on and the police themselves laid bombs at the doors of peaceful citizens in an endeavour either to intimidate the Catalan Nationalists or to produce a state of affairs in which the Constitutional guarantees could be suspended. By 1923 the situation had so deteriorated that the Lliga were almost glad to see their worst enemies, the Army, come into power 'to restore order'. But since it was during these years and out of this confused struggle that the forces which led to the civil war were prepared, it will be necessary to examine them in greater detail.

The first reply to the Catalan movement was the rise and rapid spread in Barcelona of a Left-wing Republican party, known as the Radicals. Their leader was a young journalist called Alejandro Lerroux. The extraordinary violence of his speeches, his incitements to kill priests, to sack and burn churches and to overthrow the rich generally brought him large audiences in this excitable and predominantly Left-wing city.[1] The police did not interfere with his meetings, the Governor and the military obligingly stood aside and in 1903 he defeated the Lliga at the elections. Lerroux was acclaimed as the *Caudillo* or 'Leader' and as Emperor of the Paralelo—as the quarter of slums and brothels in Barcelona is called—and the politicians in Madrid continued to shut their eyes mysteriously to his violent incitements. For he was an anti-Catalanist and the Catalan Nationalists could not make much progress so long as he controlled the lower-middle classes of the city.

But events were now developing rapidly. In 1905 the Government of Antonio Maura refused its support to Lerroux and the Radicals

---

[1] Some idea of Lerroux's oratory in these days may be gathered from the following extract: 'Young barbarians of to-day, enter and sack the decadent civilization of this unhappy country; destroy its temples, finish off its gods, tear the veil from its novices and raise them up to be mothers to civilize the species. Break into the records of property and make bonfires of its papers that fire may purify the infamous social organization. Enter its humble hearths and raise the legions of proletarians that the world may tremble before their awakened judges. Do not be stopped by altars nor by tombs....Fight, kill, die.' Quoted by Fernández Almagro, op. cit. from an article by Lerroux in *La Rebeldía* for 1 September 1906.

were therefore defeated by the Lliga at the elections. In the excitement produced by this some Army officers raided and burned two
newspaper offices which had published cartoons reflecting discredit
upon the Army, and the incident led to a situation in which a Liberal
government was forced, by the threat of a military rising, to pass a law
(the Law of Jurisdictions) by which every offence however trivial
against the Army, the Police, or the Nation (*la Patria*) was to be tried
by court martial. Since the Army was the most uncompromising
opponent of Catalan Nationalism or of any derogation, even slight, of
central authority, this law was naturally interpreted as a threat to
Catalan interests and the various Catalan National parties, from
Carlists to anti-clerical Republicans, formed a united front (*Solidaridad Catalana*) with Cambó and the Lliga at its head. This was so
effective that in January 1907 they won an overwhelming victory at
the elections, in spite of the Government's employing every possible
device to prevent it, including an attempt on Cambó's life.

Spanish political history is full of the strangest paradoxes. The
Government responsible for keeping order at these elections and for
the police terror that followed was that of Don Antonio Maura. Now
Maura was a man of distinction and integrity—who in certain respects
occupies a niche above all the other politicians of Alfonso's reign.
His mere presence when he came into a room silenced people: although of Jewish origin (he was a *chueta* from the Balearic Islands) he
was the only Spaniard whom the King did not address as *tu*. It is true
that, even by Spanish standards, he was a reactionary. He was autocratic, clerical, opposed in his whole nature to compromise. Spain
abounds in men who believe that they alone can tap the pure and
unadulterated source of Spanish traditions and project it upon the
future and that everyone who disagrees with them is necessarily per-
verse and wicked and must be overridden. This was Maura's case. He
was a Carlist who accepted the parliamentary system and the King.
But he also believed that government can only exist with the consent
of the governed. At the time of the Cuban War, he had strongly
urged that the Cubans must be given home rule and now he saw that a
certain measure of devolution must be offered to the Catalans. This
was also a Carlist position. And Maura further believed in purifying
the elections and destroying the caciques and thus restoring to political life the dignity and disinterestedness which, he believed, it had
once long ago possessed. His Government, therefore, when it took
office in 1907, came in on a wind of hope and faith in better things,

very refreshing after the feebleness and disreputableness of the Liberal governments. By the mere force of his personality, it was thought, Maura would overcome the old dragons of parliamentary corruption and sterility, settle the Catalan question and give the country pure standards of political life.[1]

And then, to the surprise of everyone, he chose for his Home Secretary La Cierva, the most notorious of all the politicians of the period and a master in the arts of electoral falsification. In every subsequent Government of Maura's La Cierva was his right-hand man and the elections held under him were the most corrupt of the century. We shall come, when we deal with the Anarchists, to other cases in which the pure idealist is linked to and necessarily depends upon the man of base or violent instincts. For Maura's ideal of pure elections was based upon his belief that free electors would necessarily return him to the Cortes with a large majority. As there was not in fact the least prospect of their doing so, it became necessary, if Maurism was not to destroy itself, for some of his followers to forget their ideals and fake the returns.[2]

The first year of La Cierva's rule at the Home Office saw therefore an extraordinary outburst of bomb throwing and assassination in

---

[1] Most of the pure idealists, the quixotic and disinterested figures who have come to the front in Spanish politics in recent times, belong to the Left, so that there is a special interest in understanding the character of one who belongs to the extreme Right. Maura is a figure who could not have existed in any other country. His distinction, his reserve, his humanity put him in another world from French royalists such as Maurras; also his extraordinary egotism—his belief that his party was so profoundly rooted in the Spanish conscience and in Castilian traditions that it did not need to put forward a programme. *Nosotros somos nosotros* he declared in an election speech that has become famous: 'We are ourselves. We have no need of any other symbol: that is our ensign. Let us be moved as patriots by the desire to serve Spain.' He preached a 'revolution from above': *Nosotros somos incompatibles con las digestiones sosegadas.* Yet his followers were simply those middle-class provincial families, the inert or 'passive classes' as they are called, who believe that good government consists in keeping everything as it is and in suppressing by force anyone who has a grievance. Maura, with all his Jewish-Iberian self-confidence, simply did not know what to do when he came into power. If it is true that, since Cánovas, there has been no Spanish politician of the same calibre, it is also true that no politician has been so ineffective.

[2] Cánovas had of course been in the same predicament and had solved it in the same way by allowing Romero Robledo to organize the elections for him. But Cánovas had chosen this path deliberately, as Walpole had done in the reign of George I, because it was the only means open to him of securing a spell of peace in which the country could develop its material resources, free from the squabblings of generals and court officials and from the periodic revolutions which their rule always ended by bringing about. This situation, once established, ceased to be in his control. Yet, but for the early death of Alfonso XII, it is possible that a real parliamentary regime based on free elections might have grown up.

Barcelona. Within a short space of time some two thousand bombs exploded in the streets. They were for the most part directed against the premises of Catalan factory owners belonging to the Lliga. But there were certain peculiar features about these crimes which aroused suspicion: no dynamiters were ever caught in the act and the workmen who were accused by the police spies could often prove alibis. In the end, after an English detective had been brought over to investigate, it was discovered that they were in nearly every case committed by a band of gangsters and agents provocateurs in the pay of the police. The leader, Juan Rull, and his chief accomplices were tried and convicted, but though the complicity of the late Governor of Barcelona, the Duke of Bivona, was made clear, nothing was done to bring him to justice and the further ramifications of the affair were hushed up.[1] But the bomb throwing went on and La Cierva, who had already introduced repressive measures, was able finally to suspend the Constitutional guarantees and to place the city under military law—a situation which was of course prejudicial to the Catalan Nationalists.

An impartial reader may well wonder whether such a story as this can be true: it was not at this time a normal practice for Conservative governments to pay gangsters to intimidate rich factory owners. But even such a writer as Señor Madariaga, anxious, as he always is, not to give a bad impression abroad of his country, fully admits it. It cannot be accidental, he says, that anarchist outbursts have invariably occurred at moments when Catalan Nationalists have been giving signs of special vitality, thus leading to repressive measures which reacted chiefly against Catalan national interests. And he attributes the freedom from anarchist outrages during the Dictatorship to the fact that Catalan Nationalism was then suppressed.[2] One might add that the outrages again ceased when the Catalans were allowed to govern themselves. Indeed the first bombs thrown in Barcelona coincide with the promulgation of the Bases de Manresa, the earliest

[1] See on these incidents Madariaga, Spain, p. 379; Ciges Aparicio, op. cit. p. 404; Fernández Almagro, op. cit.; F. Madrid, Ocho Meses y un Día en el Gobierno Civil de Barcelona.

[2] This is Cambó's opinion. 'In order', he wrote, 'to fight against a Catalonia which was beginning to lift its head Spanish governments set on foot every kind of demagogic agitation. But, as was only to be expected, the bacillus which was scattered through the country did not keep to the field allotted to it. If one day we discover what were the deepest causes of the acts to which Cánovas, Canalejas and Dato amongst others fell victims, it will come to light that there existed a bond between them and those anarchist ferments which have been cultivated in Catalonia by the Madrid governments themselves.' Quoted by Sieberer, Katalonien gegen Kastilien, pp. 152-155.

manifesto of Catalan Nationalism, in 1892, and acts of violence continued to grow and to wane in intensity with the periodic rise and decline of Catalan national feeling. As an English observer remarked in 1909, if one asked a workman in Barcelona where the bombs came from, he replied, 'Don't you know? They are made by the Jesuits.'[1]

In July 1909 there occurred one of those small disasters in Morocco which the incompetence and lack of organization of the Spanish Army were always provoking. A column of troops advancing a few miles beyond Melilla to take possession of some iron mines for which the Conde de Romanones had recently obtained the concession was ambushed by a handful of Moors and almost destroyed. To replace them the War Office called up the reserves in Catalonia.

It was a stupid and no doubt a deliberately provocative act. Since the disastrous war in Cuba and the return of thousands of starving and malaria-ridden troops, the whole country had been strongly pacifist. The reserves consisted of married men of the working classes, for in Spain no one who could afford the small sum required to buy himself out was ever conscripted. The iron mines were believed to be the property of the Jesuits, who in the eyes of one half of Spain occupied much the same position as they did in England after the Gunpowder Plot. There were painful scenes at the station when the troops left, and the next day the whole city rose.

For six years Lerroux had been urging the populace to sack, burn and kill. Now that the moment had come he and his fellow-Radicals kept out of the way, but his young followers, the *Jóvenes Bárbaros*, or 'Young Barbarians' as they called themselves, let themselves go. The result was five days of mob rule, in which the union leaders lost all control of their men and twenty-two churches and thirty-four convents were burned. Monks were killed, tombs were desecrated and strange and macabre scenes took place, as when workmen danced in the street with the disinterred mummies of nuns.

The riot was suppressed severely by La Cierva. One hundred and seventy-five workmen were shot in the streets and executions followed afterwards. Among the victims was Francisco Ferrer, a theoretical anarchist who had founded a school, the *Escuela Moderna*, where anti-religious instruction was given. There was no evidence to show that he had been implicated in the rising, which was a spontaneous affair, not part of an anarchist plot, and he was not even living in

[1] Rafael Shaw, *Spain from Within*, pp.133-180.

Barcelona at the time.[1] But he was generally regarded as having been the instigator of an attempt on the life of the King three years before by a young pupil and intimate friend of his called Morral and the opportunity was taken to get rid of him. However, this was a political error, for Ferrer was well known abroad and his death made an impression which in his life he had done little to deserve. Maura's Government fell and such was the aversion that his name had created that he had to resign the leadership of his party and it was nearly ten years before he and La Cierva were able to come back. The era inaugurated thirty months before with such hope had ended in complete failure; even the law giving a feeble measure of autonomy to the Catalans had been thrown out by the Chamber, though Canalejas was able to pass a similar law conceived on more generous lines three years later. But one effect of the riots in Barcelona was the ruin of the Radical party. The workmen who had followed Lerroux believed, when they saw him fail to stand up to his word, that he had sold himself to Madrid and they abandoned his party for the Anarchists. The Radicals became mild and respectable and the Emperor of the Paralelo himself exchanged without too deep a regret his wooden tribune and his open shirt for the comfortable armchairs and starched collars of the plutocracy.

[1] According to the Civil Governor, Señor Ossorio y Gallardo, the riots were not anarchist, but had confused objects. They were made much worse, in his opinion, by calling out the troops. A letter from the veteran anarchist Anselmo Lorenzo to his friend, Tarrida del Mármol, dated 31 July, confirms this: 'What is happening here is amazing. A Social Revolution has broken out in Barcelona and it has been started by the people. No one has instigated it. No one has led it. Neither Liberals, nor Catalan Nationals, nor Republicans, nor Socialists, nor Anarchists.' (*Anselmo Lorenzo*, by Federica Montseny, p. 30).

FURTHER NOTES ON CHAPTER II

A (p. 35). Some quotations from foreign observers will enable one to appreciate the very similar character of Spanish administration in the seventeenth century. *The Relations of the Venetian Ambassadors* are particularly enlightening.

Pietro Basadonna (1649–1653): 'One must put away entirely the common idea that the Spaniards are prudent and understand that there is no nation in the world more ignorant of good government, or more inclined to destruction: indeed it is only when one has seen how execrably they manage their private affairs that one finds it possible to believe all that one is told of public affairs' (p. 202).

Frederico Cornaro (1678–1681): 'To begin with the tax collectors retain most of the revenues. Then officials' salaries absorb large sums of money: there is not a person scarcely who does not live on the King or who, if he lacked a salary from him, could maintain himself on his own income, whilst the chief nobles, supported at court by remunerative posts, have entirely abandoned their own properties' (p. 455).

Giovanni Cornaro (1681–1682) repeats this at greater length. I have put a quotation from him at the head of the chapter.

Sebastiano Foscarini (1682-1686): Everyone who can lives at the expense of the State. The number of all the Government posts has been increased. In the Treasury alone there are more than 40,000 clerks, many of whom draw twice the pay that is assigned to them. Yet their accounts are 'wrapped in impenetrable and perhaps malicious obscurity' and it is impossible 'to get any order or number out of them'. Exorbitant pensions are granted to important persons: only the poor pay taxes: of those taxes and of the gold of the treasure fleet only a fraction ever reaches the Treasury. It is remarkable that the kingdom is able to carry on at all.

The Marquis de Villars, who was French ambassador from 1679 to 1681 and who had a long experience of the country, fully corroborates this. The taxes were crushing, yet only a fraction ever reached the King because 24,000 men were employed in collecting them. Three-quarters of the King's share of the treasure ships was never put down. Such money as did reach the Treasury was spent upon the infinite numbers of officials and pensioners, who did nothing whatever to earn it. The Inquisition alone had 20,000 familiars in its pay. To such extremities was the King reduced that one year all his servants gave notice and the ladies and gentlemen of the bedchamber could not get meals in the Palace. The cost of living in Madrid was enormous because the municipality imposed such customs and taxes, spending all the money they got on themselves. All the judges took bribes and no one who could pay was ever sentenced. Those who could not pay were not sentenced either, as there was no money to maintain the prisons, so that both thefts and murders went unpunished.

'Une partie de l'Espagne vit de...frauder les droits du Roi; l'autre vit, c'est à dire vole, dans les emplois de finance ou de justice et le reste meurt de faim....Ceux qui n'ont point vu l'Espagne en cet état auront de la peine à le comprendre.'

It may be said that these accounts apply only to a period of extreme decadence. But all the beginnings of this state of affairs existed a hundred years before—in full Siglo de Oro. It was only the degree that differed. Such was the price that Spain had to pay for being, in gold and silver, the richest nation in the world.

Chapter III

THE LIBERALS AND THE CHURCH

The Anarchists have destroyed many churches,
but the clergy had first destroyed the Church. JOSÉ CASTILLEJO.

The next seven years represent a pause in Spanish history. A few days of rioting and the fall of the Government responsible for it had released the tension that, since 1906, had been accumulating in Barcelona. The Anarchists were busy organizing a new trades union, the *Confederación Nacional del Trabajo*, in imitation of the French C.G.T. and in rivalry with the Socialists. The Catalan Nationalists had been frightened by the riots and were keeping quiet. Their united front, *Solidaridad Catalana*, had broken up over the religious question (that is to say, the tactics of the Government had been successful) and the Lliga, with somewhat reduced enthusiasm, became once again the only serious representative of Catalan ambitions. But it had been momentarily appeased by a new schedule of tariffs which gave Catalonia a complete monopoly of the home market and by a moderate measure of devolution (the Law of Mancomunidades) which after endless discussion in the Cortes it had obtained by decree in 1913. The King, too, had been warned at Edward VII's funeral of the danger of moving too far along the path of reaction and with a change of tone that came easily to him he proclaimed himself a good Liberal and even flirted with the Republicans.

For several years therefore Conservative and Liberal governments peaceably succeeded one another and, though most of the faults of the regime remained, a real public opinion was growing up in the large towns and occasionally even asserting itself in the elections. The omens for the commencement of a more healthy state of affairs began to appear favourable. In the industrial and mining centres a series of strikes raised the wages of the workmen, and the Conservatives interested themselves in improving their condition by legislation. In fact little could be done, but the Institute of Social Reforms and the National Assurance Institute (*Instituto de Previsión*), two autonomous bodies set up by previous governments, were encouraged to explore the ground and to prepare schemes which could be adopted. The work performed by these bodies was admirable and the encourage-

ment given them by the governments, which rarely had the strength
to put in practice their feeblest proposals, was at least a proof of their
good intentions.

The Liberals, on the other hand, resumed the monotonous struggle
with the Church which, since they first came into existence in the
Cortes of 1810, had been their main business in life. The contest suddenly became acute after 1900. During the last twenty-five
years the Church had been steadily growing in strength and financial
resources. Its militants—the monastic orders and the Jesuits—were
more numerous and more disciplined than ever and its treasure chest
was full. It had never resigned itself to the loss of the dominating
position it had once held in the State and now the death of Cánovas,
who had kept it out of politics, and the appearance of the clerical
party of Maura seemed to offer it an opportunity for taking another
step along the road to power. On the other hand the forces of anti-
clericalism had been growing also: they had on their side the whole
trend of contemporary European thought, and the recent triumph of
their party in France and the disestablishment of the French Church
had greatly encouraged them.

The first shock came in January 1901 with the production of Pérez
Galdós' anti-clerical play *Electra*. The young King's tutor and confessor Father Montaña had written an article in *El Siglo Futuro*
asserting that Liberalism was a sin. Feeling against the Church ran
high and this play by the greatest of Spanish novelists polarized
opinion. The struggle at once began. The chief points at issue were
the limitation of the number of the religious orders, the toleration of
other religions and the control of education. But far from gaining
ground the Liberals found that they were barely able to hold their
own. Two years of struggle (1910—1912) to compel the religious
orders to conform to the Concordat of 1851 and to the established law
of the country failed. A circular ordering the collection of taxes from
unregistered religious communities which were engaged in trade and
industry had to be withdrawn. The only advance made (and that was
not made without the violent protest of the bishops, processions by
fashionable ladies through the streets of Madrid and remonstrances
from the Vatican) was the permission granted to the Protestant
Churches to erect a cross or other symbol over their doors. It was
said that the English king refused to visit Madrid unless this were
allowed. The support given by the richer classes to the Church
enabled it to withstand the pressure of public opinion. But if the

religious question and the violent feelings it aroused are to be made clear it will be necessary to speak at greater length of the history of the Catholic Church in Spain and of its relation with the State.

In the sixteenth and seventeenth centuries there was no real political unity in Spain. Half a dozen kingdoms, each with its own administration, its own laws and Cortes, lived side by side. The only political link between them was the King, and his power, wherever individual rights or local liberties were concerned, was very limited. The cement that held them together was the Church.

This Church of the sixteenth century was a very different thing from a modern Church that stands aside from and often in opposition to the State. On the contrary it then embraced everything. Through it the King became a semi-sacred figure—a Pharaoh, as a Portuguese historian has put it: his wars, in Flanders and in Germany, became sacred wars and the discoveries and conquests in the New World missions of evangelization. Spain lived then for an idea and everything was sacrificed to maintaining that idea in its purity. The Inquisition, which was the organization set up for this purpose, was naturally given a supreme position in the State. The analogy of Spain then with the totalitarian states of to-day is obvious. The militant attitude that forced it to undertake costly wars for ideological reasons, the severe censorship, the burnings of books, the secret Cheka, the system of purifications, the ban on persons who had heretic or Jewish blood, the ban on foreign study and travel, the discouragement of foreign trade and the gradually increasing isolation—all these modern symptoms were first to be seen in sixteenth-century Spain. Only the economic and political centralization was lacking.

But if the Church so affected and penetrated the State, the latter also reacted upon the Church. It was essentially a national Church. A Spanish army captured and sacked Rome and humiliated the Pope. Both Inquisition and King were often at sharp variance with the Vatican. The doctrine of the Immaculate Conception, which was still refused credence in most Catholic countries, was in Spain an article of faith. No serious attempt was made to convert the Moors, and the children of converts down to the third generation were not considered full Christians and were refused admittance to holy orders. Had the Protestant schism not come when it did, the Spanish Church might have been the one to secede from Rome.[1] Yet in that case everything

[1] The reform of the regular clergy carried out before 1510 by Cardinal Ximénez, the desire of the Spanish clergy to be allowed to marry, the dislike of the Italians and

would have been different, for the Spanish totalitarianism of 1580 was essentially a reaction formation, like German National Socialism to-day, which could scarcely have come into existence but for the Protestant revolt.

Within Spain itself, religion was not only the link between the different provinces and the music that made them all move together, but it was the great leveller. Never has Marx's statement that religion was the opiate of the poor been more untrue. In all the social conflicts of the time—the Germanía of 1520 at Valencia, the rising of the Basques in 1631 against the salt tax and the exactions of the rich—it was the monks who led and supported the people. As in Germany to-day the mere strength of the national religion caused a country where hitherto the divisions between nobles and plebeians had been very great, to become by 1620 remarkably egalitarian. Under weak but increasingly beloved and increasingly sacred kings there lived an anarchic mass of people, who, provided they did not mind tightening their belts, could do very much as they pleased. Class distinctions ceased to have the same importance. French and Italians were horrified at the insolence with which the lowest tradesman, got up with cloak and sword even if there was nothing at home to eat, jostled the highest grandees in the land. The nobles, of course, had their troops of servants, but these servants or retainers prided themselves on doing no work and on treating their masters with familiarity. The poor, begging in the streets or fed at the innumerable convent kitchens, were just as haughty. Hungry, ragged, idle, amazingly ignorant, but also amazingly free—that is the verdict of travellers towards 1660. 'The country of Europe', wrote a French Protestant, Antoine de Brunel, 'where there is greatest social equality.'[1] And for this the Church, with its unifying religious idea, must be given a large part of the credit. The magnificent independence of the Spaniards, which strikes every traveller to-day, is no doubt a legacy of the early Middle Ages; but the fact that it was not destroyed by the rise of absolutism must be put down mainly to the influence of the monks, who for three centuries made themselves the defenders of personal and local liberty

the disapprobation of the corruption and luxury of the Papacy, the very strong following that Erasmus had in Spain down to the 1530's all point to the beginning of a Reformation movement in Spain before Luther. The antagonism to the Popes in particular. After the sack of Rome in 1527 there was a strong movement in Spain to deprive the Pope of his temporal power.

[1] *Voyage en Espagne*, 1665, usually attributed to a Dutchman, François van Aerssen, but actually written by his tutor, a French Protestant, Antoine de Brunel, who accompanied him. It is one of the best books on Spain of this century.

against both the encroachments of the State and the arrogance of the upper classes.[1] Southey, visiting Spain in 1795, full of the ideas of the French Revolution and of the Rights of Man, was, I believe, the first person to make the obvious (though not necessarily correct) deduction that, since the Spanish poor had attained a spirit of liberty and independence quite unknown among the same class in England, they were more fitted than other races for free institutions.[2]

To go back, however, to 1700, Spain was then bankrupt: her sacred king, mad and childless: her population shrunk: her land uncultivated: her trade non-existent. The old religious idea had run its course. The new idea brought in by the Bourbon kings was that of political unity and centralization and, as the century wore on, of economic revival. The Church had lost its political function. And gradually, painfully, Spain began to live again, but with a very different kind of life.[3]

[1] This statement must be qualified. Spanish independence of character, Spanish civil liberties go back to the early Middle Ages and were the result of social conditions brought about by the continual war against the Moors and by the necessity for repopulating huge stretches of waste country. They declined in the fourteenth and fifteenth centuries with the decay of the municipalities, but revived under Ferdinand and Isabella, who to counterbalance the power of the nobility encouraged the growth of a class of small hidalgos by means of laws permitting the entailing of even very small estates. That they did not come to an end altogether under two centuries of absolutist rule, but on the contrary revived in a strong upheaval of popular feeling accompanied by a rejuvenescence of popular culture, must, I think, be put down in the main to the moral support given to the people by the Church.

[2] See Southey's *Letters from Spain*, 1797: 'I like the familiarity of these people. They address me with cheerfulness and without any of that awkward silent submission which ought never to be paid by one human being to another. How often in England have I heard a tavern waiter cursed by some fellow who would never have dared to insult him if his situation had permitted him to resent the insult. I have observed nothing of this in Spain. The people show civility and expect to receive it.' But Southey was naturally unable to distinguish between the ideological tyranny of the Church and its liberating and levelling power in other respects and he goes on to state that 'with Padilla expired the liberties of Spain', and to express the hope that 'in a more enlightened age some new Padilla may arise with better fortune and with more enlarged views; then, and not till then, will Spain assume her ancient rank in Europe'. Some verses on Padilla, 'the Martyr to Freedom', follow.

[3] The moral and intellectual decline of the Church was already far advanced by 1700, though for a little longer exceptional men continued to appear in it. Yet the year 1700 is the year of the Church's greatest numerical extension in Spain: one man in every nine belonged to it. It is from this time on that the Spanish monk and priest ceases to be a support of humanistic learning and becomes, as a Portuguese historian has put it, an African medicine-man, whose powers depend on his ability to work up the passions of the uneducated classes. When one considers the greatness of the Spanish Church from 1500 to 1630—a greatness still altogether unappreciated in England, and which has perhaps no equal in ecclesiastical history in any other country or century—the rapidity of the decline amazes one. Undoubtedly a large part of the blame for this must be laid to the stultifying action of the Inquisition.

The Church however did not submit easily. The Jesuits resisted and were turned out in 1767. The Inquisition, which had to be handled with circumspection, resisted too. It still had sufficient power to ruin Olavide, the enlightened Commissioner of Charles III, who was attempting to repopulate the empty fields, for the Church was the largest landowner in Spain and felt itself threatened by his agrarian policy. And in this it had the great mass of the country behind it. The small group of enlightened men under the direction of the King who were endeavouring to impose a new economic structure and a new outlook on the people found that this people—liberty-loving and anarchic—had no wish to change and that they were led by the Church, and especially by the monks, in their resistance. This resistance of the Church to the State,[1] which begins to appear towards 1760, has been continued without a break down to the present time. And that has had several effects: first, that the natural development of the country has been checked and stunted: then, that the Church has come to regard its normal attitude to the civil powers as one of opposition: and, finally, that the State has been forced to consider as one of its principal functions the struggle with the Church.

When, therefore, in May 1808, the Spanish people rose against Napoleon, there was no king and no government to direct them. The richer classes and the nobles hedged or went over to the French. It was the people under the leadership of the Church who took up arms. Priests and monks, blacksmiths and chair-menders led the *partidas* or guerrilla bands and sat on the provincial juntas. It was even a rule in many of the *partidas* that no gentleman (hidalgo) should belong to them, because in the fight against the invaders men with property to lose could not be trusted. This was the last occasion on which the Church played a national role in Spain. Yet curiously enough the Cortes, which met in 1810 at Cadiz to carry on the war against the French and to draw up a Constitution, proved to be simply a continuation (in a somewhat modernized form, now that the King was a prisoner in France) of the old bureaucratic and anti-clerical councils of Charles III. The Liberals brought nothing new to Spain except the

[1] One can see the beginnings of this resistance a century earlier, when the monks supported the risings in Catalonia and elsewhere against Olivares' plans for a more centralized State. That fear and mistrust of the State which has always been so strong in Spain and of which the Anarchists are the chief exponents to-day was shared by the Church whenever it appeared that the State was endeavouring to increase its powers. Until it lost its hold over the people the Spanish Church invariably stood for a weak central authority.

idea, natural under the circumstances, that sovereignty emanated from the people and with it a kind of excitement about liberty—but they passed after weeks of furious discussion a law which the Bourbon kings had longed to pass but had not dared—the abolition of the Inquisition. All the other articles of this Constitution, however drastic or innovating, were put through almost without discussion. This was passed by only a small minority and, as Wellington at the time prophesied, it at once sealed the fate of the Cortes, of the Constitution and of the Liberals, as they were now called, who had passed it.

Religion from this time on lent its venom to the terribly savage repressions and civil wars of the next thirty years. All the fury which Napoleon had aroused was transferred to the Liberals, and the cowardly court circles which at first had flocked to Joseph joined fully in it. These Liberals, encouraged and maddened by persecutions, and hiding in the lodges of the freemasons where they could plot more easily, gradually emerged as the party of the new and weak middle classes and found in the Army, whose officers were mostly drawn from their ranks, a champion to defend them.

The Carlists, who were the party created by the Church to defend their interests and the ideas of the seventeenth century, were in the end defeated. Indeed they could never have resisted so long as they did, if these interests had not coincided with those of the Basque and Catalan Nationalists, whose *fueros*, or local privileges, the Bourbon kings had reduced or taken away, but which the Church, true to its pre-Bourbon attitude, had always supported.

In the middle of the Carlist War a significant thing occurred, which if the Church had not long ceased to be able to take in new impressions, might have opened its eyes to the gravity of its situation. There was a cholera plague in Madrid and a rumour spread that the monks and the Jesuits had poisoned the springs. A mob collected and burned convents and Jesuit churches and killed any monks it could find. Next year (1835), as if on a sudden signal, churches and convents were burned in all the large towns of Spain. And here one must note two things—first, that the men who burned them were most of them practising Catholics—and secondly, that the convents were burned not by the Liberal middle classes, but by the people. Anger against the Carlists had made the monks, who supported them, unpopular.

A few months later Mendizábal passed a law breaking up the convents and confiscating most of the landed property of the Church.

This law was not merely an anti-clerical or rather an anti-Carlist law: it was also part of the general policy of the Liberals of breaking up the entailed estates that then, together with the common lands, covered almost the whole of the country. Mendizábal, who from a long residence in England (he had gone successfully into business there) had come to understand the economic basis of Liberalism, hoped in this way to destroy the old Spanish inertia and to force his country-men to create wealth by exchange, commerce and speculation. It was this measure, which, by making the landowners and provincial bour-geoisie who bought up at a temptingly low price the estates of the Church his accomplices, decided the war and secured the Liberal Revolution, just as in England the sale of the monastic lands had decided the Reformation.

It had another effect. By cutting off the clergy and the monks from the possession of land, it alienated them from the people, forced them to think of other methods of enrichment and so threw them into the arms of the wealthy classes, on whom alone through the greater part of Spain they have depended ever since. Thus the struggle which from 1814 to 1840 had made the Church savage and bloodthirsty now made it grasping. Intellectually it had been degenerating since 1700— like indeed every other institution in Spain—and morally it was degenerating still more rapidly as a result of the violently aggressive attitude it had taken up. I need only cite in support of this the Society of the Exterminating Angel, founded in 1821 and revived in 1834 under the presidency of the Bishop of Osma to exterminate all Liberals: the hanging of a deist schoolmaster in 1827 by the Archbishop of Valencia after his trial for heresy,[1] or the miserable imposture of the Bleeding Nun and Father Claret at the court of Isabella[2]—

[1] Cayetano Ripoll, the schoolmaster in question, one of the first of the great army of anti-clerical and revolutionary dominies, was tried and convicted without being heard in his own defence or being allowed to give evidence. He was condemned to be burned alive, but at the last moment the mode of execution was changed to hanging, though buckets painted with flames were placed at the foot of the scaffold to symbolize the original sentence. After death his body was pulled to pieces by the mob and burned.

[2] One has only to compare the quality of the advice on political matters given by the Bleeding Nun, Sor Patrocinio and her shady confederate, the Queen's confessor Father Claret, to Queen Isabella with the letters of Sor Maria de Ágreda to Philip IV, to appreciate the enormous intellectual and moral degeneration of the Church in the course of two centuries. Or one may contrast Claudio Moyano's dictum (1853) that 'the poor should be respectful and humble with the rich and the rich charitable and generous with the poor' with Father Vitoria's declaration (c. 1534) that the 'com-munication' by the rich of their goods was the indispensable preliminary condition to their protection by the State.

all of them things which could never have occurred at this time in any other Catholic country. Thus one has the spectacle of the most naturally religious people in Europe—the Spanish pueblo—although isolated from the dangerous influences of the century because they cannot read—gradually and reluctantly separating themselves from the Church when it is forced upon them that it is a purely self-seeking institution with no real care for their interests. By 1870, although the great mass of the people was still Catholic, the priests in most of the large towns had lost their hold upon them and monks were hated. These were the symptoms which in Germany preceded the Reformation.

And yet, one cannot help thinking, it might have been different. In the sixteenth and seventeenth centuries the Spanish Church had been, as I have said, a levelling institution. Its close connection with the State had given it an interest in social and political questions such as the Church in other Christian countries had never possessed. The amazing success of the colonization of America and the humane methods by which, after the first violent conquest, the conflicts between the Indians and the planters were resolved, were largely due to its influence. Its missionaries returned to Spain with a practical experience of social problems and the strong idealism of the monastic orders led to their weight being usually thrown on the side of the under dog (in America the Indians, in Spain the workers) against the powerful and the rich. There is nothing surprising therefore to find the Spanish Church going farther than any of the Protestant Churches of the time in providing a platform on which social theories of a communistic sort could be freely discussed. Father Mariana, for example, the greatest of Spanish historians, whose books are the bible of the Right wing to-day, proclaimed the illegality (*ilicitud*) of private property in land and demanded the intervention of the State in the distribution of natural riches. Other Churchmen of the time held similar views. The folly and injustice of the unequal distribution of land were proclaimed by a host of monks, theologians and lawyers in much stronger terms than the mediaeval schoolmen had ever permitted themselves to use. In America the Inca collectivist state drew deep admiration both from the missionaries and from the civil servants engaged in reorganizing the country. The Jesuits seem to have been particularly impressed by it—it was, for example, a Jesuit, Father Acosta, who in his history of the Indies, published in Seville in 1590, first seriously recommended the application of Inca state socialism to

Spain—a train of thought which led a few years later to the establishment of the famous Jesuit concessions in Paraguay, which provide the
earliest example of a communist state set up by Europeans.[1]

The seventeenth century saw a great development and clarification
of socialist or collectivist ideas both among the clergy, who recommended them on moral and religious grounds, and of officials and civil
servants, who saw in them a remedy for the catastrophic economic
conditions of the country. The State in the end took up these ideas
and, though the extensive socialist measures which it passed (beginning with the Pragmatic of 1633, fixing the conditions for the leasing
of pasture land so rigidly as in effect to nationalize the greater part of
the surface of Spain) were never carried out, that was not the fault of
the people who directed public opinion in the country.

But what I wish to stress now is the immense part which the Church
had played in furthering these ideas and in insisting that it was the
moral duty of the King and Government to secure, compulsorily and
if necessary without compensation, a more equal distribution of property. It was only the too rapid collapse of the whole economic and
moral fabric of the country, the weakness of the Government and
its inability to get any of its economic decrees carried out against the
silent opposition of the landlords, that prevented Spain in this century
from advancing a considerable way along the road to a socialistic
organization.

But the collectivist tendencies of Spanish economists disappeared
just when the moment for deciding the agrarian question at last
arrived. The theories of Adam Smith made their appearance in Spain
in the last quarter of the eighteenth century and through the influence
of Jovellanos, the most famous economist of the time, they won a
complete victory. In the Cadiz Cortes of 1810–1814, when the
question was again taken up, his views prevailed and it was decided
that all the land that would become available through the sale of
common lands and, later, of Church property should be thrown on to
the open market. This policy, which continued to be carried out all
through the following century, was very unpopular with the peasants
and poor labourers, who saw the large estates increasing everywhere
at their expense. Had therefore the Church put forward a land policy
of its own in keeping with its traditional views and with the old
communal practice of the villages, using the immense experience it
had acquired in its American concessions to devise some scheme for

[1] For further information on this see Appendix II.

the interior colonization of Spain, it might well have checked the spreading of the Liberal ideas, which in many respects were unsuited to Spanish conditions. But the Church was no longer able to invent anything: its land policy was a mere obstinate clinging to the past and provided no guidance for the change from semi-pastoral life to agriculture which was everywhere taking place with a great increase of population. Hence Carlism failed except in Navarre and along the southern slope of the Pyrenees, where the combination of middle-sized farms and of large communal pastures suited it. The Church in Spain was ruined by its inability to react intelligently to the ideas of the French Revolution, while the low standard of education in the seminaries (the universities were secularized in 1837 and theology ceased to be taught there) prevented its ever recovering.

From 1874, then, to 1931 the Church, though losing every year its influence with the poor, was gaining steadily in riches and in political power. The death of Alfonso XII led to a great strengthening of its position. In return for Leo XIII's special protection (which kept off the danger of a Carlist rising during the King's minority) the Queen Regent dealt out money and patronage with a lavish hand. Indeed as she was herself entirely under the influence of her confessor she scarcely needed this encouragement. At the same time the French regular clergy, who had been compelled to leave their homes by the Jules Ferry laws secularizing education, established themselves in Spain and a concerted effort began to save at least one country in Europe from 'liberal atheism'. Within a few years the Peninsula was studded with almost as many convents, colleges and religious foundations as it had seen during its palmiest period and the court, the universities, the press and indeed a large part of the governing classes went down before a wave of clericalism.

The leaders of this movement were, of course, the Jesuits. Theirs was the policy—originated three centuries before by their founder—of winning over the rich and the powerful. For this they needed money. And indeed Spain provided a tempting investment for the general funds of their Society: money laid out there would bring not only a good return but also immediate political power. And so their wealth in the Peninsula began to mount up—composed as it was of the investments of the Society abroad and of the new bequests made by the pious in Spain—until it reached really immense proportions. In 1912, according to Joaquín Aguilera, Secretary of the Fomento, they controlled 'without exaggeration one-third of the capital wealth of Spain'.[1] They owned railways, mines, factories, banks, shipping companies, orange plantations. There came to be something almost mythical about their industrial activities. One was told that they ran the antique furniture business, supplied Madrid with fresh fish and controlled the liveliest of the cabarets. Their working capital was said to amount to £60,000,000 sterling. There is of course no reason why the Jesuits, with their colleges and missions to provide for, should not be wealthy. They would not be able to carry out their work if they were not. And there is a Spanish saying: *El dinero es muy católico*: 'Money is a good Catholic.' But it seemed scarcely in the national interests that one section of the community—and that a militant one— should control so large a share of the industrial life of the country, and then one must remember that a good part of this wealth had to be acquired by cadging for gifts and bequests among the rich and that these favours were not given for nothing. In return the Church was expected to defend the interests of the rich against the poor. How close, how intimate, how unbecoming this connection between some of the religious orders and the very rich could be is scarcely to be credited by those who have not lived for some years in Spain. For more than a century now all contact with the rich, with the court, and with politics in Spain has been corrupting.[2]

On the other hand the country clergy were poor. Their salaries, fixed by the Concordat of 1851, were paid by the State and the cost of living had been rising. Some of them scarcely received more than a manual labourer. But poverty is never humiliating in Spain. On the contrary, it is apt to bring out the best in the Spanish character, so that though badly educated and somewhat lax by modern standards (there were many who still adhered to the mediaeval custom of

---

[1] See article in *La Revue* by J. Aguilera, 1912, cited by A. Marvaud, *L'Espagne au XXIème Siècle*, p. 189. The statement so often made in propagandist books, that the Spanish Church is a large landowner, is not of course true.

[2] 'In the early nineteenth century', wrote the Conde de Romanones, 'the influence of the monks in society was undoubtedly less than it is to-day; though they visited every house daily, their action was individual and not as now the result of a *táctica admirable de conjunto y estudiada en todos sus detalles*' (*Notas de Una Vida*, p. 303).

In another passage he says more upon these tactics: 'The existing rivalry between one order and another has been attenuated: there has been established among them what in the financial world is called a trust.... Each is given its region, its locality and its social class. Some work the aristocracy, others the middle classes and others the poor.'

This is the comment of Cánovas: 'I will not deny that the manner of understanding and practising the Catholic religion to-day may not be more correct in its form... but it has very little that is Spanish about it' (*El Solitario y su Tiempo*).

barragania and kept a 'housekeeper')[1] they were usually plain, honest men, who in an age when faith was dead did their best to carry out their duties.

There were then the monastic orders. By the provisions of the Concordat only three orders were allowed in Spain—two of which were specified and one which was left to the Pope to choose. He never chose and so every order that wished to established itself. On various occasions the Liberals attempted to regulate this position—to compel them at least to register and so submit to inspection, but each time such furious protests were raised, there were so many threats from Rome and from the Archbishops, that the attempt had to be dropped. Actually the number of monks was never very great—some 10,000 when the Republic came in, most of them schoolmasters— but the number of nuns rose to be 40,000, more than had ever been known in Spain before and at least twice as many as in the time of St Theresa.[2]

But the main struggle with the Liberals was over education. Until 1836 education had been almost entirely in the hands of the higher clergy and the religious orders. The Church at this time had not yet recovered from the shock which the French Revolution had given it and had a mortal dread of learning. Science, mathematics, agriculture and political economy were therefore not taught, as they were considered dangerous subjects for any but trained theologians. The Jesuits frowned on history, which offered so many bad examples to the young and innocent. Almost the only subject that could usefully be studied at the universities was law. For though medicine was taught, it suffered from the suppression of that erroneous Lutheran notion upon the circulation of the blood, whilst if one touched on physics one had to remember that the Copernican system was still a *cosa de Inquisición*. In the elementary schools the children of the poor were deliberately not taught to read, but only to sew and to recite the

---

[1] In the Middle Ages it was an established custom, permitted by the bishops, for Spanish priests to have concubines. They wore a special dress and had special rights and were called *barraganas*. When the Council of Trent forbade this practice to continue, the Spanish clergy protested. And in fact they have never paid much attention to the prohibition, for they continue to have 'housekeepers' and 'nieces' to this day. Their parishioners, far from being shocked, prefer them to live in concubinage, as otherwise they would not always care to let their womenfolk confess to them. This was so in the fifteenth century, when the Basques regularly refused to receive priests who did not bring their *barraganas* with them (Álvarez de Colmenar, *Délices de l'Espagne et du Portugal*, 1707), and to my knowledge it was often true until a few years ago.

[2] See Luís Morote, *Los Frailes en España*, 1904.

Catechism.[1] As the University of Cervera—the only university in Catalonia—declared in its famous address to Ferdinand VII: 'Far be from us the dangerous novelty of thinking.'

The Liberal Revolution changed this. Successive Governments gradually freed the universities from clerical control and laid the foundations of universal elementary education. The religious orders then turned their attention to secondary schools. The Church set itself the task of educating all the sons of the upper and upper-middle classes. The colleges of the Jesuits and Augustinians became what the public schools are in England. One cannot altogether say that it was a good education that they gave. 'The Jesuits do not educate, they domesticate', wrote the Conde de la Mortera,[2] whilst those who did not take the imprint preserved bitter memories of the corporal punishments and of the system of sneaking and espionage which prevailed in their colleges. Some of the most intransigent of the anti-clericals owed their hatred of the Church to these early impressions. Nor was the purely scholastic side of the education they gave what might have been expected. The humanities (Latin, history and literature) were all badly taught and so was religion, but there was a high standard on technological subjects. The Jesuits, for example, had two universities that gave degrees in law and commerce and a large and efficient institute for engineers and electricians. The most important technical electrical magazine in the country was run by them. On this territory the Government did not compete. The *Institución Libre de Enseñanza*, one of the best and most famous educational establishments in Europe, which has done more to raise the level of Spanish culture than any other single institution, was founded in 1876 by private enterprise.

But it was over primary education that the main battle took place. The field was a wide one, for in 1870 something like 60 per cent of the population was illiterate. Though the majority of existing schools belonged to the civil authorities (the policy of the religious orders in the early nineteenth century had been to prevent the poor from learning to read) both sides claimed a monopoly. The tactics of the Church were to force the State schools to close down from lack of funds. As the upkeep of the schools was then a charge on the munici-

---

[1] See Note A on p. 55 at end of chapter.
[2] *Recuerdos de mi Vida*, by Gabriel Maura Gamazo, Conde de la Mortera, p. 13. Maura Gamazo is the eldest son of Antonio Maura, and a strong Catholic and Conservative.

palities, by its influence on the caciques and local administrations the Church was able to prevent any payments from being made. It was then that the saying 'to be as hungry as a schoolmaster' first came into existence. In a country where more than two-thirds of the population are permanently under-nourished, it conveys a good deal. This state of affairs was only remedied in 1901 when Romanones made education a charge on the State, but the amount devoted to it on the budget was still scandalously small.[1]

To appreciate the full intransigeance of the attitude of the Church one must remember that at all events down to 1910 the immense majority of schoolmasters were sincere Catholics and went to mass regularly: that the Catholic religion and catechism were compulsorily taught in all the schools and that the parish priest had a right to supervise this. So far did this sometimes go that parents used to complain that in State schools the children passed half their class hours in saying the rosary and in absorbing sacred history and never learned to read. The difference between a convent school and a State school was not one of religion but of politics. To put it bluntly, the children in convent schools were taught that if they associated with Liberals, they went to hell. This attitude is expressed very clearly in the complete Church catechism, republished in 1927.[2]

'What does Liberalism teach?' it begins. 'That the State is independent of the Church.' And it goes on to point out that the State must be subject to the Church as the body to the soul, as the temporal to the eternal. It then enumerates, among the false liberties of Liberalism, liberty of conscience, of education, of propaganda and of meeting—all of which it is heretical to believe in. It continues:

'What kind of sin is Liberalism?'—'It is a most grievous sin against faith.'

[1] In 1900 the amount budgetted for education was 17 millions of pesetas: this naturally included the State subvention to monastic schools. In 1930 it was 166 millions and still utterly insufficient: in Madrid alone more than 80,000 children did not attend school.

[2] *Nuevo Ripalda enriquecido con Varios Apéndices*, 14th ed. 1927. There is a long quotation in Professor Trend's *Modern Spain*, p. 61.

Other catechisms taught precisely similar doctrines. See, for example, *Una Explicación Breve y Sencilla del Catequismo Católico*, by R. P. Angel María de Arcos, S.J.—a book with a circulation of several hundreds of thousands of copies.

Fear of Protestantism also remained to an extraordinary degree. H. B. Clarke, the author of a well-known history of modern Spain, declared that in his time (i.e. in the nineties) Spaniards who ate with Protestants were excommunicated. The Spanish Church deliberately refused to adapt itself to the modern world, preferring to exist as a sect, cut off from all contact with reality, to modifying in any way its peculiar interpretation of the text: 'Those that are not with me are against me.'

'Why?'—'Because it consists in a collection of heresies condemned by the Church.'

'Is it a sin for a Catholic to read a Liberal newspaper?' He may read the Stock Exchange News.

'What sin is committed by him who votes for a Liberal candidate?' —'Generally a mortal sin.'

When one remembers how timid, respectable and conservative was the Liberal party of those days, how the very most they demanded were those liberties current in all other civilized countries of the world, one sees how difficult it was not to be thrown into an attitude of violent resistance to a party which in the last three centuries had forgotten everything and learned nothing. The Church presented in Spain an insoluble problem, and when in the end the majority of the population abandoned it in despair at its political intransigeance and burned churches and killed priests in revolutionary—I might almost say in true Catholic and filial—anger there is surely nothing to be surprised at.

It may be argued, of course, that only by an attitude of rigid intransigeance can a religious body survive in the destructive air of the modern world. The attractive power of a Church lies to a large extent in its air of certainty, which translated into action means intolerance. But the errors of the Spanish Church have not proceeded from the depth of its conviction, but on the contrary from its lack of religious feeling combined with pride. Just as in the sixteenth century it showed neither the will nor the patience necessary for converting the Moors, but used its influence with the State to have them driven out altogether, so to-day it has refused (until too late) to take the appropriate measures for arresting the steady de-Christianization of the working classes. Disdaining the slow work of example and persuasion, it has preferred to fall back upon the authority of the State. Thus instead of meeting the Socialists and the Anarchists on their own ground, with labour organizations, friendly societies and projects for social reform, it has concentrated its efforts upon the search for a government that would suppress its enemies by force and restore to the Catholic religion the privileged position it held two centuries ago. This has meant that its action has been mainly political and, since its allies have naturally been taken from the wealthiest and most reactionary classes, that it has drawn upon itself in the course of the struggle the hostility of every decent or progressive force in the country. This hostility has done it untold harm. The educated classes have been driven to regard the Church as the enemy not only of parliamentary government but of modern European culture: the working classes have seen in it a barrier to their hopes of a better standard of living. Behind every act of public violence, every curtailment of liberty, every judicial murder, there stood the bishop, who either in his pastoral or in a leading article of the Catholic press showed his approval and called for more. When one remembers that this political intransigeance often covered the greatest laxity of conduct and a more or less total absence of the Christian virtues, one cannot be surprised that the Church became to large sections of Spaniards the symbol of everything that was vile, stupid and hypocritical. The devotion of individual priests and monks, the sincerity and humanity which large numbers of Spanish Catholics have always shown, were obscured by the militant and reactionary attitude of the hierarchy.

Under these circumstances it is perhaps natural that, over more than two-thirds of its surface, Spain was ceasing to be a Catholic country. Already in 1910 civil marriages and funerals, almost unheard of in the previous century, were becoming common. The majority still made use of religious ceremonies at births, deaths and marriages and flocked to the great festivals, but they expressed open incredulity on Church dogmas, never attended mass and never confessed. Among the middle classes (that is to say among the men, for the women less readily lost their faith) scepticism was becoming common, and a certain contempt for the Church and clergy and for all that pertained to them had become the fashion even among those who passed as believers. By 1931 this process had reached surprising lengths. According to Father Francisco Peiró only 5 per cent of the villagers of New Castile and Central Spain attended mass or carried out their Easter obligations: in Andalusia the attendance of men was 1 per cent: in many villages the priest said mass alone. The position in Madrid was no better. In the parish of San Ramón in the quarter of Vallecas, out of a population of 80,000 parishioners, only 3½ per cent (excluding the children in the convent schools) attended mass: 25 per cent of the children born were not baptized. Of those educated in convent schools, 90 per cent did not confess or hear mass after leaving school. Yet this parish was one of the richest in Spain and spent large sums on charity and education. The situation in other parishes was worse: in that of San Millán, for example, though the church-goers were mostly drawn from the old, more than 40 per cent died without sacraments.[1] And Barcelona and Valencia had the reputation of being more irreligious than Madrid.

[1] *El Problema Religioso-Social de España*, by P. Francisco Peiró, 1936.

A large part of this decay of religious belief was due of course simply to the spirit of the age: much the same thing was taking place in other countries. There were, however, two points that distinguished the situation in Spain from that elsewhere: first the village priests had failed (except in the north) to hold their parishioners, who had lost their faith even before Socialist or Anarchist propaganda began to reach them: then the attitude of the working classes and of the petite bourgeoisie in the towns towards the priests and monks was not one of indifference but of hatred. The reason for this was, as I have said, the militant attitude of the hierarchy in political questions; that is to say, it was a reflection of the attitude of the Church towards them and their claims. But the degree of hatred shown was often startling. If the Spanish Church is to be described as fanatical, the same word must equally be applied to many of the anti-clericals. And since fanaticism leads to credulity, on each side there grew up a firm belief in the power and wickedness of the occult forces of their adversaries: in the one case of the freemasons and supposed Russian agents and on the other of the monks and Jesuits. Of all the many antagonisms that during the last forty years have flourished in Spain, none was more bitter or envenomed than that between the Catholic Church and its opponents. The Civil War has shown to what tragic consequences it could lead.

I have said that the Church made no serious effort to keep the loyalty of the working classes by means of Catholic associations and friendly societies. This statement requires some modification. It began to take a few tentative steps in this direction in the eighties and nineties as part of the new labour policy inaugurated by Leo XIII. The Catholic associations founded then had certain initial advantages over Socialist and Anarchist trade unions: they had considerable sums of money at their disposal and by their influence over employers and landowners they could obtain a privileged position for their members. But the landlords and employers showed their usual inertia and indifference and, except at periodic moments of alarm following strikes or labour disturbances, they did not back the Catholic associations effectively. Moreover, the organizers of these associations often found themselves placed in a difficult position. They could not get sufficient members unless they could make it clear that at moments of crisis they really stood for the interests of the workmen against the employers. But this they obviously did not and could not do. The employers, who provided most of the money and guaranteed jobs to the unemployed, expected in return to use the Catholic unions to break strikes. This the workmen disliked doing. And so, at the end of years of spasmodic work and effort, the Catholic associations were forced to admit their complete failure except in certain districts in the north of Spain—Navarre, Old Castile, the Basque provinces—where the gulf between rich and poor was not so unbridgeable. Elsewhere it either happened that the Anarchists or the Socialists ousted them, or that the peasants continued without organizations of any kind. In other words the Church was so deeply compromised with the employer classes that workmen and peasants could not be lured into their associations.[1] However, one must admit that, even if this had not been the case, the role of the Catholic leaders would not have been an easy one: given the economic situation, the wide gulf between rich and poor and the Spanish temperament, strong class antagonism was inevitable in a large part of the country. Taking sides had become necessary. And had the Church been drawn into serious support of the working classes, they would undoubtedly have seen the greater part of their present allies, the *gente de orden*, leave them.

So that one may say that the year 1912 marks the end of the long struggle between the Church and the Liberal parties. The Church was drawing closer to the Army and to the Crown and was seeking in them a means to its complete triumph. It had made its choice between the poor and the rich and there was no turning back. It did not of course wish to. The rich would provide it with the money needed for winning over the poor and in return it would guarantee 'social respect and order'. That was the policy. Unfortunately the bargain did not correspond to the real circumstances or to the state of opinion in the country and there was no possibility of its being carried out.

[1] The Catholic labour organizations have been more fully described on pp. 227–228.

FURTHER NOTE ON CHAPTER III

A (p. 50). The low level of education in Spain goes back to the beginning of the eighteenth century and the Church, which controlled the curriculum in the universities and provided most of the teachers, has a special responsibility for it. Readers of Saint-Simon will remember the story of Cardinal Borja, who when someone spoke to him in Latin, replied that he did not understand French.

In 1773 the University of Salamanca still ignored Descartes, Gassendi and Newton, and its theological classes debated such subjects as what language the angels spoke and whether the sky was made of bell metal or of wine-like liquid. (Ballesteros, Tomo VI, p. 288.)

A generation earlier it had refused to establish a professorship of mathematics at the request of Philip V, and one of its professors, the Jesuit Father Rivera, had declared that Science was quite useless and that its books should be regarded as smelling of the devil.) (Altamira Tomo IV, p. 257.) One of the charges on which Olavide, the famous Commissioner of Charles III, was condemned and forced to do penance by the Inquisition was that he believed in the Copernican system.

But towards the end of the eighteenth century a great revival took place. In 1770 the King founded the *Estudios Reales de San Isidro* at Madrid as a secondary school, and the *Colegio Imperial* to provide higher education for a select number of pupils, and before the end of the century the Council of Castile was discussing schemes for compulsory State education. A plan for setting up Pestalozzi schools all over Spain was adopted in 1806. But these reforms were brought in by the small set of enlightened men who then governed the country against the wishes of the Church and of the people, and the wars that followed destroyed the promising beginning that had been made. In 1840 Spanish education was much what it had been in 1740. See J. Tanski, *L'Espagne en 1843 et 1844* and G. Hubbard, *Histoire de L'Espagne*, Tome I, p. 296.

The state of primary education for the working classes was naturally far worse: indeed it scarcely existed. The attitude of the governing classes towards it is not unfairly illustrated by the remark of Bravo Murillo, one of Isabella's more intelligent ministers: 'You want me to authorize a school at which 600 working men are to attend? Not in my time. Here we don't want men who think, but oxen who work.' When a few years later (in 1854) a reactionary and clerical government passed a law making education compulsory for all, it was understood that the primary schools should be under the control of the Church. That indeed was the purpose of the law, and no money for other schools was voted.

Chapter IV

THE ARMY AND THE SYNDICALIST STRUGGLE IN BARCELONA, 1916–1923

Considering the circumstances in which the country finds itself, the most conservative thing is to be a revolutionary.

FRANCISCO CAMBÓ.[1]

The European War made a deep impression on Spain. Opinion was divided along the obvious lines: the Army, the Church, the aristocracy and the landowners were, with rare exceptions, pro-German; whilst the Liberals, the intellectuals, the parties of the Left and the big industrialists of Barcelona and Bilbao were pro-Ally. The King successfully sat on the fence and till the end of the war was claimed by both sides. But no one wished to intervene: the Allies did not press their Spanish friends for help since this might have led to a claim for Fez or Gibraltar, whilst the pro-German party felt Spain to be too isolated to be able to give effective support to their side.

Besides, the whole country was enriching itself at a tremendous rate. Never had so much wheat, so many potatoes or onions been grown before or sold at such high prices. The landowners doubled and trebled their capital. The workmen's and even the agricultural labourers' wages rose, though an even greater rise in the cost of living usually offset this. By the end of the war most of the industrial and national debt had been redeemed and the gold reserve in the Bank of Spain had risen from 23 to 89 millions sterling. But since Spain was a sick and disjointed country (invertebrate, as Ortega y Gasset called it) the first effect of this addition of strength was to increase the power of each separate organ to fight the others.

The King was now a mature and experienced man. His early taste for political changes had grown into a settled desire to rule without a parliament. All the well-known symptoms were there—the frequent military parades, the changing of clothes four or five times a day, the rigid court etiquette, the free and easy manners at other times. But he had far more talent and, when he pleased, far more personal charm, than his prototype the Kaiser. His political skill was quite exceptional, only unfortunately he had no understanding of and no care for the

[1] Cambó in the *Boletín de Información*, quoted by Burgos y Mazo, *Páginas Históricas de 1917*, p. 109.

real interests of Spaniards. His attitude, like that of many of the grandees, brought up by foreign nurses and governesses and knowing nothing of the world but Paris, Biarritz and Madrid, suggested that of a foreigner, chosen to rule over a poor but unfortunately barbaric country. As one of the court doctors remarked: 'The King is so enthusiastic about Spain.'

'Only myself and the *canaille* are on the side of the Allies' was one of his sayings that has become famous. It was not every King who would habitually have spoken of the immense majority of his subjects—both the middle classes and the workers—as the *canaille*. But Alfonso was an imitative, impressionable man and absorbed the manners and point of view of the deplorable class in which he was brought up.

The event which precipitated the inevitable crisis was the formation in the spring of 1917 of the *Juntas de Defensa*, or 'Officers' Syndicates', in the Army. But before explaining what these syndicates were it would be better to say something of the Army's previous history.

When the First Carlist War ended the officers of Don Carlos' forces were taken on at full pay in those of the Queen: this indeed was one of the principal clauses of the Convention that brought the hostilities to an end. The result was that by 1843 there were, in spite of the bankruptcy of the State, more officers in the Spanish Army than in any other army in Europe. The other ranks were less numerous. The proportion of officers to men, which lasted with slight variations for the next seventy or eighty years, was one to six or seven. The state of the commissariat was so low that the soldiers frequently went barefoot.

It goes without saying that such a force was of little value in defending the country. Since 1660, both from lack of training and discipline and from lack of equipment, Spanish armies had been unable to face good European troops. At most they could keep their end up against their hereditary enemies the Moors. But the real function of the Army was to protect the people against the Carlists, and as such it was tolerated and was even on the whole a popular force. The generals ruled the country and quarrelled among themselves. Isabella's reign shows eighteen major *pronunciamientos* and thirty-nine different cabinets within twenty-five years. To these one must add two popular revolutions, also led by generals. Military rule in Spain has always been even more unstable than civil government.

The stormy years of 1868-1874 discredited the Army and allowed the middle classes to eliminate it from politics. Then, like the Church and like all the upper layers of society, it underwent a change. Without gaining in efficiency as a fighting force, it became more of a closed corps, cut off from the rest of the nation. It began to imitate the German Army and to assume a Prussian arrogance that in no way suited it. For the Spanish Army had always been democratic. In its great days in the sixteenth century noblemen served as privates in the infantry and officers and common soldiers messed together. The close comradeship between the ranks and the excellent discipline that resulted from it were, according to English and French observers, one of the chief causes of its victories. During the Napoleonic Wars this democratic spirit increased till it became fatal to discipline. Generals ceased to have authority except when they acted in unison with the feelings of their men, and both in victory and in defeat lost all control over them. Nor did this cease when the fighting was over. The Army remained a people's army with a popular spirit of its own and promotion open to talent. A considerable proportion of its officers, among them Generals Espartero, O'Donnell and Prim, were *chusqueros* or rankers. It had all the prestige of having saved the country from Carlism. Its political role too made it more plastic, more attentive to civilian opinion. It acted almost as often in the interests of the Moderate Left as of the Right, and in its repressions of riots or of local revolutions it generally showed moderation and humanity. No doubt it remembered that it had itself a revolutionary past. But with the Restoration this changed, and the decrease of promotion from the ranks, as well as the regulation by which anyone could buy himself out of military service for a small sum, increased the gulf between the officers and men.

The disastrous Cuban War of 1896–1898 produced a general revulsion in the country against military service. Two hundred thousand Spaniards are said to have died of disease and wounds in that island, and the ragged, fever-stricken survivors had terrible tales to tell of hardship, military incompetence and corruption. The nation became pacifist and the Army unpopular. This feeling crystallized in 1909 in the rising, already described, in Barcelona against the calling up of the reserves for service in Africa.

The Army itself (or rather the officers that led it) resented this attitude. They had become increasingly sensitive to any criticisms upon themselves and showed this by forcing the Government to pass a law making all offences against the armed forces subject to trial by court martial. They also resented their loss of popularity in the country and blamed this upon the intellectuals, the workmen and the politicians, especially the politicians. With disgust they looked on at their place-hunting, their corruption and their ineffectiveness and remembered how not many years before they themselves had ruled the country and had had the pick of all the best posts. It was, after all, a very natural feeling, and when the Catalan question came to the front and the politicians seemed ready to make terms with the Lliga, they felt their opportunity. For the Army officers were mostly Castilians and Andalusians and—it was the only remnant left of their old Liberalism—were strongly centralist. They were opposed to any concessions to regionalist feeling and in this they found that a strong wave of opinion supported them. The King was on their side and they had long before made their peace with the Church.

But how was the Army composed at this period? In 1912, in full peace time, there were rather more than 12,000 officers on the active list to about 100,000 men. This figure rose in 1923, during the Moroccan War, to some 25,000 officers for about 200,000 other ranks. Even in 1931, when the war was long over, there were still 21,000 officers—as many as there were in the German Army when the European War broke out. Among the higher ranks may be mentioned 690 generals, of whom nearly half appear to have been on the active list, and colonels in proportion—on the active list alone there were over 2000. Yet these figures show a falling off, a degeneration: in 1898 there had been a general for every hundred men.[1]

This Army was expensive. In peace time it took up, together with the small Navy, a quarter of the budget. In 1922 it is said to have taken 51 per cent. Yet it had no equipment. Even in artillery, an arm which has a fine tradition in Spain (Spanish artillery goes back more than a hundred years before Roger Bacon and in the sixteenth century was the best in Europe), it was absurdly weak. There were no modern aeroplanes and not a single tank in Spain down to 1936, although the long rolling slopes of the Riff seem made for tanks and a dozen of them would have saved many thousands of lives. When I visited Xauen in 1924 I found neither reserve trenches nor barbed-wire and only one road, so narrow that two limbers could with difficulty pass on it and so badly constructed that the bridges collapsed whenever it rained. There appeared to be no precautions whatever against a sudden attack and when, not long after my visit, it was decided to shorten the line, the confusion that arose led to heavy loss of life.

[1] See Note A on p. 76 at end of chapter.

To what then were the huge army estimates devoted? Not certainly to the pay of the men, who except for the sergeants and for a few native levies in Morocco, were all conscripts. For the sake of economy great efforts were made to keep the number of these down. Military service, though normally for two years, rarely in practice exceeded eighteen months. For a small payment this could be reduced to nine months. Long periods of leave were also given, so that an army that on paper consisted of 80,000 men would in fact be reduced to 50,000 or even less. That is why an attack by a couple of thousand Moorish tribesmen would often lead to a disaster and to a calling up of the reserves.

No, the greater part of the military estimates was spent on officers' pay. And even they, since there were so many of them, did not get much per head. A young married officer could not support himself on what he got and had to look round for supplementary means of existence. Very few had private incomes. In other words the Spanish Army was not a modern military force, but was simply one more example of the ordinary over-staffed, under-paid Spanish Government institution. Just as successive ministers had struggled without success to limit the number of the monks and clergy, to control the Government employees, the railway directors and holders of sinecures, so they were also faced with the insoluble problem of cutting down the Army.[1]

Low pay and little work in positions of responsibility lead everywhere to the same results. Just as Government clerks took bribes, so peculation was rife in certain departments of the Spanish Army. In Melilla, for example, the money for the roads, for barracks and for equipment disappeared into the pockets of the colonels and generals; officers of lesser rank traded in soap, bricks, tiles, fruit and sausages and even held a monopoly in them. Private persons who wished to put up houses were obliged to employ military engineers, who charged exorbitant fees for their work. Others paid their gambling debts by selling rifles and ammunition to the tribesmen.[2] Thus in 1922 it was

---

[1] See Note B on p. 76 at end of chapter.

[2] See Ciges Aparicio, *op. cit.* p. 412, on the state of affairs at this time in Melilla. He also gives this anecdote. The only officer casualty in a small Moroccan campaign in 1893 was the Commander-in-Chief, General Margallo. He was reported killed in action. Actually he was shot with a revolver by a young lieutenant, Miguel Primo de Rivera, later the Dictator, who was indignant that the rifles with which the Moors were killing Spanish soldiers had been sold them surreptitiously by the General. Señor Ciges Aparicio has been made to pay dearly for repeating this story. He was Republican Governor of Avila in July 1936 and was one of the first to be executed there.

discovered that 77 million pesetas had been spent by the Ordnance depôt without any record appearing on the books.[1] The corruption of the politicians could be and occasionally was exposed in the press: the Army was sacred and anyone who said a word against it went to prison.

But now that we have looked at the Army from the outside, let us try to see things through the eyes of a typical officer. As a young man of the middle classes he is attracted to the Army by its glamour: he enters it full of high ambitions and patriotic ideals and at once finds himself in a very agreeable situation. He wears a smart uniform, is the idol of the girls, occupies a much higher social position than he did before and has plenty of spare time for enjoying himself. He sees his college friends who have chosen to become lawyers or doctors or engineers still sweating among their books and, socially speaking, left far behind. That is a position that appeals very much to young Spaniards. Then one day he gets caught and marries on his captain's pay. Everything at once changes. His pay is utterly insufficient. His social position is gone. More and more children arrive. Promotion is slow. The Spanish Army, which is very inefficient and very badly equipped, does not provide the consolation of serious work. The recruits spend half their time under the sergeants learning to read. There is no money for manœuvres. The captain naturally becomes a discontented and disillusioned man. He has already of course joined the vast assemblage of those who sit in clubs or cafés talking politics. Any Spaniard will tell you what they say: however much the opinions of the café politicians may differ, they are all invariably agreed upon one thing—that the Government is deliberately ruining and dishonouring the country. But the captain also remembers that he belongs to the Army, to that noble and patriotic corps of officers which once gave orders to the politicians, and that he has men with rifles and machine guns under his command. And he begins to think of all the nice jobs and of all the prestige that come in Spain from government. No wonder that he is only waiting for one of those six hundred generals to give the word to rise. And those generals have not often been backward. In a life of the famous General Weyler his biographer remarks that, whatever may be said about him in other respects, 'he had the noble distinction of never having risen in arms against the Government'.[2]

[1] See *The Martyrdom of Spain*, by Alfred Mendizábal, p. 63. The Dictatorship, so eager to expose scandals among the politicians, hushed up this one.
[2] His biographer spoke too soon, however. In 1925, at the age of 87, Weyler joined a plot against Primo de Rivera and was heavily fined for it. The punishment was all the harder to bear for his being a notorious miser.

We come then to the spring of 1917 and to the setting up of the *Juntas de Defensa* or 'Officers' Syndicates' in the Army. 'The Army Officers', says Señor Madariaga, 'took a weapon from the arsenal of Syndicalist labour and turned against the State the force which the State had entrusted to them.' The first object, however, of these Juntas was not unreasonable. It was to reform abuses that had grown up within the Army itself. They were determined to protect themselves against the *caciquismo* or favouritism that had its seat in the *Casa Militar* or 'Military Household' of the King, to insist on the reorganization of the medical corps and commissariat and, like any labour union, to obtain an increase of pay for themselves.[1] They forced one government to resign and in June compelled the head of the new government, Dato, to accept their ultimatum and to legalize them.

It was by no means, however, at first apparent that the Juntas would take a reactionary direction. Some of their leaders were spoken of as Republicans. They had grown up as part of the Renovation movement, as it was called, which swept across Spain that summer and whose objects were to get rid of the corrupt political regime and to call a freely elected Cortes that would draw up a new Constitution. At the head of this movement were the Catalan industrialists of the Lliga under Cambó, the industrialists of Bilbao and Oviedo under Melquíades Álvarez, and the Socialist party. The Radicals too supported it, and all over Spain it had the sympathy of large sections of the middle classes, especially of the more intelligent and progressive men under forty. In July the members of the two Chambers of the Cortes who favoured the movement (there were 71 out of 760) met at Barcelona and announced that they considered themselves permanently constituted as an Assembly whose object it would be to prepare the way for a freely elected Constituent Cortes. The Assembly was forbidden by the Government, but continued to meet in secret.

This was a critical moment in Spanish history. The large industrialists of Spain, in alliance with the Socialists and other Left-wing parties, had come out in open revolution against the Government. It

---

[1] The sudden rise in the cost of living, due to the submarine campaign and to the influx of gold into the Bank of Spain, was the immediate cause of the discontent in the Army, which led to the formation of the Juntas. This, of course, affected other classes besides the Army as the Juntas of Government employees, doctors, engineers and even of priests that sprang up in imitation of the military Juntas show. The workers' protest had come a year earlier, in 1916, when a series of strikes all over Spain led to an increase of wages.

was not any longer a mere question of Basque or Catalan regionalism. What was to be decided was whether the factory owners of the north or the large landowners of Castile and Andalusia should have the chief share in governing the country: it was the same question that had been settled a century before in England by the Reform Bill. The rotten boroughs of 1832 had their equivalent in the *caciquismo* of 1917. For Cambó no longer asked merely for an autonomous Catalonia. He voiced the general demand for a regenerate Spain, ruled by governments which should be modern, decent and efficient and which should make a serious attempt to solve the fundamental economic problems of the country. He was prepared to see this happen either within a monarchy or within a federal republic.

At this moment the deciding factor was the Army. Both the Renovation parties and the King were trying to attract it. It was uncertain which way the Juntas (who represented what one might call the Left wing of the Army) would move. For though they were in general sympathy with the Renovation movement, they were strongly opposed to Catalan autonomy or to any form of federalism and did not see with pleasure the rising excitement of the working classes. The Socialists and Radicals of Lerroux had made efforts to attract the rank and file. Juntas of sergeants, of telegraphists, of postmen and Government clerks, modelled on those of the officers, sprang up everywhere, and it was believed that, if it came to street fighting, the troops would refuse to fire.

At this very delicate moment there happened to be in progress a strike of the Northern Railway workers who belonged to the Socialist union, the U.G.T. The strike was on the point of being settled when the Government, which wished to provoke a general crisis before the new movement should come to a head, refused to accept the agreed terms. The Socialist party took up the glove that had been thrown down and called a general strike of all its workers. The Anarchists, rather half-heartedly, joined in. On 10 August 1917 the strike began.

The veteran leader of the Socialist party, Pablo Iglesias, had thought the moment inopportune and therefore opposed it, but he was old and at the moment ill in bed and the effective leadership passed to a younger man, Francisco Largo Caballero. In those days the theory of the general strike, which had been developed by the French Syndicalists and then been tried out by the C.G.T., was very much in the air in Spain. It was believed to be the one effective weapon of the working classes, a sure means to the socialist or anarchist goal. So hopeful were the leaders of success that Lerroux, it is said, expected to be President of the Republic within a week. But the troops were called out and used their machine guns against the strikers. The strike collapsed in three days, leaving seventy dead, hundreds of wounded and two thousand prisoners. The troops were thought to have behaved barbarously and the Juntas lost all the popularity they had acquired among the people as enemies of the Government—but the Army had 'saved the nation' and from now on was, with the King, the only real power in the country.

The Assembly met again in October. But there was no longer anything to be done. Cambó had always seen that against the Army no revolution was possible. No doubt too, as a Conservative banker and industrialist, he was not anxious to see a middle-class revolution brought in by a general strike. He therefore allowed himself to be drawn over to the King. To avert the immediate danger of a military dictatorship, for the new Cortes was unmanageable,[1] a 'government of concentration' was formed of the leaders of all the parties—Maura, Romanones, Cambó, Santiago Alba and so on—but apart from releasing the Socialists' strike leaders, Largo Caballero, Besteiro, Saborit and Anguiano, who had been given a life sentence, it accomplished little.

From now onwards the only solution had become a military dictatorship. As Maura said: *Que gobiernen los que no dejan gobernar*: 'Let those govern who prevent anyone else from doing so.' But there were still one or two obstacles that delayed it. The King wished for a regime that would allow him to rule himself through the Army: he by no means wanted to give the Juntas complete power. Then the victory of the Allies and the fall of kings all over Europe made him pause a little. But he saw to it that there was no political revival and that the decay and breaking up of the political parties went on. One result of this was that when, many years later, Primo de Rivera fell, there was not a single politician of any party except the arch-cacique and reactionary La Cierva who would stand up for him.

The scene now shifts to Barcelona. The failure of the Lliga to support the general strike had ruined it in the eyes of many of its supporters. The rich bourgeoisie were more ready than before to rest content with that secret pact, which, in the phrase of Cambó, had been

---

[1] Although 36 millions of pesetas were spent by La Cierva on buying votes in the elections of March 1918, the majority required by the Government was not obtained. The electorate was refusing to be deceived and coerced any longer. See S. Canals, *Crónica de Política interior en nuestros tiempos*.

sealed between Madrid and Barcelona; the pact by which Castile became the economic tributary of Catalonia whilst Catalonia remained
the political tributary of Castile.[1] In all matters of tariffs, and indeed
in the economic sphere in general, Madrid now gave Cambó a free
hand. Thus the Lliga, which had always been a Conservative party,
became more and more clerical and reactionary and lost supporters,
whilst a number of new Catalan parties sprang up everywhere with Left
sympathies. It was these small parties that later on merged together
under Colonel Maciá to form the Esquerra or Left party of Catalonia.

Meanwhile, however, the labour troubles that have given Barcelona
such a bad repute abroad had begun again. And once more, as in
1906-1909, they had a complex origin. In the first place the German
Government during the last year of the war had spent large sums on
seditious propaganda among the working classes: Barcelona had become the refuge of every sort of international criminal: a horde of
spies, agents provocateurs, gangsters and *pistoleros* intervened in
labour disputes and offered their services to anyone who might desire
them. There was then the immense stimulus of the Russian Revolution to the Anarchists and of the Peace Treaties with their principle of
racial determination to the Catalan Nationalists. The factory owners
too had been making large sums out of the war, whilst the workmen
had received increases of wages. Every section felt strong enough to
push their claims.

During the past year the Anarchists, disappointed by the failure of
the general strike, had been reorganizing themselves in syndicates.
Their new trade union, the *Confederación Nacional del Trabajo*, or
C.N.T. as it is usually called, had converted most of its craft unions
into factory unions, or *sindicatos de ramo*, which became known as
sindicatos unicos. They were tactically more effective than the old
unions and led to more violent action: in theory their strikes were not
merely a downing of tools, but were acts of open war against their
employers and the police who supported them. In practice, however,
one has to distinguish between two elements—one the new syndicalist
or trade-union element embracing the vast majority of the workers,
which under its leaders Seguí and Pestaña was opposed to violent
action, and the other consisting of more or less dissident anarchist
groups who still clung to discarded ideas of individual action: it was

---

[1] See Cambó's speech at Saragossa in December 1911, quoted by A. Marvaud,
L'Espagne au XXième Siècle, p. 160. 'What can you expect of a party', exclaimed
Unamuno, 'which is capable of selling its soul for a tariff!'

among these that, in reply to police repression, terrorist centres of action were formed.

But the employers had been organizing themselves too. Industry in Barcelona was still—foreign firms excepted—in a primitive stage; there were few large enterprises or factories, but a great many small ones, competing together in an anarchical manner.[1] The factory owners were usually self-made men—often they had risen from being foremen—and were therefore very hard and uncompromising with their workmen. Up to the war they had followed an oblique line of attack on the C.N.T. by organizing blackleg labour from the unlimited reservoirs in the villages and in the starving provinces of the south as well as from certain unions which had a Catholic label. Then in 1914 they held a congress of employers' federations which laid down a definite plan of action and now, seeing the more aggressive attitude of the workers' unions and the immense and alarming increase in their numbers, they decided to give battle to the C.N.T. by means of a lock-out. In the usual Spanish style they began to prepare the ground by employing agents provocateurs.

In the complicated series of events that now follows, a difference of opinion between the civil and military authorities in Barcelona was one of the principal factors in exacerbating the situation. The Civil Governor, Señor Montañés, with the support of the Government in Madrid, disapproved of the employers' conduct and took up a conciliatory attitude towards the workmen. In this he was, of course, merely continuing the policy which had led his predecessors ten years before to back the Radicals against the Catalan Nationalists, though it was also in accord with the conciliatory attitude of Conservative governments at this time and with their genuine desire to see an improvement in the condition of the working classes. But the military Juntas, through their representative General Milans del Bosch, the Captain-General of the Province, whose office made him a sort of Viceroy, sided with the employers and even urged them on to 'give battle'. It was a paradoxical situation, this union of the Catalan Nationalists with the anti-Catalan Army and a proof, if any were needed, that for the Lliga the social question took precedence over the Catalan one. For the Army it was a way to win over the Catalan bourgeoisie to their camp, and, if not, so to discredit them in the eyes

[1] See Joaquín Aguilera, secretary of the *Fomento del Trabajo Nacional* and of the *Cámara Oficial de la Industria de Barcelona*, on the lack of organization amounting to anarchy of the Catalan industries and banking system (*El Trabajo Nacional*, 16 March 1910).

of their countrymen that they would be harmless. It therefore placed no limit to the support it would give. Whereas in 1908 the bombs had been laid by men in the pay of the Civil Governor, the *pistoleros* were now organized from the Captain-General's headquarters.

These terrorist gangs, who worked at different times under the orders of the civil and military authorities in Barcelona, require some further explanation. They grew up in close association with the police. The Spanish political police or *Brigada Social*, formed in the nineties to investigate the anarchist bomb outrages, was, as one would expect, a lazy, incompetent body without any technical training and therefore very badly informed. It relied largely upon private denunciations for its information and as it had few scruples it seldom took the trouble to investigate them on its own account. Thus there grew up in close touch with it and indeed under its orders various gangs of professional *confidentes* or informers, who were paid for their information. These gangs also co-operated with specially interested bodies, such as the Federation of Employers. When a crime occurred, they gave information as to the supposed authors—and, as it was usually easier to inculpate an innocent man than to find the criminal, they became adepts at faking evidence and at planting bombs or incriminating material upon innocent people. For this purpose they would of course choose workmen whose activities as strike leaders or as propagandists of anarchism made them objectionable to the owners and to the police, and from this it was not a long step to incriminating such people as were officially indicated to them. But this was not all. The business of a police informer is exposed like all others to the ups and downs of the trade cycle. In the dead seasons crimes would become scarce and it then stood to the interest of the informers to create them by laying bombs themselves. This had been the case with Rull in 1908, with the addition that he had received encouragement if not actual orders from the Civil Governor for his acts of terrorism. It had also been the case with at least one famous bomb outrage in the nineties.

Now the conditions in Barcelona in 1918 were especially suited to the growth of terrorist gangs of this description. During the last years of the war, when the city had become a refuge for criminal elements of every kind, collected from all over Europe, German money had been lavishly spent on organizing strikes in munition factories and even on murdering factory owners who refused to stop making munitions for the Allies. A certain Bravo Portillo was at the head of an organization of this sort and controlled a gang of *pistoleros*. He had been found guilty of supplying Germany with information of the sailings of Spanish ships from Mediterranean ports, which had led to their being torpedoed, and had been sentenced to a short term of imprisonment. In spite of this serious conviction, he was, on his release from prison, taken on as a police agent by the Captain-General, Miláns del Bosch, and by the Employers' Federation. When a little later he was killed as a reprisal for the particularly brutal murder of a syndicalist leader, Pablo Sabater, which he had organized, his place was taken by a German adventurer, who went by the name of the Baron de Koenig, but whose true name seems to have been Colman. This Koenig or Colman, who had also acted as a German spy during the war, worked on the orders of General Arleguí, the chief of police of the Captain-General's office, and of the Marqués de Foronda, one of the leading figures of the Lliga and a close friend of the King. His job was not only to make away with leading syndicalists or to produce faked evidence that could lead to their incrimination: it was also to provoke the working classes to retaliation, which would lead to conditions that would force the Government to give up negotiating with the strikers and suspend the constitutional guarantees: this would reduce to nothing the powers of the Civil Governor and make the Captain-General sole ruler in Barcelona. The desired lock-out could then be brought off. But Koenig had his own way of interpreting his mission. He was a man who lived on a lavish scale and needed money. He therefore took to blackmailing the factory owners, warning them that their lives were in danger and that they must pay him certain sums to ensure their safety. Those who refused to pay were shot. His relations with the Captain-General's police gave him immunity for more than a year, but in the end his murders became too daring, his band was broken up and he was forced to flee from Spain.[1]

---

[1] In *Los Archivos del Terrorismo Blanco*, by Pedro Foix (1931), are published photostat copies of documents taken from the secret dossier of the Captain-General's police agents. One of these documents inculpates the police in laying bombs in the house of a syndicalist named Bueso so as to have a case against him. F. Madrid in *Ocho Meses y un Día en el Gobierno Civil de Barcelona* gives the whole story of these events and quotes from the official reports of two Civil Governors, Amado and Carlos Bas, as well as from statements made to the press by Pestaña and Seguí Most enlightening of all is Burgos y Mazo's *El Verano de 1919 en Gobernación*. This is an account by the Conservative Minister for Home Affairs in Sánchez Toca's Government of the almost unbelievable difficulties put in the way of a settlement of the disorders in Barcelona by the military Juntas, the Catalan federation of employers and the Captain-General of Catalonia, who wanted only one thing—an open conflict with the workmen—and were prepared to stoop to any means to obtain it. See also Madariaga, *Spain*, pp. 414–416 and p. 218; M. Buenacasa, *El Movimiento Obrero Español*, and M. Fernández Almagro, *op. cit.*

On the other side the workmen had their *pistoleros* too. During the last two years the C.N.T. had enormously increased its membership: all kinds of doubtful characters, including many professional criminals, had entered into it. Then the Anarchist movement had always, since 1882, included groups who believed in individual acts of terrorism, though the members of these groups never or rarely occupied positions of influence in the syndicalist organization. They were free lances, whose action was generally disapproved by the leaders, but who enjoyed a certain popularity and support whenever they were considered to be avenging acts of oppression—in other words when a strike had taken place and failed and the leaders were in prison. For the fact that the Spanish syndicalist organizations do not give strike pay means that their strikes are conducted in an atmosphere of hunger that easily leads to violence. A prolongation of the strike produces acts of sabotage and of conflict with the police, whilst a failure produces an atmosphere of resentment and a loosening of solidarity in the syndicates that gives individual terrorists their opportunity. In the present case, therefore, though it was the employers' gunmen who began hostilities, the syndicalist gunmen were not behindhand in replying.

Such then were the conditions under which the struggle between the syndicates and the factory owners began. In February 1919 the workers of the large electrical company of Riegos y Fuerza del Ebro, generally known as the *Canadiense*, struck work. Their grievances were not very serious ones: they demanded the reinstatement of seven men who had been dismissed for political reasons and higher wages for certain of the employees, but the strike had been carefully organized by Seguí and Pestaña and had a certain symbolical importance. It followed on a spectacular propaganda campaign throughout the country and was the first important test of the C.N.T. and of the new *sindicatos únicos*. The English manager of the company was prepared to compromise, all the more so because the conditions of work in the Canadiense were below the average, but on the advice of the Captain-General he changed his mind and refused all conversations. The strike, which had begun with only a partial stoppage, became more drastic and light was cut off, but there were no disturbances. It is here that one sees the Spanish military mind at work. The reply of the authorities to this perfectly peaceable strike was to imprison all the syndicalist leaders, to declare military law and to call up the strikers to the colours. But this was not what the Government wanted.

Romanones, then Prime Minister, sent down to Barcelona a special emissary; the men and the owners met and terms were agreed on. The strike ended. But the Captain-General refused to release the imprisoned leaders, which was one of the terms that had been agreed on, so that the next day a general strike in Barcelona began. It lasted a fortnight and was carried through with perfect solidarity by more than 100,000 workers.[1] What is more, it was peaceable: not a revolver was fired, not a person was injured—a remarkable tribute to Seguí's influence in that unruly city. However, the military arrested many thousands of workmen and, in the usual Spanish style, gave sentences of imprisonment amounting to seventeen hundred years—sentences which of course would not be carried out. The end of the strike was inconclusive: neither owners nor men could claim a victory, but the day after it was over General Miláns del Bosch put the Civil Governor, Montañés, and his chief of police, Doval, on the train and sent them back to Madrid. Romanones resigned before this act of violence and Maura came in on the insistence of the King (April 1919).

But Maura was now old and out of touch with affairs and his ultra-reactionary colleagues, La Cierva and the rest, had the real control. Military law was declared, more labour leaders were imprisoned and Bravo Portillo's gangs of *pistoleros* let loose. The syndicalist *pistoleros* replied and the situation went from bad to worse. In Andalusia, where there was a general effervescence, military law was declared and troops were sent down to suppress the strikers on the large estates. Very corrupt elections were held, but such was the state of opinion in the country that most of the official candidates failed to get in. The outcry led to the fall of Maura's Government and a Conservative Government under Sánchez Toca took its place.

This set about dealing with the situation in Barcelona in a sensible and tactful way. Señor Amado, the new Civil Governor, perceived that the terrorist groups among the workers did not have the approval of the syndicalist leaders. They could only act because the latter were in prison. He therefore saw to it that the leaders were released and set up conciliation boards to adjust conditions with the employees. The position at once improved and assassinations came to an end. After

---

[1] See Fernández Almagro, *op. cit.* for this figure. But owing to the cutting of the electric current a far greater number than this were thrown out of work. Indeed the stoppage was total. Such a strike had never been seen in Spain before. When it was over the Government in alarm passed laws decreeing an eight-hour day and obligatory pensions for workers.

endless difficulties—for the employers were unwilling to negotiate and there was opposition among the syndicalists too—terms were agreed on and seventy thousand men went back to work. But the group of extremists who controlled the employers' federation and who had all along worked to prevent agreement, refused at the last minute to take back the workmen's leaders and so the strike began again. The Government, undermined by a campaign in the reactionary press and by the intrigues of the military Juntas and of the King, fell (September 1919), and a feeble administration took its place.

This was the opportunity long awaited by the employers to 'give battle'. They at once declared a lock-out. Syndicalists were arrested in large numbers, the constitutional guarantees were suspended and a campaign of murder and counter murder began. Rival gangs of terrorists roamed the streets and assassinations took place every week. This situation continued without respite all winter till in March 1920 a new government under the Conservative leader Dato came in. By that time a great many people on both sides, including the new reactionary Civil Governor, had been assassinated.[1]

Dato came in with a policy of appeasement. He appointed as Civil Governor a humane and moderate man, Carlos Bas. But now that passions on both sides were roused, appeasement was much more difficult. The employers asked that the C.N.T., the trade union to which 80 per cent of the workers in Catalonia belonged, should be suppressed and that the syndicalist leaders should be shot. Bas observed, however, that though the C.N.T. had been declared illegal more than six months before, it still existed in secret and received regular contributions from the workers, and as to the syndicalist leaders, far from shooting them, he was anxious that they should be released from prison and restored to the control of their organizations. He had convinced himself that Seguí, Pestaña and the rest were opposed to acts of terrorism, but that in the circumstances they could not restrain their gunmen. He also broke up Koenig's band which had been shooting both syndicalists and such employers as refused to be blackmailed, and set up machinery for settling the new strikes that had

---

[1] There was an economic motive too in the growth of *pistolerismo*. After the general strike of March 1919 the employers began dismissing the more unruly of their workmen. Some of these left Barcelona, but others stayed and, not being able to obtain work, were organized as *delegados de taller* by the Syndicates. They were given pistols and their weekly pay, and their chief duty was to see that the workers, who were beginning to fall off, paid their subscriptions. When the lock-out came and the Syndicates ceased to be able to pay these men, they turned to ordinary assassination.

broken out. But the employers' federation had other terrorists in their pay besides Koenig's (in July one of these threw a bomb into a crowded workmen's music hall, the Pompeya) and after the Governor's decision that the principal strike, that of the transport workers, was justified because the employers were not complying with the law that regulated the hours of employment, the federation refused to meet him. A scene between the Civil Governor and the Captain-General, Martínez Anido, followed which made further collaboration between them impossible. The King intervened and compelled the Government to dismiss Bas and to appoint General Martínez Anido Civil Governor, with full authority to apply any means he thought necessary for putting an end to the disturbances in Barcelona.[1]

The means chosen by Martínez Anido were neither legal ones nor even those sanctioned by military law, such as arbitrary imprisonment and trial by court martial. The employers had founded shortly before a small trade union subservient to their interests which called itself the *Sindicato Libre*.[2] It contained a fair proportion of gunmen. General Arleguí, Martínez Anido's chief of police, reorganized and armed these and gave them a list of the syndicalist leaders whom they were to shoot at sight. In the first thirty-six hours twenty-one leading syndicalists were killed. Another method was the so-called *ley de fugas*. The police arrested syndicalists and shot them as they were being conducted to the police station: they were reported as 'shot trying to escape'. A third method was to arrest workmen and then release them: a gang of *pistoleros* would be waiting for them outside the prison and they would be killed before they could reach the comparative safety of the workers' districts. As the murders increased on both sides (for the syndicalists exacted strict reprisals—in sixteen months 230 people were shot in the street) feeling in Barcelona and all over Spain rose to a pitch of hysteria. Cambó applauded all Martínez Anido's acts. But the assassinations went on and in May 1921 the Prime Minister, Dato, was killed in Madrid as a reprisal for the

[1] Martínez Anido's character was well known and his appointment was an act of defiance to all moderate and humane opinion in the country. His disagreement with Bas was due to the fact that he had supported extra-legal means for dealing with terrorism: he is said to have shown Bas a list of 675 syndicalists whom, he declared, ought to be shot outright. Unamuno describes him as follows: 'The man is a pure brute—he can't even talk, he can only roar and bray, though his roars and brays always mean something.'

He was appointed Minister for Home Affairs by Primo de Rivera and again, in 1937, by Franco. He died in 1938.

[2] See Note C on p. 76 at end of chapter.

terrorist acts of the Civil Governor of Barcelona.[1] Dato was the third Prime Minister to be assassinated in revenge for police atrocities within little over twenty years. Until a military disaster in Morocco weakened the prestige of the Army and Martínez Anido could be got rid of, the terrorism in Barcelona continued and indeed got worse.[2] Even his removal did not end it, for his *pistoleros* no longer required his hand to guide them, but continued the war on their own account. Thus in March 1923 Salvador Seguí was murdered in the streets of Barcelona and not long after the Cardinal Archbishop of Saragossa was killed in revenge. It was not until the coming in of the Dictatorship with its suppression both of the Anarcho-Syndicalists and of the Lliga and of all traces of Catalan Nationalism, and with at the same time the setting up of those compulsory commissions of employers and workmen which were so distasteful to the militants of both parties, that peace was finally restored.[3]

The disaster in Morocco was the last episode of the old parliamentary regime. The King was anxious for a striking success which would enable him finally to get rid of parliament. He was impatient at the slow methods of political penetration employed in the Riff and decided to direct operations himself over the heads of the War Office. His nominee for the work was a cavalry officer, General Silvestre, whose brusque, daring ways he admired. Silvestre was to march his column across the Riff from Melilla to Alhucemas, a distance of about forty miles. The date of his arrival was timed to coincide with a speech

---

[1] It is typical of Spain that though the police could murder syndicalist leaders who were trying to restrain the gunmen on their side, Dato's murderer could not be executed. The death penalty could be imposed for merely wounding in self-defence a policeman or an officer, but not for murdering a Prime Minister in cold blood. And, as usual in anarchist crimes, the penalty fell upon a man who had little responsibility for what was done during his term of office. 'I did not fire at Dato', the assassin confessed, 'but at the Government which permitted the *ley de fugas*.' Those most responsible for the reign of terror in Barcelona—La Cierva, Martínez Anido, and, one must add, the King—escaped unhurt.

[2] The recall of Martínez Anido occurred in this way. Angel Pestaña had been seriously wounded by the General's gunmen and was taken to the hospital at Manresa to recover. A band of *pistoleros* was posted at the door to shoot him as he came out. When this became known and was published in the press a scandal was created. At the same time the Government became aware of the details of an attack which Martínez Anido had staged upon himself, with the object of creating an atmosphere which would allow him to intensify the terrorism against the Anarcho-Syndicalists. This seemed too much, and his resignation was demanded. For two years he had ruled Barcelona like a dictator, allowing no interference from the Government in Madrid, and, when he left, the state of the city was worse than when he came in. The number of political assassinations in Catalonia between January 1919 and December 1923 totalled over 700.

[3] See Note D on p. 77 at end of chapter.

which the King would make at the solemn translation of the remains of the Cid to Burgos Cathedral. This would also coincide with the day of St James Matamoros, Kill-Moor—the old patron saint of Spain. But two days before this date (23 June 1921) Silvestre's column, which had advanced without precautions, was ambushed by a much smaller force of Abd-el-Krim's tribesmen at Annual. Ten thousand were killed, four thousand were taken prisoner, all the rifles, artillery, machine guns and aeroplanes were captured. Scarcely anyone escaped. Silvestre himself committed suicide. A week or two later the fortified position of Monte Arruit was compelled to surrender. The men, some seven thousand, were massacred: the officers were carried off in chains and held to ransom. Melilla itself was only saved with difficulty.

The commission of enquiry found that the advance had been undertaken in the most reckless manner, without proper political or material preparation. Also that a state of great indiscipline and confusion had prevailed: that many of the leading officers had left their units in the field to attend the opening of a Kursaal at Melilla: that others were on leave in Malaga and that the airmen slept far away from their machines. But certain information could not be published—for example, the letter of the King to Silvestre found, so it was said, among his papers, which ordered him to 'do as I tell you and pay no attention to the Minister of War, who is an imbecile'.

A long contest now began. The country wished to expose the King, the King to conceal his responsibility, the Army—which also felt itself attacked—to protect him. In the end it appeared as if the King would lose. A new commission of enquiry had finished its labours and was about to publish its report. Everyone knew that it threw the chief responsibility on Alfonso. Twelve days later the Cortes was to meet to discuss it. A week before the report of the commission was due (on 13 September 1923) Primo de Rivera, the new Captain-General of Catalonia, proclaimed himself Dictator.

Ever since 1917, when the only legitimate or honest solution—the calling of a freely elected Cortes—had been turned down by the King and by the landowning classes that supported him, it had been obvious that either a military dictatorship or a Republic was inevitable. The syndicalist terror at Barcelona had reduced the Catalan bourgeoisie to quiescence or even to approval. The King's own responsibility for Annual had made further delay impossible. But two things may at least be noticed—the Dictator took power with the permission of the

Army, but not as its nominee. And the King, who had been saved by him from an ignominious situation, was condemned to something that he very much disliked—playing second fiddle.

FURTHER NOTES ON CHAPTER IV

A (p. 60). I rely chiefly on A. Marvaud (*L'Espagne au XXième Siècle*) and Madariaga (*Spain*) for these figures. That for 1923 is confirmed by Nicolo Pascazio, an Italian journalist who obtained his information from Right-wing sources. The statistics supplied by various Spanish Governments to the *League of Nations Armament Year Book* are intended less to enlighten than to conceal. Thus, till the Republic came in, the figures for troops in Morocco are not given and, after its entry, the statistics are so drawn up as to have as few points of comparison as possible with those of the previous period. However, so far as they go, they agree with the other figures.

For those who are curious on these matters, here are the figures for 1851 collected by an industrious German historian. In that year there were 10 captain-generals, 203 field-marshals, 78 lieutenant-generals and 345 brigadier-generals. The war strength of the Army was 180,000 and its peace strength about half. (*Spaniens Verfassungskampf, seine Parteien und hervorragendsten Staatsmänner, 1812-1854,* Leipzig, 1854, p. 6.)

Even civil war and a complete change in personnel could not alter this system. The New Model Army formed by the Republic in 1937–1938 contained one officer to every ten men.

B (p. 61). The Navy, according to Antonio Maura, was just as bad. In 1890 the technical education of the Navy (upkeep of academies, etc.) cost 3,484,948 pesetas. The total amount spent on civil education in the country (including the upkeep of museums, archives and libraries) was only 5,949,396 pesetas. Yet the Navy had no engineering or technical instruction. The ships, always anchored in the port, were fitted with telephone lines to the shore. There were only 597 naval officers appointed to ships for 1900 who had shore appointments. (Speech by Maura in the Cortes, 14 May 1890. Quoted in 35 *años de Vida Publica*, vol. I, pp. 96-114.)

When Maura came into office a dozen years later the first thing he did was to remedy this.

C (p. 73). The *Sindicatos Libres* were founded in October 1919 by a young man called Ramón Sales with the collusion of the employers' federation. The majority of its members were workmen who for one reason or another were tired of Anarcho-Syndicalist methods and wished to belong to a union which would defend their interests without forcing them along a revolutionary road. Its leaders held many ideas that would to-day be called fascist—for example they professed extreme patriotism and maintained that their rivals were being supported by German-Jewish bankers. The Anarcho-Syndicalists naturally regarded them as yellow and from the first moment there was bitter enmity between them.

When in November 1920 Martínez Anido became Civil Governor of Barcelona he took them under his protection and reorganized their *pistoleros*. They then expanded rapidly. Not only were their rivals, the *Sindicatos Únicos*, suppressed, but the Catalan employers hastened to dismiss such of their workmen as had belonged to them and to put others from the *Sindicatos Libres* in their place. In the war of *pistoleros* that followed the *libres* had the full support of the Civil Governor and his police, and immunity for all the murders they might commit.

Very soon, with the encouragement of the military authorities, they began to take their syndical functions more seriously. They launched a series of strikes which alienated the employers' association, and created a bank clerks' syndicate in spite of the strong opposition of the bankers. Thus at the moment of the *coup d'état* that brought in the Dictatorship, Primo de Rivera, who had succeeded Martínez Anido, held the balance of power in Catalonia. When later they became the only trade union in Catalonia and were joined by almost all the workers in Barcelona, they were used to keep the Lliga quiet. That is to say, just as Madrid politicians had supported first the Radicals and then the Anarcho-Syndicalists against the Catalan bourgeoisie, so the Army found a similar lever in its own creation, the *Sindicatos Libres*. Madrid can only rule Catalonia by dividing it.

D (p. 74). The attitude of the employers (or rather of the small section of extremists who had led them during the past few years) has this to be said for it. They saw the immense increase since 1917 of the Anarcho-Syndicalist trade union and the success of its propagandist campaigns. This union was led by convinced anarchists, who, though they might disapprove of terrorist acts, were only awaiting the first opportunity to attempt a social revolution. In Russia the Bolshevists had just seized power. In Italy the workmen had occupied the factories. They were terrified lest such a thing might occur in Spain. Had they been guided by their intelligence they would have seen that there was then no possibility of a successful revolution in their country and that the best means—indeed the only means—of weakening the revolutionary movement was to show themselves ready to satisfy some of the claims of the workers. Instead they decided to see if they could not forcibly arrest it by giving it battle in a lock-out and defeating it: the workmen, they believed, would then desert the syndicalist ranks and the movement would decline.

But the methods of combat they chose were not such as employers of labour usually adopt. By the use of agents provocateurs and of terrorist bands they deliberately set out to stir up the violent elements on the other side. This, they knew, would not only impair the solidarity of the workers and undermine the position of their leaders, but would create a state of alarm through the country which would allow them to call on all the powers of the State to suppress the Anarcho-Syndicalist movement. And that is why, at the height of the repression, it was not the gunmen of the other side whom Martínez Anido's *pistoleros* had orders to shoot, but rather those very leaders who were doing what they could to put an end to the assassinations.

There is, of course, nothing new about such tactics in Spain: since 1812 they have been the traditional procedure of all extreme Right-wing parties. The Apostólicos employed them in 1822, the Carlists whenever the opportunity offered, the Falangists in the summer of 1936. In the present case they were, for the time being at least, successful. They led to the demoralization and disintegration of the whole labour movement in Catalonia. But the employers' federation, whose policy this had been, paid for their success in the ruin of their own party, the Lliga, and in the suppression for seven years of all Catalan liberties. Their ally, the Army, whose triumph they had prepared, when it came into power had no pity on them.

If that were all, it would not be much. But when two bodies within the State fight *à l'outrance* in this manner, without rules or limits or regard either for the law or for the most elementary decencies, it is the whole nation that suffers. The decline of moral standards that follows cannot be measured, but one may say that the present civil war with all the hatred and savagery it has produced is the direct outcome of a century and a quarter of blind struggles of this kind in which the protagonists have been prepared to go to any lengths of violence or provocation to achieve their objects. Not only have the Anarchists, who in Spain are for the most part embittered and poverty-stricken workmen, with many good reasons for feeling as they do, resorted to 'direct action'—that is to sabotage and murder: the Church, the Army, the employers, the landowners, the State itself have all at different times, whenever their interests have appeared to them to be jeopardized, put their hands without scruple to actions of this sort. If therefore I have devoted so much space to these five sordid years in Barcelona, it is because they can be regarded as a sort of rehearsal for the recent infinitely more destructive and tragic civil war.

Chapter V

THE DICTATORSHIP

The time has come for Spaniards to be governed in accordance with the spirit of their history and the feelings which make up their better character.
NARVÁEZ in 1867, inaugurating a severe
repression that led to a revolution.

The Dictatorship of Primo de Rivera came in on a wave of good wishes and optimism. It reached its highest point in 1926, after a run of three years, and then began to decline. By 1928 it was unpopular even in the Army and by January 1930 it had come to an end.

The causes of its initial success and subsequent failure are mainly economic, for its period coincided with that of the world boom, of high prices and cheap money and expanding markets, and its premature decline was due to over-spending on public works and to the incompetent management of finances by a gifted but not very intelligent young man, Calvo Sotelo. There were other causes also: the Dictatorship came in with almost everyone's good wishes because it destroyed the old corrupt regime and because it was thought to be a temporary phase that would end in the summoning of a Constituent Cortes. Primo again and again asserted this. When it was seen that his promises would not be fulfilled opinion began to change, whilst the increasing interferences with liberty, the lack of any kind of law but the Dictator's word and the miserable expedients of espionage and repression into which he was drawn lost him the support of one group of Spaniards after another. The severe censorship was especially damaging to him: the last few years had seen a great advance in the culture and confidence in their own powers of the élite of the Spanish middle classes and it was scarcely to be expected that this movement could be suppressed indefinitely.

Primo's own personality was not an unattractive one. He was an Andalusian landowner from Jerez: the province where a hard-drinking, whoring, horse-loving aristocracy rules over the most starved and down-trodden race of agricultural labourers in Europe. It is a region where the hatred of the poor for the rich has been accumulating for generations. But Primo evidently did not share the feelings of his set. All his actions show a desire to remedy the condition of the poor within the rather narrow framework of what was possible to him. As a general too he was something of a pacifist. He stood out against the strong feeling in the Army for a *revanche* in Morocco and began a withdrawal of the troops to the fortresses of the coast. And he was humane: although his six years of rule had their share of plots and risings, on only one occasion were there executions.

Señor Madariaga has well defined him as a glorified café politician, the genius of his species, aspiring like all café politicians to save his country by making himself its ruler. His model was not Mussolini but Haroun al Raschid. He issued decrees right and left, broke them whenever he felt inclined, behaved as a complete anarchist. Like so many Andalusians he was a man of immense optimism and felt an unlimited confidence in himself because he was always sure of his own good intentions. At first his Robin Hood justice on the old politicians and caciques (he liked to make the punishment fit the crime) was thought amusing, but people soon began to get tired of this and to wish for a return to law and order. Then, as soon as things ceased to go well, his garrulous decrees and his fussiness made him ridiculous.[1] Spaniards do not like a ruler who is undignified and as his health declined poor Primo lost what dignity he had ever possessed.

As regards his intelligence, one may say that he was a man of good natural parts but of little instruction. He had had no preparation whatever for government. He despised intellectuals and specialists, hated politics and held a host of superficial ideas on every subject. As he was very impulsive in putting his ideas into practice, decrees published one day had often to be revoked the next. His ignorance of economics gave rise to a number of anecdotes: on one occasion his finance minister had adopted the device of producing two simultaneous budgets—one ordinary and the other extraordinary: on the second figured the huge expenditure on public works and upon the Seville and Barcelona Exhibitions which was labelled 'reproductive after a long period'. As a result of this the deficit usual in Spanish budgets disappeared. Primo was so delighted by this feat of wizardry that he announced that to celebrate it he would redeem all the mattresses which the poor had pawned in the State pawnshops.

His personal habits were as undisciplined and as bohemian as his mind. Though he worked long hours, these hours were very irregular.

[1] Primo's loquacity had always been famous. As a young general he once talked for two hours over the grave of a sentry who had been accidentally killed in Tetuan; Ciges Aparicio, *op. cit.* 'He is simply a parrot', said Unamuno. 'One always knows what he is going to say beforehand.' Some of his more preposterous decrees were written when he was drunk.

He sat up talking every night in clubs or cafés till three or four in the morning, slept till eight or nine and then took a siesta after lunch—putting on a cotton night dress and nightcap and going to bed in the old Spanish style till five. His only form of exercise was riding, but every now and then he would have a good *juerga* or drinking bout. He and a few friends (including women) would shut themselves up in a country house, disconnect the telephone and let themselves go for a couple of days. Then he would return to work with renewed energies. But his most troublesome vice was over-eating. As a diabetic he was supposed to eat sparingly, but he was always forgetting this and then his temperature would rise. The doctor would come and put him on a strict diet, but this was more than he could stand and in the middle of the night he would get up, steal down to the kitchen and finish the remains of his servants' supper. Next morning his temperature would have risen again. His last days in Paris, days of physical prostration and of bitterness, were passed between the church and the brothel.

Primo was really an anachronism in the Spain of his time. His simplicity, his *bonhomie*, his disorderly habits belong to the period before 1874, when the rich and the poor had not yet begun to drift apart. He had none of the *señorito* airs of so many of the landowners of to-day. He wore the cheapest clothes, preferably mufti, and when he grew fat, instead of ordering new ones, he had the old ones let out. His biographer has recorded the sort of horror with which he fingered a silk shirt. Never, he declared, had he worn such a thing in his life. There are many small Spanish landowners who live in this way to-day, but Primo, a man of good family, the favourite nephew of a captain-general, had always occupied a privileged position. His greatness—for he had a kind of greatness—came from his being a typical Andalusian, drawn larger than life.

The most successful of the achievements of the Dictatorship was the pacification of Morocco. Millions of money and thousands of lives had been sunk in that country to no advantage. Abd-el-Krim was increasing in strength every day and the Spanish troops were undisciplined and unreliable. Primo decided to cut his losses and effect an immediate withdrawal to the fortresses on the coast, and for that purpose assumed both the military and the civil command in Morocco himself. The withdrawal took place at the end of 1924, at a cost of 16,000 casualties, in great disorder. But in May Abd-el-Krim made the fatal mistake of attacking the French and plans for a joint offensive by France and Spain were drawn up that summer. In September, whilst the French, advancing from Fez, drew the main body of the Riffian forces, the Spaniards landed 8000 men at Alhucemas Bay in the face of opposition. It was a hazardous attempt, for though there was only a weak force to oppose it, the Spanish troops were demoralized and there was a long tradition of failure for exploits of this kind in the Spanish Army. Everything depended too upon the prevailing wind, the levante, not blowing. But Primo asserted it would not blow and his luck held good. The landing was successful. Abd-el-Krim's capital, Axdir, was taken a few weeks later and the whole Riff was overrun and pacified. The Moroccan War, which from 1911 to 1929 had cost £160,000,000,[1] was at last over, though one may add that at any time during the past few years a division of good infantry equipped with bombing aeroplanes and tanks could easily have settled it. As a result of this victory the military dictatorship was suppressed and with the approval of the King a civil dictatorship set up in its place. The change of name was the only difference.

Another success of Primo's regime was the relations which he established with labour. Since the general strike of 1917 governments had begun to pay more attention to labour conditions. Industrial tribunals had been introduced in 1918, the eight-hour day established in 1919 and a ministry of labour set up in 1920.[2] Primo amplified and invigorated all this legislation, establishing—to the disgust of landlords and employers—compulsory arbitration boards (comités paritarios) at which wages were adjusted. The workmen gained considerably by them. He also allied himself with the Socialists. He sent for Largo Caballero, the secretary of the Socialist trade union, the U.G.T., and invited him to collaborate in the regime. The Socialists were the only political party he would tolerate: he admired their discipline and their sincerity and hoped by their means to wean the working classes from the impossible Anarcho-Syndicalists. It was a sensible policy and had Primo been able to carry it further by breaking up the large estates, which were the fomenters and maintainers of rural anarchism, the history of Spain might have been different. But his dependence upon the Army and upon the landlords made this, even had he desired it, impossible and, since agriculture

---

[1] See El Debate, May 1929. The League of Nations Armament Year Book gives approximately the same figure.

[2] Yet in 1928 there were still 24 per cent of full-time employees who worked between 54 and 60 hours a week. Such is the gulf between law and fact in Spain! This percentage was higher than in any other country in Europe. See 'Hours of Work' in the Encyclopaedia of Social Service.

was booming and land values were rising, the cost of expropriation would have been excessive.

With this policy went a lavish public works scheme which almost did away with unemployment. The roads built by previous Governments were surfaced and made fit for motor cars.[1] Other roads were built, electricity and irrigation schemes were inaugurated. An admirable system of State hotels was set up in out of the way regions to encourage tourists. Ancient monuments were restored. The Seville and Barcelona Exhibitions were opened on a scale quite out of proportion to the wealth of the country. This excessive expenditure produced a false sense of prosperity, caused the public debt to rise from 15,000 to 20,000 millions of pesetas and led to the economic crisis of 1929, when the peseta fell from 33 to the £ to 47. This was a level it had not reached for half a century.[2]

Had Primo retired in 1925, after the successful termination of the Moroccan War, he would have gone down to history as one of the saviours of Spain. But in fact his rule rested upon an absolute contradiction. Spain needed radical reforms and he could only govern by permission of the two most reactionary forces in the country—the Army and the Church. He had come in with the consent of, but not as the representative of, the Army to cover up the responsibilities of the King. His dependence upon it prevented a solution of the agrarian

[1] This is not the only time when Spain has had 'the best roads in Europe'. In the third quarter of the eighteenth century Charles III's minister Floridablanca built roads and post-houses on a scale that was not to be seen anywhere else. English travellers such as Townsend and a few years later Southey were astonished by them. But before these new roads with their embankments, cuttings and stone bridges could be carried very far, the money ran out.

[2] Another aspect of this tremendous expenditure was the graft which often accompanied it. Primo had come in to purify the Government, but the policy of granting monopolies in one commodity after another led to a great deal of corruption. Madrid became full of adventurers. The most famous of these was the millionaire Juan March, who had made a fortune during the war by supplying German submarines. There was also a scandal over the construction of the Santander Railway in which certain members of the Royal Family were involved. See *Solidaridad Obrera* by Cánovas Cervantes and *The Civil War in Spain* by Frank Jellinek, 1938.

This graft, however, may be regarded as an indication of a change that was taking place in Spanish industry. During these five years Spanish and especially Catalan industry was passing from a stage of small concerns competing together anarchically to larger concentrations of capital—cartels and monopolies. The reorganization of the hydro-electric industry in one trust known as the *Chade*, linked to immense German and American interests and under the presidency of Cambó, is one example of this process. Another, which was much criticized, was the handing over of the state-owned telephones to an American company. As a result of these operations the cost of telephoning and of electric light to the ordinary consumer rose by approximately 50 and 30 per cent respectively.

question and made him the oppressor of Catalan liberties: his relation to the King made it impossible for him to return to legality by summoning a Constituent Cortes. The hostility of the Liberals and intellectuals which this brought him threw him into the arms of their enemy the Church. His repression of Catalan aspirations was particularly severe. Primo had come in with the connivance of many elements of the Lliga, who had been terrified by the anarchist disturbances in Barcelona.[1] This did not prevent him from dissolving the Mancomunidad, the very mild form of local government granted in 1912, and curtailing even the most elementary liberties of the Catalans. Their language was forbidden in schools and in public assemblies as well as in official notices or announcements of any sort. Their flag could not be flown. Even their national dance, the *sardana*, was prohibited, and with childish virulence the name plates of the Barcelona streets, which were written both in Catalan and in Spanish, were cut in two. One effect of this was to ruin the Lliga and to prepare the way for the victory of the Left-wing parties. More than anything else it was the overwhelmingly Republican vote of the Catalans in 1931 that brought the Monarchy to an end.

Primo was further driven—by the necessity for a severe censorship, by the whole nature of his dictatorship—to quarrel with the intellectuals, who, in a country where so few are well educated and where, owing to the feeble economic structure, ideas have always been very important, carry a great deal more weight than they do in England. This threw him more and more into the arms of the Church. The Church is such an extreme body in Spain that no government that is too closely dependent upon it can hope to govern the country. This soon became apparent. His project for allowing the Jesuit and Augustinian colleges to grant degrees raised an uproar in the universities, which, followed as it was by his hasty retraction, did a great deal to bring him down.

The Dictatorship had meanwhile failed to secure the active support

[1] In August 1923 Puig y Cadafalch, President of the Mancomunidad, and other leading members of the Lliga offered their support to Primo in his *coup d'état* in exchange for his promise to grant a measure of autonomy to Catalonia. But the feeling in the Army prevented this promise from being realized. A week after Primo came into power, he published regulations against those very Catalan Nationalists who, trusting to his often expressed regionalist sympathies, had helped him in. The setting up of mixed labour commissions to determine hours and wages was another blow to the employers on the Lliga, who disliked State mediation in industrial disputes as strongly as did the Anarchists. On the other hand the upper bourgeoisie gained financially under Primo's rule by the development of Catalan finance and industry.

of the middle classes. Spain is not a country where patriotic feelings
are easily placed at the service of a government: Spaniards can rise in
fury against an invader because he is there and interferes with their
lives and they can cling frantically to an idea, but active support for a
regime is scarcely within their capacity. The Unión Patriótica, which
was founded in feeble imitation of the Italian Fascist party, was a
failure: only doubtful characters went into it. The middle classes,
sluggish, inert and pessimistic, stood aside. The *sindicatos libres* or
patriotic trade unions organized by the Dictator (a development of the
unions set up in 1919 by the Catalan employers) proved also to be a
mushroom growth and gave no support worth having. So, as a space
opened round him, Primo was driven more and more to repressive
measures and to such un-Spanish devices as spying on the conversation of respectable people and opening private letters, and as his
popularity waned even those people whose interests he represented,
the Army and the King, began to plot against him. The last two years
were a *corrida* in which students, ex-politicians, Liberal journalists,
generals—anyone who wanted to figure in the lime-light—took up his
banderillas and challenged the Dictator, while an apathetic crowd
looked on. It was a typically Spanish *dénouement*. No race is so given
to hero-worship: no race so quick to pull the unsuccessful hero down.
And in Spain no one can be successful nor keep himself above the
crowd for long.

From Primo's dictatorship one can, I think, draw three conclusions. No government which has to depend on Church, Army and
landlords can secure more than a temporary support in Spain. No
government which represents a purely material well-being at the cost
of liberty can satisfy Spaniards. And in a country where half the
population sits in cafés and criticizes the Government no dictator can
prosper for long. Primo de Rivera came in with every possible advantage and had all possible luck, but after three years of successful
rule it was only a question of how much longer he would last.

Primo went to Paris and died and his place was taken by another
general, Berenguer, with the mission of 'bringing back the waters to
the river bed'—in other words saving the King. But the ease with
which the Dictator had been brought down encouraged the Liberal
middle classes who had done it to think that Alfonso could be got rid
of too. He had practically no supporters. He had alienated almost
every politician in the country, and even Conservative leaders such as
Sánchez Guerra, a lifelong royalist, would have nothing to do with

him. The fact that the Dictatorship had come in to cover up his personal responsibility for the disaster in Morocco was fatal to him. It was therefore with little hope of success that he began his fifteen months' fight for the throne. And he made mistakes. His worst mistake was in executing two officers, Captains Galán and García Hernández, who had risen for a republic in Jaca.[1] Military risings have so long been a part of the political game in Spain that if they fail without causing much loss of life public opinion is opposed to death sentences. A weak or failing government incurs odium by carrying them out. This had been the mistake which, in 1843, had brought down Espartero, and Isabella had lost her popularity in 1866 for the same reason. Indeed, Spanish opinion has always been strangely sensitive to executions in time of peace, whatever the crime may have been, and in 1911 a Monarchist paper *El Mundo* gravely censured the King for being at Cowes Regatta 'amusing himself, whilst one of his subjects lay under sentence of death'.[2]

One by one Alfonso tried various expedients for returning, without the risk of elections, to normal constitutional government, but could not obtain the necessary promises of support from political leaders. In the end, after infinite hesitations, it was decided to hold municipal elections to see which way the wind was blowing. To the surprise of everyone, not least to that of the parties of the Left (for municipal elections are more easily manipulated than parliamentary ones and the Socialists had at first decided to abstain from voting) they showed an avalanche. Every provincial capital in Spain except four voted Republican. In Madrid and in Barcelona the vote was overwhelming. The middle classes as a body had deserted Alfonso. The fact that the country districts, outnumbering the towns, voted royalist was of no

---

[1] A court martial found them guilty and imposed the death penalty. The Government was divided as to whether or not the sentence should be carried out. But the King insisted and the same afternoon (Sunday, 14 December) they were taken out and shot. This hurried execution on a Sunday afternoon of two young officers did more to turn opinion against the Rey Caballero than anything else he could have done.

[2] See Fernández Almagro, *op. cit.* When shortly after this the King pardoned E Chato de Cuqueta, an anarchist who had risen at Valencia, he became more popular than he had ever been before or since.

Spaniards have always hated cruelty or severity in their governments. The Spanish governments of the seventeenth and eighteenth centuries were far more lenient towards political or social misdemeanours than the French or English. And even in the nineteenth century, when risings occurred every year or two, it became the rule that any government which shed blood in Madrid had to resign. Why not, when, as an Italian historian has said, the Spanish idea of fair play is to allow everyone a little revolutionary activity against the people in power?

importance: their votes were largely controlled by the caciques or else they were politically indifferent, and in any case no king or dictator could hope to hold Spain if the towns were against him.[1] The Army and the Civil Guard, commanded by General Sanjurjo, withdrew their support. Even the grandees kept silent: they were afraid that if the King did not go there might be a 'red revolution'. But only when every possible resource had been exhausted, when it was clear that not a general would draw his sword for him, did the King leave.[2]

Thus ended the Monarchy. In the words of Nicolo Pascazio, an Italian journalist who has given a vivid account of its fall, it was 'simply a vested interest consisting of clergy, military and aristocracy at the expense of everyone else.... It had no support among the middle classes.' For the famous fidelity of the Spaniards to their kings had been broken long before. Of the immediate predecessors of Alfonso XIII, four, including a Queen Regent, had been compelled to abdicate, one (Ferdinand VII) had only been kept on his throne by French arms and one (Alfonso XII) had died young. Since 1789 not a single Spanish sovereign had had a natural reign.

[1] In many towns over 90 per cent of the electorate voted: the average in previous elections had been 40 per cent. Of the 50 provincial capitals, 46 voted for a Republic.

[2] It is often asserted in this country that the King withdrew to avoid plunging the country into a civil war. The fact is that his withdrawal became inevitable from the moment that Sanjurjo, the Commander of the Civil Guard, who happened also to be the most influential general in Spain, refused him his support. A useful martyr once he had left, whilst he was still in Spain hardly anyone wished to keep him. This is not a question on which any doubt is possible. How lukewarm was even the aristocracy may be seen from the appeal of the Duke of Almenara Alta, President of the Nobles' Club, to the upper classes of society to increase their pro-Monarchic campaign in the coming municipal elections. The grandees of Spain, he declared, had 'the firm intention of serving the King *to the point, if need be, of sacrifice.*'

See Nicolo Pascazio, *La Rivoluzione di Spagna*, for an entertaining description of their attitude and of their wholesale flight from the country when the Republic came in. Pascazio's caustic accounts of the behaviour of the Spanish upper classes are all the more telling for his being himself an Italian Fascist, who had no sympathies or contacts with the parties of the Left.

Part II

THE CONDITION OF THE WORKING CLASSES

> Everything was rotten in Spain except the hearts of the poorer people. NAPIER, *History of the Peninsular War*.

～

Chapter VI

THE AGRARIAN QUESTION

> It is a duty of humanity for us to open to all men the riches which God gave in common to all, since to all he gave the earth as a patrimony, so that all without distinction might live by its fruits. Only unbridled greed could claim for itself this gift of heaven, appropriating as its own the foods and riches which were intended to be the property of all.... God wishes then, and it is laid down by his laws, that now that human nature, corrupted as it is, has proceeded to a partition of common goods, they should not be monopolized by a few, and that a part should always be set aside for the consolation of the people's infirmities.... In a Republic in which some are overstuffed with riches and others lack the very necessities, neither peace nor happiness is possible.   FATHER JUAN DE MARIANA, *De Rege et Regis Institutione*, 1599.

Before commencing on the history of the Republic it will be necessary to stop and give some account of the position of the peasants and working classes in Spain at this time. I shall begin with a discussion of what is really the fundamental problem in Spain—the agrarian question—and its relation to industry, and shall then in succeeding chapters trace the history of the two great working-class movements, the Anarcho-Syndicalists and the Socialists, who between them comprise the great majority of the workers in the country. Finally, I will give a brief account of the Carlists, who if not exactly a working-class movement, are to a certain extent an agrarian one.

The first thing to notice is that Spain is one of those countries with an undeveloped, primitive economy which is divided by a fairly definite line into two sections. Above are the upper and middle classes, say one-fifth of the population, who vote, read newspapers, compete for Government jobs and generally manage the affairs of the nation. Beneath are the peasants and workmen, who in ordinary times take no interest in politics, frequently do not know how to read and keep strictly to their own affairs. Between these two completely different worlds there is a gulf, imperfectly filled by the small shop-keepers and artisans.

These two classes lived side by side in towns and villages, but without any very close contacts. The lack of education and the backwardness and inertness of the economic structure prevented any upward movement from one to the other. In England and France, for example, it has for a long time been common for men to rise from the humblest rank to the class above them. In Spain this has rarely happened. The workman who put by money, the peasant who added to his holding, the artisan who went into business became the exception as soon as one crossed the Pyrenees and scarcely existed at all in the south. The few one could point to as having 'bettered themselves' had generally made their money in America. And this had one effect which every traveller to Spain during the last hundred and fifty years has admired. The working classes showed no desire to imitate the customs or ways of thought of their social superiors. They had the independence of mind to prefer their own. For if they had been impoverished by the loss of their common lands in the nineteenth century, they had at least not been crushed and uprooted as the English poor had been nor demoralized by parish relief. They had been left very much to themselves in the large villages or towns where most Spanish peasants live and here they had maintained the traditional ways of life that had come down to them from their ancestors. This gave them a solidarity with their own class that had no parallel in England or France. And, as I have said, the industrial revolution that in the long run came to the help of the English poor, matured very slowly in Spain, so that opportunities for improving their lot did not as a rule exist for them. Thus, except in a few of the larger towns, society remained sharply divided into two classes—the large class of those who worked with their hands and the small class of those who did not.

It is easy to see therefore why Spanish politics of the last two hundred years give such an impression of inconsequence and futility. The people took no part in them. If they voted it was for fear of losing their jobs or to earn the peseta or two offered them by the cacique. So convinced were they that the Government and its laws were no concern of theirs and that politicians existed only in order to feather their own nests, that they regularly turned their backs on all suggestions held out by Republican candidates for the amelioration of their condition. And yet one would be wrong to regard this huge silent mass as necessarily inert and inexpressive. The Spanish pueblo has a totally different character to any other body of peasants and labourers in Europe. At regular intervals in the course of its history, whenever it has considered its deepest interests to be threatened, it has risen and carried everything before it. It was the people who, by tumults and massacres all over Spain, insisted on the forcible conversion of the Jews in the fifteenth century: it was they who expelled the Moriscos in the sixteenth century against the wishes of the large landowners and, a century later, drove out the Austrian Archduke and his English allies in the War of the Spanish Succession. Again, it was the people and not the nobility or the middle classes, who fought with such fury against Napoleon. In all these cases they rose, not so much to satisfy any material claims of their own as on the leading and at the instigation of the Church (and especially of the monks and village priests) in defence of certain ideals, and as soon as their object had been attained they returned to their former apathy.[1] In the twentieth century there were other risings which, except in the case of the Carlist Rebellion, were not led by the Church—but these were half-hearted affairs, owing no doubt to the fact that in their new orientation they were still weak and uncertain of themselves.

However there is one thing to be noted about all these popular movements, and that is that in each case the object they had in view was not a positive redressing of their grievances, but simply the expulsion of a foreign body which provoked and irritated them. Once the Jews and the Moors, then the Austrians and the French, we have recently seen them turn with the same destructive fury upon the landlords and the priests who had exhausted their patience. In all these cases one may observe the same process: the sudden spontaneous rising against the enemy in their midst and, when his destruction or expulsion has been achieved, the rapid subsidence. It would almost seem as though the long history of the 'purification' of Spain had given Spaniards the feeling that, to live as they wished, they needed only to get rid of someone.

And, again one may note, whenever they rose they proved irresistible. Spain then acted as a whole, and not from the surface only. Even the upper classes admitted this. The pueblo was recognized by them as being the great repository of the virtues of the race, the source from which everything that was sane and healthy in the country

---

[1] See Note A on p. 126 at end of chapter.

sprang. No act in which it did not take part had its roots in the national life. Even when it was too late, even after it had abandoned them, they continued to appeal to it, searching for the 'true pueblo', the pueblo that was still 'faithful to its ideals' and which had not been 'corrupted by foreign gold', with the same pathetic fervour with which orthodox Marxists search to-day for the pure proletariat. For they suffered, these Spanish middle classes, from a deadening sense of inferiority, of superficiality, of lack of substance. They had lost faith in themselves and in their religion. Under their air of self-confidence they felt themselves cut off from the true sources of life in their country and dwindling every day. No wonder then that the more sensitive of them were inclined to attribute to this pueblo—which seemed for all its ignorance to be so much stronger and healthier than they were (strong and healthy enough perhaps to end by devouring them)—a kind of mystic force such as the Russian Slavophils had attributed to their peasantry in the last decades before the Revolution. Certainly they had far better historical reasons for doing so.

The process therefore that we shall trace during the following chapters is the gradual transfer of the allegiance of the peasants and workers from the Church to revolutionary ideologies hostile to it. The effect of these new social theories was to make the workers regard the landlords and the factory owners very much as in the past they had regarded the Jews and the Moors—that is, as foreigners who interfered with them and prevented their free development. Such an obvious view scarcely required any novel arguments to sustain it, seeing how gross and unmitigated had been the parasitism of the Spanish upper classes. But Spaniards long ago formed the habit of fighting for ideas. For a thousand years Spanish history has been the history of a crusade, punctuated by intervals of indifference and torpor. An ideology was therefore needed to rouse the workers and to lead them to victory. In Socialism and perhaps even more in Anarchism they found what they needed.

The first thing to get clear is that though Spain is predominantly an agricultural and stock-breeding country (there are $4\frac{1}{2}$ millions of workers on the land compared to only 2 millions in industry) the value of the greater part of this land is very low. The fact that certain small irrigated regions scattered round the edges of the Peninsula contain the most productive land in Europe must not make one forget that a large part of the centre consists of heath, thin steppe pasture or desert. The area of cultivated land in Spain in 1928 was between 50 and 60 million acres: that of pasture and underwood was somewhat larger, whilst 15 million acres were totally unproductive. Of the pasture land more than one half was extremely poor—incapable, that is, of maintaining more than two sheep per acre.[1]

To understand the reason for this we must consider the physical conditions of the Peninsula. The core of Spain is a tableland of ancient rocks whose average altitude is over 2000 feet above sea level. This high tableland is parched with heat in summer and swept by icy winds in winter. Much of it is nearly soil-less, and granites and primary rocks lie close to the surface. The northern boundary of this region, formed by the Pyrenees and the Cantabrian Range, is a wild mountainous district resembling Switzerland and ending in the broken granite region of Galicia where heaths and small patches of cultivated land alternate as in Brittany or Ireland. The Guadalquivir Valley on the south consists of rolling country with a good soil, but with insufficient rainfall to counteract the high evaporation. On the east coast there is excellent soil, composed of miocene formations originally washed down from the central tableland and deposited in shallow lakes, but here the rainfall is so slight that, except where there is irrigation, the land can scarcely be used at all.

Rainfall is thus the critical factor in Spain. The sketch map on p. 333 will give an idea of its distribution. It varies from 60 or even 80 inches in Galicia to less than 10 near Teruel or along the east coast, whilst in some parts of the provinces of Murcia and Almería there is often no rain at all for several years on end. That is to say, drought is the prevailing weather type through most of the country and is so distributed that it is the worst soil that gets the greatest rainfall, whilst the best is rainless.

It is obvious that these varying physical conditions must give rise to very different agrarian systems. And that is in fact the case. The sketch map on p. 334 will show how closely the area of small holdings and long-term leases coincides with that of sufficient rainfall, whilst the area of large estates and short-term leases coincides with drought. The small man cannot live without difficulty in a dry area, because he is not able to stand the seasonal variation of the crops. There exist therefore two main agrarian problems in Spain: that of the small holdings in the centre and north, which are sometimes too exiguous to

---

[1] See Madariaga, *Spain*. A. Marvaud (*L'Espagne au XXième Siècle*, p. 294) gives 42 million acres as the area of cultivated land in 1903-1907 and 64 million acres for pasture and underwood.

maintain the men who work on them, and that of the large estates in the south, which are run on a factory system that keeps down wages to starvation point by means of huge reserves of unemployed labour. A third problem is that of the leases.

GALICIA

Let us examine first the question of the small holdings. The classic example is Galicia. In the Middle Ages most of the land in Galicia belonged to the Church. They let it out on a special type of lease known as the *foro*, which was a form of hereditary emphyteusis. The tenant paid a quit-rent, usually about 2 per cent of the capital value of his holding, and kept his house and farm buildings in repair, but could not be ejected. This was a form of tenure that came into use over the greater part of Central Spain in the thirteenth and fourteenth centuries and is known in Castile as the *censo*. The *foro* differed from the *censo* in being limited to a definite period—usually *por tres voces y veinte nueve años mas*—that is, 'for three lives (either of tenants or kings) and twenty-nine years more'. This limitation seems to be connected with the fact that it was introduced by Cistercian and Premonstratensian monks in the twelfth and thirteenth centuries as an inducement to free peasants and serfs to settle on the moors and waste lands, and not, as was the case with the *censo*, during the conversion of feudal tenures to a system of yearly rentals. That is to say, whilst offering favourable terms to settlers, the Church wished to retain some control of its property. Galicia, with its holy city of Santiago de Compostella, and Catalonia, which bordered on Languedoc, were naturally more subject than other parts of Spain to the new ecclesiastical influences coming from France.

In the seventeenth and eighteenth centuries the population of Galicia began to increase rapidly and land values went up. The tenants, who leased their land from the Church and from the nobility, began to find it profitable to subdivide their holdings and re-let them at a greatly increased rental—in some cases for ten or twenty times more than they themselves paid. Thus a new class of land profiteers grew up, and under them a new class of tenants, the *subforados*. The Church and the nobles then attempted to put into practice the clause which limited the leases to a definite period, but which had gradually fallen into desuetude. The *foreros* resisted and a dispute began which lasted in the law courts and in the royal councils for a hundred and thirty years (from 1629 to 1759) without any ruling being arrived at.

In 1763 an order in council suspended the whole question, which meant that the *foreros* had won. However, the entire civil and criminal jurisdiction of the lands still belonged to the Church and the nobility, so that when the Cortes met at Cadiz in 1810 the middle-class *foreros* ranged themselves on the Liberal side. Then, after the Carlist War, the Church lands were sold and most of the *foros* were bought up by the *foreros*, who thus became themselves the legal owners of the land or *foristas*. The *foro* question then resolved itself into a struggle between these new *foristas*, who were generally lawyers and lived in the towns, and the people who actually worked the land, the *subforados* or *foreros*.

To see how this question affected local politics, one must understand how the land is worked. The climate of Galicia is moist like that of Ireland, which in so many respects it resembles, but the soil is poor and more suited for grazing than for cereals. The pressure on the land, however, does not allow the soil to be worked in the most productive way. The country is dotted over with little farms each containing just enough land to support one family. The type of rural economy of each of these homesteads is necessarily therefore one of strict self-sufficiency. Each family has its own cow, which does the ploughing and provides a little cheese and milk; it grows its own rye or maize, out of which it makes its bread, ferments its own wine and even in some districts makes its own cloth. Each family eats what it grows—there are no export crops. The only means by which a little money can be raised to pay the taxes is by selling a calf every year or by going off to other parts of Spain to work at the harvest. All this might be well enough if the closing of the old outlet of emigration to America had not increased the already excessive subdivision of the land and led to a great many families living in a condition of semi-starvation.

It was in these circumstances that the Galician peasant was asked to pay a *foro* for the land on which he lived and which, since he could not be turned out of it, he considered that he owned. The *foro* was collected by agents and was paid to people whom, as a rule, he had never seen and who had no rights whatever over his property. For this reason, like the collection of tithe in England, it was felt as an injustice. And it had other evils attached to it. Although the land was very subdivided, the *foros* were not, so that endless disputes and lawsuits occurred between the tenants in deciding the share that each had to pay. These disputes were fomented by the lawyers with the object of driving the peasants into debt. As both lawyers and money-lenders belonged to the class of *foristas*, they soon got considerable numbers of the peasants into their hands and compelled them to vote for them at elections. So strong was the cacique system in Galicia that it survived even the coming of the Republic.[1]

Till recently the *foros* dominated every other political question in Galicia. As long ago as 1905 the *foristas* were finding it difficult to obtain payment because their agents were intimidated and the members of the tribunals that confirmed their claims were persecuted and sometimes even killed. At about this time the *foreros* founded two very different organizations to defend their rights. One, *Solidaridad Gallega*, believed in redeeming the *foros* by paying some compensation: the other, the *Unión Campesina*, which originated under Anarchist influences at Corunna, demanded their cancellation. The first, which one may call Republican and Liberal, believed only in political action: the second had a policy of boycotts and violence and turned its back on politics. One more example of the fact that wherever the cacique is found he promotes a-politicism and anarchism. But what makes this conflict unique in modern Spanish history was the attitude of the Church. Generally speaking, wherever the rural population in Spain is concentrated into large villages or towns, the clergy are upon the side of the middle classes and caciques against the people, whereas when the peasantry are dispersed in hamlets and small farms, the clergy associates itself with them. This was the case in Galicia. The rural clergy were fanatically anti-*forista*—cases have even been known of their refusing the sacraments to *foristas*. Only the town clergy, sons of *foristas* and caciques, preached peace and submission. The result of this was that although, with the advent of the Republic, socialist doctrines spread among the peasants, the political situation in Galicia never came fully into line with that in the rest of Spain. Politics, veering round the question of the *foros* and confused by the double attitude of the Church, remained a local issue.

There was also a regional movement based partly on the fact that the special interests of Galician agriculture were thought to be neglected in Madrid. The duty on foreign maize prevented the development of cattle breeding, which was the natural industry of the country and its one hope of emerging from its primitive economy. But in spite of the fact that the Galicians speak a language and have a culture of their own, it was not deeply rooted. So that, generally speaking, one may say that the remoteness of Galicia from the rest of Spain and from its social and political problems (a remoteness accentuated by an execrable railway system) has been its chief characteristic.

[1] Primo de Rivera decreed compulsory redemption of the *foros* in 1926. This was completed shortly before the Civil War.

ASTURIAS, THE BASQUE PROVINCES AND NAVARRE

Moving to the east along the Cantabrian Mountains one comes first to Asturias, an Alpine region of small peasant farmers. Here conditions are somewhat better than in Galicia, because the family holdings are larger and because there still exist extensive communal pastures. The only exports are cattle and dairy produce. The *foro* is rare. One arrives then at the four Basque provinces, of which the most easterly, which has developed separately from the others, is Navarre. Beyond them lies the Pyrenean half of Aragon, extending to the borders of Catalonia. All this region has a simple type of rural economy that has come down more or less unchanged from early times and is not derived from the decay of feudal institutions. It is a country of small proprietors or tenant farmers, working on a family basis and possessing sufficient land to maintain themselves adequately. Contrary to the custom in most other parts of Spain they are not grouped in small towns or villages, but lie scattered in isolated farms and hamlets. As the rainfall is abundant and the soil adequate, they are fairly prosperous.

Two forms of land tenure are in force here, according to whether the land is owned by the family that work it or rented by them from someone else. The first, common to the whole Pyrenean region, is the 'family community system', in which the property belongs to the family and the head of the family council chooses his successor among his sons or other relatives. The house, known as the *lar* or *llar* (derived from the Latin *lar*), with its orchard, fields and vineyards, is unalienable and descends from one generation to another. This system, which to-day is not so strict as it used to be, is the primitive form of land tenure that once prevailed through the whole of the mountainous region of Northern Spain. It can be traced back to the tenth century and may be much older. With it goes a strong sense of solidarity between neighbours, who are regarded as having certain duties towards one another which they must fulfil at the risk of being boycotted. In Navarre much of the land is held in this way and the result is the most conservative peasant society in Europe.[1]

---

[1] Corresponding to the 'family community' of the Pyrenees is the now moribund *compañía gallega* of Galicia, in which a family society, occupying perhaps a whole hamlet, cultivates their land in common. This existed in Catalonia also, but has now almost died out there. The fact that neither *foro* nor *censo* ever took root in the Basque provinces, in Asturias or along the southern slopes of the Pyrenees is an indication of the cohesion of this rural society, isolated in its mountain valleys and cut off from all influence of the towns. The *rentier* living on an income derived from land, but dissociated from all care in its management, could not come into existence.

Merging with these peasant proprietors are other peasants who rent their land. The form of lease most commonly used belongs to a type that was once general over a large part of Spain and is called *aparcería a medias* or share-cropping. The landowner provides the land, the tenant does the work and pays the taxes: the incidental expenses and the crop are shared. It is a system that requires, if it is to work properly, a good deal of confidence between labourer and owner, since both have to be in agreement as to the crops that are to be sown each year. It also works best in climates where the rainfall is fairly regular, for whereas the owner must always gain something, the labourer may not get sufficient to support him if the weather is unfavourable. In the Basque provinces, and indeed through all this mountainous country in the north, the *aparcería* system prevails, the contracts being often oral and descending from father to son as though it were the labourer's own property. In the three original Basque provinces, Vizcaya, Guipúzcoa, and Álava, most of the land is held in this way. The owner lives as a rule in the neighbouring small town or village and the relations between him and his tenant are invariably excellent. The terms are less onerous for the tenant than they are in Navarre or in Aragon—indeed one may say that the *aparcería* system here has come to be less a lease than an association contract. The prosperity of the Basque provinces and the liberal and reasonable spirit which they have developed may no doubt be put down in part to the success they have had in this form of co-operation.[1]

To this system of small farms one must add the communal forests and grazing lands. Along the slopes of the Pyrenees, or wherever the mountains are high enough, they are abundant. As Arthur Young noticed in 1787, they contribute greatly to the prosperity of the peasant communities.

The Basque provinces, Navarre and Upper Aragon cling then to a primitive rural economy, based on small farms handed down in the same family from generation to generation or rented on long leases which are in practice hereditary. They are enabled to do this by the fact of their regular rainfall and because the family community system has not permitted that extreme subdivision of the land which is seen

---

[1] Such at least is the opinion of Angel Marvaud, who speaks of their management of these share-cropping leases as the 'admiration of economists' (*La Question Sociale en Espagne*, 1910). One may note that in many parts of North Italy the same lease, known as the *mezzadria*, has had a long and successful history, often supplanting the *livello* or emphyteutic tenure, which was general until the fourteenth century.

in Galicia. These are the satisfied areas of Spain—the only ones, apart from a few irrigated districts of the south-east, where one can say that there is no social problem. They are also the most Catholic: in them the village priest still has immense influence with his flock and Catholic benefit associations protect the peasants against those three miseries of rural life—sickness, failure of crops and money-lenders. Yet there are differences between them. The old Basque provinces do not produce the same type of Catholicism as Upper Aragon and Navarre. The Basques with their large industrial capital at Bilbao, their mercantile marine and their active commercial relations with foreign countries, are the most European of all Iberian races. Their language is the only primitive thing about them. Though conservative in a political sense, their conservatism is that of an active commercial race such as the English, which believes in individual effort. Their Catholicism, too, is modern; if one wishes to see monks who are not engrossed in political propaganda, well-educated clergy, unfanatical bishops, this is the part of Spain where one is most likely to find them.

Navarre, on the other hand, though inhabited by a race that was once Basque-speaking, has had a very different history from its three sister provinces. The last region of Spain to come under the rule of the Catholic kings, it has always been the most faithful to the Monarchy. This is to be accounted for by its self-subsisting economy, based on small but relatively prosperous farms, owned for the most part by their proprietors, and by its remoteness from large centres of commerce. The very prosperity of the Navarrese and the success they have made of self-government have made them hate change, so that during the past hundred years they have been the chief upholders of that fanatically conservative and religious attitude that is known as Carlism and which is nothing else than the hostility of a sturdy race of mountaineers and farmers to industrial life.

OLD CASTILE AND LEON

The same can be said, though to a lesser extent, of the plains of Old Castile, around Burgos and Palencia as far south as Valladolid. These are mainly areas of small proprietors or tenant farmers, eking out a scanty but still fairly regular existence from the soil. Palencia, for example, has been a district of small holders from remote times: it was the capital of the Iberian tribe of Vacceos who divided up their lands yearly.

At first sight it may seem surprising that this region of Spain should be so strongly Catholic. Scarcely anywhere do the peasants suffer more from short leases, land speculators and usurers. Rents are fixed in money, which means that they are not dependent on the size of the crop, so that every bad year leaves the peasant in debt. Such was the state of Old Castile in the seventeenth century, such again in the eighteenth century, and such it still is to-day.[1] But Castilians, who feel themselves the master race in Spain, have a long tradition of Conservatism. Their complaints, too, have never gone altogether unheard in Madrid. There has always been a section of the Conservative party which combined an insistence on low wages for agricultural labourers with a demand for easier credit for peasants. The interests of landowner and small farmer were assimilated. Then the Church, when it found itself losing the adherence of agricultural workers in other parts of Spain, mustered its forces in an effort to retain the loyalty of the Castilians. Catholic agrarian associations and rural credit banks were started, schools for peasants' children were founded and a great deal of money poured out. On the whole this policy has been successful. The Old Castilian peasant of to-day looks on his fellow-workers in the east and south much as his ancestors looked on the Moors and infidels, and it is only when one enters an area of large estates that one finds the *Casa del Pueblo* competing with the priests and drawing the poorer of the labourers towards Socialism. This is especially the case to the south of Valladolid, where the rainfall decreases and the soil gets poorer, and when one travels west and north-west into Leon.

ARAGON

The old province of Aragon consists of a Pyrenean belt, where conditions tend to resemble those in Navarre, the irrigated valley of the Ebro, where properties are small and the peasants relatively prosperous, and a large dry area with a very low rainfall, which includes the flat steppes of the Ebro Basin and a sparsely inhabited mountainous region known as the Maestrazgo, running south to Teruel. Large estates, debt-ridden peasants and impoverished agricultural labourers characterize the steppe country, which has been strongly affected by the Anarcho-Syndicalist movement. The Maestrazgo, on the other hand, has Carlist traditions. It should be added that the physical appearance of the Aragonese is very different from that of

[1] See Note B on p. 126 at end of chapter.

either the Basques or the Catalans: they seem to be of a more primitive stock and through the whole of Spain they are famous for their obstinacy.

CATALONIA

The only remaining province of Northern Spain is Catalonia. Here agrarian conditions are good. The land is for the most part owned by small proprietors who let it out to the peasants, though there are also peasant owners. There are two main types of lease, one the hereditary emphyteusis or *censo* (which originally, like the *foro*, had a time limit) and the other a special kind of *aparcería* or share-cropping contract which is employed for land used in the cultivation of vines. As vines are the most remunerative crop, this lease has given rise to a special class of peasants, the *rabassaires*, who rent their land under it. The peculiarity of this lease is that its duration is based on the life of the vines. The land reverts to the owner when three-quarters of the planted vines have died (*rabassa morte*) and he can then renew it or not as he thinks fit. Formerly the life of the vines averaged about fifty years, which assured the labourer a contract that would cover his working life and remunerate him for the six or eight years of fruitless labour that young vines require before they mature. But the phylloxera plague in the nineties killed the old vines and led to the introduction of a new American plant which required more care and labour and lived only half as long. This grievance of the *rabassaires* led, as we shall see, to serious consequences in the third year of the Republic.

Apart from this claim, which in any other country but Catalonia would be easily adjusted, the peasants are hard-working and prosperous. They have a large market to hand in Barcelona and a fair rainfall, and though the soil is poor, the intense industry of the Catalans (remarked by Young in 1787—they were the pioneers of small holdings in Spain) has made every yard productive.[1]

The regions whose agrarian features have so far been described—that is, Galicia, Asturias, the Basque provinces, Aragon and Catalonia, all mountainous or heath-covered districts, with Old Castile and Leon

---

[1] 'We saw, everywhere, signs of much industry; and, amidst a poverty which hurt our feelings, we generally saw something to convince us, that it was not the fault of the poor people that greater exertions were not made' (Young's *Travels*, p. 318). Young's piercing eye detected at once the main scourge of Spanish agriculture—the absentee landlord. On the large estates less than 1 per cent of the land was cultivated. Small holders only existed when they had been able to buy land from the Communes.

adjoining them on the Central Plateau—have (if we except a part of Aragon) two characteristics in common: a fair rainfall and Christian traditions that go back to the tenth century. Either they were never conquered by the Moslems or they were held by them for a comparatively brief period. They thus form the nucleus of an older Spain which, both geographically and culturally, has always been closer to Europe than to Africa. Their forms of land tenure and of local government reflect this. In the main, and in spite of certain later importations of feudalism, they derive their spirit and vigour from the days of the Spanish Mark, when the most urgent task of the kings and nobles was to repopulate the empty territories and when a peasant was often as much needed to fight as to plough. It is from then that one must date that love of local liberties and personal independence which have characterized Spaniards to this day.

Among these forms of land tenure one which was very general, especially in the old frontier provinces of Castile and Leon, was the communal ownership of all the land in the village. Such communes, of course, have existed at various times in other parts of Europe, but what is remarkable is that in Spain they have not only persisted in isolated districts down to the present day, but that the communal or co-operative spirit has shown such vitality that on various occasions during the last four centuries, and more especially during the last twenty years, it has thrown out new and vigorous shoots. Since, however, these communes are no longer numerous enough to exert any general influence, but merely display certain tendencies that have been or are at work, I have relegated the discussion of them to the appendix.

THE LEVANTE

As one travels down the east coast the rainfall drops to 15 inches and makes the cultivation of cereals a precarious task. Sometimes there is no harvest for years in succession as the corn either cannot be sown or, if sown, does not come up. But Tortosa, Valencia and Murcia mark the sites of *vegas* or irrigated plains—oases in the general sterility—which show the highest level of agricultural productivity in Europe. From three to five crops can be grown on them in one year and a very small area is sufficient to support a family. (The average holding is about $1\frac{1}{2}$ acres and 10 acres makes a rich man.) The *vega* of Valencia produces not only the oranges exported to England, but all the rice that is eaten in Spain. The land on it is worked by small farmers who, since the expulsion of the Moriscos in 1602, have rented their plots on leases called *censos*, granted at a fixed money rate. To-day they have most of them saved enough to buy them outright. As they are prosperous they vote either Republican (Valencia has a strong tradition of anti-clericalism) or Catholic-Conservative. Agricultural wages are higher here than in any other part of the Peninsula. The famous anarchists of these provinces do not come from the irrigated zone, but from the dry rainless areas where the poverty and hunger are very severe. Most of the men in these regions emigrate to the large towns, leaving their families behind them, whilst the women employ their time in lace-making.

Valencia is the seat of the remarkable *Cort de la Seo* or Water Tribunal, in which infractions of the complicated irrigation rules are judged and fines levied by a jury elected by the farmers of the district. The fines, though they cannot be enforced by law, are invariably paid. This tribunal, which has come down from the early Middle Ages, is simply one out of many proofs of the capacity for organization and discipline possessed by Spanish rural communities. Incidentally one should note that water rights here are attached to the land: in other places, such as Lorca and Murcia, they are separate from it—a system which leads to great abuses.

GRANADA

The only remaining district that need be mentioned before going on to the question of the latifundia or large estates is the fertile irrigated plain of Granada. This, with the smaller *vega* of Murcia, is the only irrigated district in Spain which is not in the hands of small peasant proprietors. Considerable fortunes have been made here in recent years by the cultivation of sugar beet, and rents (from which taxes must be excluded: it is the tenant who pays them) are as high as 8 per cent on the capital value of the land. The result is that the social conflict has been more severe here than in any other agricultural district in Spain, for the labourers and farmers are not the half-starved, down-trodden serfs of the Andalusian Basin, but well-educated and organized socialists, whilst the landowners (who here live on or close to their land) form a compact body belonging, like nearly all Spanish landowners, to the extreme Right.

This concludes my survey of the agrarian conditions of the north and east. With the exception of Galicia, parts of Leon and Old Castile and the dry lands of the east, these may be described as the fortunate districts of Spanish life, where the conditions can be compared not too unfavourably with those in other parts of Europe. There remain the centre and the south, the area of short rents and large estates. This may be divided into the plateau region of New Castile and La Mancha, where the estates are usually of moderate size, and the lower, more fertile region of Andalusia, where the estates are often enormous —reaching to 20,000 acres and in exceptional cases to 200,000 acres. Extremadura on the west forms a transitional region. But it will be impossible to understand the character of these two main regions, that together make up the core of Spain, without saying something of their agrarian antecedents.

HISTORICAL RETROSPECT

The history of Spain until the coming of the industrial age a generation or two ago can be explained as a contest between the rich agricultural districts of Andalusia and the Levante and the poor, semi-pastoral tableland of Castile. Andalusia was thickly populated and had a high level of civilization long before the Romans arrived and they made it one of the granaries of Italy. But with the decay of trade and agriculture during the latter years of the Empire, the importance of this province declined and the centre of gravity of the Peninsula began to move northwards.

The battle of the lagoon of Janda reversed this situation. A Mediterranean power, with a natural talent for commerce and manufacture, regained the mastery of Spain and Andalusian civilization rose to a point it had never reached before. Great industrial centres arose in Cordova, Seville, Malaga and Almería to provide the silk and cotton fabrics, the paper, lustre pottery and glass for which Western Europe, just emerging from the stagnation of the Dark Ages and full of the optimism of new eras, felt an inexhaustible appetite. Almería with its humid climate became the Manchester of Europe with a population of 250,000 (to-day it has 54,000) and a highly developed factory system, whilst Seville and Cordova were among the richest and most civilized cities in the world. But this population could never have been supported if there had not at the same time been a great development of agriculture. Under Persian and Nabathaean influences the land began to be intensely cultivated, whenever possible by a system of irrigation channels, and new plants such as sugar cane, rice, oranges, lemons and cotton were introduced. The large estates of Roman times gave way to small holdings and wealth was relatively well distributed. The decline came in the thirteenth century when the

market for silk stuffs fell off because the cities of Northern Europe had
set up factories of their own, and the political structure of the Moslems
disintegrated.[1] The semi-pastoral Spaniards of the north were then
able to conquer the greater part of Andalusia and of the Mediterranean coast.[2]

The irrigation channels got filled in; the land was devastated by
border wars; famines and epidemics further depopulated the country,
till by the end of the seventeenth century immense tracts, indeed
almost the whole of this once fertile land, had become a wilderness
ranged over by herds of sheep and cattle, and many towns and
villages (the *despoblados*) had ceased to exist at all. The only provinces
in which the irrigation channels were kept up were Valencia and
Murcia, which were held by Aragon and where exceptional fertility
and proximity to the Mediterranean provided easy markets. And
although to-day there is certainly more land under irrigation in Spain
than there was in the twelfth century, the Guadalquivir Valley from
Cordova to Seville—the heart of the old Baetican province—has
never recovered. *Castilla ha hecho a España y Castilla la ha dese-
chado*: 'Castile made Spain and Castile unmade it.'[3]

Why was this necessary? In the first place the nobles who, under
Ferdinand III, had conquered Seville and were rewarded by his son
with huge tracts of the best land in Andalusia, were, like their predecessors of Visigothic and Celt-Iberian times, mainly the owners of
flocks and herds. This at least was the only part of their patrimony
which they exploited directly. Then the emigration of the better
part of the Moslem population from their new lands made them
dependent upon slave labour. The decline of the towns too, due to the
inability of the Castilians to carry on their industries or to sell in the

---

[1] Those curious about industrial conditions at this time should read the account
in Chrétien de Troyes' *Le Chevalier au Lion* (c. 1172) of the silk loom set up by two
demons, *fils d'une femme et d'un luiton*, in a feudal castle in France.
The conditions of this sweated labour are described minutely. Three hundred
maidens captured in war, piecework paid at 4 deniers the pound woven, not one is
able to earn 20 sous a week. They work all day and a large part of the night, eat only
bread and are dressed in rags. The cloth they were making was the gold and silk
tissue which Almería had made famous. After a terrible combat with the two capitalist demons who are described as *noirs et hideux*, the knight errant Yvain delivers
them.
I take this episode with its circumstantial detail, quite out of keeping with the style
of the poem, to be based on an experience by the poet of the first attempts by feudal
barons to break the Andalusian monopoly by setting up factories of their own. Even
the word *luiton*, derived from Netun, meaning Neptune (sea-borne), is significant.
[2] See Note C on p. 126 at end of chapter.
[3] See Note D on p. 127 at end of chapter.

foreign market, led to a decrease in the demand for agricultural products. Aragon with its Mediterranean fleet might have saved Andalusia as she saved Valencia, but Castile could not.

Moreover, a new factor was appearing which threw the balance decisively against agriculture. The foreign wool trade was becoming profitable and was taking the place of the trade in silk fabrics which had been the rage in Europe a century before. One of the last innovations of the Spanish Moslems had been the introduction of the merino sheep from Africa, and its fine wool was more valuable than any other. The Castilian nobles saw that the easiest and most profitable use to which they could put their new territories would be to turn them into sheep runs. The kings saw that it would be profitable for them also, because the wool trade provided an easy means of levying taxes. The Castilian towns favoured it because their factories (and not those of Andalusia) would weave it. And so the famous sheep-farmers' guild, known as the *Mesta*, was founded and wool became the staple industry in Castile and in all the provinces ruled by her. The day of Andalusian civilization, with its complex but fragile economy based on a balance between large-scale industry and agriculture, was over.

Nor was this all. The kings had given liberal charters to the Andalusian towns and large grants of common lands to those who settled in them. Thousands of needy Spaniards flocked in from the north. But the country was still crowded with Moslems, many of them slaves, and the large estates were worked exclusively with slave labour. In this atmosphere the Christian peasant could not live happily: work in the fields had a stigma attached to it. Besides the tendency to turn arable into pasture was very strong: soon the *poderosos* with their large herds controlled the greater part of the common lands. So little corn was grown that before long this once rich and prosperous country had become a byword for misery and starvation. Every few years during the sixteenth and seventeenth centuries there was a plague or epidemic at Seville due to undernourishment and thousands died. 'Líbrete Dios' one reads in *Guzmán de Alfarache*, 'de la enfermedad que baja de Castilla y del hambre que sube de Andalucía!'

And yet one cannot help feeling that behind this victory of the sheep farmers of Castile there lies some deeper and more permanent cause. The soil of the Central Plateau is a very poor one—*dura tellus Iberia*, as Pliny calls it—and except in certain favoured spots it requires great industry to make a living by cultivating it. So uncertain is the rainfall that crop failures and their attendant famines are frequent. Often it is only by practising a kind of village communism that the peasants are able to get along at all. At the same time there are immense steppe lands ranged over by flocks and herds which at certain seasons become migratory. The shepherds wage a perpetual war on the agriculturalists, whom they regard as their inferiors, whilst both together feel a fierce envy of the city dwellers and cultivators of the rich oases and contrast their greed and wickedness with their own free and simple way of life. Now this is a type of society which is not confined to Spain but appears wherever certain climatic conditions prevail. It is strongly developed in Persia and in North Africa. One of its chief characteristics is its instability: it alternates violently between a centralized tyranny and an anarchic tribal or local life. With every bad drought or economic crisis there is either a revolution or a wave of religious exaltation, whilst at longer intervals there are great upheavals in which all the energies of the country are poured out in a war of conquest, leaving it inert and exhausted afterwards.

Seen in this light the triumph of the sheep farmers of Castile after 1248 is simply one result of the victory of those restless, explosive elements in Spanish life which were the heart and soul of the Reconquista. Their spirit was to dominate Spain down to the eighteenth century and to block the path to economic recovery. The famous orientalism of the Spaniards is not due to 'Arab blood' but to climate and geography.

During the next four centuries sheep farming not merely took precedence over agriculture, but to a great extent displaced it through all the lands ruled over by the Crown of Castile. So much was this the case that a large part of the sparse population of the country lived on the verge of starvation. The sheep passed the summer on the great plateaux of Northern Castile and descended in autumn to Extremadura. Similar migrations took place in other parts of the Peninsula. The huge clouds of dust that accompanied their movements became one of the characteristic sights of Spain. As fences did not exist, there was a continual struggle between agriculturalists and sheep farmers over mutual encroachments and especially over the *derrotas*, as the rights of grazing on stubble were called.[1] In these struggles the Mesta nearly

---

[1] The custom of the *derrotas* is that by which all the flocks and herds of the community are allowed access to the stubble after the corn has been cut. It is a natural consequence of the communal ownership of the land that existed in gradually diminishing degree all over Spain until recent times. References to it are found in Visigothic laws: it was almost certainly Iberian. Indeed such customs, like that of

always got the best of it, with the result that agriculture declined so rapidly that by the end of the seventeenth century the French Ambassador was reporting that the area of cultivated land around Seville, which was then the largest and most prosperous city in the country, had shrunk to one-twentieth of what it had been a century before. Good corn lands were overgrown with palmetto; broom and esparto were replacing olive trees and the pernicious goat was taking the place of the local (*estante*) sheep who, in contrast to the migratory (*transhumante*), were necessary for well-balanced farming.

This state of affairs naturally produced a great many suggestions for curing it. What Costa calls the 'collectivist school of economics' made its appearance and the Government accepted and even endeavoured to put into operation far-reaching plans for controlling and nationalizing the greater part of the land in Spain. But the decline had by this time gone so far that the State no longer possessed either the economic resources or the authority required for making its decrees effective, and moreover it still clung to the old Castilian view of the moral superiority of sheep farming to agriculture.

The eighteenth century saw a complete reversal of this opinion. The new ideal was expressed by Campomanes when he declared that he wished to see every Spanish peasant owning a house and garden, a yoke of mules or oxen and 50 *fanegas* (70 acres) of land to plough. Moreover, he said, it was the business of the State to see that this was carried out. These views gradually won acceptance among the enlightened group of men who surrounded the King, and after the serious economic crisis of 1766, which led to riots all over Spain and to the expulsion of the Jesuits, the Government of Charles III decided that the moment had come for a serious attempt to solve the agrarian question and so to revive agriculture.

Almost all land in Spain was at this time divided between the Church and the nobles and hidalgos in the form of *mayorazgos* (entailed estates), or else it belonged to the communes. Except in the Basque provinces and Navarre and in one or two special districts such as Palencia, the small owner scarcely existed: where he did, it was

gleaning, were common all over Europe. When, however, this right was claimed, as it frequently was, by migratory herds (*ganado trashumante*) it constituted an abuse. One may see in it then the record of a contract forced upon poor settlers on the land by powerful owners of flocks—whether invading Celts or Visigoths or Knights of the Military Orders or rich magnates of the Castilian Mesta. This abuse was carried by the latter to such a point that by the middle of the seventeenth century the local oxen and sheep had been almost driven out of existence in the southern provinces of Spain by the migratory herds, and the whole equilibrium of agriculture destroyed.

because the communes had recently sold or given away some of their uncultivated land. The amount of this uncultivated land in Spain was enormous. In Castile the Venetian ambassador speaks of riding for days without seeing a house.[1] Even on the once fertile plains of Andalusia one went for hours without coming to a ploughed field; whole towns had disappeared, yet the misery and famine were so great that in 1750 the entire population of Andalusia decided to emigrate *en masse* and could with difficulty be prevented. This was apparently because the large estates existed then just as they do to-day, but were used for pasturage, whilst the communes had allowed their land to be monopolized by their richer members. Everywhere in Southern Spain the best land had been taken by the sheep and cattle owners.[2]

The problem presented to Charles III's ministers was that of disentailing the *mayorazgos* or entailed estates (though not as a rule those of the nobles, which until the Cortes of 1812 were still sacrosanct) and also the *bienes de propio* or rented lands belonging to the communes.[3] These lands, which were then for the most part uncultivated, were to be colonized in a systematic manner. The collectivist theories of the sixteenth and seventeenth centuries, which condemned individual property and favoured State ownership with some degree of communal management, were still in vogue and at La Carolina and other places near Cordova Olavide founded colonies of Germans on this principle. In 1771 a collection of reports, the famous *Expediente Consultivo*, was drawn up to act as a basis for the preparation of a new agrarian law. Its chief recommendations were the giving of proper securities for tenants, such as the fixing of rents and the forbidding of

---

[1] See Note E on p. 127 at end of chapter.

[2] Actually some two-thirds of all the land in Andalusia was *baldío* or common land (See Jovellanos' *Informe sobre la Ley Agraria*, 1787) but the best land and all that lay near the villages either belonged to the Church and the nobles, or else was occupied by the flocks and herds of the local *poderosos*. In dry farming districts peasants without capital cannot cultivate any except the best land, since they starve with the first drought. And one must add the weakness and low vitality of the labouring classes, frequently mentioned in documents of the period, due to hunger and epidemics. This and the insecurity of the open country discouraged squatters. As to the large estates we have the definite assertion of Jovellanos that it paid the owners to cultivate them badly and to turn large areas over to cattle.

[3] The communes owned two kinds of land in Spain: the *bienes de propio*, which were lands rented out and the rents applied to paying the expenses of the municipality: and the *tierras comunes* or *concejiles*, which are common lands at the disposal of everyone in the village and rarely rented. The *bienes de propio* originally covered those services which are paid for in England by rates (a feeble equivalent here is the 'parish land'). But by the law of 1 May 1855 they were all sold and the sum obtained (after the usual deductions by caciques and local officials) placed in Government stock, where it has now greatly depreciated.

sub-letting or eviction: the obligation of landlords to let uncultivated lands: the dividing up of the *bienes de propio* in unalienable lots among the poorer neighbours and the creation of special allotments of good land near the villages. These were all measures which, though moderate in comparison to the suggestions of the seventeenth-century economists, had to await the coming of the Republic in 1931 to be given the force of law. Other recommendations (especially those of Olavide, the Commissioner for Seville) referred to the creation of new villages of small holdings which should be unalienable and indivisible on the *bienes de propio* and even in some cases on the large estates. These reports were accepted by the Council of Castile and some steps were taken to put them into force, but the dismissal of Aranda by María Luisa in favour of Godoy and then the French Revolution and the Napoleonic invasion put an end to the whole programme.[1] When the Cortes of Cadiz took up the question again in 1812 they followed the advice of the economist Jovellanos,[2] who was a disciple of Adam Smith, refused all truck with old-fashioned ideas of national ownership and began selling up the common lands on the open market to pay the national debt. This opened the sluice-gates. For there existed a large middle class anxious to find a good investment for its savings and to enhance its prestige by becoming landowners. Up to this time their chances of doing so had been slight, since almost all land in Spain that did not belong either to the Church or to the communes was entailed. Now they saw their opportunity, and since the peasants and small men lacked the capital to take up their share, the area occupied by large estates began to grow.

This fatal agrarian policy of the Liberals was resumed when they returned to power in the thirties. The Church property (some 12 million acres) was at once sold up at very low rates. A further sale of common lands followed. For an agricultural revolution was now beginning in Spain. Almost for the first time in her history since Roman days, Spain began to export agricultural products and land rose in value. Just as had happened in England in the sixteenth and eighteenth centuries, the more enterprising of the landlords and local capitalists began to look with longing on the common lands. The Cortes gave them every facility. They could not simply pass acts allowing them to appropriate them, as had been done in England— municipal authority and local feeling in Spain were too strong—but

[1] See Note F on p. 128 at end of chapter.
[2] See Note G on p. 129 at end of chapter.

by the law of 1836, and still more effectually by the laws of 1855 and 1856, all the *bienes de propio* and such of the common lands as were not claimed by the villages for their immediate use were ordered to be sold on the open market.[1] This was a very unpopular law and was resisted in towns and villages all over Spain down to the end of the century. It deprived the peasants of their common lands, especially of their grazing, and of their rights to game, firewood and charcoal. Again, the result, especially in Andalusia, was that the number of the large estates increased until the greater part of the land in Spain had passed into the possession of a class of *nouveaux riches* who worked it with a sharper eye to profit than the feudal landlords had done. At the same time peasant risings began in 1855 and recurred with increasing frequency during the next sixty years.

Thus, in the space of a few decades, this huge heritage of national property preserved from the past was squandered, the foundation laid by generations of enlightened legislators was destroyed, and the Spanish peasantry were handed over to the tender mercies of a new class of landlords who henceforth were to live at their expense. That has been the real meaning of parliamentary government in Spain. A doctrinaire Liberalism totally unsuited to Spanish conditions, united to a swarm of lawyers, tradesmen and petty capitalists anxious to enrich themselves by cultivating the land, brought this about. This is the class that since 1843 (the dictatorship of Narváez) has held political power in Spain—a middle class enriched not by trade or industry but by ownership of land—and though one must admit that it broke up the stagnation of Spanish rural life and brought with it a degree of prosperity that had not been known before, it led also to greater inequality in its distribution and to a destruction of those safeguards (among which must be numbered the power and wealth of the Church) that the poor had before possessed.

The twentieth century gave a new impetus to this development.

---

[1] The only dissident from the law of 1836 was Flórez Estrada, a Liberal deputy and landowner, who forms a bridge between the ideas of the previous century and those of the Socialists. He proposed that the large estates and common lands should be nationalized and rented to those who worked them. 'This', he said, 'would provide a collective agrarian solution in accordance with Spanish tradition.' Although this was the obvious way of dealing with the question, the Liberal deputies and their supporters were longing to buy up the land at low prices and no one listened to him.

Another act which hit the peasant severely was the forbidding of *derrotas* on private property by a decree in 1853. The right of the poor man to pasture his cattle in winter on the rich man's stubble and fallow had from time immemorial been one of the corner-stones of Spanish agriculture.

There was a great rise in the prices of agricultural products and fortunes were made all over Spain by owners of land. In many parts of
the country the price of land rose to ten times its former value within
a few years. The increase in the size of the industrial centres brought
large areas of poor and dry land under wheat, for since the sixteenth
century cereals have been protected by a fixed price, the *tasa*, which
allows them to be grown under otherwise unfavourable conditions.
The European War saw the culmination of this prosperity: every
cultivable acre of land was then sown, though the expansion had
occurred so rapidly and Spanish landowners were as a rule so deficient in capital and so little supported by the banks that there was still
great room for improvement in the quality of the crop.[1] Since then,
and especially since the slump that began in 1930, there has been a
considerable decrease in the area cultivated.

It should now be possible, after this long excursion back into
history, to view in better proportion the problem of the large estates.
They extend, as I have said, over the whole of the centre and south of
Spain, beginning at Salamanca, Valladolid, Cuenca, Albacete and
getting larger as they approach the south-west. In the three provinces
of Extremadura, Andalusia and La Mancha alone 7000 proprietors,
the greater part of them absentees, possess over 15 million acres.[2]

CASTILE

Let us take first the central tableland of La Mancha and Castile.
In Old Castile and as far south as the Tagus Valley the estates still
belong for the most part to the nobility. The poorer the land the
more nobles there are on it, as a Spanish proverb says, and few of
these estates are large. Their origin goes back to the tenth and
eleventh centuries, to the first stage of the Reconquista, when the
kings and nobles, needing urgently to repopulate what were then
uninhabited wastes, granted land on easy terms both to individual
farmers and to communities of peasants. For this reason a considerable proportion of the soil (especially to the north of the Guadarrama)
belongs to small peasant farmers and certain villages still own their
own land and work it communally.[3] The peasants live in mud-
coloured houses built of sun-dried bricks and roofed with red tiles:

---

[1] The yearly value of agricultural production rose from 81½ million pounds
sterling in the period 1897-1901 to 306⅔ in the period 1927-1928 (Madariaga,
Spain).   [2] See Pascual Carrión, *Los Latifundios en España*, 1932.
[3] See Note H on p. 129 at end of chapter.

the villages, smaller than in most parts of Spain, have an average population of under four thousand. Each owner or tenant farmer (for the estates are almost invariably let) has his plot of land, his yoke of oxen and his house in the village. The only crops are wheat and barley: the peasants grow few garden vegetables and often in the whole village there is not a single tree. The soil, too, except in the *Tierras de Campos*, is poor and the rainfall uncertain. Droughts are common and even a total failure of the crop. Since there is no effective system of agrarian credit[1] and no spread of crops the farmers must often have recourse to money-lenders. These are one of the worst plagues of the Castilian farmer or small peasant. The other is the short, unjust and insecure form of the lease.

The long, share-cropping leases of the north, in which the owner and tenant live on intimate terms and take a common interest in the land, seem never to have existed in Castile. The typical lease here is, or rather used to be, the *censo*, a hereditary emphyteusis or quit-rent which came into vogue with the breakdown of feudal conditions.[2] Towards the end of the Middle Ages the feudal dues which the village communities paid to the lord of the manor in return for a grant of land, which they held in common and (so it would seem) divided up by lot every few years among their members, were converted into a fixed rent or canon in kind which each separate villager paid into the manor barn, in exchange for the right to occupy his house and culti-vate his strip of land in perpetuity. Generally speaking, wherever similar feudal conditions prevailed—that is in Leon, parts of Catalonia and Aragon and (after the expulsion of the Moriscos) in Valencia, but

---

[1] See on this the Vizconde de Eza, minister in various Conservative Govern-ments and a famous authority on land reform. 'In spite of all the associations, syndicates and deposit banks scattered through Spain—all of them Catholic—and the State Credit Bank, one must admit that a mechanism for agrarian credit simply does not exist' (*Agrarismo*, 1936, p. 178). The *pósitos* or rural credit funds of the municipalities, first set up in the sixteenth century, were quite insufficient. And one should add that the Catholic credit associations, when they existed, were not altogether a pure gain, since like the caciques they made trouble for anyone who did not vote for the Catholic candidate. See on this J. Chamberlain, *El Atraso de España*, 1919. The only province where they really took root was Old Castile.

[2] The Castilian *censo* is the *bail héréditaire* of the French, which under the name of *emphyteusis* was introduced into the public lands of the Italian communes and on the imperial *latifundia* during the late Roman Empire. To counteract the lack of slaves the land was let in perpetuity at a fixed rate to anyone who would cultivate it. The rent or canon, as it was called, was low and the tenant was obliged to keep the property in repair. The practice of letting land on this system, though it goes back to the eleventh century, became general in Castile in the sixteenth century, when the nobles gave up living on their estates and took houses at the court or in the nearest town.

not in the mountains of the north and not in Andalusia—similar conversions took place. Later, for the greater convenience of the lord, who had gone to live in a town, payment of the canon came to be made in a fixed annual sum of money. Now, as has already been explained, the tendency of the *censo* or *foro* is to separate the landowner from all connection with his land and to make the peasant the virtual owner of the soil he cultivates. But in Castile this did not occur. Partly owing to the bad agricultural and climatic conditions of the central tableland, which prevented the Castilian peasant from acquiring the same independence as his Galician and Valencian brothers, partly owing to the proximity to Madrid and to all kinds of special psychological factors, the Castilian nobility never lost their connection with their estates. During the last century frequent bankruptcies and failures to pay rent resulted in the conversion of many of the *censos* to short-term leases. Special legislation was passed to assist this and to-day the *censo* is becoming a thing of the past. The short lease, which under the conditions that prevail in Spain is necessarily productive of poverty and deterioration of the land, has become the rule. In such leases everything is loaded against the tenant in favour of the landlord, who, one must insist again, has no obligations whatever, since he does not pay the taxes and cannot even be compelled to keep his houses and farms in proper repair. Yet he can evict and raise rents as he pleases. This situation has grown much worse in recent years with the appearance of the land speculator and with the increase of hate between the classes. It leads to innumerable abuses. New landlords, who wish to take advantage of the land hunger, can subdivide the lots till there is not enough on each to support a family. Other landlords who live in Madrid and rarely visit their estates are unaware that their tenants frequently have to pay a second rent to the stewards. As the history of Ireland in the last century shows, this is a common accompaniment of absentee landlordism. And one can well understand how under this system few labourers or farmers dared to vote for any candidate who did not have a Conservative ticket.[1]

What was particularly serious was that this system of short leases, with all its accompanying abuses, was spreading. Owing to the loss of confidence between classes the *aparcería* or share-cropping system, which is the only satisfactory form of short contract, now only worked in the north. Many small farmers owning their own land had, for lack of a proper credit system, been squeezed out. The first Govern-

[1] See Note I on p. 129 at end of chapter.

ments of the Republic imposed restrictions upon landowners with a
view to rectifying these abuses, but the succeeding Governments of
Lerroux and Gil Robles either repealed them or allowed them to lapse.
Thus the condition both of the peasant who owned his land and of the
small tenant farmer has been growing steadily worse.

Two examples of the wretched level on which these men live will
suffice. In that part of Spain which had been assessed by 1929, out of
1,026,412 landowners or tenants paying taxes, 847,548 earned daily
less than one peseta. And in the typical Castilian province of Avila,
out of 13,530 land-tax payers, 11,452 had a daily income of less than
one peseta and only 320 had more than five pesetas.[1] These figures
show a high degree of poverty.

LA MANCHA AND EXTREMADURA

As one travels south of the Tagus towards La Mancha and Extremadura the estates increase in size and the number of small proprietors and tenant farmers diminishes. These estates have a different
origin to those of Old Castile. They were formed during the second
stage of the Reconquista, between 1085 and 1248, when the kings had
begun to incorporate territory that already had a settled Moslem
population. The land so conquered was given not to individual nobles
but to the newly constituted military orders, who, forming as they did
the principal force of cavalry in the realm, were better able to defend
it. Instead of settling on it communities of free peasants, they worked
it partly with Moorish slave labour and partly with labourers who
drifted in from the north, and turned the rest over to pasture. That is
why these estates are larger than those in Northern Castile and organized on a different basis. Their peculiar name, later transferred to
the slave-worked estates of the American colonies, was *encomienda*.[2]
In 1837 these lands were sold by the Government and bought up, as
already described, by the middle classes in the towns.

Conditions in these districts are, on the whole, worse than in Old
Castile, since the land is poorer and the rainfall less. Round Valdepeñas the vineyards give some prosperity. Round Albacete there
are huge tracts of rough steppe pasture and underwood used as

[1] Pascual Carrión, *op. cit.* Also Madariaga, *Spain.*
[2] An *encomienda* was an estate given by the King in *señorío*, or with full manorial
rights, for one lifetime or for some determinate period only. The Comendador was
the title of the temporary possessor, who enjoyed all or most of the rights of the
King. After the twelfth century *encomiendas* died out except in the military orders,
in which they were the recognized form of land tenure.

shooting estates or for breeding mules. Elsewhere the short lease has become general.

Extremadura, on the Portuguese frontier, is also a region of very large estates and of abject poverty. It is a great stock-breeding country, and the old conflict between the agriculturalist and the nomadic herdsman still goes on. One can trace this back as far as the Roman Conquest and the war of Viriathus. In more recent times, however, the main agrarian question has been different. On the plains round Badajoz is the rich corn-growing land that once helped to give its prosperity to the city of Mérida. This land belongs almost entirely to large absentee proprietors who cultivate it badly, whilst the typical peasant is the landless *yuntero* who owns a team of ploughing mules which he grazes on the commons. Thus when the landowners wish to reduce the *yunteros* to order, they have only to let some of their land go out of cultivation. This problem of the landowner and the *yuntero*, which was so acute in the eighteenth century that the State had to intervene to solve it, is just as acute to-day, and we shall see the Republic forced in May 1936 to a hasty repartition of the large estates to avoid their being seized forcibly. In Spain kings and governments legislate, centuries pass, yet the fundamental problems remain unchanged.

The remaining parts of the province are so poor that only catch crops can be grown once in about twelve years. One crop exhausts the soil completely.[1] Yet the rivers are full of water and have a steep fall. Large tracts of this country could be irrigated.

ANDALUSIA

There remains only Andalusia, the classic land of the *latifundia* or slave-worked estates. Here we at once find ourselves on very different historical and geographical ground. These great estates, which cluster round the Guadalquivir Valley near Cordova and occupy wide areas along the lower reaches of the river, have come down in much their present form from Roman times. Ruined by the Roman fiscal system and by the pastoral habits of the Visigoths, reconstituted on a more

---

[1] Extremadura provides an extreme example of those multiple rights in land which are so typical of Spain. Much of the country consists in park-land, thinly planted with cork oaks. The right of winter pasturage may then belong to one person, of cutting cork to another, of collecting the dead branches to a third, of pasturing swine to a fourth and of growing a catch crop every five or six years to a fifth. All these rights may be absolute and hereditary: the ground landlord, if one exists, receives only a peppercorn rent.

magnificent scale by the Arabs, the property first of the Arab and Moorish tribes and then of princes and kings, they were handed over intact by Ferdinand III to the feudal lords who accompanied him in his conquest of Seville. Since that day they have provided the revenues of the great aristocratic houses of Castile. But not more than a third of the large estates that one sees in Andalusia to-day have this origin. The greater part were formed out of the break-up of the lands of the Church and the common lands in the nineteenth century. Bought at very low prices they made the fortunes of the middle-class families who acquired them and gave political power to the class which has ruled Spain since that day. And since the new estates rapidly took on the worst characteristics of the feudal latifundia that stretched alongside them, one may say that to-day there has ceased to be any real distinction between them.

The old province of Andalusia or Baetica is formed by the basin of the Guadalquivir and the mountains that contain it. It is a land of rolling country, of both good and indifferent soil and of moderate rainfall (20 to 40 inches and even more near Cadiz), but the high degree of evaporation and the long rainless summer make the conservation of moisture the main problem for the agriculturalist. This fortunate region of Spain, as it is called by those who have only a passing acquaintance with it, offers a greater variety of crops than the central tableland, where as a rule only wheat and barley can be grown. The chief crop of the upper basin is the olive: round Cordova and Jaén are to be found the largest and richest olive estates in the world. Other crops are wheat, maize, leguminous plants and especially grapes. Near Seville the conditions are favourable for cotton. This variety of crops gives or could give a considerable spread of labour, but it must be remembered that their cultivation is conditioned by the dryness, which limits the productivity per acre and the possibilities of rotation. This is above everything else a country of dry farming.

The special exigencies of dry farming are not always understood by people from other parts of Europe. For example, travellers in Spain have in all ages been struck by the vast amount of untilled soil or fallow land and have put this down to the laziness or incompetence of the Spaniards. That is not necessarily the case. As we have seen when dealing with Extremadura, there are many parts of Spain where the soil is so poor and so dry that one catch-crop exhausts it for eight or twelve years. Through a large part of Castile the custom used to be to sow land only once in four years. In Andalusia the classical system has been what is known as *al tercio*, by which land is left for one year in stubble, then ploughed and left for another year fallow (*de barbecho*) and only in the third year sown. The tendency to-day is to sow at least every second year (*año y vez*).[1] But there are difficulties in that. Not only is there the problem of refertilizing the soil, but there is also that of replenishing its moisture. These are not easy to solve simultaneously. Excessive use of artificial manures leads to over-salinity, whereas if cattle are turned on to the land, the weeds they feed on (besides being very short-lived) dissipate the water. Fallows to-day are therefore mostly clean ones and the refertilizing of the soil is left to bacteria produced by the sun's rays. Experiments with special types of agricultural machinery which pulverize the soil and so diminish evaporation have shown the possibility of getting good crops out of dry lands every year with scarcely any help from fertilizers, but how far these methods can be applied to any but the best soils is still uncertain. Intensive dry farming is a scientific problem that must be solved by Spain. The great dry-farming districts in the Middle West of America have not approached it, because they do not have to support more than a fraction of the population. For this is the fundamental problem of Andalusia—how to support a large population on a dry soil.[2] But it is complicated to such a point by bad organization and by appalling social conditions that the merely geographical factors are apt to fade into the background. These social conditions are what we must now investigate.

As one descends the Guadalquivir Valley past Cordova to Seville and Cadiz the number of large estates increases.[3] They account for about 41 per cent of the total area of the province of Cordova, 50 per cent of that of Seville and 58 per cent of that of Cadiz. In three of the *partidos* or administrative districts of the province of Cadiz the large estates occupy 77, 84, and 96 per cent of the total area. And what is more significant, the large estates occupy the best land.[4] In Castile,

---

[1] See Note J on p. 129 at end of chapter.

[2] The population of Andalusia is only relatively large: excluding the principal towns, it is under 50 to the square mile. (Compare Belgium 264, Germany 137, Italy 134, for agricultural areas only.) But then Huesca and Guadalajara have only 17 and Teruel and Cuenca only 18.

[3] For purposes of land survey, estates of over 250 hectares (625 acres) are classified as large estates or latifundia. I shall keep to that definition here. Unless otherwise stated, figures given in this chapter are from Pascual Carrión.

[4] The concentration of property in a few hands is really far greater than these figures show, because they are based upon the areas of individual estates and there are no figures that show the numbers of estates held by the same family. The amount of land owned by individual proprietors is a jealously guarded secret in Spain. The

New Castile and the Levante, the capital value of the large estates is not more than 5 per cent of the total value, showing that they occupy the bad land. In La Mancha the figure is from 21 to 26 per cent and in Extremadura it is from 25 to 30 per cent. But in Andalusia it is much higher—49 per cent for Seville and Cordova and more for Cadiz. In Seville therefore one finds that 50 per cent of the area of the province belongs to the large estates and produces 49 per cent of the total wealth—the medium-sized estates producing 33 per cent and the small estates only 18 per cent. Since the small and medium-sized estates are more intensively worked, this would show that the large estates occupy most of the best ground.

Arranging the figures in another way one finds that in the province of Seville 2344 proprietors (i.e. all those possessing more than 25 acres), constituting 5 per cent of the total number of proprietors, produce 72 per cent of the total agricultural wealth. Further that, taking Andalusia as a whole,[1] the average yearly income of a large proprietor from his estates is 18,000 pesetas, whilst the average yearly income of a small proprietor (possessing under 25 acres) is 161 pesetas.[2] Since there are 4101 such large proprietors and approximately 200,000 such small proprietors in this area, it is clear that these figures (even when one allows for the fact that the small proprietor consumes yearly some 700 pesetas worth of his own produce, which should therefore be added to the 160 pesetas he spends) show an enormous disparity of wealth. Yet it is not the small proprietor who is the characteristic problem of Andalusia, but the completely landless men, descendants of the slaves and 'poor whites' who once worked them—the agricultural proletariat of the large estates.[3]

State has no record of it. E. H. G. Dobby in the course of an investigation into conditions at Ecija and Carmona was given figures that showed that, on an average, every proprietor in those districts owned four estates there. It is common knowledge that rich families often hold property in several provinces, sometimes under different names. Pascual Carrión estimates that some 10,000 families own nearly half the land that has been surveyed in Spain. The unsurveyed part (north and north-east) would of course show a far more equal distribution of property.

[1] For the purposes of the Land Survey Andalusia (Baetica) comprises the five provinces of Jaén, Cordova, Seville, Cadiz and Huelva, but not Granada, Malaga or Almería.

[2] The average yearly incomes for Old Castile show even greater extremes—23,000 pesetas for the large proprietors and 102 for the small. But then the number of large proprietors is far less, whilst the average holding of the small proprietors is smaller. Everywhere in Spain, except in one or two favoured districts, the land belongs either to large landowners or to small poor peasants: the yeoman farmer is the exception.

[3] As I have already pointed out it seems likely that the peculiar demoralization of the landless labourers of Lower Andalusia was due to the fact that Christian peasants

The inhabitants of Andalusia are not scattered in farms or villages (there are very few villages in the Guadalquivir Basin and the occasional farms one sees are new), but are concentrated in towns that have a population of from 8000 to 25,000. In between these towns, which generally occupy ancient Iberian sites and lie at some distance from one another, there is open country. An English or French town that has 12,000 inhabitants is a busy place. Not so an Andalusian pueblo of the same size. Let us take, for example, Osuna in the province of Seville with a population of 16,000 or else Morón with 19,000 or even Carmona with 22,000.[1] The first impression is one of decay and stagnation. A few wretched shops selling only the bare necessities of life: one or two petty industries—soap-making, weaving of esparto mats, potteries, oil-distilleries that between them employ some couple of hundred men: the ancestral houses of the absentee landowners, dilapidated and falling into ruin: then a few bourgeois families—the overseers of the large estates or the farmers who rent from them—and who only remain here because their interests compel them to: from eight to twelve hundred families, mostly poor, who own or rent a small property or have some settled employment. And then the landless proletariat. Three-quarters of the population consists in these men and their families, who are hired by the day, by the month, by the season—rarely for longer than that—by the overseers of the large estates or by the tenant farmers who rent from them. For more than half the year they are unemployed.

The more closely one examines the conditions in this area of large estates, the more terrible and shocking they are seen to be. Till the

cultivated their share of the common lands side by side with the Moslem serfs who worked on the large estates. The tendency to turn arable into pasture then spreading, the *poderosos* monopolized the common lands for their large herds and the peasants were thrown out of work. Many of them gravitated to the large estates and, mixing with the serfs employed on them, sank to form a Christian race of inferior category. There were still serfs of the glebe in Andalusia down to the middle of the eighteenth century.

This did not happen in Valencia and Aragon because there almost all the land was owned by the nobles, who cultivated it with Moorish labour, and when these Moors were expelled in 1602 their place was taken by tenants who rented it on the *censo* system.

[1] Compare Newbury with 13,000, Bideford with 9000, Cirencester with 7000, Wantage with under 4000. Ecija, a town of 30,000, has far worse shops than Wantage. Yet these provinces are the richest in Spain. The *liquido imponible*—i.e. the yearly product of the land after the costs of production have been deducted—of the province of Seville amounts to 71 million pesetas, more than that of any of the other provinces that have been surveyed. Compare Toledo 35 millions, Granada 40, Cordova 42, Malaga 27, Avila 16. Yet Seville is, with Cadiz, the province where the poverty of the men who work on the land is more extreme than in any other part of Spain.

European War the landlords generally worked their estates directly under overseers. They cultivated only the best land and left the rest untilled. Starving labourers who attempted to plough it were beaten by the police. During the war it paid them to cultivate the whole of it, but since 1918 the area of uncultivated land began inevitably to grow again. In 1931, for example, there were 33,000 acres uncultivated at Osuna and 50,000 at Utrera: at Jerez de los Caballeros a certain duke kept 56,000 acres uncultivated as a shooting estate.[1] No doubt a considerable proportion of this land was only fit for rough pasture. However, near Seville there are still 75,000 acres of the very best land given up to bull breeding, and in the province of Cadiz, where there is good rainfall, the amount of arable land employed in horse and cattle breeding is enormous.

Such a lack of self-interest in rich landowners living in Madrid or Seville may appear extraordinary, but the average aristocrat simply took the advice of his steward and did not bother his head about estates where he knew no one by sight and which he regarded very much as if they were in some distant colony. When for example the Duke of Alba, who has not got the reputation of being a bad landlord, visited his ancestral acres he did so with an equipment of lorries and tents, as though he were travelling in the centre of Africa. Very often, too, the owner did not have the capital to develop the land, and the banks would not lend it to him. And then, as Señor Madariaga has pointed out, there were sometimes special reasons for reducing the area under cultivation. By taking advantage of the unemployment so caused he could knock something off the wages and so 'reduce the rebellious workers to submission'.

Since the slump that followed the war and especially since the coming of the Dictatorship the tendency of the large landowners has been to rent out more and more of their estates. In 1930 between 70 and 80 per cent of the large Andalusian estates were rented in farms of from 100 to 1000 acres. The rents paid were high—at Carmona, a typical Sevillian district, they were 6½ per cent on the capital value of the land.[2] And it must be remembered that the landlord had no obligations—he neither paid taxes, nor kept his houses in repair nor

[1] See Nicolo Pascazio, *La Rivoluzione di Spagna*, 1933. As to the bull pastures, these have existed from the remotest antiquity. Strabo describes the black bulls feeding by the river just as one sees them to-day and speaks of their descent from the oxen of Geryon.
[2] Information given me by E. H. G. Dobby, who made a special study of the agrarian conditions in this district.

spent money on improving his estate. E. H. G. Dobby describes how he once pointed out to a large tenant farmer the encroaching palmetto scrub on his fields. 'Let the landlord see to it', was his angry reply. And so the condition of the land was slowly deteriorating. The position since 1928 of these tenant farmers, caught between a falling market and a rising wages bill, has been intolerable.

We can now approach the question of the *braceros* or landless labourers, who make up three-quarters of the population. Their wages to begin with: in 1930 they were earning on an average from 3 to 3.50 pesetas (i.e. 1s. 6d. to 1s. 9d.) for an eight-hour day during four or five months of the year. In summer—under the terrible heat of the Andalusian sun—they earned from 4 to 6 pesetas (2s. to 3s.)—for a twelve-hour day during two or three months.[1] During the rest of the year—that is during four, five, or six months—they were unemployed. Since there were no small holdings for them to work in, no allotments, not even a patch of garden to their houses and absolutely no system of municipal or Church or State relief, they would have starved during their spells of unemployment, but for the credit given by the shops. As it was they lived in a state of chronic hunger and the deaths from malnutrition, which reach a high figure in almost every part of the Peninsula, were here particularly numerous. One cannot, even in Spain, bring up a family on from 600 to 1000 pesetas (£15 to £25) a year, without the resources that the English country-side gives of a garden or allotment, wiring a rabbit, doing an odd job here and there.

And I have not given the lowest figures. On the distant farms and in the mountain hamlets wages dropped to 2.25 pesetas a day for men and to from 1.0 to 1.25 pesetas for women.[2] In out-of-the-way places the eight-hour day was not observed. The periods of unemployment were often even longer than five or six months, especially when there were spells of wet weather or drought, and any men whom the land-lords had a grudge against failed to get work at all except during harvest.[3] In 1930 there were over 200,000 labourers unemployed in Andalusia during the greater part of the year and after 1930 this figure increased rapidly.

---

[1] See Note K on p. 130 at end of chapter.

[2] See Note L on p. 130 at end of chapter.

[3] At Montilla, with a population of 16,000, in a district which has a high standard of farming and a considerable variety of crops, there were, in 1924, 3000 labourers unemployed for a considerable part of the year. This was in a period of boom, at the beginning of the Dictatorship. The minimum number of days of unemployment was 90. In other parts of Andalusia it was 150. (F. de los Ríos, *Agrarian Problems in Spain*.)

During the ploughing and the harvest, which occupied several months, the labourers would leave their families and sleep at the large *cortijos*, which would often be some ten or twenty miles away from the village. They slept, men and women together, sometimes a hundred at a time, on the floor of a long room called the *gañanía*, which had a fireplace at one end. The landowner fed them: except at harvest time, when they were given beans, the only dish was *gazpacho*, a soup of oil, vinegar and water with bread floating on the top. They took it hot for breakfast, cold for lunch, hot again at night. Sometimes to this diet of maize bread and oil, potatoes and garlic would be added. When the landlord provided the food, the wages were rarely more than 1.5 pesetas, for which they generally worked 12 hours, with rests. These conditions, first described in 1904 by Blasco Ibáñez in his novel *La Bodega* and, later, by A. Marvaud and other investigators, had not appreciably changed by 1930 in Lower Andalusia, as I can testify from personal experience.

And the housing conditions: great numbers of these families did not own any furniture except a cooking pot and ate their meals like animals on the ground. But I will quote E. H. G. Dobby, whose impartiality is evident to anyone who has read his monographs.

'I recall an incident during a visit (in 1935) to an experimental pig farm in an out-of-the-way part of Andalusia. From the darkness at one end of the building came a red glow. I went along and found a labourer's family crouched on the floor round a twig fire with smoke so thick that breathing was difficult. The malodorous squalor contrasted with the carefully washed sties that I had been seeing. To my query an old woman mumbled: "Yes, we live here. Worse than the pigs." At which the owner beside me exclaimed indignantly: "You have a roof over your head. What more do you want?"'[1]

Such wages, such conditions to-day may seem almost incredible. They are unique in Europe.[2] And yet the tenant farmers, under the pressure of high rents and taxes and falling markets, cannot afford to pay more. For since 1850, and indeed from far earlier times, there has been a steady competition between landowner and labourer, the first to see how little he can pay, and the latter to see how little he can work. Andalusian workmen, given the opportunity, are the hardest working and most skilled manual labourers in Spain. After all they are many of them the descendants of the 'industrious Moors' of the

[1] See Note M on p. 130 at end of chapter.
[2] See Note N on p. 130 at end of chapter.

history books, few of whom ever came from Morocco.[1] But when so many of their comrades are unemployed, it becomes a point of honour with them to do as little work as possible. And they are also well aware of the manner in which they are exploited. In these towns the atmosphere of hatred between classes—of tenant for landlord, of landless proletariat for everyone who employs him—has to be seen to be believed. Since the Republic came in many landlords have been afraid to visit their estates. And the labourers are all Anarchists. What else can one expect under such conditions—miserable pay, idleness for half the year and semi-starvation for all of it? The herding together of labourers for months at a time away from their families also increases their receptivity to revolutionary ideas. And legal methods of protesting are ruled out: the cacique system is at its worst in Andalusia and regularly at every election Catholic-Conservative deputies are returned for Anarchist constituencies. When force ceases to be possible, bribery takes its place, and down to the last election of 1936 tens of thousands of starving labourers took the money or promises of work of the landlords and voted for their candidates.[2]

What is the remedy for these conditions? In the first place something could be done by compelling landlords to cultivate their land better, by insisting on a greater variety of crops and by facilitating credits. In Lower Andalusia, as in Castile, there are no olives and no vines—only wheat and barley, which give little spread of labour. The standard of cultivation is usually low: intensive methods (especially in the vineyards) would double the employment.[3] Local industries could

---

[1] See Note O on p. 130 at end of chapter.

[2] Lower Andalusia is probably the only region in Europe where the condition of the agricultural workers has not improved in the last hundred and fifty years. Towards 1780 Campomanes wrote: 'In Andalusia the inhabitants are nearly all simple labourers who have only temporary and precarious occupation and live the rest of the year in poverty, plunged in inaction, for lack of remunerative work. Their wives and children are without work and all, piled up in the towns and large villages, live on charity . . . in a wretched starvation—which does not correspond to the fertility of the soil and certainly is not caused by their idleness' (*Cartas político-económicas*, Carta III). This is an exact description of the state of affairs to-day.

[3] One of the intensive methods of culture proper to Andalusia, but rare in Castile, is the repeated hoeing (*escardar*) of wheat and oats. It was not as a rule practised by the ancients, but was introduced by the Arabs in the twelfth century. Abu Zacaría quotes a book of agriculture by Kutsami, a Nabathaean (i.e. a Chaldean), who recommended it. Since then it has been the custom in Andalusia to hoe all sown land twice and this gives a good deal of employment. But landlords, to cut their labour costs, have recently been reserving it for the best land. The same thing applies to ploughing. In dry farming areas the land needs to be ploughed several times between crops to pulverize the soil and reduce evaporation. This has been the custom since early times, but lately many landowners have neglected it.

also be stimulated. Why, for example, should Spain, the largest producer of olive oil in the world, send so much of her oil to be refined abroad? Then considerable tracts of land could be irrigated. Andalusian landowners have usually objected to irrigation because they feared that their lands would then be expropriated in favour of small proprietors, who work them better; round Seville and Cordova, for example, they for a long time opposed every scheme. Altogether there were some $3\frac{1}{2}$ million acres in Spain under irrigation in 1931 and on a conservative estimate this area could be doubled without an unreasonable outlay. Since irrigated land produces from six to thirty times the amount produced by unirrigated land, the gain is obvious, but a whole generation of peace and prosperity would be needed to build and pay for the necessary engineering works. The Civil War has put off such projects indefinitely.

The other more fundamental remedy is the breaking up of the large estates and their cultivation by the men who at present work on them. In most cases the land could not be divided among individual families. The only reasonable solution through wide tracts of Spain is a collective one. This, as I have explained, has respectable antecedents in Spanish history, and it has recently been adopted in many parts of Southern Italy (the *affitanze collective*), but the fact that such methods have come to be associated with Soviet Russia has not recommended them either to the Right or to the Republican parties. In many districts the peasants are themselves averse to it, but the anarchist ideology in Andalusia has made it the favourite solution there and this is a factor which any sensible government would take advantage of.

For the advantages of communal ownership of the land are enormous. Under present conditions one has agricultural labourers dying of hunger on estates where large tracts of corn-growing land lie fallow because it does not pay to cultivate them. The high labour costs (due to geographical conditions) of Spanish wheat forbid export abroad, and as much as can be sold at the price current in Spain, though not nearly as much as could be eaten, is already grown. If the villagers could cultivate their land collectively, using modern machinery, they could feed themselves and sell the surplus. Hunger would disappear and, without injury to the State, their anarchist ideology, or all that matters to them of it, would be satisfied. Moreover, that division of interests between peasants and town workers, which exists in every European country except Spain and which the middle classes so much desire, would at once make its appearance. Only the incurable stupidity of the Spanish ruling classes and their governments and the ignorance of the traditionalist parties, who seem not to have the slightest notion of the conditions under which Spaniards really lived in the age which they profess to imitate, have prevented agrarian reform from being carried out long ago.

Since the refusal of the Spanish upper classes to yield an inch in this question has been the most important single cause of the Civil War, it is necessary to emphasize it. Their obstinacy is, moreover, at complete variance with the times. In most parts of Central and Eastern Europe the estates of the nobles that down to 1918 covered the land have been broken up and handed over to the peasants. It was those same peasants, who, in the troubled years of 1918-1923, formed, as they still form to-day, the barrier against Bolshevism. One might have supposed that the Spanish Church and the ruling classes would realize this. But Spain is a peninsula, cut off from the rest of Europe, psychologically and climatically at variance with its neighbours, and this isolation has produced among certain classes an obstinacy and resistance to change which neither facts nor arguments have any effect upon.

There is not much that need be said here about the industrial workers. Although numerically they were nearly half as numerous as the land workers, the greater part of them were agricultural labourers and sons of poor peasants who had flowed into the towns, and still kept the habits and ways of thought of countrymen. This was especially the case in Barcelona, where about half the factory workers were immigrants from the drought-ridden provinces of Almería and Murcia. This greatly helped to give that city its revolutionary character, so surprising when one considers its prosperity. Generally speaking the conditions of life of the industrial workers were much more favourable than those of the peasants and agricultural labourers. In the large centres of Catalonia and Asturias, and especially at Bilbao and in the Rio Tinto mines, they had obtained quite recently by organization and strikes a relatively high standard of living. In the smaller mining and industrial centres their wages were still miserable when the Republic came in, and the working conditions in the mines themselves were often very bad. But this was remediable. The poverty and unemployment among large sections of the middle classes presented a more serious problem, for here the cause lay in the disorganization and inertness of the whole Spanish economic structure and in old hereditary vices which could not be remedied in a moment.

Yet there is perhaps no country in Europe whose economic organization presents fewer difficulties than that of Spain. To begin with, the Spaniards are to a very great extent self-supporting. They grow all their own food supplies except coffee. The factories at Barcelona, which produce only for the home market, furnish most of their other needs. Many of their chief exports, iron ore, mercury, potash, copper, pyrites, olive oil, early potatoes and onions, Canary bananas, command ready markets. Others such as oranges and wine could be more easily sold if they were not so badly organized. The Spanish economic problem can be summed up as that of how to increase the buying power of the country districts so as to give more work to the towns. It must of course be borne in mind that the principal food stuffs, such as bread and meat, can only be produced at figures that are substantially above world prices, and that this in turn raises the wages of the industrial workers and becomes a fixed charge on the standard of living of the country. To decrease the duties on corn and meat would be to ruin Spanish agriculture. But Spaniards do not ask to live on the same scale of comfort as Englishmen: both the climate and the frugal customs make that unnecessary, so that this disadvantage is more apparent than real. And even within the capitalist framework a proper organization of the banking and industrial system would reduce the present unnecessarily high manufacturing costs.

But it is obvious that the closed economic system of Spain lends itself with particular aptness to a socialist experiment. The Spanish temperament also points that way. The famous individualism of the race does not apply to economics. Liberalism failed in Spain because Spaniards are essentially anti-capitalist and uncompetitive: they have neither the bad nor the good qualities, neither the attachment to money for its own sake nor the suppleness and perseverance required for success in the modern capitalist world. As a rule they are happier in the shelter of Government posts, where they multiply readily, or in those professions where they can devote themselves to serious ends, than in what they consider to be the sordid struggle of business life. If there has been so much corruption in Spain, it has been due partly, of course, to poverty, but also to the fact that Spaniards do not naturally distinguish between the money transactions that are practised by every European business man and simple stealing. In these matters they have a mediaeval conscience more delicate than ours, which tells them that all sudden or unjustified gain, unless of course it comes as the will of Allah in the form of a lottery prize, is a crime.

Such a frame of mind invites Socialism, and one can not help thinking that if the Russian Revolution had not linked that word to the most terrible savagery and misery and if Marxists had not narrowed it down to the most rigid and doctrinaire of creeds, a moderate Socialist regime might have come into existence in Spain without bloodshed. There are many factors in Spanish character and history that point in that direction.

FURTHER NOTES ON CHAPTER VI

A (p. 89). The people and the clergy against the ruling classes—how often this situation recurs in Spanish history! To dismiss it however, as the Marxists do, as an example of a Lumpenproletariat led by monkish agitators for their own ends is seriously to misunderstand the whole business. In most of these risings there was a community of interests and the people gained materially. An early example of such an alliance occurs in Moslem times when the *faquis* and the people regularly combined against the legitimate rulers (at first the Caliphs, then the Taifa kings) in favour of some more religiously minded dynasty. Here religion and self-interest were closely intermingled, for the Koran forbade the imposition of any other taxes than the poll tax and a fixed land tax, and the Caliphs and kings with their expensive courts and large armies to support had had the impiety to break this law. Again, under Christian rule, the rising against the Jews was indirectly a movement against the nobles who protected them and intermarried with them, whilst the expulsion of the Moriscos in 1602 was a deliberate attack on the large landowners who worked their lands with Moorish slaves and were now forced to let them on generous terms to small holders. In fact this expulsion is simply the last battle of the social struggle called the Germanía. In the War of the Spanish Succession one has a different situation: this was a civil war, Castile fighting Catalonia and both clergy and people divided. The monks and priests led the popular forces on both sides, because long custom had made them the natural leaders of the people and Spaniards cannot conceive of wars which have no ideological significance.

B (p. 98). All travellers to Spain in the eighteenth and early nineteenth centuries speak of the terrifying poverty and ignorance of the peasants of Old Castile, in spite of their having an abundant rainfall and a good soil. There were many reasons for this, one a crushing land tax, farmed out to ruthless collectors and another an inheritance law by which the land had to be equally divided among the children. The Conde de Cabarrús, who was one of Charles's III's ministers, writes of it as follows: 'I turn again with horror to that immense and incoherent mass of theocracy, republicanism, military despotism, feudal anarchy, ancient errors and modern extravagances, that mass of 36,000 laws with their formidable commentaries, and I say that to such a monstrous tyranny I prefer liberty and, with all their risks, the laws of nature.' (*Cartas sobre los Obstáculos que la Naturaleza, la Opinión y las Leyes oponen á la Felicidad Pública*, 1808.)
Anyone tempted to decry the innovations brought by the Liberal regime should compare the state of Old Castile in 1808 with its state in 1932 and again with its state to-day.

C (p. 103). It may be of interest to contrast the character of Moslem and Christian Spain in the eleventh and twelfth centuries as reflected in their different forms of land tenure. The intensive cultivation of the land in Andalusia was merely the inevitable consequence of the springing up there of large-scale industry. This in its turn was due to the commercial instincts of the Arabs and to their control of the

Mediterranean Basin. It was natural therefore that land should be regarded by them as a merchandise, capable of being bought and sold and susceptible to appreciation and depreciation. Although some large estates remained from the first partition after the conquest, the greater part of the land was either state property or belonged to small peasant farmers, mostly of Berber origin, who had squatted on the *baldíos* or commons that at the time of the Visigothic Kingdom covered three-quarters of the country. The state lands (which included most of the best soil) were at first cultivated by serfs, who worked them for their own benefit, but paid a fixed proportion (usually two-thirds) of the crop to the State. The same was true of the private properties, where the proportion paid was higher. But the tendency was for these serfs to improve the conditions of their labour and to liberate themselves, so that gradually there grew up a class of small farmers and peasants who either owned their own lands or rented them on the share-cropping principle. Large-scale private property did not increase because the State early adopted the practice of allotting life rents to its beneficiaries out of certain estates without alienating or losing control over them. These peasants were the stabilizing influence in the Caliphate.

In Christian Spain one of these tendencies is observable: serfs were replaced by free peasants paying a fixed rent in kind and this change took place earlier and was more thorough-going than in Moslem lands. But there were two great differences. The Moslems lacked even the most elementary feudal system. Landlords there had no jurisdictional rights and their estates, far from being entailed (as they were in Christian Spain down to 1822), were usually broken up on their death among the various members of their family. They also lacked the free communes, i.e. the towns and villages with charters, which were very common in the north and which, of course, were a perfectly normal development of the feudal age. That is to say, in Christian Spain local liberties and feudal privileges developed side by side, whilst among the Moslems nothing was permitted to infringe upon the powers of the central government.

The history of Spain can thus be interpreted in the light of two different conceptions of land tenure. In the north the possession of land stood for power and authority; in the south it stood for profit and well-being. In the former case the feudal idea became in time, through the medium of the free communes and the increase in the number of *mayorazgos*, democratized. even the humblest aspired to power, to nobility, to family permanence, and the result was a society in which the gentlemanly ideal of leisure and authority took precedence over that of material well-being. In the latter a much more expansive and hedonistic frame of mind prevailed and work was regarded as the only road to prosperity. (See especially E. Lévi-Provençal, *L'Espagne Musulmane au Xième Siècle. Institutions et Vie Sociale*. Paris, 1932.)

D (p. 103). How rapidly the condition of the land in Andalusia deteriorated may be judged from this example. In Moslem times Ecija was the centre of an agricultural district with a certain amount of irrigation. In 1275, only twenty-eight years after the conquest of the country by the Christians, a successful *razzia* here by the Sultan of Morocco produced a vast booty of sheep. In 1707 the principal wealth of the town lay in sheep farming (Álvarez de Colmenar, *Délices de l'Espagne et du Portugal*). To-day, though there is no trace of irrigation, most of the land is arable.

We get a close-up of the same process after Granada was taken in 1492. Thirty-four years later the Venetian ambassador Andrea Navagero visited it and wrote an account of what he saw: 'Hidden among them' [the waters, fruit-trees, woods] 'are the farms of the Moors, many in ruins, for the Moorish population is diminishing and it is they who kept everything in order: the Spaniards, here as in other parts of Spain, are not industrious and disdain agriculture.'

If this could happen at the height of the vitality of the new Spanish Empire after the occupation of a small very fertile region, what must have been the disorganization in 1248 when the whole of Andalusia had to be absorbed?

E (p. 107). The first impression made upon every traveller in Spain in the sixteenth and seventeenth centuries was its extraordinary and almost terrifying barrenness.

'Only what is near the villages', wrote Francisco Guicciardini of his visit in 1512-1513, 'is tilled and that badly, and the rest remains uncultivated.... The poverty is very great and in my opinion is due less to the nature of the country than to the character of the inhabitants, opposed to all work.'

Federico Cornaro, 1678-1681: 'One can travel for days on end without passing a house or village, and the country is abandoned and uncultivated.'

Giovanni Cornaro, 1681-1682: 'Spain gives the impression of being a desert of Libya, so unpopulated is it.'

Carlo Ruzzini, 1690-1695: 'The nobles never visit their estates, which for that reason are ruined, and in order to dress themselves they have to sponge on the revenues of the Kings.'

The Marquis de Villars, who visited Spain three times between 1671 and 1692, declared that not only Castile but Andalusia too was almost uninhabited. And there are few travellers after 1650 who do not remark on the large numbers of French labourers (70,000 according to Villars) who came every year to Spain, not for the harvest only, but also to sow and plough.

One may argue as to the ultimate causes of this decay, but the immediate cause is clear. The sheep farmers of Castile, encouraged by every king since the thirteenth century and especially by Isabella and Philip II, had spread over almost the whole of the country. And no one thought this mattered. Down to the eighteenth century stock breeding was believed to be the natural industry of Spain, the source of her superior nobility and of her military prowess, on which her position in the world depended. Thus, although there were famines every few years from 1500 and corn had to be imported from abroad, little regard was paid to the decline of agriculture: again and again one finds the Cortes demanding that land which had recently been ploughed up should be compulsorily returned to pasture: the only thing that really roused public opinion was when it was thought that horses and mules were being exported to France.

In the seventeenth century, it is true, the increasing deterioration of agriculture caused a good deal of alarm: the country could no longer feed itself, but the decline of sheep and cattle breeding (especially in the herds of the small farmers) was thought to be even more dangerous, and in 1633 and again at recurring intervals through the century decrees were issued forbidding the breaking up of the pasture lands (which then occupied about six-sevenths of the surface of Spain) and regulating their use very strictly. One may judge the attitude of the time on this question from Caxa de Leruela, an *alcalde mayor* of the Mesta and a man of some influence, who recommended, as a cure for the poverty of Spain, the turning over of almost the whole land to pasture, and a distribution of flocks and herds among the peasants. And the reason he gave was that for making life agreeable and redeeming it from poverty there was nothing like a pastoral occupation. 'The bread of the ploughman is bitter and it is kneaded with sweat. No herdsman was ever seen to beg: for his cattle are the staff of his old age, whereas the peasant, as soon as his bodily strength is wasted in hoeing and ploughing, even if he be the owner of a little land, will have no other remedy but to die of hunger or to beg on the high roads.'

F (p. 108). The first aim of the eighteenth-century statesmen was to give the peasants the full advantage of the immense tracts of uncultivated land belonging to the communes, which were in practice appropriated by the caciques or *poderosos* for pasturing their cattle. Two methods of doing this were suggested.

(a) The lands were to remain in the possession of the communes and those which were arable were to be divided by lot among the poorer neighbours every few years (*sorteo periódico de las tierras de labor*). This was the traditional system which had come down from the early Middle Ages and which was still practised in many parts of the country. The laws of 1770 and 1771 dividing the *baldíos* of Extremadura and

New Castile among the *yunteros* (or possessors of a yoke of mules or oxen) are examples of this method of solving the question.

(*b*) Individual holdings (*cotos*) were to be created which would be unalienable, indivisible and unaccumulative and which would pay a fixed rent or *censo* to the State. This was the system which, as has already been described, had in many parts of Spain taken the place of the old feudal tenures, generally of a communal nature, on the large estates. In the settlement of the Alpujarras after the expulsion of the Moors in 1571 the State had for the first time adopted this method and it had been repeated in the colonization of the Sierra Morena with Germans in the eighteenth century. The majority of Charles III's ministers inclined to it.

As regards the large estates the general opinion was that the landlords should be compelled to let them in small lots in perpetuity at fixed rents: that is to say, the contract should take the form of an emphyteusis or *censo*. This was regarded as being more prudent than expropriation, and it would in time have led to what, from the reign of Philip II to the establishment of the parliamentary regime, was usually looked on as the solution to be aimed at—the ownership of the land by those who worked it.

Yet all the efforts of the eighteenth-century reformers came to nothing. The reason for this was that, in the first place, they did not have sufficient time to carry them out nor power to overcome the passive resistance of the caciques. Then the State lacked the capital to buy mules and equipment for the new settlers and to establish an efficient credit system. This is the rock on which all agrarian reform in Spain has broken down. Poverty of soil and aridity of climate make the existence of the small farmer almost unbearable. And it is to be doubted whether a good agrarian credit system can by itself overcome this difficulty. In many districts the only real solution would seem to be, either the direct cultivation of the land by the State or collective cultivation by the community in one form or another. It is not for nothing that the working classes of Central and Southern Spain—for all their marked individualism—have strong tendencies to communal organization. Those who wish to change this are swimming against a strong current.

G (p. 108). Jovellanos' *Informe sobre la Ley Agraria*, published in 1787 as a reply to the *Memorial ajustado del Expediente Consultivo* of 1784 (the great summary of eighteenth-century ideas on agrarian questions), is the most famous book in Spanish economics and marks the beginning of the Liberal era.

H (p. 110). In Castile and Leon only 27 per cent and in New Castile only 33 per cent of the land belongs to estates of over 250 hectares (625 acres). The figure for La Mancha is 61 per cent, for Extremadura 62 per cent and for Andalusia 55 per cent. Of the different provinces Cadiz has the largest figure 68 per cent, and Seville 59 per cent. In La Mancha and Extremadura a high percentage of the land is only fit for pasture, whereas in Cadiz and Seville it is as a rule very fertile. (Pascual Carrión, *op. cit.*).

I (p. 112). See Madariaga on the 'totally unrestricted right of the landlord to arrange the terms of the lease as he wishes' (*Spain*, p. 196). Also A. Marvaud, *La Question Sociale en Espagne*, pp. 176-180, and Unamuno in the *Revista Católica de las cuestiones sociales*, December 1905.

J (p. 116). Mr E. H. G. Dobby has kindly given me these figures, obtained by him from the engineers of the Bureau of Agrarian Reform, of the proportion of fallow (*barbecho*) to cereals in the year 1924:

Andalusia	669/1412	New Castile	1268/1594
Old Castile	904/1231	Extremadura	492/745
Catalonia	111/375	Basque Provinces	10/70

Here we see that whereas in Andalusia land was usually sown twice in succession and then left for one year fallow, in New Castile a year of rest followed almost every crop. But clearly these figures are based upon only the good lands and disregard those large areas of poor soil which are more irregularly cultivated.

K (p. 120). In Valencia and Catalonia at this time agricultural wages rarely went below 4 pesetas (5 was the average) and rose to 8 in harvest. As crops were more varied, labour was less seasonal. Agricultural labourers generally had a strip of land which they cultivated themselves. In the Basque provinces wages never fell below 5 pesetas and were sometimes 7 or 8. Only in the most favoured parts of Andalusia, close to the large towns, did they ever rise to 4 or 5.

L (p. 120). The Report of the official enquiry of the Institute of Social Reforms published in 1905 gives agricultural wages in Andalusia as being on an average 1·50 pesetas without food, sometimes descending to 1·00, but scarcely ever rising above 2·00. Women got much less. Working days did not on the average exceed 280 in the year. (In 1930 they were well below 200.) In harvest the men worked from 15 to 16 hours. Quoted in A. Marvaud, *La Question Sociale en Espagne*, p. 136. Since then the cost of living has more than doubled itself, so that the labourer's wages in 1930 were slightly less than they used to be and his annual income, owing to greater unemployment, at least 30 per cent less. On the other hand the *rancho*, or food provided by the landlord when working away from their homes, has improved except in those two black areas—the provinces of Seville and Cadiz.

M (p. 121). See E. H. G. Dobby's 'Agrarian Problems in Spain' published in the *Geographical Review of the American Geographical Society*, April 1936. His visit to Andalusia took place in 1935, during the Lerroux-Gil Robles term of Government.

N (p. 121). Yet once, one should not forget, under the operation of exactly the same causes (the breaking up of common lands and a high tariff on corn that made agriculture extremely profitable) the same terrible state of affairs prevailed in England. When prices fell in 1814, exactly as they did in 1930, the English village 'did not contain a mass of decently paid labourers and a surplus of labourers, from time to time redundant, for whom the parish had to provide as best it could. It contained a mass of labourers, all of them underpaid, whom the parish had to keep alive in the way most convenient to farmers' (J. L. and B. Hammond, *The Village Labourer*, p. 174). In other words, the English landlords averted a revolution by pauperizing the peasants. This hypocritical prudence, parading as generosity, was alien to the character of the Spanish landlords. They preferred to double the number of the rural constabulary. But one may observe that in both cases the same assumption was made—that in order that the landlords might get high rents, the peasants must starve.

O (p. 122). The idleness of the Andalusians is a pure legend. That observant traveller Joseph Townsend, rector of Pewsey in Wiltshire and a well-known savant, exposed it in 1787. Of Malaga he wrote: 'The peasants of no country upon earth are more patient of heat, of hunger and of thirst, or capable of greater exertions than this very people who have been accused of indolence' (*Journey through Spain in 1786-1787*). He puts the idleness of Spaniards in other provinces down to bad government.

Chapter VII

THE ANARCHISTS

I shall die and the worms will eat me, but I want our idea to triumph.
I want the masses of humanity to be really emancipated from all
authorities and from all heroes present and to come.   BAKUNIN.

Spanish Anarchism traces its origin to a Russian aristocrat, Michael
Bakunin. In Herzen's *Memoirs* we find a vivid account of this man.
A giant in size, with the energy of ten ordinary men when roused,
wildly exuberant and unmethodical in all his acts, living among a
medley of unfinished articles, uncompleted plans, night-long Russian
conversations and tea drinking—that is the picture Herzen paints.
The attractive side of his character stands out—his generosity, his
lack of malice that amounted to innocence, his simple and natural
bearing with other men, but we are left with the impression of a
student—a Russian student too—whom ten years of prison had done
nothing to moderate.

There were, however, depths in Bakunin's character which Herzen,
a caustic and disillusioned exile, comfortably installed in London, did
not appreciate. Bakunin was a man of action deprived of the power
of action—a natural leader of guerrilla bands or peasant revolts. But
he was also a man of unusual sympathetic imagination. He had an
instinctive understanding for certain primitive classes of people—
Russian and Italian peasants, brigands and outlaws of all sorts. Not
only was he ready, like Garibaldi, to lead them at the barricades and to
risk his life for them, but he felt a genuine respect and liking for their
ideas and way of life. It was on just this feeling for simple and liberty-
loving people that he founded his gospel, his vision of the future,
which was to lead them, after many vicissitudes, to a heaven upon
earth.

The Anarchist movement in Europe is thus the product of Bakunin's
imaginative insight into certain classes of human beings, coupled with
a strong moral and revolutionary fervour. It has for this reason a
directness, an immediate appeal which Marxism lacks and which was
bound, wherever the conditions were appropriate, to bring it disciples. And it bears everywhere the original stamp of its founder.
For whereas Godwin may be said to be the father of American Anarchism, an ultra-liberal doctrine suited to industrial countries with a

middle-class standard of life, Bakunin is the creator of the peasant Anarchism of Southern and Eastern Europe. This is especially true of Spain, the only country where his ideas took root in a mass movement. It is no exaggeration to say that, slight as the points of contact may seem to be, everything of importance in Spanish Anarchism goes back to him.

In 1864, the year of the foundation of the International, Bakunin left Switzerland and settled in Naples. He was at that time a man of fifty, prematurely aged by his sufferings, but still with the enthusiasm and vitality of ten other men. His huge strength and height, his vivid personality, his romantic career made him the most celebrated revolutionary of his time, the Garibaldi of Socialism, and disciples collected round him. But as yet he had not very much to teach them. By his imprisonment in the Czar's dungeons he had missed the long reactionary period that had followed the '48 and which had forced most revolutionaries to alter their methods, and he still lived among the ideas of his youth. In the north of Europe these ideas were now out of date. It was not till he went to Southern Italy with its revolutionary atmosphere of secret societies and Garibaldian insurrections that he saw how they could be adapted to modern conditions. Then his creed of anti-authoritarian collectivism, or, as it later came to be called, anarchism, took shape. Italian carbonarism, Proudhon's theories, the Slavophils' cult of the peasant and his own childish mania for secret revolutionary brotherhoods, all played their part. When he returned to Geneva in 1867 his social philosophy was complete.

The next four years (1868-1872) witness the struggle between the ideas of Marx and those of Bakunin for the control of the International. The two points round which their disagreement turned were whether or not there should be participation in the political struggle, and whether the organization of the International should be centralized or federal. These points of tactics concealed, of course, deep divergences of aim and of conception, expressed at the time in the saying that whereas Marx wished to conquer political power for the proletariat, Bakunin wished the proletariat to destroy it. But we shall not understand the true nature of Spanish Anarchism unless we examine Bakunin's ideas at some length.

Bakunin's social philosophy divides itself into three parts, his criticism of the present capitalist age, his vision of the new anarchist (or, as he called it, collectivist) society and the methods by which he hoped this could be attained. As to the first, anarchism is a protest not merely against the inequalities in wealth of the present world, but against its tyranny. 'All exercise of authority', wrote Bakunin, 'perverts and all submission to authority humiliates.' And the worst kind of authority is that of the State which is 'the most flagrant, most cynical and most complete denial of humanity because... every state, like every theology, assumes men to be fundamentally bad and wicked'. He therefore wishes to do away with it, putting in its place a free federal regime in which autonomous bodies (societies, groups or municipalities) contract voluntary pacts with one another. This was, of course, Proudhon's system. He also inveighs against the organization of modern industrial life by which men are made the slaves of machines and are cut off from the possibility of leading complete human lives. Liberty, absolute and complete liberty, is a necessity for everyone.

Bakunin therefore wishes to destroy the State. And he wished to destroy God also. A passionate atheism runs through all his writings. God is the creation of men's slavish instincts and man will never be free until he has ceased to believe in him. For theology too assumes, just as does the State, that men are fundamentally bad and wicked and that they must be continually corrected and kept down. Here we come upon a rather important point of Bakunin's system. It is often said that anarchism would never work because it assumes men to be naturally good. That, however, is not an assumption of Bakunin's. He merely believes them to be good enough to live in a free society, which of course would have its own ways of exercising pressure upon them. Every society produces men after its own likeness, and those of the present time are corrupted by the struggle for power and money. But human beings are very plastic and under a different system they would behave otherwise. In the new world imagined by Bakunin public opinion would be strong enough to deal with all infractions of its code without recourse to any central authority. The analogy is to the peasant village or primitive tribe, where justice, like everything else, is organized locally.

We have seen that Bakunin laid the greatest stress upon liberty. But he does not mean what Liberals mean by that word. The Liberal or bourgeois theory of liberty, he declares, is derived from 'that vile book', Rousseau's *Contrat Social*. The isolated individual with his desire for illimitable liberty is there imagined as coming together with other individuals and contracting to live in a society with them. Each agrees to give up that part of his natural inheritance of liberty which will conflict with the liberty of the others. Out of this contract, so the theory runs, has grown up in time the modern state with its laws and institutions and indeed every form of tyranny. But, says Bakunin, this contract is, historically speaking, a pure fiction. It was not individual men who by coming voluntarily together created society: on the contrary, since men are by nature social animals, it has always been society which created them. The concept of liberty is therefore unthinkable outside a community. Man cannot be free when he is alone. He can only be free when he lives in community with other free human beings, each of whom is earning his right to that freedom by work.

'Je ne suis vraiment libre que lorsque tous les êtres humains qui m'entourent, hommes et femmes, sont également libres. La liberté d'autrui, loin d'être une limite ou la négation de ma liberté, en est au contraire nécessaire et la confirmation.'[1]

If this seems paradoxical, he adds, it is because people, thanks to their bourgeois up-bringing, are so accustomed to thinking in terms of the isolated individual that they do not realize that man only becomes a complete human being when living in a free society. The isolated individual is a fiction, but in so far as he exists he is necessarily a completely immoral creature, the personification of egoism. And Bakunin traces the responsibility for this attitude back through Descartes to the Christian notion of the immortal soul, which has produced a fatal split in the personality. Thus the chief cause of the evil of bourgeois society is that man has need of other men materially, but does not need them morally. That is why he exploits them.

One will see from this that if Bakunin wishes to destroy the State, he compensates for it by attaching a new importance to society. For society is or should be the fluid in which men must live if they are to draw their proper nourishment. In the present bourgeois world men are starved without knowing it. He therefore maintains that a free society will necessarily create strong, open, outstanding men and accepts without fear a strengthening of those great conservative forces that govern societies—custom and public opinion, which are good 'because they are natural'. Something must be said about this word 'natural', for it is one of the keys to Bakunin's ideas. He was greatly

---

[1] *Dieu et l'État* (begun in November 1870 but left unfinished). See also *Trois Conférences faites aux Ouvriers du Val de Saint Imier* (May 1871), *Oeuvres*, vol. v. These ideas are, I believe, to be found in Fichte. But that they were deeply rooted in Bakunin's personal experience is shown by a letter written to his family in 1831, when he was only seventeen, and by other letters written at intervals through his life. See *Bakounine*, by H. E. Kaminski, p. 25.

impressed by the growing artificiality of modern life, which he thought could only be arrested by some very deep transformation in the structure of society. And just as all artificiality in his eyes was bad, so all 'nature' was good. That is why destruction plays so large a part in Bakunin's theories and planning for the future so little. (The passion for destruction, he once said, is also a creative passion.) He believed that if the State, and rule of force it stood for, could only be destroyed, with all those little compartments that separate men from one another, nature would cause new and better social organisms to arise to fill their place. He forgot, no doubt, that once just such a catastrophe occurred in Europe and that what grew up was not anarchism, but the horrible and cruel anarchy of the early feudal age. As we shall see later, there lies at the root of anarchism a fatal paradox.

It should now be clear that the kind of life which Bakunin had in mind was the small peasant community as he had seen it in Russia. A few years later that other great anarchist, Kropotkin (who was also a Russian aristocrat), was to find historical precedents for his social theories in the village communities of the Middle Ages and even in Greek city life. That is to say, there is in anarchism a strong element of reaction against industrialism, of return (though without re-nouncing the advantages of modern industrial processes) to the freer, more human life of the Middle Ages. It was with this in mind that Bakunin substituted for the idea of 'the masses', so dear to Marx's Germanic mind, that of the small group. For it was only in small groups, he thought, that a proper regard for human rights and human dignity could be found. In his remarks upon this, upon the respect that is due to every man, however stupid, however wicked or con-temptible, simply because he is a man, one is at once reminded of mediaeval Christian teaching, which was based on the democratic theory of the equality of all souls in the eyes of God. Bakunin, whilst eliminating God, kept the same mystical equality of rights and indeed made it the kernel of his whole system. It led him to deny the validity of the Marxian dialectic and to insist that human needs and desires should always have precedence over economic laws. Nature for him was the nature of that semi-gregarious animal Man and not the general historic process.

There remains to be considered the manner by which, according to Bakunin, the revolution would come and the form of organization best adapted to secure this. He had no faith in the revolutionary temper of the proletarian masses in the great industrial countries of the North. He foresaw that, as their material conditions improved, they would tend more and more to adopt bourgeois modes of life and thought. He relied rather upon the poor peasantry and town workers in countries such as Italy, Russia and Spain, where industrial development was still very primitive. They alone would have sufficient spirit for revolutionary action. In this matter time has shown that Marx was wrong and Bakunin right.

But though he liked to picture the coming revolution as the 'spontaneous uprising of an infuriated town mob or a peasant *jacquerie*', he knew that such events require leadership and preparation. For this he counted on a 'phalanx 40,000 strong of young folk of the educated classes'—that is to say, of the young men down from the universities who could not find jobs, school teachers, *petit bourgeois*, *déclassés* who 'whether they know it or not belong to the Revolution'. These were, of course, the people who at that time were undermining the Czarist regime in Russia and working for the independence of Italy. Later it was they who would bring in Fascism. The underground action of these young folk would, he thought, stir up incessant revolts, strikes and acts of sabotage till, the temper of the whole people catching fire, a general rising would occur and the Government would fall. In this scheme of things there was no place for the legal intervention in the political struggle demanded by Marx. In Bakunin's eyes such action could only serve to destroy the revolutionary temper of the people; besides, in the countries where his ideas were to take root, political intervention was impossible because the people had no votes. The development of Marx's programme was as impossible at that time in Russia, Italy and Spain as was that of Bakunin in England, Germany and Northern France.

The quarrel, however, came over the question of the organization of the International. Marx wished to see the trade unions which subscribed to it organized hierarchically and obedient to the orders of the General Council. If this could be done the labour movement throughout the world would move solidly forward under one leadership. Bakunin's idea was different. According to him the General Council should be nothing more than a statistical bureau. The unions of workers that composed the International should be federated loosely together and the impetus to action should always come from below. Thus, not only would the International offer the same plan as the society of the future, but the local organizations would preserve that independence and spontaneity which, as Proudhon had taught, were so essential in all popular movements. However, something more was required to provide the necessary revolutionary fervour. To facilitate this Bakunin founded at Geneva in September 1868 among a few friends a secret revolutionary society, which he called the Alliance of Social Democracy. At the top of this were to be the Hundred International Brothers (a secret society which he had already founded in skeleton form at Naples) whose 'only country was universal revolution and whose only enemy reaction'. Under these would be the national members, chosen among the most devoted and energetic leaders in the local federations. The function of this body, as he explained to one of his Spanish adherents, would be to act as 'a secret society in the heart of the International, to give it a revolutionary organization, to transform it and all the popular masses which exist outside it into a power sufficiently organized to destroy the politico-clerico-bourgeois reaction and the economic, juridic, religious and political institutions of the State'.[1] We shall see later, when we consider the development of Bakunin's ideas in Spain, that this combination of federations of working men, forming, in the Proudhonian language of the time, free pacts with one another, with a small secret revolutionary body that permeated and controlled them, has been the typical organization of Spanish Anarchism down to the present day.

But events did not move exactly as Bakunin wished. When the Alliance of Social Democracy asked for permission to enter the International, without abandoning either its programme or its organization, this request was refused by the General Council. The Alliance was therefore forced to dissolve itself only three months after its inauguration (December 1868). Or rather it pretended to dissolve itself—the fact that it comprised at this time only a few dozen people, all members of Bakunin's intimate circle, making this dissimulation an easy matter. One of its local sections, however, that of Geneva, continued to exist in a non-secret form and was admitted to the International.

The year 1868 is an important one in the history of the working-class movement. For the first time, at the Congress of Brussels that summer, the ideal of Communism (or, as it was then called, Collec-

---

[1] Letter of 21 May 1872 to González Morago (Max Nettlau, *La Internacional y la Alianza en España*). In an unfinished letter to Francisco Mora found among his papers Bakunin describes the Alliance as 'a Society of brothers, solid to the death and whose only aim is to bring in the revolution. . . . It is in fact a religion, the religion of humanity' (*op. cit.* p. 97). In reality the Alliance had two distinct purposes: to maintain and direct the revolutionary instincts of the proletariat and to combat the ideas of Marx within the International.

tivism) was accepted by the International. That is to say, the moderating influences of French Proudhonism and of British trade unionism
were defeated. Immediately after, as we have seen, Bakunin founded
his own organization, the Alliance of Social Democracy. And at the
same moment, in September, a revolution broke out in Spain. The
Army, supported by practically the whole country, rose against Isabella and drove her out, and the calling of a Constituent Assembly was
announced for the spring. It was obvious that here was a situation
which the International might take advantage of. Up to that time no
revolutionary work had been done south of the Pyrenees. To European
Socialists Spain was a *terra incognita*. Bakunin therefore suggested
to his friend Elisée Reclus, afterwards the famous geographer, that he
should go and spy out the country. Elisée was unable to go and sent
his brother Elie instead, but it was to another person, an Italian
engineer called Giuseppi Fanelli, whom Bakunin had met several
years before at Naples and enrolled in his International Brotherhood,
that the important mission of evangelizing Spain was entrusted. After
some difficulty about raising the money for his railway fare, he left for
Barcelona in October 1868.

Up to this time Socialist ideas, properly speaking, were almost unknown in Spain. There existed a strong and growing federal movement, influenced by Proudhon, which will be described later. But
this was a movement exclusively of the lower-middle classes and had
no social implications that went beyond a benevolent radicalism. And
it was definitely un-revolutionary. There was also a small band of
Fourierists, of whom the best known was Fernando Garrido, the
author of several voluminous books on social questions and the editor
of a small Socialist newspaper in Madrid. It was he who had introduced the Co-operatives to Spain. But this movement had made no
headway except in a few places near Seville and in Catalonia.
The trade union movement was also very backward. At Barcelona
there existed two unions of cotton spinners, the rather conservative
Federación de las Tres Clases de Cataluña, which at this time claimed
6000 members out of a total factory population of 70,000, and the
more aggressive *Unión Manufacturera*, which was smaller. These
were the only trade unions of any importance in the country and both
were feebly led and organized. Strikes in factories were almost unknown. The real area of working-class discontent lay in the country
districts of the centre and south. Here the breaking up of the common
lands had caused acute misery. In 1840, in 1855, in 1857, in 1861 and
in 1865 there had been large peasant risings in Castile and Aragon and

above all in Andalusia. That of 1857 had been led by a few students from Seville, who called themselves Socialists. Narváez had encouraged it to mature and then drenched it in blood, shooting a hundred and sending many more to the penal settlements. Then in 1861 a body of 10,000 peasants assembled secretly and occupied Loja near Granada as a protest against low wages and unemployment. It was a peaceable movement—neither man nor property was injured—and O'Donnell put it down with unwonted mildness; only six of the ringleaders were executed. But those starving and yet rebellious peasants, whose heroes were the brigands and whose bitter enemies were the rural constabulary set up by Narváez, were clearly only waiting to hear of Bakunin's ideas to welcome them.

Fanelli arrived at Barcelona and, being unable to make any contacts there, went on to Madrid. He had a letter of introduction to Fernando Garrido, who passed him on to one or two young men, typographers and printers, who frequented a working-class educational club called the *Fomento de las Artes*. They belonged to a group of federalists, who read Proudhon and Pi y Margall and took in the latter's paper *La Discusión*. None of them had so much as heard of the International. A small meeting was arranged so that Fanelli could address them upon it. One of the young men present, Anselmo Lorenzo, has given a vivid account of what followed.

'Fanelli was a tall man with a kind and grave expression, a thick black beard and large black expressive eyes which flashed like lightning or took on the appearance of kindly compassion according to the sentiments which dominated him. His voice had a metallic tone and was susceptible to all the inflexions appropriate to what he was saying, passing rapidly from accents of anger and menace against tyrants and exploiters to take on those of suffering, regret and consolation, when he spoke of the pains of the exploited, either as one who without suffering them himself understands them, or as one who through his altruistic feelings delights in presenting an ultra-revolutionary ideal of peace and fraternity. He spoke in French and in Italian, but we could understand his expressive mimicry and follow his speech.'

For except for González Morago,[1] who knew a little French, not

---

[1] Tomás González Morago was the first Spanish Anarchist. Anselmo Lorenzo gives a vivid account of him. His father was a Carlist and he was drawn to Anarchism because it seemed to him to realize the teachings of the Gospel. He had brilliant qualities (Malatesta considered him to be the greatest of Spanish Anarchists) but an unstable character which led him to spend whole days in bed in a state of depression. He never quite got over his religious feelings. He died of cholera in Granada gaol while still a young man.

one of those present understood a word of any foreign language and it
had not occurred to them to bring an interpreter. Yet twenty years
later Lorenzo could recall the very accent with which Fanelli had said,
rolling his black eyes above his black beard, 'Cosa Orribile! Spaven-
tosa!'[1]

The conversion of all present was, needless to say, instantaneous.
Spaniards had long been waiting for this moment. After three or four
sessions and a few conversations in the café, Fanelli, whose money
was running low, took the train to Barcelona. He left behind him
copies of the statutes of the Alliance of Social Democracy, the rules of
a Geneva working-class society, a few numbers of Herzen's *Bell*
and various Swiss and Belgian newspapers, containing reports of
speeches by Bakunin. These were the sacred texts on which the new
movement was to be constructed. At Barcelona his success was
repeated, but, his money again running short—Bakunin had been
unable to raise the few pounds needed—he took the boat for Mar-
seilles. Within the space of less than three months, without knowing a
word of Spanish or meeting more than an occasional Spaniard who
understood his French or Italian, he had launched a movement that
was to endure, with wave-like advances and recessions, for the next
seventy years and to affect profoundly the destinies of Spain.[2]

The enthusiasm generated by Fanelli did not die down after his
departure. The initiates at these marvellous Pentecostal scenes studied
the texts he had left and at the end of a few weeks felt themselves ready
to hold meetings of propaganda. Enthusiasm spread rapidly. The
word was carried to Andalusia, where groups sprang up at Lora del
Rio, Arahal and at Arcos de la Frontera in the province of Seville
among the organizers of the new co-operative stores, and then at Cadiz
and in all the small towns of the Lower Guadalquivir. Converts were
made by the thousand. Those who went to the meetings came away

---

[1] Anselmo Lorenzo, *El Proletariado Militante*, vol. i. Before Fanelli left Madrid
the whole group of twenty-one went to a photographer's and had their picture
taken. This historic photograph has been reproduced in a little book by Federica
Montseny, *Anselmo Lorenzo*, Barcelona, Ediciones Españolas, 1938.

[2] Fanelli was by profession an architect and an engineer, but he had given up his
career to work for the revolution. He had fought under Garibaldi and against the
Pope and was one of Mazzini's emissaries. This led to his being elected deputy
to the Italian Parliament. In 1866 he met Bakunin at Ischia, was converted to his
ideas and became a member of the International Brotherhood. The Government
gave him a pension of 97 lire a month as a compensation for having lost his health
in a Bourbon prison, and as a deputy he had a free railway pass all over Italy. He
therefore spent his time travelling about, preaching social revolution in the villages
and returning at night to sleep in the train. He died in 1877 of consumption.

feeling that their eyes had suddenly been opened and that they now possessed the absolute truth upon every subject. This gave them a boundless self-confidence. They defied in open debate eminent Republican politicians such as Castelar, grave professors and economists, and patriarchal Socialists like Garrido: they intervened on every possible occasion in discussions on sociology, economics and jurisprudence. And, if one is to believe their newspapers, they invariably emerged victorious, leaving their opponents speechless and dumbfounded.[1]

A well-known writer on Socialism, the Baron de Laveleye, has left an account of one of their assemblies at Barcelona: 'Visiting Spain in 1869 I was present at several of the meetings of these socialist clubs. They generally took place in disused churches. From the pulpits the orators attacked everything that had once been exalted there: God, religion, priests, riches. Many women were present, sitting on the ground, knitting and suckling their children, as if it were a real sermon. It was indeed the image of '93.'[2]

Yet perhaps the Baron was not quite correct in his comparison. As we shall see later, this atmosphere of intense emotionalism, half denunciation of the evils of the capitalist world and half messianic expectation of immediate bliss to come, has remained typical of Anarchist assemblies almost down to the present time, but what they have suggested to modern observers has been an American revivalist meeting.

The class from which the 'internationalists', as they were called at that time, were recruited was not, as one might at first suppose, the proletariat. Among the hundred or so militants of the next few years one can scarcely find the name of a single labourer or factory hand. Artisans of various kinds, especially typesetters and cobblers, formed the principal adherents, to which one must add a schoolmaster or two and an occasional student from the Andalusian universities. The poor city workers and peasants, those 'solid barbarian elements' on whose

---

[1] Whilst the Regional Congress at Cordova was sitting, this announcement was pasted up on the walls: '*RETO.* Challenge. The Delegates of the Third Congress of the *Federación Española de la A. I. T.* challenge to public controversy all who desire to combat the fundamental principles of the International. Therefore to-day, 1 January 1873, there will take place a large public assembly at seven in the evening in the upstairs saloon of the Café del Recreo. Workers of Cordova, do not fail to attend! Defenders of Privilege, accept the challenge! Salud, Anarquía y Colectivismo!' Since none of the defenders of privilege took up the challenge, the workers knew that their case was unanswerable. (Díaz del Moral, *Córdoba*, pp. 101-103.)

[2] de Laveleye, *Le Socialisme Contemporain*, p. 270.

'elemental anger' Bakunin counted to bring in the revolution, did not come forward.[1]

This was indeed characteristic of the early Anarchist movement everywhere. In the Swiss Jura, for example, which for the next twelve years was the principal centre of Bakunin's ideas in Europe, the members of the federations were watchmakers who worked not in factories but in their own homes. In Italy it was the artisans and the students who transferred their aspirations to the International after the termination of the Risorgimento. But in Spain it was clear that anarchism could only have a future if it became a genuine working-class movement. The comparative failure of the International at Barcelona was therefore disappointing. It was found that although several of the Catalan trade unions were ready to join it to obtain its moral support, the workmen themselves were too apathetic and too uneducated to be interested in the general aim. The group founded by Fanelli had actually to conceal their opinions when they organized a federation of workmen's unions, and the paper they founded, *La Federación*, simply supported the Federal Republican programme. It was left to Madrid, where there was no proletarian following, to maintain the pure essence of Bakuninist doctrine in its two papers *Solidaridad* and (later) *El Condenado*.[2]

But this was in fact a situation which had been foreseen by Bakunin. He had envisaged a small secret society, the Alliance of Social Democracy, made up of determined Anarchists and controlling a loose federation of peasants' and workers' trade unions. Unfortunately, by a mistake of Fanelli's, the International (that is, the whole federation) had been set up in Spain with the more advanced programme of the Alliance and it was not till the spring of 1870 that it was possible to rectify this. Then a Spanish Alliance of Social Democracy, independent of the old Genevan organization, but with the same programme, was founded. This programme ('in politics anarchist, in economy collectivist, in religion atheist') contained among other things the

[1] See Note A on p. 166 at end of chapter.

[2] Some at least of the early Anarchists felt the apparent contradiction of revolutionary theory with actual facts. 'Few indeed', wrote Lorenzo, 'of the workers with their hopeless ignorance and consequent lack of will power were able to play the part that revolutionary theory expected of them' (*El Proletariado Militante*, vol. II, p. 80). Even in the Andalusian country-side, where discontent was very great and where they could build upon the federalist movement, the result was disappointing. For the ignorance was worse than ever in the south. At the Regional Congress at Cordova in 1872 it was found that for the proper working of the various local and trade federations some 7000 delegates would be required who must be able to read. But only a fraction of such a number could be found.

express stipulation that it would refuse to take part in any revolutionary activity which 'had not for its object the immediate and direct triumph of the workers' cause'.[1]

The first act of this body was to summon a general congress. This met in June 1870 in the Ateneo Obrero at Barcelona 'in a regime of liberty for each to think as he pleased'. Ninety delegates representing 150 societies in thirty-six different localities came together[2] and constituted themselves the Spanish Regional Federation of the International, adopting as their statutes those of the Jura Federation which had been drawn up by Bakunin. The agenda had been carefully prepared by the members of the Alliance of Social Democracy and the opening speech by Farga Pellicer left no doubt as to the direction to be followed: 'We wish', he said, 'the rule of Capital, State and Church to cease and to construct upon their ruins Anarchy, the free federation of free associations of free workers.' The Congress was a success and led to an expansion of the International. The uncertainty of the political situation and the apparent inability of the Constituent Cortes to find a prince willing to ascend the vacant throne was providing a favourable ground for the spread of anarchist ideas. All over Spain the animosity between rich and poor was increasing.

But a rift was opening within the ranks of the International itself. The dissensions between Marx and Bakunin which had first shown themselves at the Congress of Basle in 1869 came to a head at the Conference of London in September 1871. The questions at issue were whether or not there should be participation in the political struggle and what the form of organization should be. As we have seen, there was a close association between this and the form desired for the future society. A decision on these matters could not be postponed any longer and when the Conference broke up after stormy discussions it was obvious that a split had become inevitable. This struggle had its reflection in Spain. The Marxian party there was known as the *Autoritarios* ('Authoritarians') and, though numerically insignificant, it contained some of the best men in the International. It ran a paper, *La Emancipación*, in Madrid and had a certain following in Castile and in Granada. Whereas the Bakuninists called themselves 'Collectivists', they proclaimed themselves 'Communists'.

The struggle became acute after the arrival in Madrid of Paul

[1] See Note B on p. 167 at end of chapter.
[2] These societies or unions contained some 40,000 workers, but it must be remembered that by no means all of them had affiliated themselves to the International. Two-thirds of the delegates represented Catalan unions.

Lafargue, Marx's son-in-law, in December 1871. He appeared in disguise, a refugee from the Paris Commune. His London connections and the fact that he spoke fluent Spanish (he had been brought up in Cuba) made him the natural representative of the General Council in Spain.[1] His first move was successful. He attacked the Alliance of Social Democracy on the ground of its secrecy (secret organizations within the International had been forbidden by the London Conference) and pressed it so hard that it was obliged to dissolve itself. To prevent it from forming again, *La Emancipación* published the names of its members, without considering the use that would be made of this information by the police. The Bakuninists retaliated by expelling the *Autoritarios*, who then formed a federation of their own at Madrid. The end came a month or two later at the Hague Congress (September 1872), when Marx, after obtaining the expulsion of Bakunin and his associates from the International, transferred the General Council to New York. Rather than allow the organization he had created to be captured by the enemy, he destroyed it.

A fortnight later the expelled members met at Saint Imier in the Swiss Jura. Switzerland, Spain and Italy stood behind Bakunin. Belgium was divided. In France the repression that followed the Commune prevented any expression of opinion. The resolutions drawn up by Bakunin and embodying his views were carried unanimously. In the place of the Marxist International there had come into existence a purely Bakuninist International, with its centre among the small watchmakers of the Jura and the bulk of its members spread out along the Mediterranean.

These developments in Europe produced immediate repercussions in Spain. The Spanish delegates at Saint Imier, González Morago and Farga Pellicer, fresh from long conversations with Bakunin, hastened to call a congress in which the aims of the anarchist (or rather

---

[1] Marx had a poor opinion of Lafargue—he called him 'the Gascon'—and it was through Engels that contact was maintained with Spain. Extracts from their correspondence together with some letters by José Mesa, the leading figure among the *Autoritarios*, have been published by Max Nettlau in *Documentos Inéditos, etc.* Engels' view of the struggle is given in *Die Bakunisten an der Arbeit*. For the other side of the story one must read James Guillaume, *L'Internationale, Documents et Souvenirs*.

Engels' view, which history might seem to have justified, was that Spanish workmen and Spanish industry were both so backward that they were not ready for revolution, but must pass through a republican stage first. For this it was necessary that they should vote. Where Engels was wrong, however, was in thinking that such a programme could possibly appeal to Spanish peasants and workmen at that time. They knew how the elections were managed.

anarchising) International should be reaffirmed. It met on Boxing Day 1872 in the Teatro Moratín at Cordova. Fifty-four delegates, representing 20,000 members in 236 local federations and 516 trade unions, were present.[1] The resolutions that had been passed at the Congress of Saint Imier were unanimously approved and the necessary measures voted to put them in practice. Thus there came into existence for the first time in Spain an organization of a purely anarchist type. The local and trade sections which composed the federation were declared to be 'sovereignly independent sections', free at any moment to denounce their adherence to the federation. The centralized federal council was transformed into 'a bureau of correspondence and statistics', without any authority. Cohesion was maintained by the close personal relationships between the leaders, the former members of the Alliance of Social Democracy, which continued to exist in fact though not in name after its formal dissolution. The Congress of Cordova, acting under the immediate influence of Bakunin, had created the typical organization of Spanish anarchism.

We may pause for a moment to consider how eminently suited this organization was to Spanish conditions. The first need was to get hold of the half-starving, uneducated field labourers and factory workmen and to fill them with a consciousness of their own grievances and their own power. These men could not, as a rule, afford to pay a regular subscription and they were suspicious of any influence from outside which might embroil them with their employers. Any regular trade-union organization with a paid secretariat, acting on orders from Barcelona or Madrid and leading its adherents like a bourgeois Republican party to the polling booths, would have been doomed to failure. But the Anarchist leaders were never paid—in 1936, when their trade union, the C.N.T., contained over a million members, it had only one paid secretary. Travelling about from place to place, on foot or mule back or on the hard seats of third-class railway carriages, or even like tramps or ambulant bullfighters under the tarpaulins of goods wagons,

---

[1] According to *El Condenado*, No. 36 of 2 January 1873, the Regional Federation immediately after the Congress could claim 45,633 members, of whom 27,894 were Andalusians. Many local federations which had held back because they did not wish to take sides in the quarrel between the Bakuninists and the Marxists joined afterwards. Resolutions were passed demanding the immediate introduction of universal education, the eight-hour day and improved sanitation in factories. This, as we shall see, was simply the programme of Pi y Margall's Federals. The manifesto issued by the Congress ended with the slogan: *Viva la Liquidación Social! Viva la Internacional! Salud, Solidaridad, Anarquía y Colectivismo!*

whilst they organized new groups or carried on propagandist campaigns, these 'apostles of the idea', as they were called, lived like mendicant friars on the hospitality of the more prosperous workmen.

Their first object was simply to enrol groups of poor workers, whatever their political or religious opinions might be, for mutual protection against employers: now and then there would be a small strike, which, if it was successful, would at once double the membership of the section and lead to other small strikes in neighbouring districts. Then gradually the leaders would unfold their anarchist creed with its hatred of the Church, its wild idealism, its generous and humane outlook, and the imagination of the hearers would be kindled. Thus it happened that, at moments of enthusiasm, the number of the workers controlled by the Anarchists would double and treble themselves and, when the inevitable reaction came, would shrink back to a small kernel of convinced militants. This plasticity of the Anarchist movement enabled it to survive persecutions and, as soon as they were over, to reappear stronger than ever.

There is another characteristic of Spanish anarchism that goes back to the Cordova Congress. That is that all movements towards strikes or revolutionary action that develop in it come from below. What occurs is this. At some critical moment, let us say, a congress of Spanish federations is called to consider the possibility of revolutionary action. The delegates of each district will arrive at the assembly with a full knowledge of the wishes and capacities of the groups of workmen they represent. Each will get up and say what the men of his province or factory are able and prepared to do. No district will be urged to take any action for which it does not feel itself morally and materially prepared. This freedom of choice has certainly acted often to the advantage of the Government, who have been able to suppress anarchist movements at their leisure in one province after another. But, at all events until the outbreak of the Civil War, its merits have more than counterbalanced its defects. The fact that no group has ever been over-ruled by another group or has had pressure put on it to act against its private convictions, but only in accordance with its own measure of enthusiasm and the number of arms it has been able to collect, has meant that the anarchists have been able to suffer defeat after defeat and yet rise again stronger than ever. If no other European party has shown such resistance, that is because the Spanish Anarchists have insisted upon basing their movement upon the free and unfettered impulses of their adherents, organized in local groups, and have not allowed themselves to become enmeshed in the deadening and life-destroying net of a party bureaucracy.

A few weeks after the conclusion of the Congress of Cordova, King Amadeo resigned from the Spanish throne and left the country. Elections were held in May and owing to the abstention of the other parties a Republican majority was returned. The Cortes that met on 1 June 1873 lost no time in proclaiming a Republic. It was clear from the first that the new Republic would have a federal rather than a centralized constitution and, in fact, after a few weeks hesitation, Francisco Pi y Margall, the leader of the Federal Party, was elected president. A period of great expansion and activity opened for the International in Spain. But the Federal movement is of such importance for the history of Anarchism, and indeed for the history of modern Spain in general, that it will be necessary to say something about it.

The French Revolution, by the destruction of so many local interests and privileges, completed the work of Louis XIV and gave France a powerful and highly centralized administration. The Liberal Revolution in Spain, as we have already seen, imitated it. In both countries a reaction towards a greater local and municipal liberty was inevitable. In France this reaction was best expressed by Proudhon, who put forward those ideas which, he believed, the French Revolution had come into existence to fulfil, but from which it had been diverted by the ruthless political action of the Jacobins. In Spain, with its intense provincial feelings and local patriotisms, one would have expected the movement towards decentralization to be even stronger, but owing to the prostration of the country after the Napoleonic Wars and to the fact that Carlism drew into its own ranks many of the forces of resistance to Liberal centralism, these feelings did not for some time make their appearance among Left-wing parties. Indeed, but for the persistent preaching and writing of one man, it is possible that they would never have done so.[1]

---

[1] The first Spanish federal seems to have been Ramón Xauradó y Fábregas, a Catalan, who began to preach Republicanism in 1820. In his *Bases de una Constitución Política*, published in 1832, he advocated a federal republic. He was shot in 1837, after a rising in Barcelona. Then, according to Ramón de la Sagra (*Les Partis en Espagne*), a small anarchist and federalist group appeared at Santiago in Galicia in the early forties. Soon after, La Sagra and Antolín Faraldo were editing a federalist and socialist paper called *El Porvenir*. It was suppressed by Narváez in 1845.

Pi y Margall was a Catalan of lower-middle class family who combined a small post in a Madrid bank with occasional journalism and writing books upon art. But his true bent was social and political, and a reading of Proudhon (who at that time was quite unknown in Spain) showed him the way he was to go. He saw how exactly this Frenchman's ideas were suited to the aspirations of his countrymen and sat down to work out a political system that would meet their case. In 1854, a few weeks after General O'Donnell's successful *pronunciamiento* against Isabella's camarilla governments, his first book, *La Reacción y la Revolución*, came out. In spite of the haste in which it had been written and the superficial nature of many of its ideas, it constitutes a landmark in the history of Spanish political thought.

Its principal theme is the iniquity of power. Spain, it must be remembered, had been governed for two generations by force in its most brutal form—the general with his disorderly soldiers or militia, the guerrilla leader who was little better than a bandit and the firing squad. Pi y Margall finds this wicked and absurd. 'Every man who has power over another is a tyrant.' Discussing the meaning of 'order'—that word which for more than a hundred years had been the excuse for every act of violence and injustice—he says that true order cannot be obtained by applying force.

'Order supposes arrangement, harmony, convergence of all individual and social elements: order refuses all humiliations and sacrifices. Can you call order that fictitious peace which you obtain by cutting with the sword all that you are too stupid to organize with your limited intelligence?... True order, let me tell you, has never existed and will never exist so long as you make such efforts to obtain it, because true order supposes cohesion, yet not a cohesion obtained by the presence of exterior causes, but an intimate and spontaneous cohesion which you with all your restrictions inevitably inhibit.'[1]

This indictment of the Spanish governing classes has been repeated in our own times by Ortega y Gasset. Its truth is only too obvious. The troubles of Spain come from the belief, shared by almost every element in the country, in violent remedies. Even the Anarchists, who hold of course the same views on power, believe in the necessity for one supreme act of violence to end all violence. But Pi y Margall was always logical. He refused to use any means but persuasion and believed that, if he were able to form a government, he could carry out the desired state of affairs by gradual reforms.

[1] *La Reacción y La Revolución*, 1854, p. 153.

'Since I cannot do without the system of votes, I shall universalize suffrage. Since I cannot do without supreme magistrates I shall make them as far as possible changeable. I shall divide and subdivide power, I shall make it changeable and will go on destroying it.'[1] In the place of the power thus destroyed there would grow up a system of pacts between free groups and free individuals.

Pi's views, as expressed in this book, were of course pure anarchism.[2] The only thing that divided him from Bakunin was his reformism. And indeed he is regarded to-day by Spanish Anarchists as one of their saints. But after the failure of the 1854 Revolution Pi's ideas began, like Proudhon's, to take on a more moderate and a more purely political shape. He became the leader of the new Federal movement, which aimed at covering only the first lap of the long anarchist road.

This Federal movement, which first appears in the early sixties, grew up as a protest against the failure of the 1854 Revolution and the loss of everything that had been gained then. In his Programme of Manzanares General O'Donnell had demanded decentralization of local government, electoral reform, a free press and, most significant of all, the formation of a national militia which should guard these privileges against the encroachment of the caciques. The success of his *pronunciamiento* had been assured by a rising of the people in Madrid and through all the towns of Southern and Eastern Spain, and their sentiments had been shown by lynchings of the recently established political police and by demonstrations against the Church and against conscription. In the Cortes elected that autumn there were twenty-three Republicans.

But the generals, who, like the politicians of a later date, were merely corrupt and ambitious, moved to the Right as soon as they were in power, and in 1856 Narváez suppressed the national militia after some street fighting and initiated a period of severe repression. It was then that the federal idea began to grow.

The reasons for its popularity in Spain at this time are not far to seek. Federalism was first of all an expression of the Spanish devotion to the *patria chica* and a protest against the strongly centralizing policy

---

[1] *Op. cit.* p. 196.

[2] 'Revolution...is the idea of justice....It divides power quantitatively, not qualitatively as our constitutionalists do....It is atheist in religion and anarchist in politics: anarchist in the sense that it considers power as a very passing necessity: atheist in that it recognizes no religion, because it recognizes them all' (*op. cit.* p. 190). The atheism came from Proudhon and was silently dropped later.

of the 'liberal' regime.[1] This desire for devolution was shared by its
enemy Carlism. But it was also a protest against the autocratic and
oppressive rule of these governments, which was only possible so long
as they could arrange the elections as they pleased. They needed for
this a highly centralized administration. Federalism, therefore, was
regarded as the system best designed to preserve the rights of municipalities and to destroy the cacique. And there was the French
influence. Ever since Louis XIV had said that there were to be no
more Pyrenees, Spanish politics, both of the Right and of the Left,
has followed with an exaggeration and a superficiality that are all its
own the lead of France. And in France, as we have seen, the federal
tendencies in the young Socialist movement were vigorous. Indeed it
was Pi y Margall's translation of Proudhon's *Du Principe Fédératif* in
1868, a few weeks before the September Revolution which drove out
Isabella, that gave the Spanish federals the theoretic background they
needed.

From this moment enthusiasm for a federal republic grew rapidly.
The *petite bourgeoisie*, who from 1840 to 1934 have been the revolutionary class *par excellence* in Spain, accepted it as their programme.
The advocates of a centralized republic, like those of State socialism,
lost their supporters. The workers gave it their enthusiastic adherence.
By the time that the constitutional monarchy, which was the solution
of the liberal *bourgeoisie*, began to crack, it was obvious that a federal
republic would take its place. Thus it came about that in June 1873
Pi y Margall, a little, timid but almost pedantically well-intentioned
and honest man, found himself at the head of the Spanish State.

The federal programme which was now to be applied to the most
unruly and divided nation in Europe consisted in the main of a plan of
extreme decentralization: the country was to be cut up into eleven
autonomous cantons: these cantons were to be divided into free
municipalities, and the whole bound together by voluntary pacts.[2]

---

[1] 'Federalism is a system by which diverse human groups, without losing their
peculiar and particular autonomy, are associated and subordinated in conjunction
with those of their kind for all common ends.... It is moreover the form of organization most suited to the character of our country, a nation made up of provinces
which once were independent kingdoms and which even to-day are deeply divided
by their separate laws and customs. Thus, in all the great crises through which this
nation has passed since the beginning of the century, the first thing that has happened has been that the provinces have sought their safety and force within themselves, without losing from view the essential unity of the whole country' (Pi y
Margall, *Las Nacionalidades*, 1882).

[2] The correct term was 'synallagmatic, commutative and bilateral pacts'. 'By a
federal government we understand a government founded on alliance. These

There was to be a Central Cortes, elected by universal suffrage, but, once the Constitution had been established, it would lose much of its authority. Conscription was to be abolished, Church and State to be separated and free compulsory education to be provided for all. The social legislation included an eight-hour day, state inspection of factories and regulations to control women's and children's work. There was also an agrarian programme, which specified the expropriation of uncultivated lands and the establishment on them of communities of peasants. Agrarian credit banks were to be set up and all short-term leases changed to an *enfiteusis perpetua* which should be redeemable at a fixed rate. But these social reforms never got beyond the stage of vague projects, nor was it decided how pressure would be brought to bear upon the autonomous cantons and municipalities, if they should refuse to carry out the reforms voted by the Cortes. For Pi y Margall's federal experiment lasted a bare two months and then collapsed in civil war and disorder.

The causes of this failure were various. In the first place the Carlist War, which had been simmering for some time on the passes of the Pyrenees, broke out with violence. This made it impossible for the Federals to disband the Army and to abolish military service. Since it was this promise which had given the Republic its popularity among the working classes, the disillusion was great.[1] Then that defect of all newly formed Spanish parties, the lack of men to fill the administrative posts, made its appearance. The Federals were recruited from the lower-middle classes, and the ministers, governors and soldiers whom it threw up were either incompetent or else were unscrupulous men who had joined the party for what they could get out of it. Finally, the provinces decided not to wait for the Cortes to pass the Federal

---

alliances are contracts for whose formation it is necessary that there exist contracting parties with sufficient power or capacity to make a contract. If those who celebrate the contract are towns or states, the capacity to contract is the sovereignty: from this is deduced the fact that the federal contract can only be celebrated by sovereign peoples' (*Idea Exacta de la Federación por el Director del Estado Catalán*, 1873. Quoted by J. A. Brandt, *Toward the New Spain*, 1933).

In Spain nothing is ever new: the various provincial juntas that sprang up during the war against Napoleon all proclaimed their absolute sovereignty.

[1] The previous decade had seen a series of colonial adventures in various parts of the world which had made military service, *las quintas*, intensely unpopular. A *copla* of this time expresses this:

> *Si la República viene—no habrá quintas en España—*
> *Por eso aquí hasta la Virgen—se vuelve Republicana.*

As the Spanish working classes had never yet found anything that appealed to them in even a revolutionary political programme, their disappointment was all the more acute.

Constitution, but proceeded to set up independent cantons on their own account. With typically Iberian impatience they revolted, and the authority of the Government ceased to exist for a time in the east and south.

We must examine briefly the character of this, as it is called, Cantonalist movement. Its leaders were ambitious soldiers and local politicians: their forces were the depleted regiments under their command and the local Republican militia known as the Voluntarios de la Libertad. The incentive was, to some extent, the Paris Commune, where, it will be remembered, the leading part had been played by the Garde Nationale. The movement broke out almost simultaneously in Malaga, Seville, Granada, Cartagena and Valencia: Federals obtained possession of these cities and declared them to be sovereignly independent cantons: committees of public safety took over the duties of the Governor. A movement of similar character broke out in Barcelona.

The feeling that rises most quickly to the surface in every Spanish revolution is anti-clericalism. For all the evils of the times the priests and monks are made the scapegoat. The Cantonalist movement was no exception to this. At Barcelona the churches were closed for several months. The militia turned one into a barracks and public dances were given in another. Priests could not go about the streets in their robes. At Seville the Cantonalists declared that the cathedral would be converted into a café. Taxes were levied on the rich and in some towns a few houses were burned. In the country districts the villagers took advantage of the general anarchy to proclaim the complete independence of their villages and to divide up the large estates or common lands. As the police wisely withdrew to their barracks, these ceremonies usually passed off quietly and without loss of life. It was only in one or two places, where resistance was offered by the landowners, that serious incidents took place. As one would expect, the movement collapsed as soon as the Government showed that it was ready to use force. In July General Pavía entered Seville with a handful of troops, and by a mixture of tact and firmness restored order in Andalusia. The Cantonalist leaders retired to Cartagena, where they defended themselves for four months. By the time the long siege was over, in January 1874, the Cortes had been dissolved by the Captain-General of Madrid and the Republic had ceased, except in name, to exist.

But what part was played by the International in these chaotic events? As we have seen, a Congress had been held at Cordova in the last days of 1872 and had been followed by a great increase in the number of members, especially in the small towns of Andalusia. The accession to power of the Federals during the summer of 1873 was naturally favourable to it. On the surface, at all events, the similarity of their programmes was very striking. 'We wish', says one of the resolutions adopted at the Cordova Congress, 'to build on the ruins of national unity free and independent municipalities bound only by federal pacts'.[1] But this identity of aims on the purely political issue could not conceal wide differences upon the social. The intentions of the Federals towards the working class did not go beyond a more or less sincere radicalism, whilst the followers of Bakunin were bound in the most specific terms to have no dealings with bourgeois political parties and to spurn all compromises in their advance towards social revolution. Yet the agreement was sufficiently great for the question of whether or not they should co-operate to invite serious considera-tion. Everyone knew that the Internationalists had fought alongside the Garde Nationale (who were not even Federals) in the Paris Commune.

The decision arrived at was highly characteristic. The Internationa-lists refused to give any general support to the Federalist movement, but they raised no objection to their local groups or individual members co-operating with it. That is to say, they were ready to get any advantage they could out of it for themselves without compro-mising either their principles or their freedom of action.[2] And when one examines the records of the Cantonalist risings one is struck by the very small part the International played in them. At Valencia they came out because the Governor had imprisoned some of their members—an early example of the famous anarchist solidarity. At Granada two of them sat on the Committee of Public Safety. (The effect of this was so to terrify the bourgeoisie that the Canton collapsed

---

[1] A. Marvaud, *La Question Sociale en Espagne*, p. 36. This had also been the language of the Internationalist groups in the Paris Commune. And on 21 October 1868 the Central Committee of the International of Geneva had issued a manifesto calling upon the Spanish people to 'proclaim a Federal Republic—the only form of government that, transitorially and as a means of arriving at a social organization based on justice, offers serious guarantees of popular liberty'.

But as the conflict with Marx developed, the a-politicism of the Bakuninists became more pronounced. The final attitude of refusal to co-operate with any political party was fixed at the Congress of Saint Imier in 1872 in a resolution written by Bakunin himself and accepted by the Federal Congress at Cordova a few months later (see Guillaume, *L'Internationale*, vol. III, p. 8 for the text of this). This must be considered the fundamental doctrine of Spanish Anarchism.

[2] See Note C on p. 167 at end of chapter.

at once.) Only at one or two small towns, where they had a following of factory hands, did they do anything on their own account. It may be worth while to describe what happened at one of these, because it provides the first example of the Red atrocity story that was to be brought up with monotonous regularity whenever the middle classes felt their position to be threatened.

Alcoy is a small town between Valencia and Alicante which manufactures paper. It is a historic industry—paper has been made here since the eleventh century—and in 1873 the factories employed 8000 hands. Under the influence of a school teacher called Albarracín, who had been converted to anarchism, they decided to give Spain its first example of a general strike. The object of the strike was, in accordance with the resolutions of the Regional Congress at Cordova, an eight-hour day. The men came out and began to negotiate with the owners. Whilst they were doing so the municipality intervened, taking, as one would expect, the owners' side. The workmen at once sent a deputation to demand the resignation of the alcalde, who, as they declared, had broken his promise to remain neutral. Bands of workmen began to march up and down the street in front of the town hall till the police, losing their heads as in Spain they usually do, fired a volley. A fight began which lasted twenty hours. During the fight some dozen people were killed on each side. The workmen were in the end victorious and as a sign of their victory they burned several factories and houses, shot the offending mayor and, *more hispanico*, cut off his head and those of the police who had been killed in the fight and paraded them round the town.

The events at Alcoy produced an enormous sensation. For the first time a group which did not belong either to the Church, the Army or the middle classes had become revolutionary. The whole press came out with stories of people thrown alive from balconies, women violated, priests crucified, men soaked in petrol and set on fire.[1] Even the Republican papers joined in. Such was the fear inspired by the working classes and by their new dreaded organization the International![2]

---

[1] See Note D on p. 167 at end of chapter.

[2] The fear was worked up artificially by the Carlists, who brought out two pseudo-anarchist papers, *El Petroleo* and *Los Descamisados*, which filled their columns with crude invocations to the people to rise and murder the bourgeois and burn their property. J. J. Morato gives some amusing extracts from these. Under the vignette on the front page of *Los Descamisados* was written: '900,000 heads! Let us tear the vault of heaven as though it were a paper roof! Property is theft! Complete, utter social equality! Free Love!' whilst the first number con-

The days of this International in Spain were now drawing to a close. But their last months were the most glorious. In Europe most people attributed to them the success of the Cantonalist rising. Everywhere except in Spain reaction reigned and the only live revolutionary force seemed to be Anarchism. In Engels' correspondence one sees how bitter was his jealousy and how great his delight when, with the disappearance of the Republic, the last glimmer of revolution in Europe was suppressed. Yet these Anarchists had, in fact, accomplished very little. The Federals—despised bourgeois that they were— had shown themselves a thousand times braver and more revolutionary. Perhaps the most terrible thing about the International had been its name. It had already brought them, even in those lax and disorderly years, four 'persecutions', and Sagasta had gone so far as to declare their organization outlawed and they themselves under the criminal code. Even their numbers were smaller than was generally thought. It is very doubtful whether they ever mustered more than 60,000 members, of whom some 40,000 were in Andalusia.[1] When in January 1874 General Serrano finally suppressed them, there was really no reason to suppose that they would ever be heard of again. The far more powerful Federal movement disappeared for good.

tains an article entitled 'Our Programme' which begins in this style: 'We, the disinherited, the pariahs, the helots, the plebs, the dregs, the scum, the filth of society: we who have no feelings, no education, no shame declare that we have reached the depths of misery and that the hour of our triumph is at hand.... War on the Rich! War on the Powerful! War on Society!.........Anarchy is our only formula. Everything for everyone, from power to women.... But first there must be a terrible, an extraordinary blood bath.'

It is easy to guess what use was made of these publications. Already, a year before this, Cándido Nocedal, the Carlist leader in the Cortes, was saying that the country would have to choose between Don Carlos and Petrol, whilst the Liberal Minister for Home Affairs, Sagasta, firmly convinced that the International in Spain was sustained by foreign gold and by three hundred foreign emissaries, was denouncing it as a 'philosophic utopia of crime'.

The facts are different. When Bakunin in 1873 wished to visit Barcelona, he was unable to do so because he could not raise the few pounds necessary to pay his railway fare. The only foreign emissaries to visit Spain for the International were Fanelli and Lafargue.

[1] The Spanish delegate at the Bakuninist Congress at Geneva in September 1873 claimed for the movement 300,000 members. Francisco Mora, one of the hostile Marxist group, gave the figure as 60,000. *The Times* correspondent on 5 September gave it as 50,000. The anonymous author of an article 'Del Nacimiento de las Ideas Anarcho-Colectivistas en España', published in the *Revista Social* (Madrid) on 14 February 1884, writing with an inside knowledge of the Anarchist movement, gave it as 30,000. But the Anarchists, true Iberians that they are, have never attached much importance to numerical accuracy. 'Let us have no more', wrote the editor of *Solidaridad Obrera* in 1937, 'of these miserable statistics, which only freeze the brain and paralyse the blood'.

The International did survive, however. For seven years it lived underground. Its assemblies ceased to be held, the links between the different sections disappeared, the Catalan trade unions were made illegal. What remained were small circles of militants in Barcelona and Madrid and groups of artisans and field labourers in Andalusia. It was Andalusia that kept the fires of Anarchism alight during the next twenty years.

To get a better idea of the situation in this part of Spain one can compare it with that of Ireland in Fenian times. In both the same factors were at work. An imaginative race, a hopeless oppression and poverty, a class of landowners who when not actually absentees were regarded as foreigners, a special constabulary living in fortified barracks and armed with rifles. This constabulary, the Guardia Civil, was important. Narváez had created it in 1844 to take the place of the militia, who were politically unreliable: its chief function was to keep down the bandits.

The bandit had always been a feature of Andalusian life and for centuries had acted as a safety-valve for popular discontent. In the eyes of the country-people he was a hero, the friend of the poor and its champion against its oppressors. But the enclosure of the common lands had so increased the discontent that it became unsafe to tolerate bandits any longer. They were suppressed and risings of peasants came instead. However, on the first sign of political disturbance, the bandit reappeared again, but this time on the other side. No longer Robin Hoods (the police made that impossible), they were now the tools of the caciques, who needed them to protect their property and to control the elections against the rising tide of popular enthusiasm. The crop of bandits which covered Andalusia between 1868 and 1873 and made travelling without escort impossible were nearly all of this type, and since, whenever they were arrested, the caciques put pressure on the judges to release them, the police were powerless. Andalusia seemed to be approaching the condition that led to the appearance of the Mafia in Sicily. It was the anarchists and the Civil Guard between them that prevented this by polarizing the feelings of the oppressed and the oppressors. From now on every Civil Guard became a recruiting officer for anarchism, and, as the anarchists increased their membership, the Civil Guard also grew.[1] One has to

[1] See Julián de Zugasti, *El Bandolerismo*, 1878. Zugasti was Governor of Cordova from 1870 to 1874 with the special mission of suppressing brigandage. He was the originator of the famous *ley de fugas*. See also Bernaldo de Quirós, *La Mafia* and *El Espartaquismo Andaluz*.

have lived in Andalusia to understand the kind of warfare that went on between them.

This Civil Guard was one of the few really reliable and incorruptible bodies of men in Spain. Carefully picked and highly disciplined, they lived scattered in small fortified posts among the towns and villages, forbidden to intermarry or to associate familiarly with the local inhabitants or to move about unarmed or alone. This rule has led to their being known everywhere as *la Pareja*, or 'the Pair'. It goes without saying that in poverty-stricken districts—that is to say, throughout a large part of Spain—their relations with the working classes were of open hostility and suspicion. Living as they did among their enemies, they became unusually ready to shoot. Again and again mild riots and demonstrations have become dangerous because the Civil Guard could not keep their fingers off their triggers. And from the moment that, in the nineties, the Anarchists rather tentatively took to violence too, the readiness of the Guardia to shoot became greater than ever. After 1931 the hatred between them and the villagers made many parts of Spain ungovernable.

The character of the rural anarchism that grew up in the south of Spain differed, as one would expect, from that developed in the large cities of the north. 'The idea', as it was called, was carried from village to village by Anarchist 'apostles'. In the farm labourers' *gañanias* or barracks, in isolated cottages by the light of oil *candiles*, the apostles spoke on liberty and equality and justice to rapt listeners. Small circles were formed in towns and villages which started night schools where many learned to read, carried on anti-religious propaganda and often practised vegetarianism and teetotalism. Even tobacco and coffee were banned by some and one of these old apostles whom I knew maintained that, when the age of liberty came in, men would live on unfired foods grown by their own hand. But the chief characteristic of Andalusian anarchism was its naïve millenarianism. Every new movement or strike was thought to herald the immediate coming of a new age of plenty, when all—even the Civil Guard and the landowners—would be free and happy. How this would happen no one could say. Beyond the seizure of the land (not even that in some places) and the burning of the parish church, there were no positive proposals.

The underground period came to an end in 1881 when the Liberal Government of Sagasta (once the Diocletian of the Internationalists) came into office and passed a law making trade unions and working-class organizations legal. The Socialists at once took advantage of this law to found their party and at an Anarchist Congress held in Barcelona in March the Spanish Regional Federation of the International came into existence. It was a federation of small trade unions and local sections, modelled on that set up by the Cordova Congress in 1872, with a strictly legal programme of propaganda and strikes.

But meanwhile repressions and persecutions all over Europe had brought about a change in the character of anarchism. The Bakuninist International had held its last Congress in 1877. Since then a crisis in the watch-making industry had led to the ruin of the small home industries in the Jura, and large-scale production at Geneva took its place. Thus the backbone of anarchist trade unionism in Europe was broken and in March 1878 the *Bulletin de la Fédération Jurassienne*, which for seven years had been the chief organ of the Anarchist movement, came out for the last time. *Le Révolté*, edited by Kropotkin at Geneva, took its place with a new theory—anarchist communism.

But the loss of its trade-union following owing to persecutions and other causes, and its consequent isolation from the masses, was leading to a movement that tended either to individualism or to small secret groups. In the congresses that were celebrated from time to time in different parts of Europe it was no longer federations of workers who sent their delegates, but small groups of militants and sometimes even newspapers and isolated individuals, who represented no one but themselves. Most of the groups were secret and some were terrorist.

It was the Italians who best represented this tendency. The factory worker in Italy had never taken to anarchism.[1] Just as in Spain, it had been the *petite bourgeoisie* and the peasants of the south who had shown most susceptibility to it. Already at the Berne Congress of 1876 Malatesta was declaring that 'trade unionism was a reactionary institution'. But the police had become more active in Italy since then and soon even the peasants hung back. To stir them up and to rouse their imaginations new and more striking methods were suggested. 'Propaganda by deed' began to be preached as an anarchist technique.[2] At first this did not consist in much more than organized risings or conspicuous acts of sabotage, but police repressions, accompanied sometimes by ferocious torture in prison, led to the formation of definitely terroristic groups, which were ready to use any means to bring down their enemies.

[1] See Note E on p. 168 at end of chapter.
[2] See Note F on p. 168 at end of chapter.

The assassination of the Czar in March 1881 by Russian Social Revolutionaries caused a profound sensation all over Europe. The reactionaries everywhere took fright and the revolutionaries were encouraged. The Anarchist Congress which met in London four months later debated under its shadow. Many of the delegates were, in Stekloff's words, 'isolated desperadoes, lone wolves, infuriated by persecution and out of touch with the masses'. Others, the most violent of all in their proposals, were police spies. Others again represented the new theorics of 'anarchist communism'. But resolutions were passed accepting 'propaganda by deed' as a useful method and recommending members to 'pay more attention to the technical and chemical sciences'. The Spanish delegate, when he went back to Madrid, took several new ideas with him.

However, the effect of this changed orientation upon their Spanish comrades was inconsiderable. Spaniards lived then at a great distance from the rest of Europe. Besides, anarchism had still a large proletarian following. Under such conditions terrorist action was madness and would not find any encouragement among the workers. The new Regional Federation had in any case no need to appeal for violent methods. Its progress during the first year or two of its existence was rapid. A Congress held at Seville in 1882 represented some 50,000 workers, of whom 30,000 came from Andalusia and most of the rest from Catalonia.[1]

Yet the fact that there was no longer any picked body of professed Anarchists, such as had been provided by the old Alliance of Social Democracy, led to a serious lack of cohesion. Two tendencies stood out—the Catalan, which was reformist to the point of believing that the trade-union struggle should be kept within legal bounds and that strike funds should be accumulated,[2] and the Andalusian, which was

---

[1] According to Anselmo Lorenzo the Regional Federation was composed at this time of 49,000 members. Of these 30,047 were from Andalusia, 13,181 from Catalonia, 2,355 from Valencia, 1,550 from Castile, 847 from Galicia, 689 from Aragon and 710 from the Basque provinces (i.e. Bilbao) (*El Proletariado Militante*, vol. II, pp. 147 and 313).

Díaz del Moral (op. cit. p. 122) gives a total of 57,934 members, of whom 19,181 were from Eastern Andalusia, and 19,168 from Western Andalusia. The discrepancy is due to the fact that for Andalusia he is including sections which were affiliated to the Federation but which did not send delegates to the Congress at Seville. These figures, whether correct or not in themselves, show clearly the distribution of Anarchists in different parts of the country and their huge preponderance in the south. It was not till the end of the century that the Anarchist federations in Catalonia began to outnumber those in Andalusia. Till then Spanish anarchism was chiefly a rural movement.

[2] See Note G on p. 168 at end of chapter.

opposed to strike funds because it could not afford them and for that reason favoured short strikes accompanied by violent action and sabotage.

The Congress held at Seville in 1882 secured a formula of conciliation, but a group of Andalusians who called themselves the *Desheredados* or 'Disinherited' and consisted of certain sections of workers from the vineyards of Jerez and Arcos de la Frontera dissented and left the Federation. They favoured more violent action. Feeling in the country districts at that time was especially tense because the last two years had been years of severe drought and famine. The starving labourers had had to stand by and watch the crops on the large estates carried off to be sold at high prices in Seville or Cadiz. Ever since 1876 discontent had been acute and had shown itself in burnings of vineyards and in assassinations. Secret groups and societies pullulated. Then came a year of exceptionally abundant rainfall. The harvest was excellent and a strike of reapers against piece-work led to a state of excitement and expectation in the whole district. All at once the police announced that they had discovered a formidable secret society, the *Mano Negra* or 'Black Hand', whose members had formed a plot to assassinate all the landowners of the district. Thousands of arrests were made, there were three hundred sentences of imprisonment and, after the usual tortures to obtain evidence, eight executions. Yet the very existence of the *Mano Negra* has been disputed. Bernaldo de Quirós, the famous sociologist sent down by the Government to investigate, doubted it. Spanish and French newspapers took it up and debated it for years. The nature of the evidence presented in court, the manifest barbarity of the procedure and the severity of the sentences seemed to show that the whole thing was an invention of the police. New evidence has, however, come to light from which it would appear that there were secret societies which condemned to death—not landlords, but informers, and that the *Desheredados* were mixed up in this. But what is also certain is that the police enormously magnified the whole matter and took advantage of it to condemn the leading Anarchists of the district without any regard to whether they were innocent or guilty.[1]

The *Mano Negra* episode and the reaction that followed it drove underground once more the anarchist movement in Andalusia. In vain did a Congress summoned at Valencia issue anathemas against criminal activities. An outbreak of bubonic plague on the east coast

[1] See Note H on p. 168 at end of chapter.

led to a brief religious revival and to nightly processions of the Virgin about the streets. In Barcelona the Federation was rapidly going downhill. Its lack of fighting spirit and the bitter dissensions between the collectivists and the 'anarchist communists' were disintegrating it.

This matter of collectivism and communism must be explained. The question was—in what form would the stateless society of the future be organized? In Bakunin's day the matter had been very little discussed: the word collectivism had been adopted because to French minds communism suggested the phalanstery.[1] In a collectivist society all property and instruments of labour are held in common, but each man has the right to what he can earn by his own work, or to join with other groups (collectives) who possess that right. Such a method of organization rather presupposes a primitive agrarian form of life and is at first sight not so well adapted to modern industrial conditions. Thus, though it was popular in Andalusia, it was questioned in Barcelona. Communism had the further advantage of being supported by most of the leading Anarchists in Europe: Kropotkin, who had taken up what had originally been an Italian theory, had won them over to it. However, another very important idea was involved in this question—that of liberty. The new dogma struck at the conception underlying the whole Bakuninist organization— the liberty that each group had to decide what it thought best. If it were adopted it would put an end to that collaboration of convinced Anarchists with large bodies of free workers which was the essence of Bakunin's system. Here and not in some disagreement about the hypothetical form of the future .... sy. Kropotkin stood f.. chist ranks that would .... masses.

The .... onal Federation broke u .... olent discussion as to .... solely of convinced .... were ready to join. T .... between 'communist .... akunin. When, with th .... , it was finally decide .... uestion of the

[1] See .... ng to him 'Spanish collectiv .... all instruments of product .... e as they think fit, accordir .... ad, p. 216).

nature of the future form of society became less important. Whilst collectivism was retained as a working basis, the distant ideal became *comunismo libertario*.[1]

The next twenty years are the most obscure and ill-defined in the history of Spanish anarchism. For one thing there was no longer any single Anarchist federation covering Spain. In different towns there existed small groups of militants and intellectuals, generally centring round some weekly or fortnightly journal, and in Catalonia there was a trade union, the *Pacto de Solidaridad y Resistencia*, of collectivist tendencies, and a smaller *Organización Anarquista*, composed of pure anarchists who were mostly communists. Barcelona, Madrid and a little later Corunna contained the strongest nuclei of militants, whilst in Andalusia rural anarchism pursued its usual rhythm: bursts of millenarian fervour leading up to some great strike or mass demonstration and followed by a decade of apathy.

One of these occurred in January 1891 when, inspired by a successful strike in Barcelona, 4000 labourers armed with sticks and scythes marched into Jerez crying: 'We cannot wait another day—We must be the first to begin the Revolution—Long live Anarchy!' and occupied it for several hours. On the arrival of the police they dispersed. Two shopkeepers were murdered in the course of this otherwise harmless exploit, but the police made it the excuse for a violent repression, condemning four to death and sentencing eighteen to long terms of hard labour.[2]

The nineties were everywhere the period of anarchist terrorism. We have seen how the loss of its working-class adherents and the stupidity of police repressions led to this. But there were other causes as well. The reign of the bourgeoisie was now at its height. Their meanness, their philistinism, their insufferable self-righteousness weighed upon everything. They had created a world that was both dull and ugly and they were so firmly established in it that it seemed hopeless even to dream of revolution. The desire to shake by some violent action the complacency of this huge, inert and stagnant

---

[1] The word 'libertarian' was invented by Sébastien Faure in 1898, when the great Anarchist periodical, *Revista Blanca*, was founded. Since at that time anarchist propaganda was forbidden, some other word had to be used to express the idea.

[2] Blasco Ibáñez's novel *La Bodega* is based on this rising. The saintly Anarchist 'apostle' who is its hero is meant as a portrait of Fermín Salvoechea, who although in prison at Cadiz at the time of the rising, was sentenced to twelve years hard labour for complicity in it. It is true that he probably organized it from the gaol. The following year there was a strike in the same district at harvest time against landowners who paid 'fifty centimes for sixteen hours'. The landowners defeated it in the usual way, by calling in blackleg labour from the mountain villages.

mass of middle-class opinion became irresistible. Artists and writers shared this feeling. One must put such books as Flaubert's *Bouvard et Pécuchet* and Huysmans' *A Rebours*, Butler's and Wilde's epigrams and Nietzsche's savage outbursts in the same category as the bombs of the Anarchists. To shock, to infuriate, to register one's protest became the only thing that any decent or sensitive man could do.[1] In Spain, however, the psychological atmosphere was different. The police were more brutal and governments were more tyrannous, but as they were also more inefficient and more careless, and as life still followed in the easier track of the previous century, the air could still be breathed. Bomb outrages tended less therefore to take the form of protests against society in general than to be strict acts of revenge for prison tortures or unjust sentences. The first bomb was thrown in 1891 at a building—the offices of the great Catalan employers' association, the *Fomento*. A strike was in progress and it was thought that a little 'propaganda by deed' would encourage the workers. After this Barcelona suffered from a perfect epidemic of petards and bombs, laid however not so much to injure as to frighten. The people responsible for this were a small group of Anarchists,[2] many of them Italians, who believed that in this way they would raise

---

[1] To register a protest! This phrase sums up almost the whole of anarchist action in Spain during the last fifty years. In their newspapers and magazines no word is so common as the word *protesta*. Spanish anarchism early adopted an attitude of moral disapproval towards the bourgeoisie and all its doings which it never relaxed. As to the assassinations, whilst there can be no doubt that Bakunin would not have approved of a *policy* of terrorism, it is also true that he did not boggle at isolated 'acts of justice'. In a letter to Herzen dated 23 June 1867 he writes: 'Why do you call Berezovsky a fanatic? "He is pure because he is a fanatic" you say. What a terrible *jeu de mots*!..........As if there were no right to passions in life! Berezovsky is an avenger, one of the most legitimate *justiciers* of all the crimes, of all the tortures and of all the humiliations which the Poles have suffered. Can't you understand? If such explosions of indignation did not take place in the world, one would despair of the human race.'

[2] It is from now on that the small group becomes the characteristic organization. Small parties or *tertulias* of people would meet every day at some café to discuss the new ideas and to make plans, and at the centre of these would be four or five initiates, usually intimate friends, who held the secrets. These groups gave themselves names, such as *Salut, Fortuna, Avant, Benvenuto,* and so on. Most of them confined themselves to discussion and propaganda, in which they were highly successful. By 1892, when the bomb outrages began, large sections of the middle classes and intellectuals in Barcelona had been won over to sympathy with Anarchist ideas. But under foreign influences other groups became terrorist.

This group organization persisted, surviving even the importation of syndicalism, and later we see the redoubtable Federación Anarquista Ibérica or F.A.I. built up of a large number of groups of like-minded persons, that reacted on one another in a complicated manner. They had their cafés too: the place at which most of the armed risings of the Republican period were hatched was the *Café Tranquilidad* in the Paralelo.

the fighting spirit of the workmen. A book of instructions for making explosives, called the *Indicador Anarquista*, was handed round and a watchmaker learned to make Orsini bombs with a time fuse. Malatesta visited Spain and held a large meeting at Madrid. But the leading Spanish militants held aloof.

The following year a young man called Pallás threw a bomb at General Martínez Campos in revenge for the execution of two well-known Anarchist journalists for complicity in the Jerez rising. Martínez Campos was only slightly wounded, but Pallás was tried by court martial and shot. His friend Santiago Salvador avenged him with a terrible act. He threw a bomb into the stalls of the Liceo theatre, killing twenty people, half of them women, and wounding many more. The police, who at first could not find out who had done it, arrested five leading Anarchists at hazard and, although it was clear that they had no connection with the terrorists, the judges found them guilty. Then Salvador was caught. However, this did not prevent the five from being executed as well.[1] The inefficiency of the police on this occasion led to the creation of a new political police force, the Brigada Social.

The first act of this police was however a rather peculiar one. The traditional procession with the Host on Corpus Christi Day, headed by the bishop, the Captain-General and other authorities, was on its way to Santa María del Mar, when in the Calle de Cambios Nuevos a bomb was thrown from a top-story window on to it. But the bomb did not fall on the head of the procession where the leading dignitaries of the city were walking: it fell on the tail, where it killed seven working-class people and a soldier. The thrower of this bomb was never discovered, but General Weyler, of Cuban War notoriety and at that time Captain-General of Barcelona, made an immediate use of the incident. Not merely Anarchists but simple anti-clericals were arrested wholesale and thrown into the Montjuich dungeons, where the new police was let loose upon them. Here without any control or any rational object the most frightful tortures were applied. Several died under them, in addition to the official executions. Yet of those

---

[1] Salvador, in order to escape from the frightful tortures that were employed, pretended to repent of his act and to be converted. The Jesuits took him under their protection: one then had the extraordinary spectacle of the aristocratic ladies in Madrid and Barcelona treating him as a 'poor unfortunate' and getting up petitions to the government for his reprieve. Not a word was said about saving his perfectly innocent but irreligious companions. However, the reprieve was refused, and on the scaffold Salvador threw off the mask and cried *Viva el Anarquismo!*

executed only one, Ascheri, had belonged to the group of bomb throwers. Of those acquitted sixty-one were sent to the penal settlements of Rio de Oro, a punishment at that time almost worse than death. The Montjuich tortures shocked Europe and a young Italian Anarchist called Angiolillo, then living in London, was so moved by the account he heard that he made his way to Santa Agueda, where the Prime Minister, Cánovas, was taking the waters, and shot him.[1]

The loss of Cuba brought this wretched era to an end. Both the Government and the Army were too discredited to take the field any longer. The terrorist groups were discredited too and most of their members were either dead or in prison. A new breeze began to stir the drooping leaves of Anarchism. First it began to be said that the general strike and not the bomb was the true revolutionary weapon; then it was passed round that the triumph of Anarchism, like the triumph of Catholicism and the triumph of Liberalism, could only come from the schools: the young must be educated in the libertarian doctrine before the conquest of power could begin. A movement for founding Anarchist schools therefore grew up in various parts of the country. At Barcelona the *Escuela Moderna* was founded by Francisco Ferrer. At this children were brought up to believe in liberty, social equality and so on, and above everything else to hate the Church which taught false and 'perverted' doctrines. There were also night schools for adults and a printing press which turned out a continuous stream of Anarchist books and pamphlets. Ferrer himself, a narrow-minded pedant with few attractive qualities, professed to have given up all belief in violence and to have abjured his Anarchist connections, but this need not be taken too seriously. The recent persecutions had made discretion desirable. Other schools were founded in Andalusia. Working men were taught to read and to abjure religion, vice and alcoholism. A woman, Belén Sárraga, founded a society for working women in the province of Málaga which had 20,000 members, mostly field labourers.

This movement corresponded to a period of intellectual expansion. Never before had Spanish anarchism contained men of education and ideas. It also began to open its ranks to the middle classes. Tarrida del Mármol, one of the leading Anarchists of the period, was the director of the Polytechnic Academy at Barcelona and came from one of the best families in the city. José López Montenegro, who edited *La Huelga General*, had been a colonel in the Army. Ricardo Mella,

[1] See Note I on p. 168 at end of chapter.

a Galician engineer, was the only Spaniard to make any contribution to Anarchist theory. Many young writers and intellectuals too were drawn into the acratic orbit. Pío Baroja, Maeztu and Azorín sat for a time in their cafés and flirted with libertarian ideas. In Spain, just as in France, anarchism was the fashion. But the intense seriousness, which seemed to them narrowness and fanaticism, of the Anarchists ended by driving most of these young dilettantes away, and the arrival of syndicalism closed the Anarchist ranks for good and all to bourgeois sympathizers. Since 1910 the attitude of the Spanish Anarchists towards the intellectuals has been consistently hostile. They have had their own writers and thinkers and have not been interested in others.

For Syndicalism was now in the air: the new belief in the efficacy of the general strike was due to its influence. It led to the formation in Madrid in 1900 of a Federation of Workers of the Spanish Region, founded on the classic model of 1873 and 1881. This culminated two years later in a metallurgic strike in Barcelona in which many other workers joined. The strike failed and was followed by a temporary set-back: the workmen left the Anarchist unions in swarms and the Federation collapsed.[1] But it had given rise to a great deal of enthusiasm all over Spain and to an unprecedented wave of millenarian fervour in Andalusia. It was clear that it was only a matter of time before the new Syndicalist methods of organization, with their superior vigour and cohesion, would cross the Pyrenees into Spain.[2]

---

[1] According to a Catholic economist, Sastre, who made a special study of the working-class organizations of this period, the number of workmen in Barcelona who belonged to the 'societies of resistance' declined from over 45,000 in 1902 to a bare 10,000 in 1909. The total number of workmen in Barcelona at this time was 88,000. Even so not all these 45,000 were affiliated to Anarchist federations: according to Buenacasa, an Anarchist Congress held at Madrid in 1900 represented only 50,000 members from the whole of Spain. The fact is that the oldest and most important trade unions in Barcelona, the hand-weavers, paper-makers, barrel-makers and half the mill hands had steadily refused, since the foundation of the International, to come under Anarchist influence. It was Syndicalism and the foundation of the C.N.T. that brought them all in.

[2] See Note J on p. 169 at end of chapter.

FURTHER NOTES TO CHAPTER VII

A (p. 142). Of the 54 delegates who attended the Regional Congress at Cordova in December 1872, 30 belonged to various trades (printers, typographers, master masons, shoemakers, carpenters, bakers), 11 were factory hands (cotton spinners and papermakers), 3 were small peasants, 2 were students and one was a school teacher. For further details see Díaz del Moral, op. cit. pp. 100 and 421. Among them were several men of talent—Pablo Iglesias, Francisco Mora, José Mesa, Juan José Morato, who later joined the Socialist Party: Anselmo Lorenzo, Tomás González Morago,

Rafael Farga Pellicer, Fermín Salvoechea, who remained Bakuninists. The books written by J. J. Morato and Anselmo Lorenzo upon their respective movements have considerable merit.

B (p. 143). This rectification of Fanelli's mistake had been prepared during the previous summer, when Farga Pellicer and Dr Sentiñon went to Switzerland to attend the Fourth Congress of the International at Basle, met Bakunin and became members of his intimate circle, the Fraternité Internationale.

The programme of the Alianza de la Democracia Social, first published in August 1872 in *La Federación* and reprinted in Nettlau's *La Internacional y la Alianza en España*, was as follows:

1. The Alliance desires first of all the definite and complete abolition of classes, and economic and social equality of individuals of both sexes. In order to arrive at this, it demands the abolition of individual property and of the right of inheritance....

2. It desires for the children of both sexes equality of education, of food and of social position (*ilustración*)....

3. Enemy of all despotism, it recognizes no form of state and refuses all revolutionary action which has not for its object the direct triumph of the workers' cause against capital; for it desires that all the political and authoritarian states at present existing should be reduced to mere administrative functions of public services....

4. It refuses to take part in any action founded upon so-called patriotism and rivalry between nations.

5. It declares itself atheistical: desires the abolition of all cults and the substitution of science for faith and of human for divine justice.

C (p. 153). It is sometimes asserted that the Internationalists 'infused their tactics and principles' into the Cantonalist movement, in imitation of the Paris Commune. There is not the least truth in this. For one thing they were too weak. Compared to the *petite bourgeoisie* with its long insurrectionary traditions, who formed the bulk of the Federal party, they were quite insignificant both in their numbers and in their lack of self-confidence. For another, it had been decided at two assemblies held at Barcelona and at Alcoy on the eve of the general elections not to take part as a body in any political action, though individual members should be allowed to co-operate with the Federals if they wished to do so. The Internationalists were to confine themselves to pressing for better conditions for the working classes in Spain, whilst keeping the social revolution as a distant objective. The Cantonalist risings that summer did not materially alter this. The only risings where the Internationalists played any real part were those led by the local federations of Alcoy and San Lúcar de Barrameda, which grew out of strikes that had purely economic objects. See J. Guillaume, *L'Internationale, Documents et Souvenirs*, vol. III, part 5, pp. 60 and 85. Also Anselmo Lorenzo, *op. cit.* vol. II, pp. 122-126. And for the view of the Marxist group, see the report written for Engels by José Mesa and Pablo Iglesias on 24 August 1873, which is quoted by Max Nettlau in *Documentos Inéditos, etc.*

D (p. 154). The Internationalists' version of what happened at Alcoy is given by Lorenzo, *El Proletariado Militante*, vol. II, p. 147.

It may be interesting to compare this quite exceptional affair with a typical Andalusian riot that occurred at the same time, but in which the International played no part. Montilla is a small town lying to the south of Cordova in a famous wine-producing district. There was a strong federal Republican movement there in 1869 and also a *sociedad campesina* or peasants' and agricultural labourers' union. But the rich families of the town had no intention of surrendering their power because the Monarchy had fallen and, as elsewhere in Andalusia, they organized what was known as a *Partido de la Porra* or Cudgel Party with the help of ruffians whose business it was to control the elections and beat up anyone who tried to make trouble for their masters. When Sagasta was in power, they called themselves constitutionals: when Ruiz Zorrilla, radicals: when Serrano, unionists. That is to say, they were always of the same party as the Government and so could count on the support of the Civil Guard. And so with their paid bands of *matones* or brigands there was no one who dared to contradict them. But on the abdication of King Amadeo and the proclamation of the republic the local federals thought it time for the alcalde and his corporation to quit their posts and hand over the municipality to them. Such is the rule in Spain, where all real changes of government are revolutions. But the *matones* prevented this. Then in one of those spontaneous movements of anger that Bakunin would have admired, without prearranged plan and without leaders, the people broke loose, sacked and burned the houses of the rich, destroyed the property deeds and killed several of their tyrants. See Díaz del Moral, *op. cit.* pp. 67-77.

E (p. 158). ' In Italy the workers, the urban operatives, are on the whole conservative or apathetic. The Revolutionary section of the Italian population is made up out of the peasantry, the *petite bourgeoisie* and those who have been miscalled by the nickname of Lumpenproletariat.' Italian delegate No. 25 (Merlino, not, as Stekloff asserts, Malatesta) at the Anarchist Congress in 1881. Quoted by Stekloff, *History of the First International.*

F (p. 158). The first reference to propaganda by deed occurs in a letter written by Malatesta to Cafiero on 3 December 1876 and published in the *Bulletin de la Fédération Jurassienne*: 'The Italian Federation believes that the insurrectionary deed, which attempts to affirm socialist principles by action, is the most efficient means of propaganda, the only one which, neither cheating nor depraving the masses, is able to make its way effectively into the lowest social strata and to direct the living forces of mankind towards support of the international struggle.'

G (p. 159). According to Buenacasa it was the insistence of the leaders of the Regional Federation that strikes should be kept within legal limits and their recommendation of strike funds that ruined it. Lorenzo and most of the older militants opposed this as leading to calculation and to a weakening of the fighting spirit.

H (p. 160). The sources for the *Mano Negra* episode are:
1. The Materials published by Soledad Gustavo in *Tierra y Libertad* during 1902. This is the official Anarchist version and denies everything.
2. Bernaldo de Quirós, *El Espartaquismo Andaluz.*
3. Díaz del Moral, *op. cit.*
4. Two articles by Max Nettlau in *Revista Blanca,* 1 December 1928 and 15 January 1929. Nettlau gives evidence to show that the *Desheredados* 'condemned to death' Farga Pellicer and other leading Anarchists of the Regional Federation. Considering the stir this affair has made, it is surprising to learn that only three assassinations (all of poor men) were ever proved. However, it had one good effect: it led to the setting up by Moret of the Comisión de Reformas Sociales for investigating the causes of industrial and agricultural unrest. The first President of this body was Cánovas.

I (p. 165). The revelation of the police tortures in Montjuich gaol made a deep impression everywhere. David Hannay, at this time British Vice-Consul at Barcelona and author of *Twentieth-Century Spain,* wrote that 'there was no doubt that torture was used to extort confessions from large numbers of people arrested at random. It was not applied as by the Inquisition and by the old criminal procedure on a regulated system and under the supervision of magistrates, but at the direction of the lowest class of political agents. These cruelties were quoted by Michel Angiolillo as his justification for murdering Cánovas. The memory of the torturings

in Montjuich has done more to excite the social hatred of the poor against the rich—
a sentiment once hardly known in Spain, but now too common.'

Hannay goes on to say that much of the violence of the Anarchist movement must
be attributed to the cruelty of the police repression. (*Cambridge Modern History*,
vol. XII, Section on Spain by David Hannay.)

H. B. Clarke, in his conservative history, says the same thing: 'Holders of
advanced opinions, though peaceable citizens, might if they fell into the hands of the
police be treated like wild beasts' (*Modern Spain*, 1906, p. 454).

These horrors were first made known by Tarrida del Mármol, a cultured man of
good family who had himself been imprisoned at Montjuich. He wrote a book on
his experiences which raised a storm in London and Paris. Mass meetings were held
in Trafalgar Square and one of the victims of the police tortures was paraded about
Europe. His toe-nails had been pulled out, his body was a mass of cuts and stripes
and his sexual organs had been burned. And these were not the worst things that
were done. When two years later an attempt was made to assassinate Portas, the
police captain responsible for these horrors, his assailant had to be released, because
no judge would convict him.

For further details see *Historia Ilustrada de la Revolución Española*, by F. Caravaca
and A. Orts-Ramos, vol. I, pp. 301-311. Also a large volume by Pedro Corominas.

J (p. 166). The period 1888-1909 is the most confused and badly documented in the
by no means clear or simple history of Spanish anarchism. Although certain
episodes such as the *Mano Negra* or the Montjuich tortures have been extensively
written upon, there is no book or article even which throws any general light upon it.
Nor is the press informative. Until Dr Nettlau publishes the material he has been
collecting, many points must remain unsettled. And since the war has delayed such
projects indefinitely, it is doubtful if this will ever see the light. Meanwhile I have
to thank him for having answered various questions I put to him.

The salient feature of the period is the attempted introduction from France of
'anarchist communism' with its conception of a centralized organization and secret
directing group. This conflicted so violently with the large but loose federations of
the 'collectivists' that after bitter disputes the Anarchist movement in Spain practically broke up. One group of the 'anarchist communists' then took to terrorism.
This conflict illustrates the fundamental dilemma of anarchist organization. When
the local federations were left to themselves they tended to isolated action and to
reformism and when they were controlled by a small central body, then the revolutionary pace became too hot and most of the members fell off. A compromise
solution was found in Anarcho-Syndicalism, but the disputes that attended the
setting up of the Federación Anarquista Ibérica or F.A.I. in 1927 show that even
this was not entirely satisfactory.

Chapter VIII

THE ANARCHO-SYNDICALISTS

Recommençons maintenant......la marche vers la délivrance.
GEORGES SOREL.

The word 'syndicalism' is simply French for trade unionism. The Syndicalist movement of a generation ago (Revolutionary Syndicalism, as it is usually called) had, however, a special character. It grew up in France during the nineties as a reaction against the parliamentary socialism that allowed such men as Millerand to represent the workers in the Chamber and to lead them along paths acceptable to the bourgeoisie. The figure chiefly associated with it was an Anarchist, Fernand Pelloutier, and, though he died prematurely in 1901, the reorganization of the *Confédération Général du Travail* (or C.G.T.) in the year following his death completed his work.

This Syndicalism was in the first place a movement that aimed at uniting all workers, whatever their political or religious opinions, in one body and in giving to that body a new fighting spirit. They were to reject all corporate political action and to keep entirely to the industrial sphere. Here they would rely upon their own resources and their own men, refusing the assistance of bourgeois journalists and intellectuals. They would cultivate a strict discipline and their only weapon would be the strike, which would be thorough and violent.[1]

Up to this point Syndicalism was simply a fighting technique for winning more and more advantages for the workers—such was its 'daily revindicative task'—until in one crowning battle, conceived in the form of a general strike, total emancipation would be obtained. But it had final aims also: like Proudhon it looked forward to a 'dissolution of government and state in the economic organization' and it saw in its own organization the image of the future society. 'The Syndicate, to-day a society of resistance, will in future be the group of production and distribution and the basis of social reorgani-

---

[1] The general strike goes back to the Chartists, but it was not till the Congress at Verviers of the Belgian Federation of the Bakuninist International in April 1873 that the theory of the general strike as the one and only means of bringing in a social revolution was first put forward. The strike that took place at Alcoy near Valencia a few months later was a consequence of this. After this the idea died down until the growth of revolutionary syndicalism in France during the nineties brought it to the surface again.

zation.'[1] That is to say, it was collectivist. But whereas the Marxists wanted the ultimate control to be exercised through the State and its organs in the interests of the consumer, the Syndicalists wanted this control to rest in the hands of the producers and to be exercised by the trade unions.

Syndicalism had a philosopher, or perhaps one should say a poet, Georges Sorel. His best-known book, *Réflexions sur la Violence*, published in 1908, had little influence among the workers and was never read in Spain,[2] though it was there that its ideas were most successfully carried into effect. It is a neo-romantic production, full of the echoes of Bergson, Schopenhauer and Nietzsche and steeped in a *fin-de-siècle* pessimism. Sorel did not desire the happiness or physical well-being of the workers, but only their moral regeneration. This he conceived in a Nietzschean sense. Out of the sacrifice and heroism of their struggle against the bourgeoisie would arise a new and superior type of man, imbued with the sense of honour and chivalry that comes from war and filled with a consciousness of the dignity and sublimity of his mission. These new men, drawn from the *corps d'élite* of militants who had led the workers into battle, would form the new aristocracy. But such a result could just as well be obtained by a reformed and aggressive middle class as by a victorious proletariat. Thus, by a natural transition, Sorel became the father of Fascism.

In the later development of Spanish Anarcho-Syndicalism one sees much that reminds one of Sorel, especially the belief, always close to the surface in Spain, in the *mystique* of violence. But the generosity and optimism of the Spanish popular movement lay in a different key to the rigid Jansenism of the retired Norman engineer, who believed that 'the great ages were the ages when men had been chaste' and put the blame on the Jews when the Russian Revolution failed to lead to an increase in chivalry. He is better represented by the Falangists, whose Catholic upbringing helped them to appreciate his sense for the penumbra and his mood of semi-religious romanticism. In the Civil War the two branches of his descendants met, and sordid firing squads and bloodstained cemetery walls then showed exactly what was to be got out of Sorelian ethics.

French Syndicalism reached its climax in a congress at Amiens in

---

[1] See the so-called Charte d'Amiens.
[2] A Spanish edition appeared in 1915, but attracted little attention outside literary circles. Later some of the Falangists read it.

1906. The 'theoretic affirmation' which this assembly made in the so-called Charte d'Amiens broadcast its aims and character to the world. In the following year an Anarchist congress met at Amsterdam in the hope of devising something that would increase the cohesion of the anarchist groups and federations in Europe: on the suggestion of Malatesta, who till then had been one of the most intransigeant of the 'communist anarchists', it adopted as a technique Revolutionary Syndicalism.

A considerable number of Spanish Anarchists were already prepared for this. Some years before, after the failure of the 1902 general strike, a federation known as *Solidaridad Obrera* had been formed in Barcelona, with the special object of introducing a syndicalist organization: in 1907 this federation was extended to the whole of Catalonia and in January of the following year it held its first Congress. It seemed that the moment had arrived, but political conditions were not favourable (the agitation in Andalusia had just petered out and Maura's Government was in power) and it had to be postponed. The events of the *Semana Trágica* and the execution of Ferrer decided the matter. The hero's legend and the martyr's crown bring recruits in Spain, and demands for the creation of a strong syndicalist organization were at once raised from all over the country. Thus in October 1910 a Congress of libertarian groups and federations at Seville created the *Confederación Nacional del Trabajo* or, as it is generally called, the C.N.T.[1]

The conditions on which this great union was formed were laid down clearly. Syndicalism was to be regarded, not as an end, but as a means of fighting the bourgeoisie. The end was of course Anarchism. The syndicates were to be organized on a local basis—that is to say, there were to be no national craft unions. The subscriptions were to be small—30 to 50 centimes a month. (In Andalusia, where the wages were exceptionally low, members were not required to pay anything.) There was to be no social insurance and no strike funds, nor were any of its leaders or secretaries to be paid. This at once gave it, in Spanish eyes, a moral superiority over the Socialist trade union, the U.G.T., which had a considerable paid secretariat.[2]

The Congress added a number of riders that might help to explain the meaning of the new syndicate to the growing army of its rivals. The material emancipation of the workers, it declared, could only

---

[1] See Note A on p. 197 at end of chapter.
[2] See Note B on p. 197 at end of chapter.

come as the result of their moral emancipation. When they had ceased to feel like slaves they would be free. And everyone who did not think for himself and act spontaneously, following his own reason, was a slave. 'But the workers cannot feel free so long as they feel the need of emancipators or leaders, who as soon as they have overthrown the old regime will inevitably set up another in which they will be privileged.'

The new confederation held its first congress in 1911 at the Bellas Artes in Madrid. 30,000 members in 350 unions were represented at it.[1] A great expansion seemed about to take place, many of Lerroux's Young Barbarians were flocking in, but the new doctrine of the general strike proved too seductive. Without sufficient preparation a strike broke out at Bilbao and was taken up at Saragossa and Seville. There was also a violent rising at Cullera near Valencia. The premier, Canalejas, acted energetically: the C.N.T. was suspended in Barcelona and in other towns, and its offices were closed. The movement collapsed and the Anarchist press went bankrupt. But Canalejas paid a heavy price for his firmness: like Cánovas before him he was assassinated. Then when in 1914 the syndicates began to reorganize and to prepare again for action the European war broke out and caused a split in the Anarchist ranks, some (especially the younger generation) being neutral and pacifist and others favouring the Allies. The difference went deep and aroused bitter feelings, and it was not till 1917 that the C.N.T. felt itself strong enough to take serious action.

At this point it will be necessary to pause in our account of the development of Anarcho-Syndicalism in the industrial towns in order to say something of what was happening in the country. The principal areas of rural anarchism in Spain are Andalusia and the Levante. With the help of Díaz del Moral's admirably objective and detailed history of the movement in the province of Cordova it should be possible to obtain a fairly exact idea of this.

The general strike in Barcelona in 1902 roused, as we have seen, a good deal of enthusiasm among the working classes in the rest of the country. Nowhere was this greater than in Andalusia. Terrorism had been tried and had failed, half a century of peasant revolts had produced no result beyond long terms of imprisonment and executions: surely the general strike was the key which would unlock the door to happiness and plenty! An extraordinary ferment, as sudden and apparently as causeless as a religious revival, swept over the country

[1] M. Buenacasa, *El Movimiento Obrero Español*, 1928.

districts. In the fields, in the farms and wayside inns only one subject was discussed and always with intense seriousness and fervour. In the midday rests and at night, after supper, groups were formed to listen to a labourer reading aloud from one of the Anarchist papers. Then came speeches and comments. It was what they had known and felt all their lives. How could they shut their ears to it?[1] An immense desire sprang up to read and learn, so as to have access to this store of knowledge and wisdom provided by the Anarchist press. One met peasants reading everywhere, on mule back, at meal time under the olive trees. Those who could not read, by force of hearing others spell out aloud their favourite passages, would learn whole newspaper articles by heart. Sometimes, after a single reading from *Tierra y Libertad* or *El Productor*, a labourer would feel illuminated by the new faith. The scales would fall from his eyes and everything seem clear to him. He then became an *obrero consciente*. He gave up smoking, drinking and gambling. He no longer frequented brothels. He took care never to pronounce the word God. He did not marry but lived with his *compañera*, to whom he was strictly faithful, and refused to baptize his children. He subscribed to at least one Anarchist paper, read the little books on history, geography and botany brought out by Ferrer's press and held forth on these subjects whenever possible. Like other uneducated people who have suddenly had their eyes opened to the possibilities of knowledge, he spoke in an inflated style, using long incomprehensible words.[2]

The assemblies of these converts to *anarquismo* were what one would expect—scenes of naïve enthusiasm reminding one of Baptist meetings in English villages fifty years ago, where country orators discussed and harangued interminably. The speeches and resolutions were often of a simplicity that would make anyone smile, yet the authorities and the landlords, judging the Anarchists through their press and their foreign reputation, imagined that terrible plots were being hatched and fearful schemes of murder and destruction debated. So great was their ignorance of their own workmen that down to 1936 the majority of the landlords believed that, in spite of all appearances to the contrary, the Anarchists were 'in the pay of Moscow'.

The miracle that was to bring in the Messianic Age was the general strike, but in their impatience to see this the *campesinos* would not wait and strikes broke out all over the country without synchroni-

---

[1] See Note C on p. 198 at end of chapter.
[2] See Note D on p. 198 at end of chapter.

zation. Each town or village struck when it seemed best to it, choosing as a rule the worst moment—when there was no work to be done in the fields. The demands were usually for a reduction of hours rather than for an increase of pay—piece-work was particularly objected to—but often they were pushed to absurd lengths.[1] For example, in the general strike at Cordova in 1905 the workers asked for a $7\frac{1}{2}$ hours' rest in an eight-hour day. The reason for this was that, since the strike was expected to bring in the revolution, they wanted to make sure that the owners would not agree to their terms. A more serious demand was for a *reparto*, i.e. for a division of lands. Whilst strikes were in progress the workers gave up drink and tobacco, observed a strict chastity and did not play cards. They either spent their time at home or parading silently up and down the streets. When there are no strike funds to be drawn, strikes are periods of tremendous strain and anxiety for the workers: the battle that the owners wage with their bank balances, the men have to wage with their stomachs. Discipline and solidarity are therefore essential.[2]

The terrible drought and famine of 1905 brought the strikes to an end. The wonder-working images, with their clockwork heads and arms, were brought out and carried in procession round the fields. But Anarchism had killed faith in Catholic miracles and few followed barefoot. The famine, which the Government did very little to relieve, was followed by a period of calm, though defeat left bitter feelings behind it and there were burnings of farms and crops. If the strikes had led in many places to an increase in wages, this was offset by the steady rise all over Spain in the cost of living.

The struggle between the C.N.T. and the Catalan employers' association in Barcelona, which began in 1918 and continued for five years until the Dictatorship put an end to it, has already been described at some length in Chapter IV. It will only be necessary here to show in what way the development of Anarcho-Syndicalism was

---

[1] The real struggle on the large estates was over *destajo* (piece-work). There was a good reason for this. The landlords could not pay decent wages so long as their labourers did so little work. The labourers would not work harder because by doing so they would increase the already cruel unemployment. The landlords got serf labour—that is, bad and unwilling labour—but the labourers did not get the one privilege of serfs, which is maintenance.

[2] Here is an example of a typical strike at Morón in the province of Seville in 1902. 30,000 labourers from the whole district came out on strike and were followed by all the workmen, servants, wet nurses, municipal clerks and so forth. The women made the round of the richer inhabitants, demanding clothes and money. The men demanded a *reparto*, i.e. a division of land. On the arrival of the Civil Guard, the strike collapsed. (A. Marvaud, *La Question Sociale en Espagne*.)

affected by it. The preliminary step was the organization in the C.N.T. of the *sindicatos únicos de ramo*, or factory unions, as a result of the failure of the great revolutionary strike of 1917 in which the Socialists had played the leading part. This measure merely gave the finishing touches to the 'syndicalization' of the new union. It had been the organization by Pelloutier in the nineties of the *Bourses du Travail*, or local unions, in a national federation and their inclusion as a separate section in the newly formed C.G.T. or federation of craft unions that had laid the foundation for the syndicalist machine. Without such a structure it could not be effective. These changes in the C.N.T. therefore, though far from complete, greatly increased the fighting power of the workers' organizations. They were, of course, a deliberate preparation for the coming battle.[1]

In the winter of 1918 a National Anarchist Conference met at Barcelona. Its object was to settle once and for all what were to be the relations of Anarchists to the syndical organization. After some discussion a Bakuninist solution was adopted, recalling the resolutions of the Congress of Cordova and the first years of the International in Spain. That is to say, it was agreed that, though a huge federation of workers such as the C.N.T. could not possibly be described as anarchist, it must be impregnated as much as possible with the libertarian or anarchist spirit and be led and directed by them. The reorganization in *sindicatos únicos* was approved and arrangements were made for launching a vigorous anarchist campaign throughout the country.

The leading figures in this movement were Salvador Seguí, the *Noi del Sucre*, as he was called, or 'Sugar Boy', and Angel Pestaña. Seguí's position was different from that of the 'communist anarchist' doctrinaires of the previous generation. Though a good speaker when occasion required, his chief talent, like that of Pelloutier, lay in organization. The C.N.T. as a fighting force was largely his creation and he dreamed of a fusion between it and the Socialist U.G.T. that would unite in one body all the working-class forces in Spain. For this end he was prepared to surrender some of his Anarchist principles.

---

[1] *Sindicatos únicos de ramo y industrias* in the large and *sindicatos únicos de trabajadores* in the small towns. At the Madrid Congress in December 1919 the question was raised as to whether the formation of *sindicatos únicos* meant that the *federaciones de oficio y de industrias* (i.e. craft unions) then existing must be wound up and 'simple committees of professional relations' put in their place. At the request of the Asturian delegation, which was under the influence of Socialist trade-union ideas, it was agreed that the old federations might remain.

But before anything of this sort could take place it was necessary to rouse the workers throughout Spain by means of some great act which would prove the strength of the new syndical organization. Enthusiasm among the Catalan workers had reached a point when it would decline if it were not given an outlet.

It was under these circumstances that the strike in the *Canadiense* (the great electrical company of Barcelona) broke out in February 1919. The strike ended in a compromise that was a moral victory for the workers, but the refusal of the military authorities to accept the terms agreed upon led to a general strike in which 100,000 came out.[1] The perfect discipline observed and the complete stoppage of all the factories and social services made a deeper impression upon Spaniards than any mere riot could have done, and though the strike again ended in a compromise (without strike pay no strike on this scale can last long) it provided a complete vindication of the syndicalist method. The agricultural labourers and small peasants throughout the south and east of Spain hastened to enrol themselves in the ranks of the C.N.T.[2]

The struggle in Barcelona continued all that summer with varying results, according to whether a reactionary military or a moderate Conservative Government was in power. In September came the employers' lock-out which weakened the syndicalist federation, but let loose the terrible war of the *pistoleros* which has already been described. In that struggle, as in all civil wars, both the contending parties lost. But in other parts of Spain, and especially in Andalusia, the agitation was now at its height and new strikes were a daily occurrence. It was in these circumstances that a Congress of the C.N.T. was called at Madrid.

In December 1919, 450 delegates, claiming to represent some 700,000 members of the C.N.T. and of the societies federated with it, met in the Comedia theatre.[3] A decision had to be taken on various

---

[1] This is the figure given by Fernández Almagro (*Historia del Reinado de Alfonso XIII*). One may compare with it the 45,000 men who came out in Barcelona in 1892 for a nine-hour day. It was of course far from representing the total number of factory workers. By the end of 1919, according to Almagro, the *sindicatos libres* (the conservative union) in Barcelona counted 100,000. Towards the end of the Dictatorship they reached, with the Catholic unions, the figure of 274,000, which one may take to be the total number of male workers of all classes in Barcelona. As Pestaña said in 1922, 30 per cent of the workers in Catalonia were convinced Syndicalists: the rest formed an incoherent mass which voted for whichever side was winning.
[2] See Note E on p. 198 at end of chapter.
[3] See Note F on p. 199 at end of chapter.

important matters—how best to continue the struggle, whether there should be a fusion with the Socialist U.G.T., what were to be the relations with Soviet Russia. As regards the first of these it was decided to call a strike of rent-payers all over Spain on 1 January and to organize among the printers a Red censorship which would correspond in intensity with the Government censorship.[1] A resolution was also passed upon sabotage: though a valuable arm in the struggle against capitalism, it was decided that it must be used intelligently and 'only when it was necessary, opportune and efficacious'. It was then agreed that the C.N.T. should adhere provisionally to the Third (Communist) International, although maintaining all the principles of the First as laid down by Bakunin. As regards fusion with the U.G.T., Seguí was strongly in favour of it and many syndicalists believed that, as the C.N.T. had at that time twice as many members as the U.G.T., they would absorb it. However, the voting was heavily against it.[2] In deference no doubt to the Bolshevik Revolution, the Congress declared its adhesion to the ideal of 'anarchist communism' or as it was now called, *comunismo libertario*. This declaration was later ratified at the extraordinary congress in 1931 at Saragossa.

We must now take up the story again in Andalusia. After the famine of 1905 anarchism seemed to disappear in the south of Spain. Only a few groups remained in the towns. But towards 1910 a certain activity began which culminated in the founding at Cordova in April 1913 of a federation of peasants and agricultural labourers under syndicalist auspices, which called itself the *Federación Nacional de Agricultores Españoles* or F.N.A.E.

It was hoped that this federation would end by enrolling peasants from all parts of Spain, and for this reason, though Anarchists had taken the leading part in its foundation, libertarian ideas were kept in the background. The aims were moderate—an eight-hour day, a minimum wage of 2.50 pesetas, an extension of the factory laws to cover accidents to field workers and to insist upon proper sanitary arrangements in the *caseríos* or labourers' barracks. Its libertarian tendencies were shown by its condemnation of co-operatives, friendly societies and strike funds, 'as tending to increase egoism in the workers': its condemnation of arbitration tribunals, which involved the intervention of the State: and the encouragement it gave to workers' clubs and unions to set up rationalist schools. This did not, however,

---

[1] See Note G on p. 199 at end of chapter.
[2] See Note H on p. 199 at end of chapter.

prevent the small Socialist unions that existed in some of the Andalusian towns (especially in the province of Jaén) from joining it. The success of the F.N.A.E. was only moderate: it did not spread to the centre or north of Spain, except for certain districts around Saragossa: perhaps its chief feat was the conversion of the Levante (Murcia and Valencia) to libertarian ideas. Hitherto this part of Spain had remained neutral. But there was no return to the enthusiasm of 1902–1905 and by 1916 the movement was languishing. By the end of 1917 it appeared to be dead, yet a few months later the whole of Southern and Eastern Spain was in a state of violent agitation. Such is the invariable rhythm in the southern provinces.

The immediate incentives were, of course, the Russian Revolution and the growing strength of Anarcho-Syndicalism in Catalonia. The 'means to deliverance' was, as in 1902–1905, the general strike. But the Messianic feeling of expectation, the childish belief that, if only work were to cease everywhere for a few days, *comunismo libertario* would drop out of the sky, had greatly diminished. All over this part of Spain there were now thousands of experienced militants, veterans of earlier campaigns, who understood the necessity for a serious struggle. The innumerable newspapers that sprung up, one to every small town, fanned the zeal of the workers and directed their operations.[1] Not only was the feeling in the towns and villages stronger and more unanimous than before, but the area affected was much wider.

General strikes began in various small towns and villages towards the end of 1917 and, since most of them ended in success for the workers, they spread in the following spring and summer to the whole of Andalusia and the Levante. As in 1903, each village or town struck when it suited it.[2] The success of these strikes was due to the fact that, except in really large cities such as Seville or Malaga, all the workers and even the small farmers and shopkeepers were grouped in

---

[1] The newspaper has always played an immense part in the Anarcho-Syndicalist movement. By the end of 1918 more than fifty towns in Andalusia had libertarian newspapers of their own. It would be quite usual for an enthusiastic member of the C.N.T. to see several papers, all of course of his way of thinking, every day and certain phrases or verses would have a wide circulation and be quoted all over the province. Many of the articles in the local papers were sent in by uneducated men and rewritten by the editor before publication. Thus the newspaper was not merely an organ of propaganda but, like the pulpit in a Baptist chapel, a platform on which the leading sectarians of each little place could air their opinions.

[2] Of the seventy-five municipalities in the province of Cordova, only four failed to take part in this movement. By May 1919 almost every town and village in the province was in full eruption. (Díaz del Moral, *op. cit.*)

one syndicate. In May a Congress was held at Seville to extend this system of local syndicates to the whole region. The adoption of *sindicatos únicos* by Catalonia, which has already been described, followed a couple of months later and the F.N.A.E. followed suit. That autumn saw therefore the immense majority of agricultural workers of the south and east of Spain, together with the tradesmen and the workers in small local industries, organized in one vast though loose syndicate. The beginnings of a peasants' confederation that would cover the whole of Spain seemed to be in sight, but in December at a Congress at Valencia the F.N.A.E. was merged in the C.N.T. This confirmed the preponderant influence of the factory workers of Barcelona in the agricultural districts of the south and east, strengthened the Anarchist influence and perpetuated the quite unnecessary gulf between the Castilian and Andalusian peasantry. In other words the interests of the peasants and field labourers had to give way to the old antagonism between Catalonia and Castile.[1]

The strikes were organized in this way. In the majority of the pueblos not only did the peasants and landless labourers join the *centro* or *sindicato*, as it was variously called, but also the artisans, small shopkeepers and domestic servants. Members of the U.G.T., the Socialist union, enrolled also. In some pueblos there were at first a certain number of dissidents. These comprised the richer peasants and also those traditional enemies of the peasants, the muleteers and *yunteros* (landless possessors of a yoke of mules or oxen), as well as those labourers who for various reasons were closely associated with the landlords. But as the enthusiasm increased, these, either willingly, or because they feared to stand out, joined the *centro* also. Strangely enough the pueblos in which there were a fair number of small peasants were more enthusiastic than those where there were only day labourers. The latter, who had no resources of their own, could not afford to undertake long strikes. Their only weapons were sabotage and violence. It was therefore in those villages where large estates existed side by side with very small ones that the strikes were carried out most energetically. In some of the earlier strikes there was intimidation of blacklegs and boycotts. But very soon this ceased to be necessary, and the strikes were carried through quietly with perfect discipline and solidarity.

During these years the local syndicates everywhere acquired immense prestige and authority. Their leading men, who sat on the

[1] The headquarters of the F.N.A.E. movement had always been at Barcelona, in the offices of its leading newspaper, the *Voz del Campesino*.

committees, were the real rulers of the district. The municipality kept only a nominal power. Every Sunday the syndicate would meet in full assembly to discuss local affairs. The whole village attended and anyone who wished to had a right to speak. Resolutions were passed and voting took place by a show of hands. During the rest of the week the committee enforced its will by a system of fines, against which an appeal could always be made to the village assembly. What one was witnessing was really the rebirth of the municipality of the early Middle Ages, before the intrusion of the nobles, the rich burghers and the King had robbed it of its democratic quality. This is not the only occasion on which we shall have to note that Spanish Anarchism, just as much in its own way as Carlism, seeks to recreate the past.

The demands of the strikers were not as a rule unreasonable. This shows that their political education had improved since 1905 and also that syndicalist, as opposed to anarchist, tendencies were uppermost. The majority of the strikes were for quite small increases of the appallingly low wages. At Castro del Rio, to take a typical example, the men demanded a minimum wage of 2.50 pesetas (about 1s. 6d.). When this was granted they raised their demands to 3.50. A compromise was reached at 3.00. Then the abolition of piece-work was pressed almost everywhere: the landlords agreed to this when obliged to, but went back on their promises later. It was a point they could not yield on. But the question that, for the first time in Spanish history, was seriously agitating the workers, was unemployment. And for the first time, too, this problem was linked with the idea of cultivating the land in common, under the supervision of the syndicates. Until now there had been no question of cultivation in common. Regularly in every revolutionary movement the villagers had demanded a new *reparto*, or division of the land. But the failure of so many small holders was showing the folly of this, except where the soil was very good, and the rise of the syndicates provided an ideal means for its organization. The strikers therefore asked the Government and the municipalities to find work for the unemployed 'until the land should be handed over to the syndicates, to be worked by them in common'—just as it had been, in fact, in the Middle Ages.[1]

---

[1] The policy of collectivizing the land, which during the Republic was the Anarchist solution for all agrarian questions, seems to have been first adopted at a Regional Congress of the C.N.T. at Cordova in July 1923. A resolution was then passed to the effect that parcellation of the land was a mistake and that the large estates at all events should be handed over to *sindicatos de agricultores*. This was the solution desired by the Catholic syndicates as well. But except perhaps in some parts of Lower Andalusia, 90 per cent of the field labourers continued to prefer parcellation.

The attitude of the employers deserves some attention. Their first reaction was the usual Spanish one of intransigeance and arrogance. They refused to parley with the strikers at all. But when they saw that this did not pay, they collapsed and granted whatever was asked. This was all the more necessary because they received no support from the provincial governors. The moderate Conservative Government then in office knew that agricultural wages were below the subsistence level and were glad to see them raised. The more sensible of the landowners therefore made a serious attempt to come to terms with the workers and to start housing schemes, schools and grants of land. But as the strikes spread and, from being sporadic, became synchronized through whole provinces, they gave way to panic. Liberals, Conservatives and Republicans forgot their ancient rivalries and drew together. The vendettas of the caciques were suspended and every house of any size became an armoury of shotguns and revolvers. With the terror so characteristic of their class whole families packed up and left the district, some not stopping till they had crossed the frontier. But in May 1919 a reactionary Government relieved them of their fears. La Cierva sent down a general at the head of a division of troops. Martial law was declared and all workers' syndicates made illegal. The movement collapsed as if by magic, and although under later governments other strikes took place, they never recovered the same force or unanimity. The results gained by these two years of agitation were inconsiderable. During the same period the Catalan workers won, and kept, large increases in wages. In Andalusia the small gains made were soon offset by a rise in the cost of living. With the end of the European War, there came a slump in agricultural produce, much land went out of cultivation and unemployment increased. It was obvious that only by far more drastic changes could the standard of life of the agricultural workers be raised.

We must now return to the Anarcho-Syndicalist movement in the large towns of the north. It was declining in Barcelona by the end of 1919 with the employers' lock-out and the outbreak of assassinations that accompanied it, and began to fall off a year later in Madrid and Saragossa. A pact signed by Largo Caballero and Seguí as representatives of the U.G.T. and C.N.T., committing them to combined action, came too late to help it. Indeed, during the short time it lasted it had rather the opposite effect. For the failure of the great series of strikes, first in Andalusia and then in Barcelona, had cast

discredit upon the purely Syndicalist elements and with the imprisonment of so many of the leaders other figures were rising to the surface.
The last years before the Dictatorship saw therefore a struggle for
leadership within the C.N.T. Seguí and his friends were losing
influence. The purely Anarchist groups held against them their pact
with the U.G.T., their readiness to accept the mediation of the
State in labour disputes and their general tendency to reformism.
There was also the new Bolshevik influence. The Russian Revolution
had naturally made an immense impression upon the Anarchist rank
and file. A group, of whom the chief figures were a Catalan schoolmaster from Lérida called Andrés Nin and an Aragonese, Joaquín
Maurín, were in favour of closer association with the Bolsheviks. Nin
and Maurín persuaded a local assembly to send them to Russia and
there, without any authority for doing so, federated the C.N.T. to the
Third International. But the suppression of the sailors' soviets at
Kronstadt in March 1921 had produced a revulsion in acratic circles
and Alexander Berkman, Emma Goldman, Schapiro and other leading
Anarchists began to denounce the horrors of Lenin's dictatorship and
in particular the war of extermination he was waging against their
comrades. Angel Pestaña, who had also been in Russia, returned to
Spain with a full account of what was happening and Nin's and
Maurín's action was disavowed.

These events culminated in a Congress held at Saragossa in June
1922 at which Juan Peiró presided. Faith in libertarian communism
was once more reaffirmed, the C.N.T. refused all connection with the
Moscow International and sent instead its delegates to Berlin to the
congress of the rival Syndicalist International or A.I.T., which was
in process of being founded by those syndicates which had never
made pacts with politicians and which had remained anti-militarist
through the War. A few months later it formally adhered to it.

Meanwhile a Congress of purely Anarchist groups held at Madrid
had resolved that all Anarchists should enrol in the C.N.T. and treat
it as their special field of action. Up to that time many had held aloof
from the syndical organization which seemed to them to represent a
narrowing of the conception of anarchism as a philosophy for all men:
it was now urgent that they should bring their full influence to bear
upon it if they did not wish to see it captured by the Bolshevists, who
were practising their usual infiltration tactics. It was not so easy to
resist the assaults of a party which had just carried out a successful
revolution in Russia and was now reproaching the Spanish Anarchists

for, of all things, their timidity and their pedantry. But in September of the following year the free development of all working-class movements was arrested by Primo de Rivera's *coup d'état*. Anticipating its forcible suppression, the C.N.T. met and formally dissolved itself. Their members enrolled in the *sindicatos libres* of the Dictator.

This dissolution however was only a feint. The framework of the syndical organization remained. The closing of all libertarian centres and the suppression of its press early in 1924 compelled it to act in secret, but conferences, or *plenos* as they were called, of delegates from the regional federations sat regularly with the members of the National Committee and, as the Dictatorship drew to an end, collaborated with the political parties in bringing about its downfall.[1]

As this moment approached, preparations were made for the revolutionary period which it was believed would follow it. Whilst Nin and Maurín were organizing from exile a tiny but active Communist party, the Anarchists founded in 1927 the *Federación Anarquista Ibérica*, or F.A.I., as it is invariably called.[2] With this the wheel of anarchist history swung full circle back to Bakunin and the Alliance of Social Democracy. For the F.A.I. was a secret or semi-secret society composed exclusively of Anarchists. Its mission was to control and penetrate the syndicalist organization as soon as it should be re-established. Comprising the leading militants from all over the country, men devoted heart and soul to the cause of the revolution, it would ensure that the mass of workers under its influence should incline neither towards reformism and co-operation with political parties, nor on the other hand towards Russian communism and the dictatorship of the proletariat. When in 1930, after the fall of Primo, the C.N.T. was allowed to re-establish itself, the Anarcho-Syndicalist forces reappeared stronger and more powerful than they had ever been.[3]

[1] See Note I on p. 199 at end of chapter.

[2] As the F.A.I. was a secret organization, no figures of its strength have been published. One may assume however that from 1934 to 1936 its membership lay round about 10,000. Every member of the F.A.I. had also to be a member of the C.N.T. and nearly, though not quite all the leading members of the C.N.T. were in the F.A.I. The opposition to the F.A.I. that grew up in 1931 and led to the formation of *sindicatos de oposición* will be explained in a later chapter.

[3] General Mola, who in the interval between the flight of Primo de Rivera and the proclamation of the Republic was at the head of the police forces in the country, describes the extraordinary efficiency of the Anarcho-Syndicalist espionage. By means of their agents in the Post and Telegraph Offices they not merely opened any letters they chose, but were able to decipher code telegrams as well. Often, he said, the secret code instructions sent out by the Government to the Provincial Governors and Captains-General were published in *Solidaridad Obrera* a few hours after they had been despatched from Madrid. (Emilio Mola, *Lo que yo Supe*, p. 111.)

They began to prepare, deliberately and systematically, for the social revolution.

We have now traced the history of the Anarchist movement up to the commencement of the Republic. All that remains to be done is to draw one or two general conclusions. First its extension. From the very beginning, as we have seen, the peculiarity of Spanish Anarchism has consisted in its having two distinct roots—the industrial workers of Catalonia and the agricultural workers of Andalusia. At first sight this might seem to be a rather unnatural partnership. For the Catalan workers were, at all events since 1920, the most highly paid workmen in Spain outside the Basque country. They had no better reason than any other body of workers in Europe to aim at revolution. But they were recruited to a great extent from the half-starving and embittered agricultural labourers of the south and east and penned up in the most unruly and excitable city in Europe. They were there subjected to the clumsy and heavy-handed rule of Castilian generals and governors and to the arbitrary and often barbarous action of the Spanish police, who are the best fomenters of anarchism. In spite of this they showed a persistent tendency towards the pure and, in practice, quite unrevolutionary syndicalism of the French C.G.T. Had Spain been able to solve her agrarian problems and settle down to ten or twenty years of peaceful development, this tendency would undoubtedly have prevailed.

Rural anarchism has an altogether different character. It is the natural reaction to intolerable conditions and whenever those conditions cease to be intolerable—whenever, that is, one finds peasants owning or renting sufficient land to support them—anarchism ceases. Thus in Catalonia the small peasants (the *rabassaires*) have never in spite of their serious grievances become Anarchists; they had a political party of their own which gave its support to the Esquerra. In the same way the prosperous peasants of the irrigated *vegas* of Valencia and Castellón de la Plana belonged either to the Catholic Right or to one of the Republican parties, whilst the peasants or labourers of the equally fertile plain of Granada, though in constant and bitter struggle with the landowners, preferred Socialism. It was only the landless labourers and small peasants of Andalusia and the dry eastern regions, struggling with hostile geographical conditions, who embraced libertarian doctrines. They comprised, of course, the vast body of agricultural workers of the south and east, and as they had constituted for a long time the chief labour market for Barcelona, they kept up the fires of Catalan anarchism and drew from it the intellectual support and stimulus that impoverished rural communities cannot provide for themselves. It was this intimate connection with Catalan industry, as well as the inequality of wages and conditions in different parts of Spain, that prevented the growth of a peasants' union or party. Any government that wished to destroy anarchism in Spain would have therefore to do two things—to solve the agrarian problem in the south and east and to allow greater scope to Catalan industry in developing these impoverished regions. So long as Castile has the last word in Spanish affairs, Andalusia is likely to remain what it is at present.

There were of course other centres of anarchism in the Peninsula. In Madrid the C.N.T. was strongly represented in several unions, especially among the builders, but had no following in the rest of Castile. Saragossa had long been an Anarchist stronghold and had managed to throw a few offshoots into the surrounding districts: the vineyard workers of Rioja, on the edge of Navarre, were one of these. In Asturias the steel workers of Gijón and La Felguera formed Anarchist islands in a sea of Socialism: the effect of their environment was to make them incline to U.G.T. methods and discipline. In Galicia there was a rural libertarian movement and a strong Anarchist nucleus among the dock workers of Corunna, which reacted upon one another. These Galician Anarchists played an active part in proselytizing South America.[1] Along the coasts of Spain fishermen, sailors and dock workers preferred Anarchism to Socialism. See the sketch map on p. 335.

The effects of this curious distribution in field and factory were seen in July 1936 when the long desired revolution came. The Anarchists stood for a system of collectivization for agricultural workers which was well suited to conditions in Andalusia. But the greater part of Andalusia fell at once into the Nationalists' hands and when the Anarchists of the large industrial towns attempted to impose collectivization upon Catalan peasants and Valencian rice growers, they met with strong opposition. The peasants, looking round for someone who would defend them against this unwanted revolution, found their champion in the Communists.[2]

And what had sixty years of Anarchist leadership brought to the workers? In the country districts, in spite of all the strikes and in-

[1] See Note J on p. 200 at end of chapter.
[2] See Note K on p. 200 at end of chapter.

surrections, it had achieved practically nothing. Whether agriculture was booming or slumping, the standard of living of the agricultural labourers in the south of Spain remained practically the same from 1870 to 1936. The small peasants—those that had survived the bad years—were only better off because markets had improved. In the industrial towns, on the other hand, it had led to a great increase of wages. But so, with much less drum-beating and agitation, did Socialism. In this respect there was nothing to choose between them.

As to its revolutionary achievements, they cannot be summed up so easily. Whilst Anarcho-Syndicalism had, as Maurín remarked, shown itself incomparably more effective than Socialism in creating a revolutionary feeling and situation among the Spanish workers, it lacked the necessary qualities for carrying a revolution out. It expressed admirably the uncompromising resistance of Spanish workmen and peasants to the conditions that capitalist society imposed on them: it provided (on a small scale) wonderful examples of solidarity, of devotion to an ideal and of revolutionary fervour: its leaders were almost the only real revolutionaries left in Europe—and yet its organization and its principles were such that it was condemned for ever to the role of Sisyphus. Even if a social revolution had by some means or other broken out, it would not have been a party that sought, as the Anarchists did, to destroy political power, but one which seized and used it, that would have come out on top. Thus while Anarcho-Syndicalism was extremely effective in harassing mild parliamentary governments, while the guerrilla warfare it maintained with the Second Republic did a great deal to discredit it and bring it down, while by weakening and undermining the Socialist party in power, it finally drove it into revolutionary channels—at bottom, taken by itself alone, all its revolutionary airs were but play-acting and childishness. When the despised U.G.T. rose at Oviedo in 1934 they shook the whole of Spain. The Anarcho-Syndicalists, through their spirit, their organization, their natural contrariness, were incapable of making a wide and concerted effort of this sort. Though they might frighten the more timid among the bourgeoisie, no government ever regarded them, in spite of their huge numbers, which mounted in times of excitement to a million or a million and a half, as anything more than a problem for the provincial governor and the police.[1]

---

[1] In maintaining that the Anarchists were incapable of making their revolution, I am by no means implying that the Socialists were any better equipped for this. This is a question that will be discussed later. Meanwhile I would point out that there is

This might seem to exhaust the subject of Spanish Anarchism. Ineffectual as a revolutionary force, only moderately successful in improving the conditions of the workers, it has dogged and hampered every government, good or bad, well-intentioned or the reverse, that has existed in Spain. By playing always for the highest stakes, it has necessarily proved on many occasions the friend of reaction. But that cannot alter the fact that it has expressed something far more deeply seated than Socialism or Liberalism in the minds of the Spanish poor and that it has had for this reason a moral influence that will not easily be brushed away. It is this aspect of anarchism—the moral and not the political—that must now be considered.

When one seeks to penetrate into the real meaning of the Spanish Anarchist movement one is struck, I think, by two main aspects that in practice fuse into one. There is first of all its strongly idealistic and moral-religious character. These anarchists are a set of men who are attempting to put into practice their utopia (which is severe and almost ascetic like the old Jewish-Christian utopia) at once, and, what is significant, by force. Secondly, they are Spanish villagers and work-men who are trying, though without being consciously aware of it, to reconstruct the primitive agrarian conditions (in this case the collec-tivist commune) that once prevailed in many parts of Spain and to recover the equality and leisure, and above all the dignity, that, to a greater or lesser extent, they enjoyed in previous centuries. That is to say, Spanish Anarchism has, like Carlism, its atavistic side: in a certain measure it is an expression of nostalgia for the past and an attitude of resistance to the slavery which the modern capitalist struc-ture of society and the strain of factory life bring with them.

I will take first the moral-religious aspect. One might from this point of view describe anarchism as the Spanish Protestant (i.e. protesting) heresy from which the Inquisition in the sixteenth and seventeenth centuries saved Spain. However violent these anarchists may be (and Cromwell's Independents were violent too) they speak the same language of love of liberty, of dependence upon the inner

a certain analogy to be found in the Napoleonic War. The French were driven out of Spain by the continual wearing action of the guerrilla bands (which, like the Anar-chist forces of to-day, were a spontaneous expression of the revolutionary feeling of the people) acting in combination with a small but highly disciplined force. Neither of these would have sufficed alone. In the same way the Anarchists and Socialists might together, under favourable circumstances, have brought off a successful revolution. But in fact no such combination of the two working-class forces in Spain was ever practicable. It took nothing less than Franco's rising to bring it about.

light that Englishmen once used to do. And they are uncompromising moralists. Every action is for them either right or wrong; they admit no such thing as expediency. When Sir Peter Chalmers Mitchell explained to his Anarchist friends at Malaga that their killings had made a bad impression in England which would perhaps affect the question of getting arms for the Republic—

'What,' exclaimed these men of the F.A.I., 'do you mean to say that we should fail to do what we believe to be right merely because people in England disapprove of it?'

I can give another instance from my own experience. I was standing on a hill watching the smoke and flames of some two hundred houses in Malaga mount in to the sky. An old Anarchist of my acquaintance was standing beside me.

'What do you think of that?' he asked.

I said: 'They are burning down Malaga.'

'Yes,' he said: 'they are burning it down. And I tell you—not one stone will be left on another stone—no, not a plant nor even a cabbage will grow there, so that there may be no more wickedness in the world.'

It was the voice of Amos or Isaiah (though the old man had never read either) or of an English sectarian of the seventeenth century.

The fanatical hatred of the Anarchists for the Church and the extraordinary violence of their attack upon it during the Civil War are things which are known to everyone. Without going far wrong one may say that all the churches recently burned in Spain were burned by Anarchists and that most of the priests killed were killed by them.[1] Such a persecution of religion has not been known in Europe since the Thirty Years' War: the Russian Revolution provided nothing to compare to it. It can only, I think, be explained as the hatred of heretics for the Church from which they have sprung. For in the eyes of Spanish libertarians the Catholic Church occupies the position of Anti-Christ in the Christian world. It is far more to them than a mere obstacle to revolution. They see in it the fountain of all evil, the corruptor of youth with its vile doctrine of original sin, the blasphemer against Nature and the Law of Nature, which they call *Salud*

---

[1] J. Langdon Davies (in *Behind the Barricades*) speaks of the 'anti-religious mysticism of the Anarchists' and suggests that the churches in Catalonia were burned in July–August 1936 through fear of the Church's black magic. He agrees with all other observers that they were burned by small groups of men who came out from the towns for that purpose. Peadar O'Donnell (in *Salud*) watched a church in a Catalan village being burned by twenty men, with the silent disapproval of the villagers.

or Health. It is also the religion which *mocks* with its pretence of brotherly love and mutual forgiveness the great ideal of human solidarity. We forget, I think, our history when we show surprise at this anti-Papist violence. Between the decapitated saints in English churches and the broken altars and blackened walls in Spain there is only a difference of degree.

But, one may ask, if Spanish Anarchism can be described, however loosely, as a religious heresy, how and at what moment did it secede from the Church? There are, I would suggest, two main classes of heresies—first, those which arise as the result of a difference of opinion, when the Church, during the course of its development, is faced with some choice upon doctrinal matters. Of these Arianism, Monophysism and Pelagianism are examples. They appear when the body of doctrine in some particular sphere is still fluid. The Church chooses its line and those who do not submit become heretics. Secondly, there are those which come from a rebellion within the body of the Church against abuses—against the failure of the priesthood to live up to its claims. If one of these should happen to take a doctrinal form it becomes far more dangerous, because it is fed by a spirit of indignation and because a genuinely religious emotion has a great advantage against a body that knows itself to be hypocritical and worldly. It was in this way that Lutheranism gained its triumphs.

But there is one sort of heresy belonging to this class of which both the Catholic and the Protestant Churches have always shown a quite peculiar terror. It is that which consists in taking literally the very frequent allusions in the Scriptures to the wickedness and consequent damnation of the rich and the blessedness of the poor. This had been the crime of the Circumcellians, a militant sect of the fourth century which sprang up on the African *latifundia* under much the same circumstances as the Spanish Anarchists, and it was also the crime of the Waldenses and of the Anabaptists. What the authorities could not forgive in these sects was the emphasis they laid on the social teaching of the Gospels. And it will be remembered with what almost insane fury Luther urged the destruction by fire and sword of those peasants who were compromising him by taking his teaching on Christian freedom in a literal sense.

The reason for this violence is obvious. The Bible, and especially the New Testament, contains enough dynamite to blow up all the existing social systems in Europe, only by force of habit and through the power of beautiful and rhythmical words we have ceased to notice it. An intelligent Chinaman has been more observant. Sun Yat Sen, when he visited Europe, was amazed that a religion which persistently extolled the poor and threatened and condemned the rich should be practised and maintained chiefly by the richest, most selfish and most respectable classes. The political skill and duplicity required for such a feat seemed to him to go far beyond anything that simple Orientals could run to. The danger has therefore always existed that any weakening in the influence of the Church, any desertion of the interests of the poor by the priesthood, would lead to a greater emphasis being placed upon the social principles of equality, voluntary poverty and brotherly love that, along with many other things, lie at the root of Christianity.[1]

And where were these conditions better fulfilled than in Andalusia in the last century? The poor labourer who bought one of those New Testaments which the British Bible Society provided for a few pence (and which have always sold so well in the south and east of Spain) could read, for example, what the Virgin Mary, the goddess of Andalusia, to whom every night when he took off his shirt he said a prayer, had felt upon these matters. In her great song of triumph, charged with an unmistakeable prophetic meaning, she had rejoiced that the mighty had been put down from their seats and the poor exalted, that the hungry had been filled with good things whilst *the rich had been sent empty away*. He might be forgiven for seeing in such words an expression of class feeling.

I would suggest then that the anger of the Spanish Anarchists against the Church is the anger of an intensely religious people who feel they have been deserted and deceived. The priests and the monks left them at a critical moment in their history and went over to the rich. The humane and enlightened principles of the great theologians of the seventeenth century were set on one side. The people then began to suspect (and the new ideas brought in by Liberalism of course assisted them) that all the words of the Church were hypocrisy. When they took up the struggle for the Christian utopia it was therefore against the Church and not with it. Even their violence might be

---

[1] The classic texts from the New Testament on which Christian communists have always relied are *Qui habet duas tunicas, det unam non habenti* and *Compelle eos intrare*. The second text, which sanctions the use of force in matters of faith, has been found equally useful by the Church and by sects such as the Anabaptists, who anticipated many of the anarchist teachings. One may remember that Emilio Castelar, the most eloquent and cultured of all Spanish politicians, declared that he was a democrat because he saw in democracy 'the realization of the Gospel'.

called religious. The Spanish Church, after all, has always been a
Militant Church and down to the twentieth century it believed in
destroying its enemies. No doubt the Anarchists felt that if only, by
using the same methods, they could get rid of all who were not of their
way of thinking, they would make a better job than the Church had
done of introducing the earthly paradise. In Spain every creed as-
pires to be totalitarian.[1]

It may be thought that I have stressed too much the religious
element because Spanish Anarchism is after all a political doctrine.
But the aims of the Anarchists were always much wider and their
teaching more personal than anything that can be included under the
word politics. To individuals they offered a way of life: Anarchism had
to be lived as well as worked for. To the community they offered a
new world founded exclusively on moral principles. They never made
the mistake of thinking, as the Socialists did, that this could be
achieved merely by providing a higher standard of living all round.
On the contrary, they were often ascetic and puritanical. I have
already described how in some Anarchist collectives they endeavoured
to suppress wine, tobacco and even coffee. This asceticism was extended to sex also. Anarchists, it is true, believe in free love—everything, even love, must be free—but they do not believe in libertinage.
So in Malaga they sent missions to the prostitutes. In Barcelona they
cleaned up the cabarets and brothels with a thoroughness that the
Spanish Church (which frowns on open vice, such as wearing a
bathing dress without a skirt and sleeves, but shuts its eyes to 'safety-
valves') would never approve of.[2]

Dr Borkenau, who in his book on the Civil War has given such an
admirable account of the Spanish Anarchists, particularly stresses this.[3]

[1] Possibly my argument is not clear. I do not deny that the new ideas brought in
from Rousseau, Godwin, Proudhon, Bakunin and so on have a source independent
of the teachings of the Church. But if that were all that Spanish Anarchism contained
it would be a very different kind of movement. The point I wish to make is that the
emotion behind these anarchists, especially the more primitive ones of the Andalusian
Valley, is derived from the social teaching of the Church and from familiarity with a
certain strain of feeling to be found in both the New and the Old Testaments. After
all, the history of Christianity is, from one point of view, the history of the capture
by the Pharisees of the religion of their enemy Jesus, who taught his gospel of
salvation to the oppressed and the poor.
[2] See Note L on p. 200 at end of chapter.
[3] 'Anarchism *is* a religious movement. It does not believe in the creation of a new
world through the improvement of the material conditions of the lower classes, but
in the creation of a new world out of the moral resurrection of those classes which
have not yet been contaminated by the spirit of greed and mammon' (F. Borkenau,
The Spanish Cockpit, 1937).

Their hatred of the upper classes, he declares, is far less econo-mic than moral. They do not want to possess themselves of the good living of those they have expropriated, but to get rid of their luxuries, which seem to them to be so many vices. And anyone who has lived for long in a Spanish village, even in one which has not been affected by anarchist ideas, will have noticed how characteristic is this disapproval of even the most elementary luxury. The vices of the men of to-day, the stern virtues of their forefathers are constantly cropping up in their conversation. Smoking, though general, is always condemned, and it is common to hear workmen boasting of the few pence a day they can live on. After all it was Don Quixote who, in his rapturous account of the Golden Age and of the state of felicity in which the men of old lived, declared that they nourished themselves on acorns.

It is hardly necessary to point out how completely the Anarchists differed in this from the Socialists and Communists. They would have nothing to do with the Marxian dialectic or with the body of theory and dogma built up on it. The strict discipline of the Communists and their practice of subordinating moral principles to expediency were regarded by them as Jesuitical. They themselves relied upon that very Spanish thing—acting from instinct. Any plan, any order, any ar-rangement that fettered the instinct was wrong. Once the battle was opened, they went straight forward, following their inner light or nature, behaving with extraordinary daring or with complete cowar-dice as they felt inclined: at certain moments magnificent, but if the conditions demanded a cohesion or a resistance they could not give, becoming unreliable. This had been the principle of the *partidas* or guerrilla bands in the Napoleonic War. If anyone doubts that much of what is called 'anarchist' to-day is merely unadulterated Iberian, let him compare the famous call for 'organized indiscipline' pasted up by the F.A.I. on the walls of Barcelona in August 1936, at the time when Durruti's column was getting ready for its march on Saragossa, with this description by an intelligent eyewitness of the organization of the guerrilla war against Napoleon.

'After the regular armies had all been beaten...one saw growing up a system of war in detail, a *kind of organized disorder* which perfectly suited the unconquerable character of the Spanish nation and the unhappy circumstances in which it found itself.'[1]

Their other quarrel with the Communists was over liberty. Marx

[1] See Note M on p. 201 at end of chapter.

had diagnosed the troubles of the world as being due to greed. The fundamental sin to him was owning property. The Anarchists agreed to this, but added that there is a second even more fundamental sin, which is love of power. They pointed out that the abolition of private property in Russia had led to an increase of tyranny. And it was precisely against the economic tyranny of the modern capitalist world, and only in the second place against inequality of income, that they made their protest.[1]

The Anarchists stand then above everything else for liberty. But here the dilemma comes. These stern moralists, these children of the categorical imperative, disapprove of the present organization of society. But what is it they demand? They demand that everyone shall be free. Free to do what? Why free to lead the natural life, to live on fruit and vegetables, to work at the collective farm, to conduct himself in the way that Anarchists consider proper. But if he does not want to do these things, if he wants to drink wine, to go to Mass, to dig in his own field and refuse the benefits brought into the world by *comunismo libertario*, what then? Why then he is one of *los malos*, *los perversos*, possibly curable but, if he does not come from a working-class family, more likely corrupt and vicious out of upbringing or heredity, and therefore unfit to partake of the Anarchist paradise. A bullet in the head for this *compañero*—without hate, of course, without hate. He can smoke a last cigarette before dying. After all, *compañero*, death is nothing.

That then would seem to be the practical consequence of anarchism. Many people whose sympathies have been captured by the Spanish anarchists, who have been moved by their heroic idealism and charmed by their sincerity and open-mindedness, forget that there is this other side to the picture. Anarchism, which puts freedom above everything else, may easily lead in practice to the worst tyranny. No one can doubt that if the Anarchists had won the Civil War they would have imposed their will not merely upon the bourgeoisie, but on the peasants and factory workers too with complete ruthlessness. There were many indications that in the country districts this would have led to a new sort of *caciquismo*.

For this is the tragic paradox of Spanish Anarchism. It aims at

[1] On 27 January 1935 the National Committee of the C.N.T. published this statement, aimed at the Communists, in *Solidaridad Obrera*: 'Tyranny and crime are equally deserving of condemnation no matter whether they exist under the red-yellow flag of the Monarchy or in the name of the tricolour of the Republic or even under the red banner of the Dictatorship of the Proletariat.'

reaching by violence a state from which even the mildest form of compulsion is to be excluded. The wicked who have so long oppressed the earth are to be eliminated and then the age of peace and mutual tolerance will automatically begin. Such hopes are surely not to be taken seriously. It argues a great deal of simplicity to believe that out of the welter of violent revolution in a modern country such a stateless form of society could appear. Only in small towns or in villages where the immense majority were labourers or poor peasants, prepared to work their land in common, would anything of the kind be possible. But what in the mind of Bakunin was a mere revolutionary's day-dream has appealed to Spaniards precisely because they are accustomed to think so much in terms of their own village. A change, that in a highly organized community would be quite utopian, might be feasible here. When therefore the Anarchist says, 'to introduce the Golden Age you have only to kill the wicked who prevent the good from living as they wish to', there is always at the back of his mind the village with its three thousand small peasants and landless labourers. By getting rid of a dozen landowners and a priest, the rest can divide up the land and live happily. And there is nothing illusory in such a belief. Anyone who has known the Spanish poor will agree that by their kindly and generous feelings for one another and by the talent they have so often shown for co-operation they are perfectly fitted for playing their part in an 'anarchist commune'. The Berbers of the Moroccan highlands, who are first cousins to the Iberians, have for thousands of years lived in small independent communes whose organization is purely anarchistic.

With this applicability of the libertarian idea to village life we reach, I think, the other root of Spanish Anarchism besides the religious one. For if anarchism is, in one sense, a utopian conception of life that opens out its arms to the future, it is also true that the Anarchists have, like the Carlists, their inner eye upon the past. Rural anarchism is quite simply the attempt to recreate the primitive Spanish communes that existed in many parts of Spain in the sixteenth and seventeenth centuries. To-day they call them collectives, but till the Russians invented this word and modern machinery gave them a new scope, it was the old commune where the land was divided every few years by lot that they hankered for.

In Appendix I, I describe some of these communes and show how indistinguishable in nearly all respects a Carlist municipality of the Pyrenees with its extensive social services can be from an Anarchist fishermen's collective in Catalonia.[1] Anarchism, I would then say, has simply rekindled the perennial instinct of the Spanish peasant, who believes that his life in the past was better in every way than it is now and who wishes to return to it. There has not been a peasant rising in Andalusia in the last hundred years when the villages did not form communes, divide up the land, abolish money and declare themselves independent—free that is from the interference of 'foreign' landlords and police.[2]

And the anarchism of the industrial workers is not very different. They ask, first of all for self-government for their industrial village or syndicate and then for a shortening of the hours, a reduction in the quantity of the work. They ask for more liberty and more leisure and above all more respect for human dignity, but not necessarily a higher standard of living.[3] After all, that is simply another way of saying that they wish for a return to the empty, leisurely conditions of the seventeenth century, when, at the expense of their stomachs, the workmen in the towns still retained their innate dignity and freedom and had not been crushed and dehumanized by factory life. Thus Spanish Anarchism, though seeming to look forward only to the future, is in fact dominated by that nostalgia for the past that is so characteristic of Spain. The Siglo de Oro—the age of glory for the educated classes, the age of liberty and leisure for all—is the Golden Age to which most Spaniards would willingly return and, without plunging too far into the unconscious, one may suspect that behind it stands the Pastoral Age, when men stood and watched their flocks by day and meditated like Hebrew prophets upon Vice and Virtue, upon Fate and God, whilst the toil and degradation of the agricultural life was left to others.

We have come here, I think, to the precise significance of Spanish Anarchism and its value both to Spain and (though this may seem absurd) to Europe. It voices more clearly and intelligently than any other Iberian movement the resistance offered by the whole Spanish people to the tyranny and soullessness of the modern machine-serving age. Unlike Carlism, which (in so far as it still means anything at all) turns its back upon modernity altogether, it accepts the benefits to be obtained from machine production, but it insists that nothing what-

---

[1] See Note N on p. 201 at end of chapter.
[2] Mr Langdon Davies has put his finger on this fundamental notion of rural anarchism: 'There it is again, this constantly recurring Spanish theme of philosophical anarchism, this practical experience that if nobody interfered all went well' (*Behind the Barricades*, p. 71).
[3] See Note O on p. 202 at end of chapter.

ever should curtail the right of all men to lead dignified human lives. There must be no sacrifice to Moloch. In the choice that has to be made between a higher standard of comfort and a greater amount of leisure, it emphatically selects the second. And this is not out of any preference for idleness. It is because Spanish Anarchism is an ascetic creed, which places the spiritual things of life above material comforts and knows that leisure is required for their development. In this it is intensely Spanish. For two centuries and more the Spanish pueblo, as every traveller since the eighteenth century has observed, has been the repository of the virtues and traditions of the race, abandoned by the effete upper classes. To-day few but the poor can speak with the authentic voice of Spain. 'The surface of our country constantly decays', said Cánovas, 'but never the depths.' And so the Spanish Anarchist movement, narrow, ignorant, often terribly ruthless, holding with uncompromising determination and unfailing optimism utterly impractical designs, is not only the most 'Hispanic' thing south of the Pyrenees, but it contains principles which must, in however modified a form, be recognized and satisfied if Spain is to become once again a great and united nation. Had a true national leader ever appeared, he would have seen this. For what Spain has to give Europe will not be given by imitating the forms of the more highly organized but in many respects less vital nations round her—forms which in any case she would be quite unable to make use of—but by developing within herself her own seeds of life. This can only be done by having some regard for what the people want. During more than a century now the weakness of Spain has come from the fact that every government has had the great mass of the people against it.

FURTHER NOTES TO CHAPTER VIII

A (p. 172). The matrix of the C.N.T. was the *Confederación Regional del Trabajo* of Catalonia. A Galician Regional Confederation joined this and others followed. The full number, eight, was not reached till the period of the Republic. The veteran Anselmo Lorenzo played a large part in winning over the editors of *Tierra y Libertad* and other anarchist groups to the new idea. From the first moment all the delegates at the regional and national Congresses were Anarchists.

B (p. 172). The C.N.T. was organized in regional federations which held yearly congresses. Under these came the local or comarcal federations and then the syndicates. Each syndicate elected its executive and administrative committee. In the small towns the syndicates were organized on a local basis and in the large towns by trades. When, owing to Government persecution, congresses were forbidden, delegates were sent by the local or regional federations to a *pleno*. The very small subscription required for membership of the C.N.T. (and in impoverished districts often remitted) was an advantage to it in its competition with the U.G.T. Poor men joined the union which cost them least. On the other hand men in regular employment preferred the U.G.T. because it did not call them out so often on strike.

C (p. 174). Díaz del Moral (*op. cit.* p. 204), speaking of the innocence of many Andalusian Anarchists, gives the following extract from one of their pamphlets: 'On this planet there exist infinite accumulations of riches which, without any monopoly, are enough to assure the happiness of all human beings. We all of us have the right to well-being, and when Anarchy comes in, we shall every one of us take from the common store whatever we need: men, without distinction, will be happy: love will be the only law in social relations. How shall we secure all this? By putting an end to authority and property, the foundations of inequality and the only sources of evil and of injustice: by organizing production through the free agreement of individuals and of groups, who will come together in accordance with their natural affinities.'

Commenting on this Moral remarks that one continually finds Anarchists who believe that the day of libertarian communism would bring happiness to the rich as well as to the poor.

'Señorito, when will the great day come?' a poor man asked a senator in 1903.
'What day?'
'Why the day on which we shall all be equal and when the earth will be divided up equally among all.'

From my own experience I can fully confirm this.

'The rich will gain, too', an Anarchist friend of mine declared in June 1936. 'When *comunismo libertario* comes in they will see that their riches have been as much an obstacle to their happiness as to ours. Except for a few perverts, all human beings prefer to live healthy and decent lives, if they are given the opportunity. But the propaganda of the Church and of the political parties has closed their minds to this.'

Nothing is more surprising, nor more touching, than this belief that the rich may some day see the light and be converted. It is a consequence of their absolute conviction that they are in the right and that, in the end, truth and reason must prevail.

D (p. 174). The books most read were *The Conquest of Bread* by Kropotkin, *El Dolor Universal* by Sébastien Faure and a novel called *El Botón de Fuego* (The Fire Button) by López Montenegro. Anselmo Lorenzo wrote novelettes in imitation of *Candide* with an anarchist moral. Other favourite writers were Elisée Reclus, Charles Malato, Malatesta, Grave, Most and several Spaniards—Federico Urales, Soledad Gustavo, Ricardo Mella, Leopoldo Bonafulla, José Prat.

Old-fashioned books such as *The Ruins of Palmyra* by Volney were also popular. Editions costing 30 or 50 centimes frequently reached a circulation of 50,000.

E (p. 177). Manuel de Burgos y Mazo, in his *Páginas Históricas de* 1917 (pp. 79–83), quotes in full the Anarcho-Syndicalist programme issued in Barcelona for the 1917 strike. This, it will be remembered, was the general strike declared all over Spain under the leadership of the U.G.T. with the object of overthrowing the regime. Its principal points were:

1. A Republic.
2. Recognition of working-class syndicates and their power to veto laws passed by the bourgeois Cortes.
3. A seven-hour day and an English week.
4. A minimum wage of 4 pesetas a day and no piece-work.
5. Pensions for disabled workmen and for those over 50.
6. Children under 14 not to work.
7. The dissolution of the Army and its substitution by a militia.
8. A declaration of war to come only after a plebiscite, and those who vote for it to be enlisted first.
9. Separation of Church and State, dissolution of convents and the closure of the churches for a certain period.

10. Divorce laws.
11. Nationalization of land.
12. Reforms in the prison system to make it more humane.
13. Prohibition of all festivals (e.g. bullfights and indecent cabarets) which can brutalize the people.

It was expressly stated that this was neither a minimum nor a maximum programme, but intended to indicate a direction.

This programme might seem to show that the Anarcho-Syndicalists were, after all, prepared in return for a few not unreasonable concessions to accept a bourgeois government. One must bear in mind, however, that the demands put forward by them in their strikes often meant very little. They anticipated Hitler in proceeding at once to fresh claims the moment those previously put forward had been granted. That is to say, they never lost sight of their revolutionary goal. On the other hand, as the standard of living of the workers rose, they showed less disposition to follow their leaders, except when the weakness of the Government or some new grievance such as the imprisonment of their comrades provided an incentive. There has been a steady tendency in Barcelona since 1919 towards reformism. Indeed the revolutionary movement could scarcely have been kept alive but for the continued influx of poor villagers from the parched regions of the Levante. In its roots Spanish Anarchism is rural.

F (p. 177). The Anarchist press claimed that this Congress at Madrid represented 800,000 workers. Pestaña gave the same number for the membership of the C.N.T. at the time of its provisional adherence to the Third International, though stating that it sometimes contained a million. In the proceedings of the Congress the number which it represented is given as 550,000 of whom 500,000 were federated. See *C.N.T. Memoria del Congreso de 1919*, 1932. But many organizations abstained from voting or from sending delegates, especially in country districts, either because they could not afford to pay their expenses or for other reasons, whilst others never enrolled in the C.N.T., though acting under its influence. Altogether one may say that if there were moments when the Anarcho-Syndicalist movement was leading from a million to a million and a half workers, its core of persistently faithful adherents did not exceed 200,000. The U.G.T. claimed at this time 250,000.

As to the distribution of the Anarcho-Syndicalists through Spain, the *Memoria del Congreso de 1919* gives the following figures of affiliated members: Catalonia 427,000; Levante 132,000; Andalusia 91,000; North (including Galicia) 29,000; Aragon 15,000; Centre 4500 (to which one must add 22,000, i.e. all the Madrid workers, not affiliated); Balearic Islands 1000.

The comparatively small number from Andalusia and the Levante is probably due to the fact that the movement there had been suppressed a few months before by the military and the syndicates declared illegal. Even so, 124 towns in Andalusia were represented as compared to 95 in the Levante and 105 in Catalonia.

G (p. 178). During the strike of the Canadiense in 1918 a Red censorship had been very effectively applied. For publishing an official proclamation by the Captain-General of Catalonia the *Diario de Barcelona* was fined 1000 pesetas and *El Progreso* 2500. The fines were paid; if not all the workers on these papers would have gone on strike.

H (p. 178). On the question of fusion with the U.G.T., the voting was 170,000 for and 324,000 against. The Asturians favoured it, Catalonia and Andalusia opposed it. On the question of introducing the *sindicato único*, 651,000 were for it and 14,000 against it. (C.N.T. *Memoria del Congreso de 1919*. Also Buenacasa, *op. cit.* p. 98.)

I (p. 184). In 1928 the *Comité Nacional* of the C.N.T. held a *pleno* and appointed committees of action which entered into negotiations with Sánchez Guerra, the Conservative ex-premier, who was plotting against the Dictatorship. This was the *Comité Nacional's* method of conspiring with politicians without committing itself. At another *pleno* in February 1930, just after the flight of Primo to Paris, a resolution was passed calling for the convocation of a Constituent Assembly, the re-establishment of constitutional decrees, an eight-hour day and the liberation of all political prisoners. (*Un Año de Conspiración*, by B. Pou and J. R. Magriña, pp. 117–130.)

That this was merely a tactical move and not a sudden conversion to reformism, events were soon to prove. At all events this flirtation with the Republicans did not prevent *Solidaridad Obrera* from publishing some documents on the projected revolutionary movement of 28 October 1930, which led to its being put off two months.

J (p. 186). One should not forget that Spanish Anarchism was merely one branch of a world-wide movement that had active adherents in almost all the Latin American republics and especially in the Argentine, Uruguay and Bolivia. There was a constant intercourse between the Anarchists in these countries and in Spain, and, particularly in times of repression or severe press censorship, South American Anarchist newspapers circulated freely in Catalonia and Andalusia. The Spanish working classes were really far more pan-Iberian in their outlook than either the Socialists or the bourgeoisie.

K (p. 186). The geographical division between Socialism and Anarchism corresponds of course to a great natural difference of climate, culture and character. The men of the south and east are optimistic, expansive, impressionable, easily roused and quick to subside: those of the central tableland are slower, more rigid, inclined to pessimism: aware, through the dominating role which their State has played in Spanish history, of the importance of strong government and organization. The first are pleasure-loving, artistic, given to commerce, with Oriental and Mediterranean traditions: the others, if not exactly ascetic, are conscientious—formed through many centuries on the doctrine of original sin. Socialism can be explained as a development of Castilian bureaucratic ideas of the sixteenth century. Anarchism, though intensely Spanish too, has something of the flavour of an evangelical Protestant heresy which the Inquisition (the servant of Castilian centralism) kept out.

L (p. 192). The Anarchists were genuinely shocked by the morals of the Spanish bourgeoisie. Replying to accusations that they wished to destroy the family, they protested that the people who said this had almost without exception mistresses or else lived in the worst vice: that indeed every member of the Government lived in that way—but that they on the contrary wished the family to be based on love and on feelings of honourable reciprocity.

'We know of nothing more cynical and repugnant, nothing more dangerous to public morals than the private lives of the champions of religion, property and family.' (Anselmo Lorenzo, *op. cit.*)

Anarchists, on the other hand, were expected to give a good example. According to *Solidaridad Obrera* (1922) the Anarchist should set out to have a moral ascendancy over others; he must obtain prestige in the eyes of the workers by his conduct in the street, in the workshop, in his own home and in strikes. Difficult though it might be in present society, Anarchism must be *lived* by Anarchists.

As regards other forms of puritanism, Díaz del Moral contrasts the Anarcho-Syndicalist organizations in Andalusia in 1918 with those of the Socialists. The Anarchists neither smoked nor drank. The *Casas del Pueblo* had taverns which were called restaurants. The Anarchists thought that the only thing that prevented everyone from thinking as they did was lack of education. They therefore attached great importance to schools and generally set up one in their *centro*. The Socialists thought that education was a matter for the State. Anarchist newspapers never inserted bourgeois advertisements nor paid their union leaders. The Socialists did both these things and, in the poorer parts of Spain, lost by it. The Anarchists opposed cock fights and bull fights. They stood for the protection of 'women, children, old men, trees and animals'. The Socialists merely frowned on gambling. This was the time when, especially in the south of Spain, naturism and vegetarianism were making many conquests in Anarchist circles. They were believed to have marvellous powers for transforming human beings and preparing them for the ineffable *acracia* which, after a few centuries of effort, would arise upon the earth.

Time did not change these dispositions. When in 1937 Dr Borkenau visited Castro del Rio ('one of the holy places of Syndicalism', as Díaz del Moral calls it) he found that the Anarchists there had abolished money payments and closed the bar and were looking forward to the moment when all the coffee would be used up.

M (p. 193). *Mémoires sur la Guerre des Français en Espagne*, by A. J. de Rocca, 1814, p. 139. De Rocca was a young Swiss officer who married Madame de Staël. Put beside the quotation from de Rocca the following: 'The Spanish pueblo, guided by its instinct, the product of its libertarian nature, which permits it without leaders to tackle and solve the most arduous problems...threw itself of its own accord into the most disconcerting Revolution which the history of popular commotions has ever known.'

That is the somewhat fanciful description by Cánovas Cervantes of the very minor part played by the Anarchists in the 1934 rising. (*Solidaridad Obrera*, p. 313.)

And just as de Rocca's phrase throws light upon modern Anarchist methods of war, so this passage from a libertarian writer perfectly expresses the spirit that led to the formation of the guerrilla bands in 1810. Yet the Anarchists had not been afraid at times to call themselves the Party of Order. At Cordova they had published a paper called *Orden*. A propagandist book came out with the title *Anarchy or the Friends of Order*. By this they meant of course that all disorder came from the principle of authority.

N (p. 196). In Appendix I on Village Communes and Co-operatives there is a description of three of these collectivist communes with some account of their origin. But it is not only on the economic but on the political side also that the anarchist movement marks a return towards mediaeval institutions. When the military rising took place in July 1936 every village in the anarchist districts of Spain threw off its municipality and began to govern itself through its syndicate. This syndicate was simply an assembly consisting of every able-bodied man and woman in the village who belonged to the working classes, whether he was a member of the C.N.T. or not. They met one evening a week and for several hours discussed village problems. Anyone who chose had the right to speak. The syndicate elected a committee which governed the village and was responsible to it, as a British cabinet is to Parliament.

This system was not a sudden invention. Many times during the past seventy years, whenever the success of a strike or a rising had made it possible, similar bodies had arisen and taken over the government of the village. The only thing to cause surprise was the ease and spontaneity with which these syndicates appeared and the deep satisfaction they gave to the small peasants and labourers. The whole thing worked as naturally as though the village had never managed its affairs in any other way.

This leads one to enquire whether this system of village administration was really an Anarchist invention. On the contrary, the syndicate and committee of 1936 were in all respects identical to the *concejo abierto* and *cabildo* of mediaeval Spanish communes. For the mediaeval town or village in Spain was governed by an assembly of all the adult men of the district, called the *concejo abierto*, and this assembly, which had full powers of debate, elected the municipal officers who in their collective capacity were called the *cabildo*. As time passed various abuses crept in: the nobles obtained hereditary posts in the *cabildo* or bought votes like the caciques of later days: the King, to resist the influence of the nobles and increase his own, appointed special officers termed *corregidores*. The democratic character of the municipalities was lost. By 1500 the *concejos abiertos* had ceased to meet in the towns except for the perfunctory ceremony of electing the *cabildo*. But in the small villages this decay did not take place and down to the middle of the eighteenth century they preserved, in the words of Ballesteros, 'all the early fragrance of the mediaeval institution'. Indeed in some parts of Castile and Leon they continued to exist down to the twentieth century: in 1891 a law was drawn up to give them legal status.

Thus again one finds the Anarchists hastening to restore the groundwork of local life from which Spain in the days of her greatness had sprung. And this was not, like certain aspects of Carlist or Falangist theory, an archaeological restoration. The Anarchists are quite unaware that they have any links with the past. But their creed has happened to express the extraordinarily tenacious desires and memories of a large part of that most conservative of all European peoples—the Spanish pueblo. Hence its success. Hence too that apparent negativeness, that belief in mere destruction that strikes most observers: Spanish workers and anarchists are as one in believing that as soon as certain obstructions are removed, society will automatically organize itself in free communes: it is a belief based not upon theory or upon Bakunin's famous phrase, but upon actual peasant experience.

O (p. 196). After pointing out that the working classes have become living machines, Anselmo Lorenzo goes on: '...We have asked that the hours of work should be shortened, because we need liberty in which to think, to study, to take up our responsibility as citizens,...to satisfy our moral instincts. The shortening of the hours of work is not idleness' (*El Proletariado Militante*, vol. i, 1901, p. 327).

Tomás González Morago, the first of the small group converted by Fanelli, also insists upon the loss of human dignity suffered by the workmen under factory conditions: 'Disequality is an ignominy that destroys human solidarity as the reason conceives it and fraternity as religion teaches it, and there neither is nor can be any material advantage capable of washing out its stain' (quoted, *op. cit.* p. 99).

If one then reads some seventeenth-century book such as Brunel's *Voyage en Espagne* or the *Relations of the Venetian Ambassadors* one will find that the Spaniards of that time showed exactly the same preoccupation with dignity—the peasant ploughing with a sword dangling from his waist, the cobbler and the mason treating the grandee as their equal, the beggars expecting to be addressed as Your Worship. And one will find the same demand for leisure too, though it would not seem that this leisure was invariably spent in study or in 'cultivating the moral instincts'.

I do not of course mean to assert that the poorer peasants, serfs and landless labourers of this time enjoyed much of this liberty and dignity. There existed then, as to-day, a down-trodden layer that had few rights or liberties. For the most part they consisted of the descendants of Moors, Jews or gypsies and their associates—people of 'impure blood' and therefore outside the pale—and even if their descent happened to be Christian, the fact that they had sunk to the lowest social level—possibly through their preferring regular hard work to the uncertain life of a *caballero mendicante* or beggar—would automatically cast doubts upon it. But it is clear that the artisan class, the servant or retainer class and large sections of the manual labourers and peasants enjoyed, for all their poverty, a degree of liberty and leisure that has left a deep and ineffaceable mark upon the character of the Spanish people.

The desire of the Anarchists for weak governments can be explained in the same way. Even in Philip II's time the Government had only a very limited control of internal affairs and until 1700, when Louis XIV sent Frenchmen to reorganize the administration, it was weaker and milder than in any other country in Europe. Spain, like China, has always refused to put up with a strong and efficient administration, finding its real strength in the solidarity of the people and in their adherence to Spanish (i.e. religious) culture. The following quotation from *Solidaridad Obrera*, September 1936, is therefore merely one more instance of the exaggerated 'hispanicity' of the Anarchists: 'Only weak nations have strong governments. To-day Spain has a weak government with no influence because the people themselves are going into action.'

Chapter IX

THE CARLISTS

Una grey y un pastor solo en el suelo,
Un monarca, y un imperio y una espada.
HERNANDO DE ACUÑA, 1540.

The Carlists first appear on the scene in 1823. In the summer of that year a French army marched into Spain to put down the chaotic constitutional regime and earn, in Chateaubriand's words, *un baptême de gloire* for the French Bourbon dynasty. But Louis XVIII had no wish to restore the old disreputable absolutism. He had Ferdinand's promise that he would give his country a *charte* or moderate constitution. When therefore Ferdinand VII proceeded to break his word and to let loose a ferocious persecution on the Liberals, the French king was placed in a difficult position. Protests produced no effect: to use force against the fanatical power of the Church seemed dangerous. But for the sake of his reputation abroad he was compelled to insist upon one thing—that the Inquisition should not be restored. Ferdinand was therefore compelled to dismiss his clerical minister, Victor Saez, which he did by making him an archbishop, and to content himself with what he wanted most—a few thousand executions.

But Saez did not resign himself to this 'betrayal of our Holy Religion'. He collected round him a party, known as the *Apostólicos*, who demanded two things—the restoration of the Inquisition and the complete extirpation of the Liberals. The majority of the bishops and many of the courtiers joined it and it was planned to depose Ferdinand and to place his stupid and fanatical brother Carlos on the throne. This plan led to a rising in Catalonia, which was put down, but the responsibility of the real leaders was hushed up in return for a promise to cease plotting and await the death of the King. Ferdinand was a widower with no children and, since his health was bad and his life dissolute, it was not expected he could live for long. But a few years later the situation suddenly changed. The King took a third wife, María Cristina of Naples, and a daughter, Isabella, was born. This happened at a moment when the July Revolution had destroyed all hope of armed support for the Carlist party from France. Then the King died, leaving the throne to Isabella and appointing his widow as regent. Even before the 'cork of the beer bottle', as Ferdinand called himself, had blown off, the Bishop of Leon and the Jesuits had called out the Carlist bands in Castile. A civil war, which was to last for seven years and to produce effects that would be felt for a whole generation, had begun.

Don Carlos' claim to the throne rested upon the question of whether the Salic Law, which had from all time regulated the right of succession in the Bourbon family, should apply in a country such as Spain which had never admitted that law. It was true that, at the time of the Treaty of Utrecht, Philip V had issued a decree by which it was declared that the throne could not descend through the female line, nor could any prince born out of Spain inherit it. The object of this decree was to prevent any possibility of the union of the Crowns of France and Spain. But some seventy years later, when this possibility had vanished, Charles IV, who had been born in Naples, called a secret meeting of the Cortes to ratify his abrogation of this decree. This Pragmatic Sanction, as the document was called, was published in 1830 by Ferdinand. Thus even if, as the Carlists maintained, one king could not with the assent of the Cortes annul the decree of another, Don Carlos was still not the rightful heir, for his father, having been born out of Spain, had no legitimate right to the throne.

But the strength of the Carlists did not depend upon legal quibbles such as these. The cause which had drawn them together was far more important than the succession of this or that dynasty. They were taking up arms against Liberalism, which in their eyes was but a second wave of the old Lutheran heresy, to resist which Spain in the past had given her life-blood. Any concession to the new ideas, any mitigation of the old Church and State absolutism would, they saw, let in the poison. What they did not see was that the times had changed and that it was impossible to use against Liberalism the same weapons that Philip II had used against the Protestants.

They made another mistake. Luther's attack on the Church had stimulated its latent energies and produced a movement so rich and overflowing in human and religious feeling that it scarcely needed an Inquisition to support it. But the Church in 1830 no longer possessed these energies: both in Spain and in Rome it lacked the moral and the intellectual power to react positively and so was driven back to a purely negative position. The Carlists therefore had no policy but to return to the seventeenth century.

It was of course natural that at this moment, when Spain was called upon to leave the cave in which, like Segismundo, she had so long been dreaming and to step out into the dangers of the modern world and steer her way among its winds of doctrine, there should have been a moment of giddiness and panic and a desire to return to the safety and tranquillity of the past. That giddiness is the essence of Carlism. It is a longing for the past because the past gave unity. 'One flock, one earthly shepherd, one monarch, one empire and one sword.' The couplet by the sixteenth-century poet which stands at the head of this chapter sums up the Carlist ideal. And looking back to-day a Spaniard who could forget for a moment the existence of Europe and the inevitable march of time might well regret the Liberal victory, for if the Carlists had had their way none of the civil wars, none of the discords and divisions that have since rent Spain would have occurred. For Carlism meant ideological agreement, unity of thought and belief, and this on such a comprehensive scale that it robbed political questions of everything but their immediate and practical content. Besides, given such unity, there could be a return to that regional and personal independence and weak central government that Spaniards love. At the bottom of Carlism, as Unamuno observed, there is a great deal of anarchism, and anarchism is only possible, as we have pointed out before, when there is agreement as to certain essentials. Under the Hapsburg kings that agreement (secured by the severest restrictions on the liberty of thought) had permitted an anarchic freedom of action. It was therefore essential, so the Carlists declared, to restore that special tribunal, the Inquisition, which had made all this possible.[1]

The Inquisition had long ceased to inspire terror (its last victim had been an old woman burned in 1781 'for having carnal converse with the Devil and laying eggs that had prophecies written on them'), but down to its first dissolution by Napoleon it had continued to exercise great political power. It could ruin and disgrace anyone whom it chose to attack and in 1780 it had with difficulty been prevented from prosecuting all the King's ministers. It was the only instrument that could be trusted to root out the freemasons and so keep back the Liberal tide. It was natural therefore that it should provide a rallying cry for the Carlists, and even when, in the first years of the twentieth century, it had become entirely a thing of the past, one finds its restoration still at the head of the Carlist programme, whilst in their periodicals it is acclaimed in rapturous language as 'that most august tribunal, brought down by angels from heaven to earth'.[2]

[1] See Note A on p. 213 at end of chapter.
[2] Jaime de Lobrera, *El Carlismo es una Esperanza no un Terror*, 1883.

But the religious and dynastic questions were not the only ones that divided Liberals and Carlists. The centralizing policy of the last Bourbon kings and their whittling down of local rights and privileges had been greatly resented. The Liberals also stood for this policy and were planning to carry it much further. The Basques and Aragonese naturally felt their *fueros* threatened. Then the land policy of the Liberals (also a legacy of the eighteenth-century kings) was unpopular. The Cadiz Cortes had proposed selling up the common lands, and the Cortes of 1822 would have carried this out if it had had more time. This drew the Church and the peasants together, for though little had as yet been said about selling Church property (which amounted to nearly one-third of the non-communal land in Spain), it was clear that before long its turn would come. If it was only in the north of Spain—the Basque provinces, Navarre, Aragon and Catalonia—that the peasants rose as a body to support Don Carlos, that was because it was only in those districts that the peasants and small farmers were sufficiently independent and conscious of the threat to their interests to react strongly. Small agricultural holdings were here balanced with communal pasture lands, and there was a large class of peasants who were relatively prosperous. Thus the religious question was linked to the land in 1833, just as it was in 1933, though in a different sense, for in 1933 the Church was not supporting the interests of the peasants but those of the landlords. Had the Church ever understood that its fate depended upon there being everywhere in Spain a prosperous peasantry, it is certain that its position would not be what it is to-day. But it never grasped this. And one must admit that it would have been difficult for it to have taken up this position without quarrelling with the wealthy middle and upper classes, whom the decline of the mendicant orders and the influence of the Jesuits had made the chief support of the Church.

The enemies of the Carlists were, as we have said, the Liberals. And just as the Carlists had an international society, the Jesuits, which directed their policy and furthered their aims, so the Liberals had the freemasons. A few words must be said about them. Freemasonry was brought to Spain by the English. The Duke of Wharton founded the first lodge in Madrid in 1728 and, though forbidden by the Inquisition, it made progress among the enlightened aristocracy and the ministers of Charles III. In 1780 the more exotic rites of the Grand Orient (founded seven years before by the Duc de Chartres) were substituted for the Scottish rites and in 1789 the Conde de Aranda, the

Prime Minister who had been the friend of Voltaire, became Grand Master. Many members of the King's circle joined it. For the lodges stood for the humanitarian ideas which were the fashionable doctrine of the age and which inspired the attitude of the Government and of the small ruling class. They thus acquired a great deal of power—for twenty years the Madrid lodge was a sort of council of state—and the road to influence lay through them.

The Napoleonic War broke up the lodges, some going over to Joseph, who became Grand Master, and others siding with the National cause. But the membership was greatly extended by the inclusion of many of the corps of officers, and when the famous Constituent Cortes met in 1810 at Cadiz a new patriotic branch, the Grand Orient of Spain,[1] was founded which at once proceeded to give birth to the Liberal party.[2] From now onwards freemasonry was the International of the revolutionary middle classes in their struggle against feudal and religious institutions.

The Army, which was the champion of these middle classes, was naturally its special stronghold. Most of the plots and *pronunciamientos* of the next sixty years were hatched in the military lodges. The first of these, Riego's rising in 1820 that restored the Constitutional regime, was pre-eminently their work. Then, in those 'three so-called years' that followed (to use the Carlist expression for them), the lodges expanded till they permeated the whole of middle-class life. They became one of those typical Spanish institutions such as the Inquisition, the Army, the civil service, that because they have jobs to offer swell almost overnight to huge proportions. For since they controlled the Government, they had in their gift all the bureaucratic and military posts in the country. No doubt for this reason they represented a moderate Liberalism, and the radicals and *exaltados*, who wanted jobs too, were driven to form rival societies.

After the restoration of the Absolutist regime by the French the

---

[1] Throughout the Peninsular War the French and English competed in installing lodges in Spain, especially in the Army and Navy. These military lodges were called *trincheras* or trenches. It may seem strange therefore that, in the Cortes which sat at Cadiz at a time when the whole of Spain was overrun with French troops, it was a French type of lodge which won. But it was precisely the success of the French arms which led to this result and the Liberals of the Grande Oriente were quite prepared, if necessity arose, to come to terms with Joseph. As recent events have shown, the patriotism of Spaniards needs certain qualifications: three-quarters of the resistance to the French was due to the hatred of the Church for Jacobinism.

[2] The Liberal party was the gift of Spain to the world. The Conservatives were known as the *serviles*—*servil* meaning not only 'servile' but also, when written in two words, 'vile being'.

masons were hunted down and killed, but on Ferdinand's death they reappeared and again took charge of the Government. This time they were more successful and by their influence in the Army enabled the weak middle classes and the somewhat thin and heady Liberalism they stood for (Liberal ideas without their appropriate economic background) to defeat the Carlists. After this the importance of the lodges declined, mainly because the victory was won and in the less oppressive days ahead their organizations no longer served any useful purpose. After 1874 they ceased to be anything more than a club for the anti-clerical section of the Conservative middle classes. When the Republic came in most of the senior Army officers and even, it is said, the King were masons.[1]

The Carlist War that lasted from 1833 to 1840 completed the ruin that the Napoleonic Wars had begun and put all power into the hands of the Army for thirty years. The stronghold of the Carlists was in the north—the Basque provinces, Navarre, Aragon, parts of Catalonia and Old Castile—where, as we have seen, a fair distribution of land and a regular rainfall had produced a prosperous yeoman class who were ready to defend their liberties. It was essentially a movement of the country districts, for the large towns such as Bilbao, Saragossa and Pamplona were Liberal. Had agrarian conditions in other parts of Spain been less wretched Carlism would have appeared simply as an opposition of the country districts to the cities, such as one has recently seen in Austria. But in the rest of Spain the priests and monks could not get the people to rise or throw off their indifference, whilst the landlords were won over to the Liberal cause through their purchase at very low prices of the Church lands.

The war settled down almost at once into a monotonous and ruthless struggle between two parties who could not come to effective grips with one another. The Basques and Navarrese fought with their usual courage and energy in their own country and produced leaders of genius such as Zumalacárregui and Cabrera. But their only form of warfare was guerrilla war and they failed as soon as they left their native mountains. The Liberal armies, on the other hand, composed of half-hearted, half-starved conscripts, led by the same incompetent generals of whom Wellington had so many bitter things to say, could make no progress against them on Carlist territory. They were ambushed, cut up and defeated whenever they advanced on to it, whilst in Madrid and through all the south of Spain a Liberal revolution

[1] See Note B on p. 214 at end of chapter.

simmered, because the Queen Regent would not, until forcibly obliged to, grant a full constitution. Carlism in the north, chaos and aimless revolution in the south and east: it was the same situation that reappeared during the First Republic in 1872 and again in the autumn of 1936, after Franco's rising had broken out. But in the Carlist War the foreign intervention (of more moral than material use) was on the side of the legitimate government.

The war was fought with great ruthlessness, prisoners and hostages being frequently killed on both sides, whilst by a solemn order of Don Carlos (especially disgraceful when one remembers that the British Navy had not long before saved his life) every English prisoner caught by his troops was shot. The end came only when the Basques and Navarrese got tired of fighting and made peace without consulting their master. By the Convention of Vergara they were guaranteed their *fueros* and their officers were taken over by the Regular Army at the same pay and rank.[1]

Carlism being now defeated, revolutionary Liberalism had accomplished its mission. It had secured power for the upper-middle classes. All that remained was to consolidate this position and to prevent the *petite bourgeoisie* from obtaining the share that, on the strength of the assistance they had given in bringing down the Carlists, they now claimed. To do this it was necessary to reconcile the *nouveaux riches*, who had bought the Church lands sold in the heat of the war, to the bishops and the clergy. The man who brought about this reconciliation was General Narváez. Three years after the conclusion

[1] A British Legion 10,000 strong, recruited with the assistance of the Government and led by British Army officers, was fighting on the Cristino side. But there were also British volunteers fighting for 'the faction'. English admirers raised subscriptions for arms, and visits from Tory M.P.'s to Don Carlos' camp took place very much as they have done during the recent war. 'The Carlists', wrote a certain Mr Wilkinson, who was fighting on their side, 'are very anxious to get stray Englishmen who enter their provinces to write something about the cause.... They lead him about and if the season be spring or summer will bid him observe how green the fields and trees are and how the peasants are busied in their occupations. All this while the individual has no opportunity of ascertaining by general enquiries the real state of things: he is feasted and wheedled by the people of the court, writes as they wish, and leaves the country with the idea that he is competent to pass a judgement upon it.'

But Don Carlos soon made the position of his English admirers very difficult: by the famous Durango Decree he condemned all foreign soldiers who were captured to be immediately shot and to the end of the war he carried this out to the letter. Several hundred Englishmen were massacred in cold blood and Tory support fell off. Only one M.P. was found to declare that 'this was their fault for going there'. And one should add that these Tories who supported the party of the Inquisition abroad were the same who by every means in their power had opposed Catholic Emancipation at home.

of the Carlist War he drove out Espartero, the victor in that war and the champion of the *petite bourgeoisie,* who under cover of the title of Regent had made himself dictator, and set up a military dictatorship of the Right instead. The Jesuits came back to Spain, a concordat was signed with the Vatican, the common lands were sold. Except for brief revolutionary intervals the upper-middle classes, who then acquired power, have ruled Spain—sometimes through generals and court camarillas and sometimes through political parties—ever since.

Carlism was dead as a serious political party after 1840, yet the idea lived on. During the dark years when Spain was ruled by 'freemasons and heretics, Jews and Liberals', which saw the introduction of such works of Satan as railways and gas light, it remained a hope for many thousands of Spaniards. Its position was very much that of the Stuart parties in England and Scotland after 1715. It lingered as a sentimental and romantic tradition in the north of Spain and among certain families. It appealed to the chivalrous and quixotic feelings to which Spaniards are so prone as well as to that *ordenancismo* or love of laying down the law to which, so long as it is not to be applied to themselves, they are equally susceptible. And it had many adherents among women. But, though occasional small risings broke out from time to time, the Second Carlist War (1870–1876) could never have taken place had it not been for the deposition of Isabella and her substitution by King Amadeo of the 'atheistical and masonic' House of Savoy, followed two years later by the Republic.

The second Don Carlos (grandson of the first) had all the qualities required for a Bonny Prince Charlie; he was young, handsome and charming—so charming that it was almost forgotten that he spoke Spanish with an Italian accent. The highlanders of Navarre and Alava rose with enthusiasm to fight for him. So once more the old heroic scenes of 1834 were repeated. Monks and priests led out guerrilla bands, nuns left off their prayers to make cartridges, whilst the young men of the farms and hamlets, eager to destroy atheists and Liberals, marched and drilled on the hillsides. But unfortunately Don Carlos was just as weak and incompetent as his grandfather had been. Before the war was a year old he had lost all authority over his bands, who roamed the borders of Castile and Valencia or made sudden descents on to the lowlands, robbing and murdering as they pleased. The Carlist tradition of violence reasserted itself and prisoners were shot with monotonous regularity, although this time the conduct of the Government troops gave little excuse for it.

'Carlism a Hope and not a Terror' is the title of a tract of this time. But outside the Basque-speaking country it was the terror which made the deepest impression. The whole eastern theatre of the war, from Huesca almost to Alicante and from Cuenca to Teruel and Tortosa, along that arid mountainous watershed known as the Maestrazgo, which had also been the scene of the Cid's operations, was given up to the most frightful anarchy. There was a priest called Santa Cruz who levied blackmail, tarred and feathered women and plundered friends and enemies alike. Another threw everyone he caught alive into a chasm. Another, called Cúcala, made the wives and daughters of Liberals march at the head of his column when attacking. In some places the churches of Liberal priests were burnt, whilst theological students destroyed trains and railway stations as 'accursed novelties'. To the mild and cultured seventies and eighties, accustomed to revolutionary movements from the Left and to the need for restraining them, but shocked by a deliberate attempt to set back the clock, Carlism seemed an extraordinary demonstration of antique fanaticism, more fitted to Thibet or Turkey than to a modern European country.[1]

The Republicans had great difficulty in containing the rising, which gathered strength as soon as they came in. Estella was taken by the Carlists and became the seat of their court. There were no troops to oppose to them, for most of the regiments had disbanded and the south and east were in the throes of the Cantonalist insurrection. But Don Carlos failed to advance on Madrid and the Republicans collected an army and drove him out of Castile. A year later the accession of Alfonso XII with the blessing of the Pope put an end to the war, which had never been popular among the countrymen: its chief supporters having always been the women and the priests. As a result of it the Basques lost their *fueros*.

Carlism now seemed doomed to final extinction. The Carlists of Catalonia and of the Basque provinces enrolled themselves in the regionalist parties of their respective provinces, which grew up largely out of its ruins. The former joined the Catalan Lliga, the latter the Basque Nationalist party. Local autonomy had always been the main incentive in the Carlist rank and file.[2] But in Navarre (where the

[1] See Note C on p. 214 at end of chapter.
[2] The claim of the Carlist pretenders to stand for local autonomy was hardly logical when one remembers that the policy of all the eighteenth-century Bourbon kings had been greater centralization. But the French royalist party, in their search for popular support, had been carried along just the same road. In his manifesto of

agrarian conditions and the lack of large industries suited it and where there was a traditional opposition to the other Basque provinces) it maintained itself as strongly as ever, and all over Northern Spain it could count adherents in every town and village. Refusing the too secular name of party, it took to calling itself the Carlist Communion and kept up a fervid stream of enthusiasm in local newspapers and journals. Its programme remained the same. The year 1900 finds the Carlists still demanding a high property qualification at elections, the abolition of religious toleration for foreigners and above all the re-establishment of the Inquisition. Then, as its prospects of success dwindled (the worst humiliation came when the new Carlist pretender, Don Jaime, announced himself a Liberal), a period of apocalypse began. Ever since 1870 Don Carlos had been spoken of as the Messiah who would come to judge the enemies of the Church and establish a reign of truth and equity. Now a certain Father Ceferino began to prophesy that the Carlists would rule Spain 'after the anarchy' which he announced was close at hand. And so in 1909, during the disturbances in Barcelona, we hear of Carlists drilling and of convents amassing arms and of *requetés* firing from the upper windows of the Rambla into the street. Not all the bombs that went off during the following years were laid by Anarchists.[1]

But all the same a change was taking place. Leo XIII's pontificate had led to a new attitude towards social and political questions in Catholic countries. This necessarily affected the Carlist ideology also. Early in the nineties a reformer appeared among them, a certain Juan Vázquez de Mella, who drew up a programme which he declared, in a phrase that bordered on blasphemy, 'was more suited to modern times'. His views gained ground with all but a few die-hards and the Carlist Communion became the Traditionalist party.

Absolutism, he declared, was dead. What was needed was a king who ruled and governed, with the assistance of a council chosen by himself. Instead of an elected parliament, there was to be a corporative assembly, composed of deputations representing the classes,

6 July 1871 the Comte de Chambord promised the French people to give them 'sur les larges assises de la décentralisation administrative et des franchises locales, un gouvernement conforme aux besoins réels du pays'.

After 1900 and the rise of Catalan and Basque Nationalism the Carlist support for local autonomy declined and has to-day ceased to exist altogether.

[1] The Carlists used bombs in Spain before the Anarchists. 'My civil conscience', said Unamuno in a speech at Hendaye in 1930, 'dates from the day in which twenty bombs were laid in Bilbao, my native city, by the absolutists of Don Carlos de Bourbon. Fifty years have passed since then.'

interests and regions, which debated in secret. Without their consent the king could not impose new taxation nor alter any fundamental law. The authorities would of course see to it that only right-thinking persons were nominated.

In the country districts the aristocracy were to be restored to their 'ancient functions and privileges'. The middle classes would be allowed to control the municipalities. Schools and universities would be under the Church, new and severe laws against blasphemy would be passed and liberty of worship would be rescinded. There would of course be a censorship of books and of the press. The leading principles of the regime would be absolute submission to the Pope and absolute devotion to the King.

That is the creed for which the *requetés* fought so heroically in the Civil War. Its resemblance to Mussolini's Corporative State will be noted. As Unamuno said, the Carlists both in their general ideas and by their methods of violence and intolerance anticipated Fascism. But there is also a profound difference. Carlism looks solely to the past: all the industrial and intellectual developments of the last century are antipathetic to it. To its adherents it promises neither glory nor prosperity, but 'order' and 'respect for the hierarchies'. Spanish Fascism, on the other hand, is an exuberant creed drunk on fantastic dreams of empire and glory in the future. That they can be reconciled for long is not probable.

FURTHER NOTES ON CHAPTER IX

A (p. 205). The Carlists aimed at restoring what Menéndez y Pelayo called the *democracia frailuna*, monkist democracy, of the seventeenth century. They were careful to distinguish, as Juan de Mariana had done, between absolutism and despotism. In the former system the powers of the King were limited by natural law and by religion. If the King ordered anything contrary to the 'eternal and immutable principles of justice', the people should reply in the well-known phrase *Se obedece, pero no se cumple*—'We obey, but we are not going to do anything about it'. Again if the humblest of the King's subjects was injured by the King, he could sue him at the courts and recover damages from him. For *Sobre el Rey está la ley*.

The Carlists also drew attention to the fact that governments which derive their powers from tradition can afford to be laxer and milder than new governments, which are forced to commit many tyrannical acts to maintain themselves. Certainly Spanish history has provided plenty of examples of the truth of this argument. What the Carlists forgot was that since methods of production in the world change, any system of government which cannot adapt itself to new circumstances becomes intolerable. No doubt it was true that Liberalism was, as they asserted, merely old Protestantism writ new. The greater scope it allowed to individual effort, the neutrality or passiveness of the State—both had their origins in Lutheran anti-authoritarianism. Yet it was not any abstract theory of liberty, but the invention of the spinning jenny and the steam engine, that were making the new political forms inevitable.

B (p. 208). In the period between 1808 and 1840 the influence of British lodges in Spain was very strong. The Scottish lodges at Gibraltar (which contained many officers of the garrison) supported all the plots against Ferdinand. After 1840 the French influence ousted the British and to-day there is no connection between British and Spanish freemasonry. This breach (according to Gould) dates from 1877 when the Grand Lodge of England separated itself from the Grand Lodge of France because the latter had removed from its Book of Constitutions the paragraph affirming the existence of a Great Architect of the Universe. In 1936 there were two Grand Orients in Spain, one of which retained this paragraph, whilst the other did not. The masons of La Linea, who were direct descendants of the Scottish lodges, seem to have kept to the old tradition. This did not, however, prevent them from being, to the number of about 200, murdered in particularly sordid circumstances by the Carlist *requetés*, under the eyes and one might almost say with the tacit approval of the English garrison and colony at Gibraltar.

C (p. 211). Don Carlos began the campaign with a proclamation to the effect that 'every Spaniard who did not obey the order to rise, however powerful his reasons might be, was condemned to be shot.' Although this was meant only as a piece of bravado, it was frequently acted upon. The histories and newspapers of the time give ample proof of it.

One may ask why the Carlists were always so violent. The answer is that, like Don Quixote, they were an anachronism in a modern world that had ceased to care for the things they lived by. They believed that they were engaged in a holy war against Liberals, freemasons and atheists: all around them were the hosts of Satan, the men of the century, the madmen who believed that the rule of life must change because time moved. They alone were faithful. They alone were entrusted with the judgements of God.

But there was also an economic reason for their violence. The Carlists suffered under a disadvantage which did not affect the Government forces. They had no regular means of raising money and thus, not only were their troops compelled to live on the country, but the principal object of most of their military operations had to be to squeeze money from the towns and villages hostile to them. This led to a deterioration in the character of the war. The guerrilla leaders tended more and more to become brigands and to adopt those methods of threat and torture to which people who raise money by force are necessarily driven. And this in turn led to a demoralization in the Carlist ranks. Whilst some of these men were fanatics who robbed for the cause only, others were simply adventurers who had entered the Carlist ranks for what they could get out of it.

The parallel to Anarchism is obvious. The Carlist terror in Aragon and Valencia was not unlike the Anarchist terror in 1936 through the same district. Durruti was the implacable Cabrera over again. The principle of action—violence to obtain 'liberty'—was identical. The main difference was that whereas the Anarchists were endeavouring to create a new world, the Carlists wished to force Spain back into the narrow framework of the past. In 1833 Carlism still had some *raison d'être*: it represented a perfectly normal conservatism and an opposition of country to town. But in 1873, in so far as it was not a rural movement confined to the farms and villages of Navarre, or a purely sentimental attitude on the part of a few families, it was simply the revolutionary action of the militant wing of the Spanish Church.

Chapter X

THE SOCIALISTS

In Chapters VII and VIII I have gone at some length into the character and history of the Anarcho-Syndicalist movement. It will not be necessary to say so much about Spanish Socialism. Unlike Anarcho-Syndicalism it is a branch of a European family whose leading characteristics are well known everywhere, whilst the course it has followed south of the Pyrenees has been a perfectly normal one.

We have already seen how a small group of *Autoritarios* or Marxian Socialists, under the leadership of an old trade unionist and typographer called José Mesa, were expelled from the Bakuninist International in 1872. This group did not survive the collapse of the Republic and the proscription of the working-class organizations that followed, but its members continued to exchange views and to correspond with one another. A *tertulia* or circle of friends met every night in a Madrid café to discuss Socialist theories, and these discussions ended in a resolution to found a party. Thus it came about that on 2 May 1879 five friends met in a tavern in the Calle de Tetuan for a 'banquet of international fraternity' and founded—in secret, of course—the Partido Democrático Socialista Obrero.

This young Socialist party consisted for the most part of members of the Madrid union of printers and typographers with a few doctors thrown in. The leading figure was a typographer called Pablo Iglesias, who nine years before, as a youth of twenty, had joined the International. The son of a poor widow who earned her living by washing clothes in the Manzanares and suffering all his life from bad health due to early malnutrition, he had developed a tenacity and will power which made his companions ready to accept him as a leader in preference to older and perhaps more talented men. Thus in 1872 he was editing the authoritarian paper *La Emancipación* in collaboration with José Mesa and Paul Lafargue and a few years later he was elected President of the (non-political) Printers' Association in Madrid. But the chief influence in the formation of the party came from abroad. José Mesa had been settled for some years as a journalist in Paris and corresponded regularly with Iglesias. Through Paul Lafargue he had come to know Jules Guesde and had joined his circle. Now Guesde was not only an intimate friend of Lafargue's but the chief representative at this time of orthodox Marxist doctrine against the opportunist influences that were creeping into it. He edited the famous weekly *L'Égalité*.[1] Mesa naturally saw that copies of this paper reached his Socialist friends in Madrid, whilst his letters of advice and explanation, which, in view of his age, experience and former position as leader of the authoritarian group, carried great weight, presented the same point of view. Iglesias was impressed by Guesde's severe, categoric style and uncompromising attitude and adopted them for the use of the Spanish Socialist party.

In 1881 Sagasta's 'fusionist' party came into office and restored to the working classes their old right of association. The Socialists could therefore appear openly. The party was refounded with 900 members of the printers' and typographers' union and a hundred members from other professions, and Iglesias was elected secretary. His first act was to organize a strike. Some of the printing establishments had refused to carry out their legal obligations towards their employees. They therefore struck work. It was a very small strike—only 300 typographers were involved—but it was the first one the country had seen since the restoration of the Monarchy, and it created a great sensation. Several newspapers had to cease publication and the whole press, Liberal as well as Conservative, resounded with denunciations of the Socialists. The Government intervened in favour of the proprietors and imprisoned the strike committee. But the men won, and although Iglesias was sentenced to three months' imprisonment for the part he had played in it, the fact that it had been won against the Government and the municipal authorities gave the Socialist party a certain prestige. One result of this strike was that many newspapers and printing establishments in Madrid refused to employ Socialists.

---

[1] Jules Guesde (1845–1922) was a Bakuninist until 1873 or thereabouts, when he went over to Marx. As soon as the reaction that followed the Commune came to an end he became the chief propagandist of Marxist ideas in France. At first these were a little vague. The general lines to be followed were not settled till 1880 when Marx, Engels, Lafargue and Guesde drew up a programme which was accepted by a labour congress at Le Havre in the same year. In this programme it was laid down that although a political party of the proletariat must be founded, a complete rupture with the bourgeoisie was necessary. The next congress two years later led to a split between Guesde and the reformist and anti-Marxist wing of Brousse (Les Possibilistes). Guesde then founded his own party, the Parti Ouvrier, which decided to participate in elections, but only as a means of agitation and propaganda. It was in this spirit that Guesde (assisted by Lafargue) edited *L'Égalité*. His influence upon Iglesias was so great that one can trace it not only in the programme and policy of the Spanish Socialist party, but in the dry and uncompromising style of their paper *El Socialista*.

An exodus of typographers followed and Socialist doctrines were carried to the provinces.

The movement, however, progressed very slowly. It was not till 1886 that it had a paper of its own: then *El Socialista* was founded as a weekly on the very insufficent capital of 927 pesetas, which it had taken three and a half years to collect. The foundation of the paper led to a small split in the party. One of the articles of its programme, as drawn up by Iglesias, expressed its intention of 'attacking all bourgeois parties and especially the most advanced'. In this decision Guesde's influence showed itself: the advanced parties were the most dangerous because they alone could attract working-class votes. But several of the most outstanding men in the party, among them Jaime Vera, the scientist, dissented and left. This did not deter Iglesias, who during the next twenty-five years never abandoned an attitude of what he called 'blessed intransigeance'.

The next step was to organize a trade union for the whole of Spain. The Anarchist Regional Federation, founded in 1881, was at that time breaking up and leaving all over the country small unions that often had not any very definite political orientation. By capturing and bringing together a number of these and adding them to the now reduced typographers' union, Francisco Mora and García Quejido succeeded in founding in 1888 the *Unión General de Trabajadores* or, as it is usually called, the U.G.T. This was a trade union of the ordinary social democratic type, moderate and disciplined and without any immediate revolutionary objects. Its strikes were peaceful and directed solely towards improving the workers' conditions.[1] But its numbers were insignificant: founded with a membership of 3300, eleven years had passed before it could double this. The comparison with the teeming forces of the Anarchists was discouraging. It almost seemed as though the Spanish working classes would never be won over to Socialism. One reason for this failure to attract adherents is obvious. The main principle that separated the Socialist party from the Anarchists was their belief in parliamentary and municipal action. Yet the fact that the elections were a sham and that their results were decided beforehand by the Government in power showed that they

---

[1] The U.G.T. was founded in Barcelona in the hope that it would absorb the industrial workers there, but its failure in Catalonia was so complete that in 1899 the central office was moved to Madrid. This was not, however, due to the competition of the Anarchists. The oldest trade union in Catalonia, the *Tres Clases de Vapor*, was in 1882 attempting to found a political party with 'possibilist' tendencies and other independent unions showed signs of joining it. It was the Castilian, authoritarian spirit of the Socialist party that made it uncongenial to the Catalan workers.

had no chance whatever of gaining a seat either in the Cortes or in the municipalities. To expect Spanish workmen to go in large numbers to the polls knowing beforehand that the results would be falsified was out of the question. Iglesias was therefore obliged to fall back upon a plan of moral preparation of such of the working classes as he was able to draw over to his party. This gave the Socialist movement a peculiarly severe and puritanical character. The Republicans, with whom they carried on a constant war, spoke of it as a *cosa de los frailes*. But perhaps monkish was not quite the word. This closed and narrow congregation, set on maintaining the purity of its doctrines, with its strict discipline, its austere enthusiasm and its unshakeable faith in its own superior destiny, could better be described as Calvinist. There was something almost Genevan in the standard of self-respect, personal morality and obedience to conscience that it demanded of its followers.[1]

The wisdom of this policy was to show itself when, in 1899, under the shock administered to the regime by the American War, the tide began to turn. Within a couple of years the membership of the U.G.T. rose from 6000 to 26,000. Up to this time the only places where the Socialist movement had shown any signs of life had been Bilbao and Madrid. In Madrid were grouped more than half the trade-union members and a still larger proportion of the party, but the possibilities of expansion were limited because, till the introduction of electric power some years later, it contained few industries and only a scanty working-class population. In Bilbao the case was different. Here a nucleus had existed almost from the beginning among the

---

[1] The Socialist party set itself to raise the self-respect of the working classes. They made it clear that members of their union had to be serious men: they could not get drunk, take bribes or go to brothels. Even bull fights were frowned on. Pío Baroja, who was no friend of theirs, said that one of the best things that Socialists had done in Madrid was that they had put an end to the *chulapería* of the poor. Madrid, as the seat of the court and the Government, had at this time a very loose standard of conduct and the working classes were infected with the vices of the bourgeoisie just as they are in Seville to-day. This moral regeneration was of course essential if the Socialists were to hold their own in these corrupt times. Equally essential was the voluntary seclusion which the party had adopted, which exposed them to the reproach of being more afraid of being absorbed by other parties than anxious to gain new adherents. The 'policy of attraction' (in other words, bribery) practised by the Government parties, which had robbed the Republicans of so many of their best men, had to be guarded against. As an example of this, one may take Sagasta's offer to give Iglesias a seat at Valmaseda if he would refrain from contesting Bilbao at the approaching elections. Iglesias had a following at Bilbao, but none at Valmaseda. Had he taken Sagasta's advice, the Socialist party would have had a representative in the Cortes many years before it actually did so, but at the cost of becoming a tool of the Government.

workmen in the iron foundries and had gained prestige for itself in a series of successful strikes. Although it had to fight to gain recruits in such strongly Catholic surroundings, its position in the largest industrial city in the country after Barcelona was decisive and Bilbao became the chief centre of diffusion for Socialism in the rest of Spain. From it the movement spread to the steel workers of Asturias and to the miners of Linares in the province of Jaén. All over Spain builders, typographers, iron workers and miners were leaning to the U.G.T. rather than to the Anarchists. But still progress was slow. Every new group had to struggle against the bitter hostility of the employers, the municipalities and the caciques, whose actions were never hindered by any scruples as to their legality. Elections still continued to be conducted in the old way so that, though the party had gained two seats in the Madrid Municipality,[1] it had as yet no representative in the Cortes. Besides, the low wages of the great majority of Spanish workers made co-operation in a normal trade union, with its relatively high subscription, difficult.

This was the time of the introduction of the *Casas del Pueblo* or Workers' Houses. They were an institution of the Belgian Socialists which Lerroux had brought to Barcelona in 1905 for his Radical party and which were then taken up by Iglesias. Every *Casa del Pueblo* contained the committee rooms of the local branch of the party, a free lending library at which not only Socialist literature but also books of general interest were provided, and usually a café as well. In the towns there was also an assembly room where meetings could be held. When one reflects that only four or five cities in the whole of Spain possessed a public library, the educational value of these workers' clubs can be appreciated. They were available to every member of the U.G.T. In Madrid the *Casa del Pueblo* was a ducal palace bought expressly for the purpose, for the Socialist party had a strong sense of its own dignity and felt itself the heir to the glories of the past. This extension of its activities led to a certain rivalry with the Anarchists, especially in the south, where the Socialists were regarded as trespassers, and with the Radicals, who in Barcelona had *Casas del Pueblo* of their own. However, these innovations were not allowed to affect the general trend of the party. Under Iglesias' leadership it

[1] In 1905 Pablo Iglesias and Largo Caballero secured their election to the Madrid Municipal Council by faking the secret identification marks on the ballot papers of the Conservative parties, which led them till the actual counting of votes took place to believe that they had won. After 1910 public opinion turned and it became increasingly difficult to falsify the results of elections in the large towns.

continued on its austere and moderate course, disdaining both the general strikes and revolutionary fervour of the Anarchists and the purely verbal violence of the Radicals.

But Maura's policy and the events of the *Semana Trágica* brought it down from its pedestal. On 26 July 1909 the Socialist party in Barcelona, in alliance with the Radicals and the Anarchists, called a general strike. On 2 August the strike was extended by the U.G.T. to the rest of Spain and Iglesias published a violent manifesto. This unexpected act gave the Socialists a sudden popularity. It was followed by an alliance with the Republicans and the Radicals with the immediate aim of putting an end to the war in Morocco and bringing the reactionary Maura Government down. The results of this new policy were immediate. At the elections held a few months later the Socialists obtained seats in forty municipalities and Iglesias was returned to the Cortes for a Madrid constituency.

The reason for this sudden change is not far to seek. The Socialist party believed that its road to power lay through parliamentary and municipal action. But it could make no progress along this road so long as the elections were corrupt and fraudulent. Like the Socialist and peasant parties in other backward, badly governed countries it stood therefore, before anything else, for honest elections, moderate reforms and a purification of the political and administrative life of the country. This was a point of view which was shared by Conservatives like Cambó and the Catalan industrialists who followed him, by Melquíades Álvarez's Reformist party, recruited in Asturias, by Lerroux's Radicals and by the small Republican party, as well as by most sane and progressive people throughout the country. Everywhere increasing disgust was felt at the corruption and inefficiency of political life and at the tyranny of the caciques, and public opinion was rising. When therefore the Socialists came to the front as the champions through all Spain of honest and decent government and did what no other political party could do—declared a general strike— they at once drew the attention of all those people who desired the same thing. And as the struggle at the polling booths became real and the caciques saw their power confined more and more to the country districts, the enthusiasm of the working classes rose, and, except in the Anarchist regions or where the caciques were too powerful, they flocked to vote.

The years 1910–1917 saw therefore a marked increase of Socialist activity. The great mining and steel-producing centres of the north—

Bilbao and Asturias—increased their membership and began to pro-
selytize the south. González Peña won over the Rio Tinto to the
U.G.T., and the mining centres of the Sierra Morena—Peñarroya and
Almadén—followed suit. These movements were accompanied by a
series of strikes at Bilbao, Linares and Rio Tinto, which were most of
them successful. Only a railway strike led by the U.G.T. and supported by the newly founded C.N.T. failed completely. The fear of
the bourgeoisie that it would be the prelude to a revolution led
Canalejas to call up the strikers to the colours. The Socialists also
began to turn their attention to the land. In the small towns of
Andalusia and the Levante *Casas del Pueblo* sprang up and a successful campaign was started in the irrigated *vega* of Granada.[1] The
Anarchists lost everywhere except in Catalonia. For this was a period
of faith in parliamentary action and of belief that it would lead, either
by peaceful means or by revolution, to a new state of things. But the
King and the reactionary forces which supported him had no intention
of taking the risks which honest elections to a Constitutional Cortes
would offer, and when in the so-called 'Renovation Movement' of
1917 all those forces making for a new Spain began to gather strength
and to demand an immediate solution, the Socialist party was manœu-
vred into declaring—against Iglesias' advice—a general strike, which
was then broken with considerable bloodshed by the Army.[2] So the
hope of regeneration by parliamentary action came to an end. It did
not return till 1931, when the conditions for its success were for many
reasons less favourable.

Every revolutionary movement, every strike that fails after courage-
ously defying authority, is a moral success in Spain and leads to an
increase in the numbers of the defeated party. That is a measure of the
difference of psychological climate between Spain and other European
countries. The four Socialists—Largo Caballero, Besteiro, Anguiano
and Saborit—who were condemned to penal servitude for their part
in the strike were at once elected to the Cortes (two of them on
Anarchist votes), at the same time as Iglesias and Prieto.[3] The
Government had to release them. In the following year the U.G.T.,

---

[1] See Note A on p. 228 at end of chapter.
[2] See Note B on p. 228 at end of chapter.
[3] One of the charges on which Besteiro, who was a member of the Junta which in
March 1939 negotiated the surrender of Madrid to Franco, was sentenced to a long
term of imprisonment by the Falangist authorities was his participation in the 1917
strike! An offence for which he had twenty-one years before been pardoned by the
King. He died in prison.

which in 1900 had only 42,000 members, could claim 220,000. Spanish Socialism was becoming a serious political force. And new men appeared on the scenes to lead it. Pablo Iglesias, *el abuelo* or 'grandfather', as he was affectionately called, though he lived on to 1925 and retained the Presidency both of the Socialist party and of the U.G.T. until his death, was too ill during the last eight years of his life to play any effective part in the movement. Francisco Largo Caballero, a Madrid plasterer who had learned to read when he was twenty-four, took over his functions in the U.G.T., whilst Julián Besteiro, a professor of logic, became Vice-President of the party. Fernando de los Ríos, a professor of law, Luís Araquistáin, a journalist, and Indalecio Prieto also began to come to the front of the movement. Prieto requires a few words to himself. As a boy he had sold newspapers and trays of pins in the streets of Bilbao. His great natural intelligence had enabled him to rise and to attract the attention of a wealthy Liberal banker and business man, Horacio Echevarrieta, to whom he became a sort of confidential agent. Prieto advised him on his affairs and managed his newspaper, *El Liberal de Bilbao*, so well that in the end he became sole proprietor. When in 1919 he was elected to the Cortes his exceptional parliamentary gifts (he was the most eloquent speaker in the house) gave him a leading role in the Socialist party. His life-long rivalry with Caballero dates from this moment. Whilst Caballero represented the severe authoritarian spirit of Castile with its narrowness and intransigeance, Prieto stood for the more liberal and flexible trade unionism of Bilbao, a commercial city whose affinities lie in the north of Europe rather than in Madrid. Thus it came about that on almost every important occasion during the next twenty years Prieto and Caballero differed. And since Caballero represented Madrid and the tradition of Guesde and Iglesias, and Prieto only Bilbao and that almost non-existent thing—Spanish Liberal opinion—it was natural that Caballero's views should prevail.

A difficult problem soon confronted the party—whether or not to adhere to the Third (Communist) International. Their reformist tendencies had received a strong check in 1917 when the attempt to clear a legal parliamentary road had failed. King, Church and Army now blocked the way, and it was difficult to see how they could be removed without violence. Besides, the Russian Revolution had established itself and was acting as a powerful magnet on all working-class movements. After two extraordinary congresses, held in the summer of

1920, had come to opposite decisions (the second voted by 8269 votes
to 5016 in favour of entering) it was decided to send two emissaries,
Fernando de los Ríos and Daniel Anguiano, to Russia to make a
reconnaissance. They arrived to find that the Congress of the Third
International had established twenty-one conditions which must be
fulfilled by anybody wishing to join it. De los Ríos, who was unfavourably impressed by everything he saw in Russia, thought these
conditions were unacceptable: Anguiano was for accepting them. On
their return a third extraordinary congress was called to hear their
reports. Before it met the Executive Commission of the party (which
in the absence of a Congress is the supreme authority) met at Iglesias'
house to discuss the matter. Iglesias, who was a democrat, made every
effort to persuade them to accept de los Ríos' report, but on putting
the matter to the vote, the majority were seen to be against it. When
the Congress assembled a few weeks later Iglesias was ill and unable to
attend, but he sent a letter in which he made a last appeal against
accepting the twenty-one conditions, on the grounds partly that this
would cause a split in the party. This appeal was successful. The
Assembly decided against affiliation with the Third International by
8880 votes to 6025 and when the Second International was revived a
few years later the party took Caballero's advice and joined it. The
dissidents, who included such active members of the party as García
Quejido, Anguiano and Francisco Mora, founded the Spanish Communist party.[1]

Another problem was soon provided by the Dictatorship. Primo de
Rivera, who had a genuine admiration for the Socialists, felt the need
for having some support among the working classes and offered them
favourable terms if they would co-operate with him in his work of
regeneration. Prieto, who had grown up in the Liberal climate of
Bilbao and was a member of the Ateneo, was opposed to acceptance.
Largo Caballero, a Madrid authoritarian, over-ruled him. So the
Socialists took what was offered them by the Dictatorship and

[1] The Communist party was founded by the dissident Socialists and by a certain
number of Anarcho-Syndicalists, of whom the best known were Andres Nin and
Joaquín Maurín. Within a couple of years all the Socialists had left and, with the
exception of Anguiano, who remained neutral, had rejoined the Socialist party. The
Anarcho-Syndicalists were equally restive in their new allegiance and Nin and
Maurín went to Russia to point out the need for different tactics. When they returned at the end of the Dictatorship they founded the Left Communist (Trotskyist)
party, which obtained a certain mass support in Catalonia. During the Dictatorship
the Communist Party was so insignificant that Primo de Rivera did not think it
worth while suppressing it and the Communist press continued to appear as usual.

Caballero, as Secretary of the U.G.T., became a Councillor of State. The real reason for this unexpected action was the hope that by so doing they could strengthen their position in the country and in particular gain ground from the Anarcho-Syndicalists, whose organizations had been proscribed by the Dictator.

During the past few years the C.N.T. had been increasing its numbers very rapidly. With the aid of its *sindicato único* and the prestige of its great strikes it had not only swept away all the recent gains of its rival in the Andalusian campo, but it had invaded the Socialist preserve of the centre and north. Here it had seized half the builders' union in Madrid, which was one of the first strongholds of the U.G.T., had drawn off many of the railwaymen and planted itself firmly in Asturias, in the port of Gijón and in the great iron foundries of Sama and La Felguera.

To Caballero, who had the whole organization of the U.G.T. in his hands, this was a serious matter: the fear of losing ground to the C.N.T. was almost an obsession with him. As a Marxist he felt the supreme importance of the unification of the proletariat. He sensed therefore in the Dictatorship a good opportunity for making some progress in this direction. Possibly the U.G.T. would be able to absorb the C.N.T. altogether.

This hope was not fulfilled. By using the *comités paritarios* (arbitration boards in industrial disputes) of the Dictatorship as a starting point, the U.G.T. greatly increased their strength in the country districts, especially in Extremadura, Granada, Aragon and New Castile, but they failed completely in Catalonia and made no progress among the industrial proletariat. The Anarcho-Syndicalists preferred to enter the reactionary *sindicato libre*, which they knew would break up with the fall of the Dictatorship. One other gain made by the Socialists was the incorporation in the U.G.T. of the shop assistants' and bank clerks' unions through a large part of Spain and the formation of a strong doctors' union. Henceforth a small though influential section of the professional classes and a large body of the lower-middle classes belonged to them.

There only remains to be considered the general character of Spanish Socialism. Señor Madariaga, himself a Liberal, writing in 1930, drew attention to its stern political outlook, its sense of authority, its instinct for government from above, for the weight and dignity of institutions. Essentially a product of the Castilian soil, it showed, he thought, an attitude of life that had been deeply influenced by the traditions of Catholic Spain.[1] He might have added that, as history shows, there has often been a definite trend in Spain towards Socialist institutions. In the sixteenth and seventeenth centuries Spain was too isolated from the rest of the world to feel the Renaissance deeply. Her history was therefore a continuation, in an expanded form, of the Middle Ages. Her Church was the all-embracing Mediaeval Church. Her State moved towards Socialism rather than towards capitalism. To such a point did this go that in the middle of the seventeenth century we find what Costa has, with some exaggeration no doubt, described as a school of collectivist economics whose projects for nationalizing the land were seriously debated by the Royal Council and on one occasion actually adopted.[2] The progress of modern industrial civilization arrested this tendency, but failed to make the current flow in the opposite direction. For all the Liberal ferment of the early nineteenth century, economic Liberalism never took root in the country. Private enterprise remained stagnant. Spain became 'backward'. Since no one can suppose that such an active and intelligent race as the Spaniards could not, if they wished, apply themselves to the tasks of money-making, the explanation can only be that, as a Venetian ambassador two centuries ago observed, they have never wished to. Indeed to anyone who has lived in Spain this is obvious. Every class has its own way of showing the repugnance it feels for modern capitalist civilization. The risings of the Anarchists and the Carlists are one form: the idleness of the rich, the lack of enterprise of the business men and the sluggishness of the bankers are another. So too are such phenomena as *empleomanía* and the swollen ranks of Government clerks and Army officers. Whatever historical causes may be assigned to this refractoriness, it remains a fact that Spaniards live either for pleasure or for ideals, but never for personal success or for money-making. That is why every Spanish business man and shop assistant is a poet manqué: every working man has his 'idea': every peasant is a philosopher.

It may be said that all this does not point to Socialism: yet by making the stress and strain of competitive life and of factory con-

---

[1] 'The Socialism of Madrid is the only true historical entity in modern Spanish politics, i.e. the only feature endowed with an inner life which gives it a permanent, growing and formative value in the life of the country.' Madariaga, *Spain*, p. 207. How far Spanish Socialism and Catholicism are plants of the same soil is shown by the fact that in Old Castile, the heart of the former Spanish Empire, the only two parties are the Socialists and the Catholics. Neither Liberals nor Republicans nor Anarchists have ever had any influence there.

[2] See Appendix II.

ditions intolerable, the capitalist system has produced a strong desire in every class for a change. What Socialism offers, what every Spaniard desires, is safety. The ethical side of Socialism too, the belief that to everyone should be given not according to his deserts, but according to his needs, is deeply rooted in the Iberian nature. This belief, which has never been current in the democracies, is part and parcel of the Spanish Catholic tradition. It is what most distinguishes Spanish from English and French Christianity. No race in Europe is so profoundly egalitarian or has so little respect for success or for property. If within the next two centuries there is a happy and peaceful future awaiting Spain, one may predict that it will be in a weak and paternal Socialist regime, giving ample regional and municipal autonomy: a regime not unlike the system under which Spain lived in the early seventeenth century.

A few words must be said about the Socialist party of Catalonia. It will be remembered that, although the headquarters of the U.G.T. had been for ten years at Barcelona, it had never caught on there. The Spanish Socialist party and its union were too authoritarian, too Castilian to please the Catalans. A purely Catalan party, the *Unión Socialista Catalana*, was therefore founded some years later by Juan Comorera. It was less centralized than the Socialist party and inclined towards the federal principles of Pi y Margall. It allied itself at elections with the Esquerra or Left Catalan party. It was always a very small party and would have little importance but for the remarkable results which it helped to produce by its support of the Co-operative movement, which had been declining since 1873, but now began to revive in a remarkable way. The work of some of these productive co-operative societies of Catalonia is described in Appendix II. Through the energy of Comorera and his associates eight large co-operative shops, each with its café, billiard room, gymnasium, reading room, cinema and baths, were opened in the suburbs of Barcelona in 1933. There were forty-two smaller co-op's in other parts of the city and two hundred in the province. Many of these were agricultural, fishing, or industrial societies where all the land, factories, houses and instruments of labour were owned in common by the associates. One may safely say that nowhere else in Europe has collectivization been so successful, yet because this work has been carried on quietly in an unpolitical atmosphere little has been heard of it. Certainly for all their drum-beating neither the Anarcho-Syndicalists nor the Socialists have ever produced anything to compare with this.

But then the Co-operatives aimed at immediate results. The others put off all realization of their theories till the day of their triumph. The Catholic Syndicates also require some notice. Catholic trade unions in Spain date from 1861, when an active and intelligent Jesuit, Father Vicente, organized the *Centros Católicos de Obreros* in Valencia and in other places and affiliated them to the International Catholic labour movement. But neither the bishops nor the employers gave him any assistance and this promising movement fizzled out towards 1874.

Leo XIII's pontificate led to a change of attitude. For the first time since the eighteenth century the Spanish hierarchy awoke to the idea that there was a social question and that some attention must be paid to the working classes if they were to remain within the Church. The clergy were instructed to organize Catholic clubs and friendly societies. Assistance in illness and in unemployment was provided as well as funeral expenses. The members contributed something, but the bulk of the expenses was borne by the honorary members—that is, the employers. This movement never came to anything because it depended upon their financial support. Either the societies declined into groups of blacklegs (as for example in Barcelona) or they came to an end for lack of funds. Those owners who did not care to organize unions of strike-breakers for use in their struggles with the U.G.T. or C.N.T. preferred to keep religion out of labour questions altogether. This was especially the case in the country districts of the east and south, where the anti-religious feeling was strongest. Here one may say that by 1905 the Catholic working-class movement had ceased to exist.

In the north the position was different. Here the Catholic unions, being able to draw on a predominantly Catholic population, were more successful. There were two types. The first consisted of working-class societies and clubs, which in 1916 were grouped together as the *Consejo Nacional de las Corporaciones Católicas Obreras* under the presidency of the Archbishop of Toledo. They were friendly societies providing assistance in case of illness, old age and unemployment. In the country districts small loans were given to peasants without interest. But strikes were not permitted: employers and workmen were both members, and the Church adjudicated and preached mutual love between them. As time passed these societies naturally fell more and more under the control of the employers, who further gained by the co-operative arrangement by which they bought and sold in common. The interest of the workers in them declined.

The other type of Catholic trade union is best represented by the *Federación Nacional de Sindicatos Católicos Libres*, a Dominican association of a European type founded by Fathers Gerard and Gafo in 1912. These were much more effective because they were genuine working-class organizations which defended the interests of their members by strikes and boycotts. They had great success in the Basque Provinces, in parts of Navarre and in the cities of Old Castile, and between 1917 and 1923 they developed an intense economic action. They had no scruples about co-operating with the Socialists and in Bilbao they regularly organized joint strikes in which Catholics and Socialists sat side by side on the strike committees. This did away with the reproach invariably levelled at Catholic associations that they supported the interests of the employers. Undoubtedly these syndicates did a great deal, especially in the Basque provinces, to keep the workers within the body of the Church and to prevent them from going over to the Socialists. Although all the various types of Catholic associations expanded greatly during the Dictatorship, these were the only ones that stood the test of the Republic.

So that we may say that the Catholic labour movement was successful in those parts of Spain where the Church was not openly associated with the defence of the interests of the rich against the poor, and that it failed completely wherever the unequal distribution of the land had created an irreparable gulf between the classes.

FURTHER NOTES ON CHAPTER X

A (p. 221). The Socialist unions that sprang up in the years 1910–1912 in Andalusia and the Levante were nearly all in places that had Republican antecedents and were therefore accustomed to vote. The Socialist party, whose propaganda was very bad (much worse than the Anarchists') did little to encourage them. The first to join were railwaymen and miners, if there were any; then came artisans and last of all agricultural workers. The hill towns were much more susceptible than those in the river valleys. Granada, which might seem an exception to this, is 3000 feet above the sea and has a distinctly Castilian temperament. In every other part of Andalusia the conquests made by the Socialists in agricultural districts reverted in 1918 to the Anarcho-Syndicalists.

B (p. 221). The best account of the events that led up to this strike is to be found in *Pablo Iglesias*, by Juan José Morato, pp. 217–233. The salient factors are the impatience of the Anarcho-Syndicalists who had promised their assistance, the skilful provocation by the Government before the ground was prepared and the overruling of Iglesias by Largo Caballero and Anguiano. Those who had thought that the Army would make common cause with the strikers (as some regiments had done in Barcelona in 1909) were deceived: the cavalry charged unarmed strikers at Cuatro Caminos and the infantry opened fire on them.

Part III

THE REPUBLIC

Inquietus est et magna moliens hispanorum animus.
MICHAEL SERVETUS.

～

Chapter XI

THE CONSTITUENT CORTES

The French took three years of struggle and shed oceans of blood to win their liberty. All we have needed in Spain have been two days of explanation and one of rejoicing.   ALCALÁ GALIANO in 1820.

As we have seen from the previous pages, the picture presented by Spain at the moment of the proclamation of the Republic was by no means a simple one. The country was split, both vertically and horizontally, into a number of mutually antagonistic sections. To begin with there were the movements for local autonomy in Catalonia and among the Basques, which were opposed by an equally intransigeant centralist block in Castile. These autonomous movements, although they had their roots deep in Spanish history, had recently taken on the character of a rebellion on the part of the industrial interests in Spain against government by landowners. Thus the revolutionary movement of 1917 had parallel aims to the English Liberal Revolution of 1832. To consider the other side, the backbone of Castilian centralism was the Army, which drew its strength from the middle-class landowners who had been the chief gainers from the abortive Liberal Revolution of the early nineteenth century. The Army naturally collected round it the other conservative forces in the country, the King and the Church, though in the latter case there was a limit to the support it would give, due to the fact that the claims of the Church were so high that no other body of opinion in the country could back them. In its own way the Army was anti-clerical. A further feature was the fronde which it carried on with the political parties, who represented exactly the same material interests and even the same families that it did itself.

The working classes too were divided among themselves into two sections—the Socialists and the Anarcho-Syndicalists. Their differences were also, to a certain extent, of a regional sort. But whereas one may safely say that on the whole Socialism represented Castilian centralism and Anarcho-Syndicalism the federal and autonomous movement of the east and south, one would further not be far wrong in asserting that Socialism stood mainly for the urban proletariat and shopworkers and Anarcho-Syndicalism for the landless labourers of the large estates—the only exception to this (a large one it is true) being Catalonia. As we have already pointed out, an agrarian settlement in Spain, if such a thing were possible, would reduce Anarcho-Syndicalism to the dimensions of a purely Catalan movement. In a Spain that had gone Socialist, Catalan Anarcho-Syndicalism would have the same relations with Madrid that the Lliga and Esquerra had had with the Monarchist parties: it would appear as a Catalan separatist movement.

Under all the unrest and revolutionary action of the last hundred years lies the agrarian question. Reactionary farmers in Navarre (Carlists), peasants with a grievance in Catalonia (*rabassaires*), insurrectionary day labourers in Andalusia (anarchists), revolutionary peasant farmers and labourers on the Central tableland and in Extremadura (socialists)—all have made their contribution to the witches' cauldron. The conditions under which they lived were such that no one could deny that they had good reasons for their actions. When one remembers that the urban masses were by this time almost all under Socialist or Anarcho-Syndicalist leaders, one cannot help wondering how it was that Spain was still governable. Clearly unless very radical land reforms were introduced, it would soon cease to be so. But it happened unfortunately that these reforms were peculiarly complex and difficult. The agrarian question could not be solved, as in other European countries, by distributing plots of land to individual peasants and advancing them credits. Collective solutions would often be necessary. This presupposed a large staff of technical advisers, a fair amount of time and patience, and an organizing capacity —precisely things which no Spanish administration has ever possessed. There were also, on the part of all the non-socialist parties, strong objections to the organization of peasants on a collective basis. Yet till the agrarian question had been solved, or at least considerably ameliorated, there could be no hope of peaceable life or development for Spain.

Between the old governing classes—Army, Church and landowners
—and the peasants and factory workers there stood a thin but politically very active layer—the lower-middle class of the towns. This was
the class which had taken the lead in all the revolutions through which
Spain had passed since 1856, yet it had never except for brief revolutionary periods enjoyed power. Recently it had lost a considerable
number of its members (especially among the artisan class) to the
Socialists and Anarcho-Syndicalists, but it had compensated to some
extent for this by the increase in the numbers of the small tradesmen
who formed the bulk of its membership. Now, though broken up into
various groups which easily combined and fused with one another, it
formed the kernel of the Republican parties. Some 80 per cent of the
intellectuals, school teachers and journalists, together with a fair
number of the professional classes, sympathized with it. Its political
centre of gravity corresponded to what used in England to be called
Radical opinions. And, like the Liberal parties of the first half of the
nineteenth century, of which it was the reincarnation, it was strongly
anti-clerical.

The task that now lay before this party and its allies was a singularly
difficult one. On the one hand there were the old governing classes
led by the Army, who would certainly seize the first opportunity to
rise against it. Having successfully overthrown every Left government that had come in during the last hundred years, they had no
reason to doubt their ability to overthrow this one also. On the other
hand, there were the working classes and the peasants, over-confident
of their strength, impatient from long waiting and inspired by revolutionary ideologies. The Republican parties, who were themselves
comparatively weak and subject to great fluctuations in their membership, would have to hold the balance between these two menacing
forces whilst the essential reforms were passed. And by essential I
mean not merely those political reforms in which the Republicans
took a special interest, but such solid satisfactions as would give them
a dependable backing in the country. They were called upon to carry
out, not a Socialist Revolution, but a long overdue Jacobin one, which
would take the power from the landowners and give it to the lower-
middle classes backed by a contented peasantry.

The chief problem that they would have to solve would be, as I
have said, the complex agrarian question. But there was another
difficulty which in its way was just as great, though it has been more
generally overlooked. This derived from the fact that they came into

power at a moment when every party in Spain, both those of the Right and those of the Left, had been steadily increasing in strength and in pugnacity for the last thirty years. The Army, though temporarily taken aback by the fall of the Dictatorship, was more aggressive than it had been in 1900. The Church likewise. Of the forces of the Right, only the Monarchy had lost. As to the Left, both the Socialists and the Anarcho-Syndicalists were immeasurably stronger and more confident than they had ever been before. It was true that the Republic came in on an irresistible wave of popularity and that among more or less neutral opinion there was a desire for reforms. So long as this feeling lasted, no threat from either side need be feared. But neutrals cannot for long be relied upon and there was no reason to suppose that their enthusiasm would outlast the first disappointments. One might expect therefore that when this first rush of popularity subsided, the revolutionary forces of the Right and of the Left would be left to confront one another, with only a weakened Republican party to separate them.

It will be remembered that it was the victory of the Republican parties in the large towns in the municipal elections of April 1931 that sent the King into exile. The elections to the Constituent Cortes followed two months later. They gave, both in the country districts and in the towns, an enormous majority to the Republicans and their Socialist allies. The Left-wing Republican groups obtained some 150 deputies: the Right-wing Republicans just over 100 (the largest party among these, the Radicals, getting 90): the Socialists obtained 115. On the other hand the parties which had not desired the proclamation of the Republic obtained little more than fifty deputies and of these only nineteen were confirmed Monarchists. But even these figures do not show how great was the landslide, for the majorities by which the Republican parties were returned in the towns were colossal: in Madrid they averaged 120,000 and in the smaller towns 30,000. The whole country had turned with remarkable unanimity against the Dictatorship and against the King.

The Cortes elected in July gave promise of being in every way worthy of the task it had been called upon to perform. The personal distinction of many of its members was high. During the past few years Spanish life had touched a pinnacle of culture and intelligence which it had not known since the middle of the seventeenth century and the new men elected—few of them had sat in any previous Cortes —were fully up to the standard required by it. It was an assembly of notables at least as much as a delegation of interests.

We have seen that the parties which brought in the Republic fell naturally into three sections: the Socialists, the Left Republicans and the Right Republicans. The Socialist party at this moment was remarkably united. Its two leading figures, Francisco Largo Caballero and Indalecio Prieto, were both in favour of entering the Government in collaboration with the Republicans. Besteiro alone, adopting what one might almost call a syndicalist attitude, dissented from this view, but accepted the post of Speaker of the Cortes.

The Right-wing Republicans consisted in the main of the so-called Radical party, whose leader was Alejandro Lerroux. These Radicals had a somewhat shady reputation. They had appeared suddenly in Barcelona in 1904 as a violently demagogic and anti-clerical party, had been pushed forward by the Liberal Governments of the time to keep out the Catalan Nationalists and during their lengthy tenure of the Barcelona Municipality had set up a building racket out of which they had made huge sums of money. After 1909 many of their supporters left them to join either the Syndicalists or one of the Left Catalan parties, and they took several steps to the Right. The fall of the Monarchy made them the party of Conservative Republicanism. All over the country the middle and lower-middle classes who were tired of the King and had little love either for the Army or the Church voted for them. Prepared at first for a few reforms, they took fright as soon as they saw the rising excitement in the country. The Radicals were moreover the only party in the Cortes to be led by politicians of the old type who were not always over particular as to the means by which they acquired money. Their *Caudillo*, Lerroux, was a man of humble origin who had risen, no one could say exactly how, to be the owner of a luxurious house and considerable property. His debts were famous. The type of vulgar Latin politician of the first decade of this century, he and most of his party were out of place in this Cortes of enthusiasts who were there to build, each according to his own ideas, a new Spain.[1]

---

[1] Lerroux was the son of a sergeant-major, but was brought up by his uncle, a priest, to whom he acted first as acolyte and then as sacristan. His youthful education left him with a detestation of everything connected with religion. After an adventurous career as a journalist and public speaker he founded the Radical party which, thanks partly to the mysterious sums of money on which it could draw and partly to his violent oratory, had an immense and rapid popular success in Barcelona.

The Left Republicans, who formed the largest group in the Cortes, were made up of the Esquerra (the Catalan Nationalist party of the Left) and of three Spanish parties whose views and antecedents were very similar: Republican Action, led by Manuel Azaña: the Radical Socialists, who included Marcelino Domingo and Álvaro de Albornoz, and the Republicans from Galicia, who followed Casares Quiroga. Their views were what in England would be called Radical. They represented the more active and progressive members of the middle and lower-middle classes and they had a programme of reforms which would, they hoped, give them the support of sufficient numbers of the working classes to arrest the revolutionary movement which had been growing steadily since 1917. They aimed, in other words, at the conclusion of the Liberal Revolution which had been begun in 1812, but which military *pronunciamientos*, reactionary courts and a Church that still lived among the ideas of the seventeenth century had long ago brought to a standstill.

As one would expect, these Left Republican parties contained a large number of intellectuals. The famous 'generation of 98', whose political convictions had been formed by the loss of the last remnants of the colonial empire, as well as the pick of the professional classes—the doctors, lawyers and university professors who owed their position to the magnificent education given them by the Institución Libre de Enseñanza—sympathized with them. They included the great majority of schoolmasters. Their headquarters were the Ateneo in Madrid, the famous literary and political club which during the last hundred years had included all the more distinguished figures of Spanish life among its members. The Ateneo had been closed by Primo de Rivera—a thing which even the most reactionary governments of Isabel II had not dared to do—and from that moment it became the focus of the Republican movement. A few months before the Monarchy fell Manuel Azaña was elected to be its President.[1]

---

[1] A great deal has been made of the freemasonry of the Republican parties. As a matter of fact nearly all the Monarchist politicians and most of the Army generals before 1931 were masons. The King himself is said to have been one and practising Catholics often occupied high positions in the lodges. That is to say, freemasonry had ceased to have any political or anti-clerical connotations and had become a mere friendly society as it is in England. Then towards 1930 the Republicans began to invade the lodges and made it their business to restore them to their old function. During the first years of the Republic the Madrid lodges formed a convenient meeting-place for Republican politicians and a link between the Radicals and the groups that followed Azaña.

Broadly speaking one may say that being a mason meant belonging, in however tenuous a way, to the nineteenth-century Liberal tradition. Thus among the Socialists

The first Government of the Republic was formed in July and included members of all the Republican parties. It proceeded at once to a discussion of the new Constitution. This was to be followed by that of certain complementary laws, of which the most important were the Catalan Statute and the Law of Agrarian Reform. For a time the work of the Cortes went rapidly and smoothly. The Revolutionary Committee which brought in the Republic had taken great pains to settle the general outlines of the Constitution, so that no unforeseen disagreement should wreck it. The failure of the First Republic in 1873 had not been forgotten. Thus one of the first acts of the Provisional Government had been to set up a commission which should cast this outline into a legal shape that could be debated by the Cortes. The result of this careful preparation was that the first twenty-five articles were passed after due discussion within three months. It was the twenty-sixth article, which dealt with the position of the Church in the new State, that provoked the first serious opposition and finally a crisis which brought down the Government.

The reason for this crisis was as follows. The Juridical Commission set up by the Provisional Government had drafted an article which declared the Church to be separated from the State but gave it the position of a special corporation *de derecho público*. By the terms of this corporation it could have its own schools and, on certain conditions, give religious teaching in State schools. Canonical marriage would be regarded as legal, and public ecclesiastical functions could take place providing that those who took part in them had sworn allegiance to the Republic. Such an arrangement would have been accepted by the great majority of Catholics. It fulfilled Ortega y Gasset's dictum that in dealing with a historical and international body such as the Church 'one must act with a certain generosity on account of the forces of the past which it represents: but one must also act with caution'.

However, the majority of the Cortes found the provisions of this draft far too lenient. They held that the granting of a special status to the Church was tantamount to recognizing that it had sovereign rights, and drew up an article by which it was to be regarded as an ordinary association subject to the general laws of the country. Further, the

Prieto was a mason, but not Largo Caballero: among Catholic Conservatives Alcalá Zamora and Miguel Maura, but not Gil Robles: among the generals, Sanjurjo, Mola, Queipo de Llano, Batet and Goded, but not Franco. A few of the Anarchist intellectuals were masons, but, it would appear, no genuine Marxists.

annual State grant to the clergy (about 67 million pesetas) was to cease, all convents were to be dissolved and their goods nationalized and all religious schools with the exception of the seminaries were to be closed.

To understand the reasons for this aggressively anti-clerical attitude one must bear in mind not only the history of the Spanish Church during the past hundred years, but also its recent attitude. The Republic had come in as a reaction against the Dictatorship and the Monarchy: the Church has been the strongest supporter of both. During the recent elections it had deliberately identified the cause of the Monarchy with that of the Catholic religion. In the Catholic press and in the pulpit the Republican candidates had often been denounced as 'sold to Moscow gold'.

Then, a bare two weeks after the proclamation of the Republic, the Cardinal Primate of Spain, Mgr Segura, had issued a violently militant pastoral against the Government. It was true that the majority of the hierarchy showed a more correct attitude, but that was thought to be due rather to prudence than to good intentions. The working classes at all events had no doubts as to who their chief enemy might be. In reply to a demonstration at a Monarchist club and to an article in the *A.B.C.*, the crowds attacked a new Jesuit church in Madrid and burned it, and on the following day the conflagration spread, as if by magic, all over Spain. Dozens of churches and convents were destroyed, especially in Andalusia.[1]

The vote of the majority of the Cortes showed that the deputies were still under the spell of these emotions. They might argue that, since not more than 20 per cent of all the inhabitants of Spain were practising Catholics, they were merely reducing the Church to its true dimensions and importance. They could further point out that it was hardly fair that Spaniards who were not Catholics should contribute

---

[1] In six large towns alone (Madrid, Seville, Malaga, Granada, Murcia, Valencia) 102 churches and convents were completely destroyed. On the walls of the new Jesuit church in the Gran Via was chalked up *La Justicia del pueblo por Ladrones:* 'The justice of the people on thieves.'

These outrages and the apparent ease with which they were accomplished (due to surprise or panic, not to indifference: the Minister for Home Affairs, Miguel Maura, was a Conservative and a Catholic) produced symptoms of strong religious emotion among Catholics. The *damas catequistas* marched through the streets singing hymns. Pilgrimages were organized to adore the Santo Sudario in Oviedo. There was also a remarkable crop of miracles. Relics abandoned to the flames turned up later unscathed; a 'communist' who had fired his revolver at a Crucifixion fell back dead. Miracles never go out of date in Spain and during the next few years there was to be no lack of them.

to the expenses of the cult. But in fact their speeches and actions showed that they saw in the Church the chief support and maintainer of reaction and wished, by striking both at its funds and at its right to educate the young, to destroy its power once and for all in the country. It does not seem to have occurred to them that, by a more prudent conduct, they might have created a party for themselves within the Church. Many of the parish priests had voted for a republic. They were for the most part extremely poor, whilst the monastic orders were rolling in money and the bishops had large incomes. The Archdiocese of Toledo alone brought in 600,000 pesetas yearly. But naturally when they saw that the Cortes, which they had hoped might do something for them, had voted for cutting off their incomes altogether, they turned and became rabidly anti-Republican. The Republic also raised hopes among the more sincere elements in the Church—the Catholic intellectuals and those who saw that religion must be more than a means of supporting the rich against the poor. These included certain of the teaching Orders whose members had been trained abroad. By favouring them the Republicans would have been assisting the Spanish Church to raise itself to the intellectual and moral level of Catholicism in other countries and incidentally would have found a badly needed support for themselves. They preferred, in the moment of their triumph, to throw down the gauntlet.

But their action split the Government. After prolonged discussion the Minister for War, Azaña, brought forward a modification of their project by which the monastic orders, with the exception of the Jesuits, were to be allowed to remain (though not to continue teaching) and the State grant to the Church was to be continued for two years. This, after further stormy discussion, was passed, but the Prime Minister, Alcalá Zamora and Miguel Maura, the Minister for Home Affairs (both Conservatives) resigned and the Basque deputies walked out of the Cortes and refused to return to it.[1]

The unwisdom of this measure is to-day evident. For one thing it has always been a serious matter to legislate against religion in Spain. The mere abolition of the Inquisition by the Cortes of 1812 led to fearful persecutions by the Church and to a long religious war. In the revolutionary Cortes of 1869 a clause permitting civil marriage and freedom of worship for non-Catholics was only passed after weeks of discussion, although none of the other measures of this radical constitution met with serious opposition. The Republicans were therefore

[1] See Note A on p. 262 at end of chapter.

asking for trouble in striking so boldly at the Church. Not only were they losing a certain number of their own supporters and alienating many waverers, but they were providing the reaction with a rallying cry which it badly needed. The logical consequence of their act was that henceforth they must lean less upon middle-class support and more upon that of the working classes, or else they would fall. But absorbed as they were in the political passions of the moment, they did not see this.[1]

Another lesser consequence was the effect which the inhibition of the religious orders from teaching had upon education. Half the secondary schools in Spain were threatened with having to close down altogether. The effect upon primary schools was almost as serious. In Madrid, for example, 37,000 children were being educated in the State schools, 44,000 in private schools mostly run by the Orders and 45,000 were receiving no education at all. To fill the place of the Church schools, 2700 new State schools were needed.[2] Yet by 1933 little progress had been made in providing them. One must admit that, in spite of all the propaganda put forward by the Republican parties, their achievements in the field of education were mostly on paper. It was not that they lacked the good will—on the contrary, they were the first body of men in Spain to treat the matter seriously—but the problem was one that required many years of preparation and a great expenditure of money if satisfactory results were to be obtained. The dissolution of the Jesuit Order likewise missed its mark. Their property was found to be for the most part invested under other names, whilst the fact that the Fathers had nominally ceased to be members of a religious order set them free to continue their work of education.

The debate on the religious question brought to the front Manuel Azaña. He was a completely new man. Until the fall of the Dictatorship he had been unknown outside a small circle of friends. In appearance he was not exactly prepossessing. A short stumpy man with a green bilious complexion and staring expressionless eyes, he reminded people who saw him for the first time of a toad or frog. His history had been uneventful. Born like Cervantes in Alcalá de Henares, in a house between two convents, he had lost both his parents whilst still a child and had had a hard and gloomy youth. The two years he had spent studying law at the Augustinian College at the

---

[1] See Note B on p. 262 at end of chapter.
[2] See Note C on p. 262 at end of chapter.

Escorial had left him with a strong dislike for the Church. Since then he had lived alone in his house at Alcalá or in Madrid, seeing few people and immersed in his books. He wrote, but without much success: his chief productions were an autobiographical novel which sold few copies and translations of Borrow's *Bible in Spain* and of Bertrand Russell. Then he turned to politics and for a time acted as secretary to one of the small Republican parties that came into existence in the years preceding the Dictatorship. His chief resort, where from now on he was always to be found, was the Ateneo: he was elected President of this famous literary and political club in 1930 and it was his activity in organizing a Republican movement here during the last months of the Monarchy and in launching a party which obtained twenty-six seats in the Constituent Cortes that brought him a post in the cabinet. As Minister for War he showed tact and firmness in purging the Army and his strong personality made itself felt among the other members of the Government. Now he became Prime Minister. During the rest of this Cortes he was by far and away the leading figure. 'The man with the brilliant future behind him', as the Trotskyist Maurín called him, until the rise of a revolutionary Socialist movement he dominated the political scene. There are various reasons for this. In the first place, he was a man of action who made himself feared by all the enemies of the Republic, whether like the Anarchists they came from the Left or like the generals from the Right. Then he showed, more than any other Republican politician, the qualities of a statesman and parliamentarian without ever compromising his honesty. It was mainly due to his drive and persistence that the huge mass of new legislation was piloted through an increasingly recalcitrant Cortes. But the cause of Azaña's greatness lies deeper than this. Just as Abraham Lincoln lived for American democracy and came to stand as a symbol for it, so Azaña lived for and embodied the idea of the Spanish Republic. 'La République, c'est moi' was the burden of most of his speeches, yet his sincerity and conviction were such that in spite of his often high-handed ways, not even his enemies ever accused him of ambition. It is less important in Spain to be liked than to be respected.

The Constitution was completed by the end of the year and the first President of the Republic was elected. The man chosen was Niceto Alcalá Zamora, who had been premier until October, when he resigned on account of his disagreement with Article 26. Don Niceto was an Andalusian lawyer and landowner, the very man to be Presi-

dent of a safely established Latin Republic—highly respectable, extremely conscientious, a commonplace but flowery orator and, at all
events in Spanish eyes, a little ridiculous. They called him *Botas*,
'Old Boots'. He had been a protégé of Romanones and had held a
portfolio in one of Alfonso's last governments. Having been shabbily
treated by him, he had nursed his pique and become a Republican. In
the elections that brought in the new regime he had received enormous majorities in several of the large towns because the Catholic and
Conservative middle classes had voted for him. For he was the
guarantee that the Republic would not move to the Left. Being a
sincere Catholic he accepted the Presidency in the hopes of some day
being able to amend the anti-clerical clauses in the Constitution. At
the same time Lerroux and his Radical party left the Government and
adopted a neutral attitude. Azaña formed a new cabinet of Left
Republicans and Socialists.

An Anarchist putsch in the Llobregat Valley near Barcelona took
place in January 1932 and the strikes which had been going on all
autumn broke out again. Azaña showed a heavy hand with the Anarchists and deported many of them to Africa—conduct which alienated
the workers but conciliated the bourgeoisie, who began to feel that the
Republic might not be so bad after all. The new divorce law was
passed in spite of further opposition from the Church and in May the
simultaneous discussion of the Catalan and Agrarian Statutes began.

Down to the coming of the Dictatorship the only political party of
any consequence in Catalonia had been the Lliga. This, as we have
seen, was the party of the bourgeoisie—Catholic and Conservative,
but with a Conservatism based like the English on industry and not on
landed estates. In 1917 it had for a moment aligned itself with the
Socialists and with the small Republican party in a revolutionary
attitude. Since the failure of this venture it had grown more Conservative and clerical. The syndicalist struggle in Barcelona in the years
1919–1923 had then driven it still farther to the Right and had shown
that its local nationalism counted for much less than its class feeling.
It had ended by allying itself with the Army, that is, with the most
anti-Catalan force in Spain, and had welcomed the *coup d'état* that
brought in the Dictatorship. When Primo de Rivera then showed his
ingratitude by destroying the Mancomunidad, as the very moderate
form of home rule then in force was called, and by rooting up every
element of Catalan culture, the Lliga lost most of its former influence.
The Dictatorship, however, strongly stimulated the growth of Catalan

national feeling and led to its spread among the lower-middle classes. The Lliga being discredited, they sought to enter one of the many small Nationalist groups with Left sympathies that existed at this time. The result was a coalition of Left groups into a single party, the Esquerra or Catalan Left. This was made easier by the discovery of a suitable leader in Colonel Maciá, a tall handsome gentleman with white hair and moustaches, who became a national hero by organizing ineffective plots from beyond the French frontier. When Primo de Rivera fell, Cambó, the leader of the Lliga, finally ruined his party by his attempts to prop up the King. At the municipal elections in April 1931, the Esquerra swept the board and Maciá returned in triumph.[1]

A far-reaching statute of autonomy for Catalonia was now a necessity. Indeed the impetuous Colonel, on the day following the announcement of the election results, had proclaimed an independent Catalan republic from the balcony of the Generalidad. This was soon after rectified, but a few months later, when the draft of a statute drawn up by a committee of the Cortes was submitted to a referendum, over 99 per cent of the votes were in its favour. The statute was brought up before the Cortes in the following May. For months it was fiercely contested, but at last, shorn of a few of its privileges, it was passed (September, 1932). The Castilian prejudices against it had been overcome only by the persistence of Azaña, and he was rewarded by knowing that the Republic had won in the Catalan people its strongest body of supporters.[2]

A few weeks before it was finally approved, a military insurrection broke out at Seville. Its leader was General Sanjurjo, a soldier who had made a name for himself in Morocco and who was very popular among the troops. A year before, as Commander of the Civil Guard, he had been responsible for the entry of the Republic without bloodshed by his refusal to place his force at the disposal of the King. His *pronunciamiento* was defeated by a general strike of the C.N.T. before he could obtain any support. A simultaneous rising of Monarchists, who attempted to capture the War Office, was put down without difficulty in Madrid. Sanjurjo's movement was a protest against the

[1] At the elections for the Cortes in June the Esquerra obtained an even more sweeping triumph. Its vote was five times that of the Lliga in Catalonia, and in Barcelona all its fourteen candidates were elected, whereas only one member of the Lliga got in. Maciá alone obtained 109,300 votes. His rival Cambó had become so unpopular through his support of the King that he had to flee the country.

[2] So intense was the dislike of the Right-wing Castilians to Catalan autonomy that Royo Villanovo, a deputy who had led the opposition to it in the Cortes, became a hero and was elected to several constituencies in the 1933 elections.

Catalan Statute and the Law of Agrarian Reform which were then being debated, and he was thought to have the secret support of various Republican politicians. His aim was in all probability not a restoration of the King, but a Conservative Republic in which the Army would have the lion's share.

The ease with which the Government put down this rising immensely strengthened it. The immediate consequence was the rapid passage of the Catalan Statute and of the Law of Agrarian Reform, which had been held up all summer. The repression, however, was thought by many to be unnecessarily severe. Of the 157 people brought to trial the majority were found guilty and deported to Villa Cisneros, a healthy but excessively disagreeable colony on the African coast. Two Bourbon princes were among them. Sanjurjo himself was given a long sentence of imprisonment. By a special bill passed through the Cortes before the trials began, the property of the rebels was confiscated and handed over to the Institute of Agrarian Reform.

The success or failure of the Republic would clearly depend upon its ability to conciliate the working classes. This meant of course that it must secure a general rise of wages without increasing unemployment. But it also meant its ability to carry into effect a serious measure of agrarian reform. This would be regarded by the working classes as the measure of its sincerity and would in the long run give the regime the stability which it needed. Let us see what success it was having in this.

It was the misfortune of the Republic that the world crisis broke just before it came in. Primo's regime had benefited by the boom—indeed without it he could never have maintained himself for so long. It produced high prices for agricultural products which led to the ploughing up of large areas of third-class land, decreased unemployment and slightly increased wages. The slump had the opposite effect: agricultural prices fell, a great deal of land went out of cultivation and unemployment reached a figure never known before.

The Provisional Government passed a number of decrees for remedying the distressing situation in the country districts: wages were nearly doubled (it must be remembered that, since in most parts of Spain agricultural labour is seasonal, the wages need to be large enough to cover unemployment subsistence): landlords were compelled to cultivate all their land: tenant farmers were given the right to appeal against an increase of rents and were protected against capricious eviction: an eight-hour day was established. Later, on Socialist pressure, other measures were passed—a *Ley de Términos Municipales* to prevent landlords from employing cheap emigrant labour[1] and a *Ley de Jurados Mixtos* which established tribunals at which workmen and employers met to decide hours and wages and to settle industrial disputes. This was a modification of the *comités paritarios* set up by Primo de Rivera, but redrafted so as to be more favourable to the workers.

The unrest spread however in the country districts as the discussion of the Constitution, which did not interest the working classes, continued and nothing was done about agrarian reform. There had been a general expectation that all the large estates would be expropriated, and the disappointment was great when it became evident that this would not be done. These two years (1931–1932) were moreover a period of Anarcho-Syndicalist expansion: their bitter attacks on the Socialists' participation in the Government and their refusal to have anything to do with the social legislation passed by the Cortes were producing a revolutionary atmosphere in the *campo*, which was unfavourable to the success of any agrarian scheme. But the chief reason for the dangerous delay in tackling this question was the disagreement between the Socialists and the Republicans as to the form it should take. Agrarian reform projects had become focused on the question of breaking up the large estates: but whereas the Republicans wished that the land so obtained should be split up into individual holdings, the Socialists demanded that it should be used to form collectives.

The difference was more than one of abstract principle: it involved the future of Socialism and of bourgeois Republicanism in Spain. The Republicans knew that the success of their regime would in the long run depend on whether or not they could create a peasantry who would be grateful to their protectors and sufficiently conservative to form a bulwark against revolution. The Socialists knew that they must at all costs prevent this and therefore proposed a collective organization of the land, which, in Castile and Extremadura at all events, would come under their influence. Except in Anarchist dis-

---

[1] The justification for the *Ley de Términos Municipales* was the use which landlords made of emigrant labourers from Galicia or Portugal or from the neighbouring hill villages to undercut local men. But its provisions were too drastic. In effect it penalized the wretchedly poor and politically unorganized peasants of the small pueblos, who depended on the money they earned at harvest to get through the year, for the benefit of the labourers on the large estates, who were usually syndicated to the U.G.T. or C.N.T.

tricts such collectives would inevitably be syndicated with the U.G.T. With this object they had organized in 1931 the *Federación Española de Trabajadores de la Tierra* of the U.G.T., which in Catalonia included the Catalan Rabassaires, whose political affiliations were not with the Socialists but with the radical Esquerra party. This Federation at once started a strong propaganda movement in favour of agricultural collectives.

As it happens, geography was on the side of the Socialist plan. For reasons that have been explained in a previous chapter, the lot of the individual small holder in a dry farming district is an extremely difficult one. He is condemned to a perpetual struggle against an unfavourable environment, and even if he does not succumb to the first drought or sink into hopeless debt, he has no prospect of rising above a crushing poverty. If, in spite of this, individual holdings were to be established on unirrigated land, the most careful preparation would be required: modern machinery must be provided on a communal basis, a credit system organized and the plots carefully surveyed and divided. Moreover, only selected peasants could be set up on these plots: certainly not inexperienced landless labourers. But unfortunately none of the materials for a large-scale organization of this kind were present. There was a great shortage of engineers and technical advisers, and among the Republican leaders a sluggishness and lack of drive that contrasted vividly with their interest in political questions, which, being more familiar to them, could be settled in discussions at café tables or in club armchairs.[1]

And there was another aspect. The world crisis, as we have said, had ruined agricultural markets. Farmers were having their work cut out to keep solvent. The prospect of confiscation under some as yet unsettled agrarian law increased the general consternation. Banks withheld credit and, in spite of all the laws and decrees to prevent it, more and more land was going out of cultivation. The Republican parties had a considerable following among the small landlords and these now made their influence felt. The result was an agrarian law of very modest proportions which in its practical results turned out to be insignificant.

Briefly, the Agrarian Statute (passed in two parts, in July and September 1932) set up an Institute of Agrarian Reform of twenty-one members and provided it with yearly credits from the State: this Institute, working through regional committees, was to decide what

[1] See Note D on p. 263 at end of chapter.

estates were to be expropriated and how the land so taken was to be settled. In principle every estate of more than 56 acres that was not worked by the owners was liable to expropriation by the State. One particular class, the grandees, lost their estates without appeal. Compensation was paid, but it was on the basis of the taxation returns submitted by the owners: so that, since nearly every landowner had for years been sending in false returns, he would tend to lose from half to a third of the capital value of his property. The State would thus regain some of the money lost to it by generations of dishonesty. As to the discrimination against the grandees, this was a political measure. Just as a century before the Church lands had been taken because the monks and priests supported the Carlist cause, so the grandees were to be deprived of their landed property to weaken the influence of the King. The rising of General Sanjurjo in August led to further expropriations against those implicated in it for which no compensation was paid.[1]

One should observe that the Agrarian Statute applied only to the centre and south—to that part of the country where large estates are common. For although in theory small properties could be confiscated, the intention was to do so very sparingly and mainly for the creation of allotments outside villages. The Statute confined itself to an attack upon the age-long problem of the latifundia. Nothing was done to assist the innumerable families in the north who had too little land or to convert the variable and usually excessive rents of Castile into a fixed *censo* or *bail héréditaire*.[2] Here one may say that the Republican parties lost a great opportunity, not only of curing some

[1] The proposals put forward by Díaz del Moral in a speech in the Cortes on 10 May 1932 suggested that expropriation should be made by converting full ownership into a *derecho real de censo*. This could be done without any disturbance of the agrarian structure: tenants would pay 4 per cent interest on the capital value and have absolute security of tenure. He also proposed that some of the large estates should be turned into experimental 'associations of land workers' and be provided with technical advisers and machinery. Further that all landless labourers should be given allotments of good land near their homes to assist them through the seasonal unemployment. These proposals would seem to have much to recommend them.

The project of agrarian reform actually adopted was based partly on the theories of Henry George and partly on the experience of land partition in Czecho-Slovakia. The collectives which the Socialists wished to introduce were to be modelled on the Russian kolkhoses (Russian Agrarian Code of 1922). No doubt the Socialists' leaders were unaware of the details of the ruthless collectivization of peasant holdings which was being enforced at that moment in Russia, though it was of course due to this that collectivization had suddenly become such a blessed word.

[2] According to Mateo Azpeitia, a Conservative critic of the Project of Agrarian Reform, 84 per cent of the small proprietors in Spain needed wages in order to be able to live: *La Reforma Agraria en España*, 1932.

of the crying abuses of the country-side, but of gaining adherents for themselves and strengthening the regime. The question that should have been put before all others was, mainly because it held little emotional interest for the lawyers and professional men who made up the Republican party, taken up late and debated in a half-hearted manner.[1] And since the solution arrived at left open the question of how the expropriated estates were to be divided, the dreary deadlock between the Socialists and the Republicans continued and nothing was done at all. Against the local opposition of the U.G.T. or C.N.T., who objected to an increase in the number of individual holdings, no simple *reparto* was possible.

The autumn of 1932 saw Azaña at the height of his career. In the eyes of Europe the new Spanish Republic had taken root and con- solidated itself. Spain, it seemed, had ceased to be the country of the Black Legend—a semi-Balkan nation with a glorious history—and had become one of the most modern and dignified states in Europe. This was the moment chosen for introducing a budget. The Dictatorship, it will be remembered, had left the finances of the country in the worst condition. Instead of taking the advice of Cambó, who had made the mistake of being born a Catalan, Primo de Rivera had chosen as his finance minister a Galician lawyer, Calvo Sotelo, whose talents were better suited to organizing rebellion than to finance. The result was an increase in the deficit of the national debt of from 417 to 924 million pesetas within four years. Hardly had the Republic come in when the economic crisis threw new burdens on the State. The railways, which were heavily over-capitalized, collapsed. Markets dried up. The am- bitious education programme, the increase in the numbers of the police, the Statute of Agrarian Reform all required additional expen- diture. Under these circumstances the finance minister, Jaime Carner (who incidentally was a Catalan), performed a miracle. In one year the deficit was reduced to 576 million pesetas and in the second to

---

[1] A Marxist and an Anarchist are both agreed as to the prime error made by the Republic:

'The Republicans', wrote Maurín, 'never understood the importance of the *ampo*: therefore they were defeated.'

'Had the Republicans', wrote *Solidaridad Obrera*, 'at once expropriated without indemnity all the large estates, as happened in the French Revolution, the bourgeois republic would have lasted many years. The workers, even the Anarchists, would have tolerated it.'

The answer is, of course, that Jacobin Revolutions cannot be made to-day and that, even if they could, the respectable and cultured bourgeois who made up the Republican party were not the men to do it. Nor is there any reason to suppose that the Army would have tolerated it.

approximately 470. Yet one should note that this was done without modifying the system of taxation. This remained almost entirely indirect and the receipts from income-tax were negligible.

The Government was proceeding quietly on its way, discussing the various laws complementary to the Constitution and impeaching, in the usual Spanish fashion, those responsible for the crime of the Dictatorship, when an event occurred which, though it was thought at first to be of little consequence, led in the end to a situation that brought down the Government. Casas Viejas is a wretched hamlet in a malarial district not far from Jerez: the land around it, belonging to the Duke of Medina Sidonia, who is the largest landowner in Spain, had been marked down for expropriation. The inhabitants, who belonged to the C.N.T., were miserably poor and ignorant, as are all the field labourers on these great latifundia. On 8 January 1933 a small rising led by militants of the F.A.I. took place in Barcelona: a general strike in Andalusia had been planned to accompany it, but did not come off. However, an old Anarchist in Casas Viejas, known as Seisdedos, Six Fingers, had heard of these projects and, in one of those bursts of millenarian fervour that are so typical of Andalusia, decided that now the great moment had arrived, now *comunismo libertario* would infallibly come in. Having inspired his friends and relatives with the same ardour, the whole party armed itself with sticks and shotguns and marched to the barracks of the Civil Guard close by to give them the good tidings and to tell them that now they could lay down their arms, for henceforth all men would be brothers and would till the fields of the rich in common. The Civil Guard did not respond to these appeals, shots were exchanged and after a solemn parade through the neighbouring village the men of Casas Viejas settled down to lay siege to the barracks.

The Government was expecting a concerted Anarchist rising in Catalonia and Andalusia and was determined to suppress the first movements rapidly. It was not long therefore before troops and civil guards were on the move through the whole province. Aeroplanes flew overhead and Seisdedos and his thirty or so followers retired to their houses. Here a siege began, and, the unfortunate men having refused to surrender, their houses were set on fire and twenty-five, including Seisdedos, were killed.

A wave of indignation swept over the country. Tragic events had often happened before in Andalusia, but this was the culmination of a long series of harsh acts on the part of the police. Had not the Republic come in precisely to put an end to this kind of thing? The Right in particular, with peculiar hypocrisy, were loud in their protests at the crime committed against 'poor innocent men'. The Government, which at first attempted to take the matter lightly, was in the end forced to appoint a committee of investigation. This committee brought to light three things—first that the orders issued by the Home Secretary, Casares Quiroga, and by Azaña himself had been unnecessarily severe, then that the Director-General of Police, Menéndez, had interpreted these as permitting the application of the *ley de fugas* (police custom of shooting prisoners when 'trying to escape') and finally that the police captain, Rojas, had acted with criminal barbarity in shooting a dozen prisoners in cold blood, for no reason at all. It was a prelude on a small scale to what would happen two years later at Oviedo.

Casas Viejas produced a terrible effect on the working classes all over Spain and made the Socialists, who shared the responsibility for it, unpopular. The credit of the Government never recovered from this blow. The only thing left to be done was to choose the first favourable moment for holding elections and then to resign. Azaña had announced that he would hold municipal elections on the new register (which included women) in April. When it came to the point, he drew back and ordered partial elections instead: some two thousand rural districts which in April 1931 had returned Monarchists and whose representation had in consequence been cancelled, were now to be allowed to nominate their municipal officers. If this were intended as a feeler to see how public opinion lay, it was a bad one. The result, by which the Government got just over a third of the nominations and the Right just under a third, proved nothing. Azaña quite naturally refused to take the opinion of the *burgos podridos* or rotten boroughs, as he called them, as a signal for resignation, but he had let loose an outcry against him that continued to augment. There were Anarchist strikes in almost every town in Spain for the release of their prisoners. The university students also struck, as they had done before at the end of the Dictatorship, whilst Lerroux and his Radical party commenced a deliberate obstruction in the Cortes.

Of the three Republican parties in the Constituent Cortes, two, the Radicals and the Socialists, were bitterly opposed to one another. The Left Republicans held the balance between them. When, after the completion of the Constitution, it became impossible for the three to sit together in the Government, Azaña had to choose with which to ally himself. He chose the Socialists, feeling no doubt that it would be impossible to govern the country if the two great divisions of the working classes were both aligned against him. The Radicals then maintained a passive attitude, not opposing the passage of the complementary laws but contesting any Socialist elements that had crept into them. For, as we have pointed out, the term Radical was a complete misnomer for their party: they were conservative Republicans, representing what were known as the 'passive classes', and the only positive elements in their programme were their anti-clericalism and the importance which they attached to education. Now that the tide had begun to turn they decided that the moment had come for putting an end to reforms and for holding immediate elections, which they hoped would return them in sufficient force to give them the leading voice in the government of the country.

Two important measures remained, however, to be passed: the Law of Public Order, which was to replace the very unpopular and severe Law of the Defence of the Republic, and that authorizing the setting up of a Tribunal of Constitutional Guarantees, which was to take the place of a Second Chamber as a guarantee of the observance of the Constitution. The Radicals consented to withhold their obstruction in the Cortes until these were passed. This was done, and after some further hesitation and delay the Government resigned, September 1933.

We have so far confined our attention to the purely political actions of the Republican Government. But this is not sufficient to enable us to grasp the full complexity of the Spanish scene at this time. Whilst the wise men of the Cortes deliberated, a succession of strikes, boycotts, acts of sabotage and armed revolts went on all over Spain without intermission. We shall best understand this if we begin by examining the part played in them by the Anarcho-Syndicalists.

We have seen in a previous chapter that the Anarcho-Syndicalists took advantage of the comparative calm of the Dictatorship to reorganize themselves. Fearing that Communist influence might obtain a hold in the C.N.T. and displace that of the Anarchists, they set up a secret association, the *Federación Anarquista Ibérica* or F.A.I., whose members must also be members of the National Labour Confederation. The F.A.I. was intended not only as a nucleus of thinkers whose mission would be to keep the movement ideologically pure, but as a council of action for organizing revolutionary movements. It would provide a much needed unification. The fact that its members were also the leading members of the different federations of the C.N.T. gave it all the influence it needed.[1]

Its revolutionary energy made itself felt from the first moment of the inauguration of the Republic. During the next four years an endless succession of strikes, armed assaults on public buildings and acts of sabotage were launched against the Republic. No previous Spanish Government had had to sustain such a continuous assault. Had the Syndicalist theories and methods of 1919–1923 been still in evidence, the Republic could perhaps have come to terms with them. But Seguí's influence was a thing of the past and against the F.A.I. there was nothing they could do but oppose violence to violence.

The difference can best be seen by contrasting the old militants of the movement with the new. Seguí and Pestaña were essentially trade-union leaders, though the unions they led were extremely militant and had ultimate revolutionary ends. Their influence was exercised mainly at the meetings of the local and national federations. Their particular skill lay in propaganda and in syndical organization, and their aim was to build up powerful working-class federations and then, by carefully prepared strikes, to confront and defeat the employers' associations. In this way they hoped to make themselves the dominant partners in industry, in readiness for the day when they could take over its management altogether. The leaders of the F.A.I., on the other hand, belonged to the type of revolutionary who comes to the front after a period of street fighting followed by police suppression. They were men who had proved their worth in pistol encounters at street corners and in hazardous coups of various kinds. Durruti and Ascaso, for example, were fanatics of the cause who by their feats of incredible daring had made themselves the heroes of the Catalan proletariat. Durruti was a powerful man with brown eyes and an innocent expression and Ascaso a little dark man of insignificant appearance. Inseparable friends, they had together robbed banks, assassinated enemies of the cause and been in the forefront of in-

---

[1] One of the principles of the F.A.I. was that it should not interfere in purely syndical matters. However, one may say that no important decision of the C.N.T. was ever taken except by its influence. Yet there was no official connection between the two bodies. The only committees on which the C.N.T. and the F.A.I. collaborated were the Comité de Defensa, which organized armed risings and the Comité por Presos (Prisoners' Committee) which liquidated their results. The real connection consisted in the fact that nearly all the leaders of the C.N.T. were also members of the F.A.I. This sometimes produced odd results, as when a certain *compañero* voted for a rising as a free member of the F.A.I. and against it as a representative of a federation of the C.N.T.

numerable strikes and acts of violence. Most of their lives had been spent in prison: as soon as they came out they returned to their humble work in the factory, for, naturally, none of the money they acquired by their forcible expropriations (on one occasion they opened and emptied a safe in the Bank of Spain) was kept for themselves. They were two saints of the Anarchist cause, showing the way by their merits and their example. García Oliver, on the other hand, belonged rather to the type of Irish revolutionary of 1919. Though a workman by origin and only partly educated, his political instincts were well developed. He was credited with a special flair for the revolutionary feeling of the masses and for the right moment for action. He thus became the leading tactician of this period and the organizer of its various revolutionary strikes and insurrections. Only, being an Anarchist, he did not remain like a general in the background, but led his men with bomb and revolver in his hand himself.

One peculiarity of Spanish Anarchism, which becomes increasingly noticeable from now on, was the inclusion within its ranks of professional criminals—thieves and gunmen who certainly would not have been accepted by any other working-class party—together with idealists of the purest and most selfless kind. Occasionally, as we have already pointed out, the two elements were combined in the same person, but more often they were separate. One may explain this historically. The bandit has always been a popular figure in Spain because he preys on the rich and defends the poor. Then during the Napoleonic Wars the guerrilla leader and the bandit fused in the same person. This tradition was continued by the Carlists. Their famous guerrilla leaders, Cabrera, Father Merino, Father Santa Cruz and Cúcala, belonged to the same type of men as Durruti and Ascaso. But the Anarchists were also lax in allowing ordinary thieves and murderers to join their organization. The first sign of this was seen during the Cantonalist rising of 1873, when the convict prison of Cartagena, containing 1500 of the most desperate criminals in Spain, was opened on the insistence of the Internationalists and the inmates were invited to join in the defence of the city. Then, during the troubles of 1919–1923 at Barcelona, dozens of pure *pistoleros* entered their ranks. No doubt most of them took care to put a certain ideological colour on their actions, but this would not have been sufficient if the Anarchists had not had a sentimental feeling for all those people who have taken to criminal ways because they have been thwarted or injured by society. A typically Spanish inability to distinguish between those who have enriched themselves by 'lawful' means and those who attempt to do so by pure robbery and violence lies at the bottom of this. It is a mentality that goes with certain political and social conditions—one finds it, for example, in the New Testament.

However, the inclusion of so many men of criminal instincts could not fail to have a demoralizing effect upon the Anarchist organizations. It was increased by the fact that the F.A.I. was a secret society. Such societies usually end by conforming to one of two types—either, like the ancient Assassins, they develop a blind obedience to a central authority (Bakunin had dabbled with this idea), or they split up into groups. This last was the real organization of the F.A.I. Behind the official committees stood small groups of like-thinking people which pulled the strings, and sometimes behind these were terrorist groups that, at certain moments, controlled the larger ones. This, at all events, was what happened when the Civil War broke out, and if one bears this in mind many of the inconsistencies between Anarchist practice and doctrine will become intelligible. This complex and shifting group organization explains, too, why a simple history of Spanish Anarchism is impossible.

A congress of the C.N.T. met in Madrid in June 1931 to settle various matters connected with the reorganization of the Confederation.[1] Hardly was it over or the new Cortes taken its seat when there was a strike of the telephone operatives at Madrid combined with an armed assault on the Central Telephone building. The assault failed and the C.N.T. operatives, on the threat of being expelled, enrolled in the U.G.T. A week later a strike in Seville led to a clash with the troops, in which thirty were killed and three hundred wounded. The Government showed that they had no hesitation in employing all the means that they had so much condemned when practised by the reactionary governments of the past. But it is in Catalonia that the Anarcho-Syndicalist action during these years was most characteristic. The Esquerra or Left Catalan party had replaced Madrid as the effective rulers of the province. Luís Companys, a lawyer who for many years had been on close terms with the Anarchists, had been elected alcalde of Barcelona at the April elections and was afterwards appointed Civil Governor. In this position he used the greatest possible tact in dealing with his old friends. 'Since you', he said to them, 'are not ready to make your revolution, why not let us make ours and use the liberty the new regime gives you for your propaganda?' When the C.N.T.

[1] See Note E on p. 263 at end of chapter.

announced a twenty-four hours' general strike, he declared the day a national holiday. The F.A.I., however, had no intention of being diverted from their revolutionary projects in this manner. All that summer their influence in the C.N.T. was increasing, and in October they were able to force the resignation of the editor, Juan Peiró, and of the whole staff of the famous Anarcho-Syndicalist daily, *Solidaridad Obrera*, because they refused to support the F.A.I. policy of revolutionary action by small groups.[1]

That summer saw therefore an interminable series of strikes with sabotage, violence and clashes with the police. Strange requests were made to the Civil Governor—that he should disarm the police and arm the people instead: impossible demands were made on employers. In short everything was done to alarm the authorities, discredit the regime and produce a revolutionary tempo.[2] A new technique was the guerrilla tactics employed against the police. They were sniped on from windows and corners, forced to mobilize at this point and that and kept in such a constant state of alarm that they could not get sufficient sleep. This made their nerves jumpy and their tempers bad and when militants were caught they were made to suffer for it. The Anarchists then complained bitterly that the Republican Government was more tyrannous than that of Primo de Rivera. They conveniently forgot that during his dictatorship the C.N.T. had been dissolved, the Anarchist press suppressed, and that in all these five years not a single Anarchist had dared to make himself seen or heard.

But one must remember that during the whole of this time the working classes were suffering very real hardships. The slump had brought terrible unemployment. In Barcelona only 30 per cent of the workmen of the builders' union were fully employed. Of 45,000 at work in 1930, only 11,000 were at work in 1933.[3] And certainly the slump alone was not to blame for this. All over Spain banks had combined to restrict credit and employers to lock up their capital in the hopes of making the Republic unpopular. According to the *Anuario de Estadística* the capital issue fell from 2000 millions of

---

[1] See Note F on p. 263 at end of chapter.
[2] For example, the demands made on the Millowners' Federation were that they should choose all their workmen through the Bolsas de Trabajo or labour exchange of the C.N.T., abandon piece-work, give pensions at fifty to all workmen, grant unemployment and sickness insurance and paid holidays and work only a six-hour day. Their manifesto, containing an exposé of their political ideals, is quoted in full by F. Madrid, op. cit. pp. 191–195.
[3] See *Service de Presse de A.I.T.*, No. 162, 15 September 1935.

pesetas in 1928 to 50 millions in 1933. At the same time the cost of living rose. In Spain, it must be remembered, unemployment means semi-starvation because there are no unemployment benefits. Yet Professor Allison Peers has seen fit to reproach the Republican Government for tolerating an increase of mendicity due, he explains, to 'the growth of indiscipline'.

The first days of 1932 saw a rising organized by the F.A.I. in Catalonia in which the newly formed *Izquierda Comunista* or Left Communist party also took part. This was a group of 'Trotskyists' led by Maurín, Nin and Andrade which had just seceded from the official Communist party, taking nearly all the Catalan Communists with them. *Comunismo Libertario* was proclaimed by the F.A.I. in the Upper Llobregat valley, the public buildings at Manresa and Berga were seized and in one or two places estates were divided up. Troops easily suppressed this rising, but not till there had been a certain amount of bloodshed. The Government thereupon arrested a hundred and twenty of the more prominent leaders of the C.N.T. and F.A.I., among them Durruti and Ascaso, and deported them without trial to Spanish Guinea. But the violent agitation, coupled with threats, that followed compelled it to release them soon afterwards.

A year later (January 1933) came a second armed rising in Barcelona, Lérida and Valencia, led by García Oliver. Its object was to secure the release of the prisoners deported to Africa and still detained there; like the previous one it took the form of an attempt by a handful of militants to seize public buildings, but it was an even greater fiasco than the first and merely led to fresh arrests and to the confiscation of the few arms that had been collected.[1] The Government declared the C.N.T. to be an illegal organization and closed its offices, but it was not strong enough to enforce this. Indeed, three months later the C.N.T. in Barcelona launched a formidable strike in the building trade which lasted eighteen weeks, whilst sympathetic general strikes took place at Saragossa, Corunna, Oviedo and Seville.[2]

---

[1] The Anarchists taken in this rising were severely beaten up at the Jefatura Superior de Policía. See F. Urales, *La Barbarie Gubernamental en Barcelona*, 1933, in which García Oliver and other arrested Anarchists describe their personal experiences. These police, moreover, belonged to the *Guardia de Asalto*, a corps formed by the Republican Government and composed of convinced Republicans and Socialists. I have been told by a member of this police force who was certainly a humane and decent man, that the guerrilla warfare that the Anarchists waged on them during strikes and the lack of sleep they suffered from so wore down their nerves that the desire to wreak violent reprisals on the prisoners became irresistible.

[2] See Note G on p. 263 at end of chapter.

These unsuccessful risings had, however, been sufficiently un-popular to lead to a split in the C.N.T. The policy of the F.A.I. had always had its opponents. Already at the Congress of Saragossa in 1922 two divergent tendencies had shown themselves—that of the 'pure' Anarchists who believed that a revolution could best be brought about by the action of small enthusiastic groups and that of the majority who put their faith in the building up of powerful syndicates in a libertarian ambience. The brutal repression of Martínez Anido followed by the Dictatorship secured the triumph of the more violent party. But disapproval of the 'tyrannical' leadership of the F.A.I. persisted. We have already seen how, only a few months after the entry of the Republic, Juan Peiró and the whole staff of *Solidaridad Obrera*, which represented the views of the 'syndicalist' group, were forced to resign. This was followed soon after by the expulsion of Angel Pestaña, the secretary of the C.N.T., from the metal workers' syndicate at Barcelona for having vented his disapproval of the insur-rection in the Llobregat Valley. A number of well-known Anarchists, among them Peiró and Juan López, supported him and published their disapproval of the policy of the F.A.I. in a document which, because it had thirty signatures, was known as the *Trentistas*' pro-clamation. The consequence of this was that they too were expelled from the C.N.T. and, as the syndicates which they represented fol-lowed them, there came about a split in the Confederation. The dissident syndicates, which comprised those of Tarassa and Sabadell in Catalonia, half of those in Valencia and one in Asturias, were known as the *sindicatos de oposición*. Pestaña himself soon after went com-pletely reformist and founded a Syndicalist party which sent one deputy to the Cortes of 1936. None of the other *Trentistas* followed him, but the split continued, mainly on personal grounds and with bitter feelings on both sides till it was healed at the Congress of Saragossa just before the Civil War broke out.[1]

One gets, however, an incomplete idea of the strength of the working-class resistance to the Republic by dwelling solely on the revolutionary attitude of the town proletariat. During the whole of 1931 and 1932 the country districts of South and South-Central Spain were in a state of effervescence. As in 1919–1923, the Anarchists made the pace, though thanks to the Socialist participation in the Govern-ment, the U.G.T. now spread to many districts that had not known it before. By 1934 there were few villages of any size in this half of

[1] See Note H on p. 264 at end of chapter.

Spain that did not have their *sindicato* or *casa del pueblo*. The increase of unemployment and the expectation of sweeping agrarian reforms increased the tension and, though strikes were less frequent than in 1921, the class hatred was stronger and gave rise to a certain amount of intimidation. Still acts of violence were rare; when from time to time there were clashes with the police they usually occurred because the peasants were prevented from holding meetings or from ploughing up uncultivated land belonging to the large estates.[1] The most tragic of these episodes was that already described at Casas Viejas. Another, in which four Civil Guards were killed in a riot and their bodies hacked to pieces, occurred in an isolated pueblo of Extremadura called Castilblanco. As it throws a certain light upon the social conditions in the campo at this time I will describe it.

The villagers of Castilblanco, a small poverty-stricken pueblo of the Sierra de Guadalupe, in the gorge of the Guadiana, were not affiliated to any syndical organization. They were still too isolated for the new ideas of working-class solidarity to have reached them. But a strike of *campesinos* of the U.G.T. was going on at Badajoz and in the corn-growing villages around, and the whole province was in a state of agitation because sowing time was approaching and the discussion of the project of agrarian reform had not yet begun.

Castilblanco, among its rocks and ilex woods, lived on the edge of this struggle: the hill villages are always the last to be drawn in and the agents of the landowners (this is a district of large feudal estates) had been successful in keeping the Casa del Pueblo out. But the villagers

---

[1] One of the places where there was the greatest tension at this time was Granada. Here the landowners of the rich irrigated *vega* were numerous and strong because the rent of a hundred or so acres sufficed to keep a middle-class family in idleness and comparative affluence. The *campesinos* too were fairly prosperous and were strongly organized in the U.G.T., but there was considerable unemployment. The tension showed itself in a riot from time to time and in petards that exploded, noisily but harmlessly, every night. Cars were sometimes stopped and their owners forced to 'make a contribution' to the fund for the unemployed, and unpopular landlords kept to the main streets after dark. At Seville, where the C.N.T. predominated, the tension was more intermittent. Motoring through a village near Osuna in the spring of 1933, I asked a woman at the petrol station how the Easter festivities had gone off. 'Very well indeed', she answered. 'Whilst the procession was going its round the Anarchists broke into the church and set fire to it. Había mucha animación.' But apart from such incidents middle-class life, even in small villages, proceeded normally. Spaniards have had for centuries to put up with so many disorders and scenes of violence that they have grown resigned to them. Only the groups of unemployed labourers standing silently and ominously in the squares and street corners and the processions of peasants carrying the red flags of the Socialists or the red and black flags of the Anarcho-Syndicalists showed the casual observer that anything unusual was happening.

had their grievances and, in imitation of the pueblos lower down the valley, decided that they would have their strike too. After downing tools they announced a general meeting in the village square.

The four Civil Guards of the place received orders to prevent this. But on their attempting to do so by force, an unexpected thing happened. In one of those paroxysms of rage not uncommon among primitive people, the crowd beat them down and killed them and followed this up with a fierce scene of exultation in which the women of the village danced round their mutilated bodies. This happened on 1 January 1932, and a few days later a court of enquiry was held to decide who was guilty. But no evidence incriminating any individual could be obtained. It had been a collective deed. One was reminded of the story of Fuenteovejuna, a village a few miles off among the Sierra Morena, around which Lope de Vega wrote a famous play. The villagers had killed their local cacique and tyrant, but when asked under torture who had been their leaders, refused to say. However insistently the judges interrogated them, the only answer they could get to their question 'Who killed the Comendador?' was 'Fuente-ovejuna'.

The object of the Socialist party in organizing strikes and mass meetings in the country districts was evident: they wished to bring the greatest possible pressure to bear on the Republican parties to grant a wide measure of agrarian reform. For the first time in their history they had grasped the importance of the *campo*. The object of the Anarcho-Syndicalists, on the other hand, was revolutionary. The F.A.I. saw in the increase of liberty given by the Republic a convenient weakening in the power of the Government which would enable them, at some not very distant date, to bring it down. Their tactics of armed putsches, acts of sabotage and guerrilla warfare with the police were intended both to make the work of the Government as difficult as possible and to rouse the whole of the working classes to the necessity for revolution. They were aided in this by the distressing unemployment (which it was the object of their strikes for a six-hour day to cure) as well as by certain just and intelligible grievances.

The Governments of the first Cortes of the Republic went out of their way to display their harshness and asperity. Azaña, the leading spirit of the various combinations, was determined that this Republic should not fail from the same causes that had brought down the last. He would defend it vigorously against its enemies, whether they came from the Right or from the Left: it must never be said that he could not keep order. The burning of churches and convents all over Spain on 11 and 12 May was a warning and the Government acted on it by enrolling a new body of police, the *Guardia de Asalto* or Assault Guards, which only men of known Republican sympathies could join. This was followed in October, when Azaña became head of the Government, by the Law for the Defence of the Republic, which gave the Home Secretary wide and drastic powers. By means of this law the heavy hand of the Republic was felt alternately by the Monarchists and the Anarchists.[1]

Of all the restrictions on liberty, that imposing a censorship on the press was the most criticized. The Monarchists, who had themselves practised a far more severe censorship in the past, were especially outraged when, after General Sanjurjo's rising, their paper the *A.B.C.* was suspended for four months.[2] The Anarcho-Syndicalists suffered more than they need have done because they refused to conform to the regulation which required that they should submit their articles to the censor before publication: this frequently led to whole issues being confiscated. But undoubtedly the strongest objection which they had to the Republic concerned its new labour legislation.

The Minister of Labour, Largo Caballero, had introduced a series of laws regulating the rights of the working classes in their dealings with capital. The most important of these, the law of 24 December 1931, laid down the conditions which all contracts between workers and employers must fulfil in order to be valid. A special tribunal was set up to decide alleged infractions. Another law, the *Ley de Jurados Mixtos*, established tribunals at which labour disputes were to be compulsorily settled: this was a principle which had been adopted by the First Republic on the recommendation of Pi y Margall and had been taken up again by Primo de Rivera. But the powers of these tribunals were now extended to allow them to supervise the working of all labour contracts. Another law required eight days notice to be given of every strike. Apart from the fact that these laws ran contrary to the Anarcho-Syndicalist principles of negotiating directly with the

---

[1] The speech in which Azaña introduced this bill is typical of the intense personal pride he took in the good repute of the Republic: 'Never,' he declared, 'while in my hands, shall authority be weakened! Never, while in my hands, shall the Government of my country be the object of contempt, scorn and reviling! Never in this ministry shall there be hesitancy in the service of the commonwealth! The Republic belongs to us all. Woe to the man who dares to lift his hand against it!' (*El Sol*, 15 October 1931). This law, intended as a temporary measure only, was repealed in July 1933 and its place taken by the more liberal Law of Public Order.

[2] See Note I on p. 264 at end of chapter.

employers and interfered with the practice of lightning strikes, it was clear that they represented an immense increase in the power of the State in industrial matters. A whole army of Government officials, mostly Socialists, made their appearance to enforce the new laws and saw to it that, whenever possible, they should be used to extend the influence of the U.G.T. at the expense of the C.N.T. This had of course been the intention of those who drew them up. In fact the U.G.T. was rapidly becoming an organ of the State itself and was using its new powers to reduce its rival. The Anarcho-Syndicalists could have no illusions as to what would happen to them if a purely Socialist Government should come into power. To that they almost preferred a military dictatorship, which would force their organizations to disband, but could not destroy them.

The last Government of the Constituent Cortes resigned in September 1933 in deep unpopularity. The prisons were full—there were said to be 9000 of the C.N.T. alone in them. The country was packed with armed police—half as many again as in Primo de Rivera's time. The unemployment was as great as ever. Capital was lying idle in the banks and strikes and labour disputes were incessant. It was not only the extreme Right and Left which protested: it was a man of the Centre, Martínez Barrio, one little given to rhetorical exaggerations, who declared that this was a Republic of mud, blood and tears. How different from the First Republic which, chaotic and farcical though it had been, had been described by one of its leading men as the Republic of wit and poetry!

What was the cause of the failure? Briefly that the Republic had alienated large sections of the middle classes without giving satisfaction to the peasants and factory workers. Had it, as Lerroux desired, contented itself with being a continuation, in a somewhat more enlightened form, of the Monarchy, it would have drawn all the middle classes round it. But it would then have united all the working classes against it and, since their claims could no longer be denied, a revolutionary situation would have developed. If, on the other hand, it had gone deeper, throwing open all the large estates to the peasants and to the political organizations that controlled them, it would have risked initiating a social revolution and being carried out of its depth. The Army would then have intervened 'to restore order'. It chose therefore a middle course—which in Spain, one must remember, is always the line of greatest resistance. Yet perhaps if the world economic crisis had not descended on it with full force at the most critical moment it might have been successful.[1]

Fate then was against it. Yet before one accepts this easy view it is worth taking a look at Spanish history. This was not the first time that 'enlightened' opinion, supported by a section of the middle classes, had endeavoured to impose its will upon that great conservative or negatively revolutionary mass—the Spanish people. It had happened in 1530–1540 with the Erasmists: more vaguely in the early seventeenth century with the 'collectivist' economists: in the second half of the eighteenth century with the reformers of Charles III's administration. In the nineteenth century the Liberal Revolution had broken out in three great spasms—1812, 1820 and 1837. Again, the years 1854–1856 and 1868–1873 had seen an eruption of the radical lower-middle classes. Yet all these movements had been abortive and had been followed by an intensification of reaction. The failure had been the same whether the masses had been composed of one solid Conservative block or had been divided into two antagonistic wings.

These abortive revolutions, these periodic turnings over of a new leaf that succeed for a year or two and then fail, are therefore peculiar to Spain. Or rather are typical of a country where, owing to the backward state of economy, the only people who can lead a movement of regeneration belong to an advanced section of the middle classes who are not themselves sufficiently strong to impose their will. They can therefore only remain in power by the consent of the working classes, whose real wishes and needs they do not understand. For these working classes, from the moment in which they deserted the cause of the feudal aristocracy, entered at once a revolutionary Socialist ambience without passing through the intermediate 'liberal' stage. The reason for this is evident. Political progress is the result of deep-felt and expanding economic activity which continually draws new

---

[1] 'The Republic', said the Anarchist writer Juan Peiró, 'came in without blood: therefore it was not a true revolution. It always lived insecurely as a result.'

Maurín made the same criticism. Certainly the fact that the old ruling classes had not been defeated, but had merely made a strategic retreat, was the shadow that hung over the Republic. Yet one may doubt whether a 'revolution with blood' would have led to anything except the victory of reaction. Companys held an intermediate opinion. 'The Republicans never realized whilst they were in power the indispensable and transforming work which the people expected of them.'

If by this he meant, as is probable, their failure to achieve a substantial measure of agrarian reform, everyone will agree with him. The first need of the Republic was to strengthen itself against the inevitable reaction by winning fresh supporters. Yet the difficulty of this reform in view of the geographic conditions, the economic crisis and the complex political situation should not be forgotten.

classes up towards the surface. So long as this activity exists each class seeks to obtain the privileges of the one above it and parliamentary government, which is the political mechanism by which these desires seek realization, becomes possible. But inertia and stagnation have been precisely the conditions of Spanish economy for many hundreds of years—since Ferdinand III's Crusaders destroyed the foundations of Andalusian prosperity and the mines of Cuzco preached the lesson that the wealth of nations consists not in industry but in silver and gold. Castile, which made Spain a united country, infected her with a Byzantine horror of time and change and of every instinct by which modern nations grow. The result has been a rigid stratification of social life which does not correspond either to the proud and independent character of Spaniards or to the conditions of modern Europe.

In the present case the irony of the position in which the Republican parties found themselves could not be more plain. These able, cultured and disinterested men who came forward to build a new constitution for their country were building in sand. Their avowed aim was to put an end for ever to the violence, injustice and corruption which had governed Spanish history during the last hundred and fifty years. With skill and foresight they prepared a document that was to be the charter of Spanish rights and liberties for generations to come. Its clauses were adopted from the most modern and best tested inventions of constitutional history and jurisprudence. They were expressed in high-sounding yet succinct language. Safeguards were provided against special contingencies, watertight guarantees were devised against violation. Everything that could be thought of was thought of—except that the people for whom it was designed might not want it. And so it turned out—for after a short trial neither the Church nor the Army nor the landowners nor the peasants nor the factory workers would have anything to do with it. To them, they said, it did not offer liberty but tyranny—Spain having so developed that one man's liberty necessarily implied his tyranny over another. The makers of this Constitution might well have pondered the words of a former President, Emilio Castelar, who had declared that he was ready to proclaim a republic 'as soon as Spaniards shall have agreed on the grounds that divide them least'—though this perhaps would have meant the postponement of that proclamation for ever.

The Spanish Republic can be compared to the League of Nations. It was an attempt to found a regime of law and justice and comparative decency in a situation where hitherto only injustice and violence had prevailed. But, like the League, it was also—quite unavoidably—founded upon certain misappropriations and acts of violence. It had all the faults, all the inevitable make-believes and hypocrisies of new attempts to lay down by one party what shall be done by all parties in the future. It was obliged to simulate a prestige which it lacked, a prestige which only time and long custom could give and which no Spanish Government since the eighteenth century has ever possessed. And so one may say that no one, except its founders, ever showed the least respect for it, that none of the Right-wing parties had the least intention of obeying it, and that oaths of allegiance to it were taken by soldiers and politicians with the secret reservation that they would break them on the first moment that it suited their convenience. As to the working-class parties, though for a time one of them supported it, that was only because it regarded it as a temporary stepping-stone on its own march to power.

FURTHER NOTES ON CHAPTER XI

A (p. 237). Salvador de Madariaga, an impartial witness, since he disapproved of Article 26, thus contrasts State and Church education: 'State education in Spain is not lay in the French sense of the word: it is religious, orthodox and Catholic.... The Church educates with a *tendency*, and gives all its teachings a profound bias and an intolerant turn. Hence the persistence of a rift in the nation, a state of mutual intolerance born of the intolerance of the Church, since one cannot be tolerant towards intolerance.' (*Spain*, 1930, p. 229.) He adds that clerical education (which in elementary schools was invariably given by nuns) was bad by any standard. And one must remember that these Church schools were maintained not by the faithful, but by subsidies from the Ministry of Education.

On the other hand the action of the Government was unnecessarily drastic and tended to defeat its own ends. As Don José Castillejo has pointed out, most of the teaching orders had entered the country extra-legally and their schools could be closed down simply by applying the law. So too the suppression of the Jesuit Order merely turned it into a secret society and enabled it to continue teaching as before. The cancellation of the annual State grant to the Church was moreover an act of manifest injustice, since this grant represented the interest on the property of the Church which the State had sold. It was intended to be applied only to the support of the clergy and to the maintenance of public worship. But Spanish love of clear-cut solutions, Spanish intoxication in the moment of fancied victory triumphed over wiser counsels, and the enemies of the Republic were given the opportunity to proclaim themselves the defenders of the Faith.

B (p. 238). The anti-clerical articles in the Constitution were supplemented by the Law of Religious Confessions and Congregations, which defined the general intentions expressed by them more precisely. This was passed by the Cortes in May 1933 and signed by the President after a long struggle with his conscience. It was allowed to lapse a few months afterwards, on the fall of the Government. The Jesuit Order had been dissolved by decree in the previous January.

C (p. 238). Statement by the Minister for Education, Marcelino Domingo, quoted by A. Mendizábal in *The Martyrdom of Spain*. The position of education in Spain is discussed in various special articles in *The Times*, one by Don José Castillejo on 10 August 1926 and others by an unnamed correspondent on 6 June 1931 and 6 June 1933. Professor Allison Peers gives a good general account in *The Spanish Tragedy* of the reforms effected and not effected by the Republic. The catastrophic consequences to secondary education of the inhibition of the religious orders from teaching have been described in *Anarquía y Jerarquía*, by Sr. Madariaga. One good thing the Republic certainly did—it raised the salaries of the schoolmasters and university professors. Up to this time the salary of an elementary school teacher had lain between 2000 and 2500 pesetas—at the current rate £60 or £70 a year. Even university professors often earned no more than 5000 pesetas.

D (p. 244). The credit allotted to the Institute of Agrarian Reform was 50,000,000 pesetas a year. This only allowed the settlement of, at most, 5000 families annually. In fact only a fraction of these had been settled before the fall of the Government. The attitude of the Republicans is well shown in an interview which a French Socialist, M. Picard-Moch, had with Azaña in October 1932—that is when he was at the height of his power.

'—Et la réforme agraire? En attendez-vous véritablement des résultats?

'—Progressivement. Car le rhythme de son application va dépendre de l'état des finances. Mais n'oubliez pas que c'est chez nous un vieux problème: il n'y a qu'une chose de changée, c'est la résignation des ouvriers de campagnes, qui n'attendaient rien de la monarchie et qui attendent tout de la République.' (*L'Espagne Républicaine*, G. and J. Picard-Moch, p. 49.)

Well might Largo Caballero call this law 'an aspirin to cure an appendicitis'!

E (p. 252). A measure for the setting up of *federaciones de industria* was approved by this Congress by 302,343 votes to 90,671. This measure, which was advocated by among others Valeriano Orobón Fernández, a young Anarchist intellectual who had been secretary of the A.I.T., set up vertical industrial federations in addition to the local federations known as *sindicatos únicos*. The opponents of this measure, among whom was García Oliver, objected that it would increase the centralization of the C.N.T. Its adherents denied this and claimed that some such a system would be necessary for organizing libertarian production after the Revolution. Such was the confidence in approaching victory!

F (p. 253). Peiró's view, put forward in an Anarchist manifesto in September 1931, was that a revolution could not come from a small prepared minority and that such putsches, if they succeeded, must inevitably lead to dictatorships. The Revolution his party desired could only come from a movement sprung from the deep desires of the whole body of workers. The C.N.T. was just such a movement and it should therefore build up its forces and hold itself ready. The text of this manifesto is quoted in full by F. Madrid in *Ocho Meses y un Día en el Gobierno Civil de Barcelona*, pp. 215–218.

It will be remembered that *Solidaridad Obrera* had originally been founded with the object of introducing French Syndicalist methods and so counteracting the tendency that since 1887 had existed in Spanish Anarchism to split up into small groups of action, without sufficient syndical backing. The view of the F.A.I. was that these putsches would have the effect of rousing the revolutionary temper of the workers and that, if this were achieved, their immediate failure would not matter. This, of course, was orthodox Bakuninism.

G (p. 254). The most obstinate and heroic strike in the annals of the Spanish working classes was that at the steel foundry of La Felguera near Gijón in Asturias during the spring and summer of 1933. 2800 workmen of the C.N.T., the entire population of the place, struck to prevent the dismissal without pensions of some old workmen. The employers refused to treat, so the strikers replied with sabotage. The children were sent away to other towns and the workers tightened their belts. For nine months they held out—nine months of semi-starvation, but which cost the equally obstinate employers millions of pesetas—and won their case. In no other country but Spain could such a strike occur, and even here only in the C.N·T. where what one might call the *pundonor* of the workers was much more powerful than any material considerations.

One should note that the motive of nearly all C.N.T. strikes at this time was solidarity—that is to say, they struck for the release of prisoners or against dismissals. Such strikes were not engineered by the F.A.I., but were perfectly spontaneous manifestations of the feeling of the syndicates.

H (p. 255). The Russian anarchist Schapiro, who was sent to Spain by the A.I.T. in 1933 to report on this matter, declared that whereas the *Trentistas* were reformists, the F.A.I. 'sought in an individualist pseudo-collectivist exaltation a solution of the deadlock in which it found itself'. The *Trentistas* contained the older leaders, whereas the F.A.I. was a youth movement. The quarrel had begun in the *Comités de Defensa* and *por Presos* of the C.N.T. and was carried on with great bitterness, the Fai-istas speaking of their opponents as *bomberos* (i.e. *pompiers*), *enchufistas*, *atracadores* and so on. The main object of the *Trentistas* was to prevent the F.A.I. from dominating the C.N.T., and in this they failed.

His comment on the general situation in Spain is as follows: ' L'Espagne est aujourd'hui, indubitablement, le foyer de la révolution. Un foyer qui ne s'éteint pas. Seulement il est mal entretenu. Le feu est irrégulier et brûle mal. La chaleur utile émise est loin d'être proportionnelle à la quantité de charbon employée. Si l'esprit de la révolution inévitable règne en maître dans l'Espagne prolétarienne et paysanne, on ne peut pas en dire de même de l'esprit d'organization de cette révolution. *L'instinct de la spontanéité révolutionnaire continue encore à primer toutes autres considérations chez les militants. L'idée que l'action révolutionnaire destructive contient en elle-même les germes de l'activité révolutionnaire reconstructive est encore profondément enracinée chez nos camarades et est un obstacle constant à l'inoculation du virus organisateur dans l'activité de la C.N.T.*' In other words the Anarchist movement in Spain was intensely Spanish.

As to constructive work, the Anarchists did not, it is true, make any experiments in collectivization before the Civil War, nor even, I believe, draw up any plans on the subject. But they did set up schools, some of which were very interesting. Those organized by the stone cutters' syndicates at Hospitalitet, a suburb of Barcelona, were of the type familiarized in this country by Bertrand Russell.

I (p. 258). It must be said that little was done to make the Republic acceptable to Monarchists. From the first moment they were exposed to all kinds of petty irritations. Not only were titles of nobility abolished, but postmen were instructed not to deliver letters so addressed. There was a purge of the Civil Service for 'incompatibility with the regime'. The King was arraigned for high treason. The names of streets were changed. Summer time was abolished because the Dictatorship had introduced it: when the Catalans refused to agree to this, there were two times in Spain.

But so it has always been in Spain. For a hundred and twenty years the first act of every new regime has been to harass the outgoing party and to undo its legislation. From the fourteenth century on new municipalities have monotonously started off by prosecuting their predecessors. For centuries it has been so much the accepted thing that every administration will rob and oppress all who are not its particular supporters that those who come into office are expected to begin by revenging themselves. In the American colonies the official institution of the Audiencias gave a legal sanction to this practice.

Indeed, one may say that justice in Spain has never aimed at more than that each party should take its turn at oppressing the others. Judged by these standards, the behaviour of the Republicans was moderate. The Dictatorship had been much more vindictive. But both made the same mistake of exasperating their enemies without disarming them.

Chapter XII

THE BIENIO NEGRO

Cuando en un pueblo se cierran las puertas de la justicia,
se abren las de la Revolución.   SAGASTA.

The elections held in November 1933 ended in a smashing defeat for
the parties of the Left. The Left Republicans were almost annihilated. Of the 120 deputies that had sat in the previous Cortes, they
managed to keep but a bare half dozen. Azaña himself only obtained a
seat through the good will of Prieto, and the largest of their groups, the
Radical Socialists, got no seats at all. The Socialist party also did
badly: its numbers dropped from 116 to 58, though it maintained and
even increased its strength in Madrid. The Catalan Esquerra declined
from 46 to 19, whilst its rival, the Lliga, mopped up the seats it had
lost. The Radicals increased their following slightly, so that, as they
usually voted with the Lliga, the Centre block can be said to have gone
up by 30. But the chief gainers from this landslide were the Right:
their numbers leaped up from 42 to 207. Spain seemed to be turning
against the Republic.

The swing of the pendulum had not, however, been nearly so
violent as these figures would suggest. The new election law had been
devised to favour the formation of two main groups in the Cortes, in
imitation of the English party system: voting was for lists of candidates and parties which combined to form a united front obtained a
great advantage over those that did not. The side which was victorious at the polls was further given a representation in the Cortes
that was out of all proportion to its voting figure. In this election
the Right had presented a united front and the Left had not. Thus it
happened that, although the Right obtained twice as many seats in the
Cortes as the Left, the number of votes cast for it was actually less
than those cast for the disunited Left parties.

The principal cause of the defeat of the Left wing parties was thus
the refusal of the Socialists to collaborate with the Left Republicans
at the elections. They had been getting on badly ever since the scandal
over the Casas Viejas affair. Their failure to put through any serious
measure of agrarian reform and the knowledge that their continued
participation in the Government was making them unpopular among

their own followers had led to an increasing dissatisfaction among the party leaders. Since the Republicans had now gone to the full length of their tether, whilst the Socialists felt that their programme had scarcely begun to be carried out, further collaboration seemed out of the question. But their going to the elections alone was an act of suicide. By doing so they lost all the advantages of the new electoral law which they had helped to draw up and of which the Right parties were quick to avail themselves. The result of this was that, although the Socialists were undoubtedly much stronger numerically in 1933 than they had been in 1931, they returned only half the number of candidates. Such was the penalty paid for putting pride before self-interest.[1]

Another cause of the defeat suffered by the Left was the Anarchists' abstention. In 1931 large numbers of them had voted for the first time in the general enthusiasm. This year they organized a strong campaign of *no votad*, backed by all the resources of their propaganda. When the C.N.T. voted it was usually for one of the Republican parties, hardly ever for the Socialists. Thus their abstention in these elections seriously affected the Esquerra, who lost the votes of the Catalan proletariat and had to depend on those of the peasants and the *petite bourgeoisie*. The feminine ballot also played its part. In the middle classes many of the women whose husbands voted Republican followed their priest's direction and voted for the Right. In the working classes it was different: here the women were just as anticlerical as the men and the Socialist vote therefore did not suffer.

The dissensions of the Left were not, however, enough by themselves to account for the new situation. The forces of the Right had also greatly strengthened themselves. In the previous elections they had been obliterated because they had been associated with the

---

[1] The Electoral Law of the Republic was briefly as follows. Each constituency returned several members, but the electors were entitled to vote only for a limited number of candidates—that is, for less than the full number of deputies to be elected. Madrid elected seventeen and the electors were entitled to vote for thirteen: Barcelona elected twenty and the electors could vote for sixteen. The party or combination of parties which obtained a majority of votes could thus in Madrid win thirteen seats and the largest minority, even if nearly equal to the majority, could only win four. The advantage given to large combinations of parties is obvious.

In this election the voting in Madrid was: Socialists 175,000: Right 170,000: Left Republicans and Radicals between them 100,000. The Socialists therefore obtained 13 seats, the Right 4 and other parties none. Here the Socialists, on account of their exceptional strength, gained. In the provinces, however, their quarrel with Azaña's party combined with the large sums spent by the Right in buying votes caused them to lose. The number of votes cast for the different parties is discussed in Note A on p. 314 of the next chapter.

Monarchy. Their followers had either stayed at home or, in the hopes of putting a brake on the Republic, had voted for the Radicals. It was only to be expected therefore that they should now reassert themselves. But the scale of their success was due to careful organization. After the destruction of the old Monarchist parties in 1931 a new party known as *Acción Popular* was founded as the political branch of a Catholic organization, *Acción Católica*. *Acción Popular* represented the reaction of the Church and especially of the Jesuits to the Republic. It was a superficial imitation of the German Catholic party and was intended by its founders to be, not simply the party of the caciques, the Army and the aristocracy, but of the Catholic masses as well. It accepted the Republic, but not the anti-Catholic laws, and the main part of its programme consisted in a demand for the revision of the Constitution. Its social programme was of the vaguest kind, because those few Catholics who saw the necessity for agrarian reform and sickness and unemployment insurance were overshadowed by the landlords. In spite of the good intentions expressed by the founders of the party, these had the principal say in policy because they provided the funds. The brain behind the party was Angel Herrera, the director of the *Debate*, a paper controlled by the Jesuits, and he put forward as its leader a young man of some talent but very mediocre personality called Gil Robles.

José María Gil Robles was the son of an eminent professor of law, who after being the *élève modèle* of the Salesian Fathers at their college at Salamanca had gone on to the staff of the *Debate*. Here he had the good luck to please his masters who, when it became evident that the Dictatorship would not last long and that bad times lay ahead, picked him to be leader of the new Catholic party. A match was arranged for him with the daughter of the Conde de Revillagigedo, one of the richest men in Spain, which gave him the position and connections that, as a Catholic leader, he required. He then took his honeymoon in Germany. In his search for new political ideas he visited first the Nuremberg Rally, where he was impressed by Hitler, and later Dollfuss. The persecution of the Church by the Nazis caused him to react against his first favourable impressions and he finally fixed his eyes on the Austrian Corporative State, which became the goal towards which he hoped to direct the destinies of Spain. But in Germany he had learned something of the value of propaganda in political campaigns and on his return to Spain he proceeded to put these lessons into practice. The Casas Viejas episode had made it clear that an election could not be long delayed and, in order to secure the majority his party hoped for, it would be necessary to take advantage of the new electoral law and form a block of all the Right-wing parties.

The first step was to group around *Acción Popular* various small Catholic bodies of like nature: the Confederation of Fathers of Families, the Catholic Youth Organization, and so on. The new party thus formed was known as the *Confederación Española de Derechos Autónomos*, or more briefly the *Ceda*. This party then proceeded to form an election block with four other Right-wing parties: *Renovación Española*, the small Monarchist party; *Comunión Tradicionalista*, the Carlist party; the Basque Nationalists and the Agrarians. The latter were a party very close in feeling to the Ceda, whose programme was confined entirely to the defence of the landed interest. They represented in the country districts very much what the Radicals did in the towns. Gil Robles, whose party, the Ceda, with 110 deputies was the strongest in the Cortes, became the leader of the new combination.[1]

The next months were spent in preparations. Dockets were drawn up in Nazi style upon every voter, giving particulars as to his opinions, where he worked and who could influence him. Political functions and rallies were organized. All this cost money. The old parties of the Monarchy had always got along without regular funds: their election expenses had been kept down to a minimum and the chief inducement offered to voters had been the hope that, if they were victorious, they would share the spoils. But now the cacique system only worked in the more isolated districts and therefore money was necessary. Money for propaganda in the towns and for buying votes in the country. The landlords were the only people who could provide it. Thus any hope of the Ceda's carrying through even the most moderate programme of social reforms was ruled out from the start. The landlords, and especially those of the Monarchist group who, being the richest, had made the largest contributions, were in a position to prevent it. Composed as it was of so many discordant elements and hopelessly divided within itself, the combination led by the Ceda was incapable from the first of any positive decisions.

The question of the composition of the Government was the first to come up. The largest party in the house was the Ceda, but it did not

---

[1] The relative strengths of the chief Right-wing parties are shown by the number of deputies they returned to the Cortes. Ceda, 110: Agrarians, 36: Traditionalists, 20: Renovación Española, 15: Basque Nationalists, 14. Nothing could show better the unpopularity of the late king than the small size of his party in this Cortes. The Monarchy had become a lost cause.

have an absolute majority. It was natural therefore that the Centre, in other words the Radicals, should form a Government. They could depend either on the votes of the Left or on those of the Right. It is significant that they chose the latter. As a result of this there was a small secession from their party. Martínez Barrio crossed the house with a group of some thirty followers and took his seat beside Azaña. The Catalan Lliga and, for a time, the Agrarians joined the Government. The latter had a policy of assisting the landowners by 'revalorizing agricultural produce'—in other words increasing the duty on foreign cereals and reducing wages—which they were anxious to put through.

The intentions of the Government were soon seen. Within a few weeks all the legislation fixing wages and conditions of employment that had been passed by the Constituent Cortes was either repealed or allowed to lapse: the tenants' guarantee against capricious eviction was thrown overboard: some 19,000 peasants who had been settled on the large estates in Extremadura were evicted: wages (which had no doubt been too high) fell by 40 or 50 per cent and landlords, to assist the process, began dismissing hands. At the same time as much as possible of the anti-clerical legislation of the last government was allowed to lapse and the substitution of lay schools for religious ones was indefinitely postponed. The expenditure on education was also drastically reduced. These measures were the more extraordinary because the Radicals had always won their elections on the anti-clerical ticket and had recently voted in favour of the laicization of education. It was the price they had to pay for the support of the Ceda.

More significant still was the passage of an Amnesty Bill, setting free all persons involved in Sanjurjo's military rising, reinstating the officers in their previous rank and awarding them their arrears of pay for the time they had spent in prison. The grandees, whose estates had been confiscated, had their property returned to them. This bill, which clearly sanctioned the right of officers to rise against the Government, was only passed after an uproar in the Cortes, and the President of the Republic signed it with a rider stating that he personally disapproved of it. An attempt by the Minister of Justice to re-establish the death penalty had to be dropped for fear that it would lead to a revolution. There was, in short, hardly an act passed by the previous Government that was not either repealed outright or permitted to lapse. Yet the Radical Government was an extremely weak one: there was a ministerial crisis every few weeks, whilst waves of small strikes all over the country prevented any possibility of trade recovery.

The Anarchists had not, however, waited for the new Government to show its hand before declaring open war against it. During the elections, it will be remembered, they had conducted a strong propaganda campaign against voting. The result was that the reactionary parties won. The Anarchists then felt that their honour required that they should answer this 'triumph of fascism' in the only way open to them—that is by an armed revolt. They would show the Socialists what was the proper way of fighting the bourgeoisie.

After the usual consultations of the F.A.I., the different regional committees of the C.N.T. met to decide what could be done. All were agreed that revolutionary action, stronger than any hitherto taken, was necessary. But most of the Regional Federations had exhausted themselves on previous risings and were without arms. It was decided therefore that the Aragonese Federation should be the only one to rise, but that it should be supported in other parts of Spain by general strikes.

The Aragonese are the toughest and most obstinate of all the Spanish peoples, as the history of their conflicts and of the famous sieges of Numantia and Saragossa shows. The Socialist party (owing perhaps to the fact that it was associated with Castile) had never had many adherents among them. The workers in the towns, the peasants on the bare wind-swept *páramos*, who a century before had flocked to the Carlist banners, now followed the red and black flag of the C.N.T. Saragossa itself was a C.N.T. stronghold, the centre of a purer brand of anarchism than could be found in half-syndicalist Barcelona.

The rising broke out on 8 December and *comunismo libertario* was proclaimed in many of the villages of Aragon and by the vineyard hands of the Rioja. In Saragossa, Huesca and Barbastro attempts were made to seize the public buildings, and barricades were thrown up. In other parts of Spain—Andalusia, Valencia and Corunna—there were strikes and church burnings. Only Catalonia, exhausted by the efforts of the previous year, kept quiet. But the insurrection did not last long. The Government hurried up fresh troops and at the end of four days all was over. Against the C.N.T. both the rank and file of the Army and the Republican police could be trusted.

What was remarkable about this rising was that for the first time in Spain clear instructions were issued for a social revolution. Mills and factories were taken over by the workers, and factory committees set up. Other committees for food, transport and so on were organized on the lines set down by Kropotkin. The rising was regarded as a rehearsal for the coming revolution, if not as the actual beginning of it But the fatal weakness of Anarcho-Syndicalism was seen in the fact that only one out of the forty-six provinces in Spain rose. What could be hoped for from that? The F.A.I. were once again playing at revolution. However it is characteristic of Spaniards to be satisfied with gestures and with petty acts of defiance and courage and to neglect the real heart of the matter. The Arabs conquered the whole of Spain in two years. It took the Spaniards eight centuries to get rid of them.[1]

The real strength of the C.N.T. lay not, however, in their armed revolts, but in their powers of syndical resistance. This was proved by a general strike that took place at Saragossa in March 1934—only three months after the suppression of the rising—as a protest against the bad treatment of the prisoners taken in the previous December. It lasted four weeks and during that time Saragossa remained a dead city. The children of the strikers were sent to other towns to be fed. A similar but shorter strike took place in Valencia. When one remembers that the C.N.T. had no strike funds, one can appreciate the courage and endurance required in these contests. If the Anarcho-Syndicalists could not bring off their revolution, they at all events knew how to keep a revolutionary situation alive.

As I have pointed out in a previous chapter, the outstanding success of the Anarchist movement in Spain lay in the moral influence it exercised among the workers. 'Whilst everywhere', wrote an English Socialist, 'the workers' movement is bent on attaining comfort and security, the Spanish Anarchist lives for liberty, virtue and dignity.'[2] That is exact. If, unlike other revolutionary parties, Anarchists cared little for strategy, that was because they believed that revolution

---

[1] In the rising 67 of the C.N.T. were killed and 87 seriously wounded. This shows the relatively small scale of the fighting. Nearly 6000 arrests were made by the police and the C.N.T. was declared an illegal organization, though the Government was too weak to enforce this. See Nos. 170, 171 and 172 of the *Bulletin of the I.W.M.A.* The first contains the text of a proclamation by the C.N.T. on the organization of the committees.

An amusing sequel to the rising was the holding up of the judges of the court who were trying prisoners and the carrying off under their noses of all the evidence that had been prepared by the police. This hold-up was organized by Durruti from prison.

[2] *Spain To-day*, by Edward Conze, p. 62. This little book, whilst misleading on many points, gives an excellent picture of the relations of Socialists and Anarcho-Syndicalists in 1934–1936.

would come spontaneously as soon as the workers were morally prepared. Their main effort was therefore directed to this preparation: it was not sufficient for them to gain converts: every worker must endeavour to put into practice at once the anarchist conception of life. From this it followed that their leaders could not, like the Socialist bosses, occupy a comfortable flat in a middle-class quarter: they must remain at their jobs in shop or factory like ordinary workmen. In strikes and armed risings they must always be at the point of greatest danger. No paid bureaucracy could be allowed to direct their huge trade union: the workers must manage their affairs themselves through their elected committees, even though this meant a sacrifice of revolutionary efficiency. Better that the revolution should fail than that it should be founded on a betrayal of principle.

This severely moral attitude was in striking contrast to the behaviour of the Socialists. For three years they had enjoyed the fruits of office: a host of new trade-union officials had grown up and many of their leaders received substantial salaries.[1] Yet little good had come to the working classes from it. During this same time the Anarchists had been giving proof of their devotion to the workers' cause by heroic strikes, by bold if useless risings, and in prison cells. The reproach was evident. Even those who disagreed with their politics were fired by their example. The U.G.T. wavered. After more than fifty years of strict reformism, the Socialist party began to turn revolutionary.

We must consider what a change this meant. Only two years before Fabra Ribas, the under-secretary to the Minister of Labour, Largo Caballero, had spoken as follows:

'It is not enough to practise Socialism. Socialism has to be won, to be deserved. The Socialist party hopes that the Republic will allow them to realize this work and that is why they have defended it with such ardour.'

And he went on to explain that the Socialist party did not expect to see Socialism in their time, nor even a purely Socialist Government in Madrid. They would be content if they could develop their ideas gradually.[2] This, of course, was simply the classic attitude of Spanish Socialism as held by Pablo Iglesias. Since then nothing had happened to make it irrealizable. There had merely been, if one was to judge by

[1] See Note A on p. 295 at end of chapter.
[2] From a speech made on 14 February 1932, on inaugurating the *Escuela de Trabajo* at Saragossa. Quoted by G. and J. Picard-Moch, *L'Espagne Républicaine*, pp. 382–383.

the surface, a swing of the pendulum which in any other country
would have been regarded as temporary. Yet by January 1934 opinion
in the party and still more in the union was veering rapidly in favour
of abstention from Government until complete Socialist domination
should be possible—that is, towards a revolutionary attitude.

To explain the reasons for this change we must go back a few years.
When the Dictatorship fell the Socialists had still been a small party.
Their trade union, the U.G.T., had been greatly inferior in numbers
to that of the Anarcho-Syndicalists. Its figure did not reach 300,000.
Then, under the Republic, it expanded enormously. Its strength in
June 1932 was over a million. By 1934 it had reached a million and a
quarter. This prodigious increase gave it a self-confidence it had never
possessed before. One thing to be noticed about this expansion is
that most of the new recruits belonged either to the small peasants
and landless labourers or to the shop-employee class. The Socialists
had been gaining ground here on the C.N.T., thanks to the new
labour legislation and to the hopes which their position in the Government had raised. The number of miners, factory workers and railwaymen showed little increase because they had mostly been under
either Socialist or Anarcho-Syndicalist influence before. The following figures, taken in June 1932, give the proportions:

> 445,411   rural workers;
> 287,245   factory workers, miners, railwaymen;
> 236,829   clerks and shop employees.

They show clearly enough why the Socialists were so sensitive to
discontent in the country districts and so anxious for a comprehensive
agrarian settlement.[1]

The refusal of the Republican parties to treat agrarian reform
seriously lay then at the root of the Socialists' disillusion with the
Republic. It was a feeling that welled up from below, affecting the
young more than the old, the recently joined rather than the confirmed party men. That it was especially strong in Madrid was
perhaps due to the small but energetic Anarchist nucleus in that city.
(Generally speaking a small but well-organized group of Anarchists
in a Socialist area drove the Socialists to the Left, whereas in predominantly Anarchist areas, Socialists were outstandingly reformist.)
This feeling found a leader in Largo Caballero. As President of the
U.G.T. he was especially alive to the danger of losing ground to the

---

[1] See Note B on p. 295 at end of chapter.

Anarcho-Syndicalists. And he had also a personal grievance. First of all he had quarrelled with Azaña. Then as Minister of Labour he had been especially disgusted at the way in which much of the legislation drawn up by him had been sabotaged. Sabotage is an old weapon in Spain, the formula expressing it, *obedecemos pero no cumplimos*, 'we obey but won't comply', dating back many centuries. Caballero had found that even the officials in his own ministry refused to obey the directions given them. There was a conspiracy to make nonsense of everything. Thus it came about that already in February 1934 he was saying that 'the only hope of the masses is now in social revolution. It alone can save Spain from Fascism.' As Maurín puts it, 'Caballero, the representative of opportunist reformism, became in 1934 the man of the masses'. Eighty years before this Carl Marx had pointed out that Spanish revolutionary movements developed more slowly than those of other countries and that they usually took several years to reach their climax. Thus there was really nothing very surprising in this new development.[1]

The first step taken to carry the new policy into effect was the organization by the U.G.T., and by Largo Caballero in particular, of the *Alianza Obrera* or Workers' Alliance. This was intended as a sort of Popular Front, confined to working-class parties and organized locally. The C.N.T. refused to join. Feeling between the two great unions was very bitter and the Anarcho-Syndicalists refused to believe that the Socialists could change their skin so suddenly and after fifty years of domesticity develop revolutionary instincts. They had also a deep distrust of Caballero, who had always displayed a strong hostility to them. They got on better with the Right wing, with Prieto. The Communists also refused to join. They were still in their wildly revolutionary phase and at loggerheads with every other group or party in the country. All that was left therefore was the *Bloque Obrero y Campesino*, or Workers' and Peasants' Block, a small group of Left Marxists confined to Catalonia,[2] and the *Sindicatos de Oposición* or *Trentistas* of Pestaña and Peiró, which had recently seceded from the C.N.T. and were also confined to Catalonia and Valencia. Later the *Rabassaires*, or Catalan Peasants' party, joined them. Thus it happened that the *Alianza Obrera* (till August at all events) only managed to come to life in Catalonia, where, like the P.S.U.C. two

---

[1] 'Three years seem to be the shortest limit to which she restricts herself, whilst her revolutionary cycle sometimes expands to nine.' (*Revolutionary Spain*, a series of articles contributed to *The New York Daily Tribune* in 1854.)

[2] See Note C on p. 296 at end of chapter.

and a half years later, it owed its *raison d'être* to jealousy of the Anarcho-Syndicalists. It was even strong enough to declare a general strike which was effective in one town—Sabadell. A strike in Catalonia that was not anarchist! And on the orders of Caballero—that is, of Madrid! Maurín, the leader of the *Bloque Obrero*, felt such enthusiasm for the new venture that for a moment he considered joining the Socialist party.

The conditions in the country districts, which had been bad enough in 1933, were rapidly deteriorating. The fall of wages, the dismissals of workmen, the relaxation of the laws safeguarding tenants, permitted and encouraged by the Government in the hopes of reviving trade and stimulating capital, had brought an enormous increase of misery. The Vizconde de Eza, a Monarchist deputy and a famous authority on agriculture, declared that in 1934 150,000 families on the land lacked the bare necessities of life. Some pueblos had almost a thousand men unemployed through nine-tenths of the year. When he asked a group of these men what solution they had to the problem, 'Let them kill half of us' was the answer.[1] The misery was so immense that the landlords themselves were petrified. Partly for economic reasons, but still more no doubt with the design of dealing the *coup de grâce* to the tottering Republic, they had dismissed large numbers of workmen and were cultivating as little of their land as possible. But in the face of so much misery they were too weak to assert themselves and the Government, which was mortally afraid of another Casas Viejas, had given the police orders to keep as much in the background as possible. Thus it happened that the Socialists were able in several provinces to take over land more or less by force from the landlords and to organize collectives on it. So feeble had the Government become since Azaña had ceased to lead it!

The collectivization was managed in this way. An official of the Land Workers' Federation of the U.G.T., at the head of a large body of unemployed labourers, would approach a landowner and invite him to lend a certain part of his land to form a collective. He himself would be enrolled as a member and would draw profits from it. All the documents would be prepared beforehand and he would be invited then and there to sign. Under the circumstances few had the courage to refuse. In this way about a hundred collectives were organized in the province of Ciudad Real and nearly as many again in that of Toledo. Others were established in Jaén, Badajoz and

[1] See Note D on p. 296 at end of chapter.

Valencia. A school with classes in the use of tractors and in book-keeping was opened at Valdepeñas by Felix Torres. Although the capital was small and few of the collectives managed to acquire tractors, most of them seem to have worked well enough to remain in existence down to the end of the Civil War.

All this misery and unrest in the country districts culminated in a general strike in June 1934. Things had been working up to it for a long time, but when it came it was too late to be effective. Hungry men do not make good strikers. The object of the strike was to compel the landlords to observe the labour charter set up by the Republic, and both the C.N.T. and the U.G.T. took part in it. The harvesters downed tools in fifteen provinces, but after nine days returned to work on a compromise.

Meanwhile the process of undermining the work of the Republic from the Government benches was steadily going on. Lerroux had ceased to be premier in March and another Radical, Ricardo Samper, had taken his place. This Government was, if possible, even weaker and more stupidly provocative than the last. One of its first acts was to quarrel with the Catalans.

The position in Catalonia was as follows. Thanks to Anarchist abstention at the polls, the Lliga had sent 25 deputies to the Cortes and the Esquerra only 19. But in the elections to the Generalidad, or Catalan Autonomous Government, which followed in January, the Anarchists repented of their hasty action and the Esquerra won a complete victory. As Colonel Maciá had died in December 1933, Luis Companys was now the leader of this party. Difficulties soon cropped up over the Agrarian question. The laws which the Constituent Cortes had passed fixing rents and prohibiting unjustified dismissals of tenants had either been repealed by the Radicals or had been allowed to lapse quietly. Evictions of tenants were going on all over Spain as in the old bad days. The Catalan landowners were not behindhand in this and, taking advantage of certain long-disputed contracts, began to evict tenants whose leases they considered were up. Within a few months more than a thousand families had been dispossessed of land which in most cases they had cultivated for generations.

There are few large estates in Catalonia: most of the land is in the hands of small propertied men who have put their business savings into it and who re-let it to a class of peasants known as the *Rabas-saires*. The type of contract they use belongs to the familiar *aparceria* or share-cropping system, in which costs and fruits are shared equally by tenant and owner. But, as most of the land so rented is used for vineyards, the duration of the contract is based upon the life of the vines. The land reverts to the owner when three-quarters of the planted vines have died (*rabassa morte*) and he can then renew it or not as he thinks fit. The Catalan peasants had made an art of prolonging the life of the vines and in the old days they lasted as a rule for fifty years. This assured the labourer a contract that would cover his working life and remunerate him for the six or eight years of fruitless labour that young vines require before they mature.

But the phylloxera plague in the nineties killed the old vines and led to the introduction of a new type of plant which required much more care and labour and had a maximum life of only twenty-five years. This created a situation which was manifestly unjust. However, when the first of the new contracts terminated during the European War, prices were so high that no disputes over the renewal occurred. It was not till the fall in wine prices came that the *Rabassaires* began to feel the injustice of their position. They then organized themselves with the assistance of Companys in a syndicate and, when the Dictatorship fell, placed themselves under the protection of the Esquerra.[1] In exchange for its political support they agreed to vote for it at elections. That support was now called for and accordingly in April the Government of the Generalidad passed the *Ley de Cultivos* to regulate the matter. It was a moderate bill, empowering tenants to acquire land they had cultivated for fifteen years and setting up tribunals for arbitration. But the landlords would not accept it and appealed to Madrid. The Spanish Government laid the matter before the Tribunal of Constitutional Guarantees to decide whether or not the Generalidad had power to pass such a bill. This tribunal, whose membership had recently been changed to bring it into harmony with

[1] The *Rabassaires* first organized themselves in 1923 as an agricultural society under Companys' leadership. In spite of their adherence to the Esquerra they took little interest in politics. Some of their members syndicated with the C.N.T. and others with the U.G.T. On the other hand a certain number of Anarchists and Socialists were members of the *Rabassaires*, which they regarded as an agricultural syndicate.

For the *Rabassaires* were simply small peasants who believed in socialization and in minding their own affairs. They had a programme of agricultural co-operatives, credit institutions and mutual aid societies in which, without any aid from the State, they had produced surprising results. Their ideas were untheoretical and were modified by practical experience, but they showed a great persistence in carrying them out. Their co-operatives provide a rosy picture of what agricultural society might have become under more favourable auspices over a large part of Spain.

the views of the Government, decided that it had not. On this Companys defied Madrid and declared that the law would be carried into effect all the same. The Lliga, which might have mediated, refused to continue sitting in the Catalan Parliament and walked out.

At the same time that the Government were breaking with the Catalans they were quarrelling with the Basques. The Basques have a long tradition of liberty and self-government. Down to 1840 they had their own parliament, courts of law and mint. They raised their own militia and the King could not send troops through their country without their permission. Their administration was distinguished through the whole of Spain for its efficiency and lack of corruption. But, as a punishment for their support of Don Carlos, they lost their autonomy, retaining only certain *fueros* or privileges. These allowed them to raise their own taxes, to have their own douane or customs and exempted them from military service. Then, as a result of their participation in the Second Carlist War, they were deprived of these also, but were given what was called a *Concierto Económico*. This, among other things, permitted them to assess their own taxes and to pay a certain fixed sum to the Treasury.

After 1900 a national party appeared in the Basque provinces just as it had done some years before in Catalonia. Like the Lliga, it was a party of large industrialists and of small Catholic bourgeois and farmers. Its desire for autonomy sprang from much the same causes —national sentiment mixed with the resentment of a modern and enterprising race at being ruled by a body of Castilian soldiers and landowners. There was also a religious motive. The Basque Nationalists, who were intensely Catholic, wished to remove their country from the corrosive influence of Spanish anti-clericalism and to govern it in accordance with the encyclicals of Leo XIII. But the feeling behind them was not so strong as it was in Catalonia, because the Basques, like the Scots, are a race of mountaineers who have long been accustomed to find a field for their enterprise outside their own country. Economically speaking, they are extroverts. Nor was the primitive Basque language such a useful rallying point as the Catalan. Not only did it lack its literary traditions, but it was spoken in only two provinces, Vizcaya and Guipúzcoa, and in the Pyrenean valleys of Navarre. In the southern province, Álava, it had almost died out and for this reason the adherence of the Álavese was tepid. On the other hand, the Basque Nationalists gained from the fact that the social problem in their territory was much less acute than in Catalonia.

Apart from a nucleus of Socialists in the iron foundries at Bilbao, whose conduct was entirely reformist and who in any case were not Basques but immigrants from other parts of Spain, their only rivals were the Traditionalists or Carlists, who were supreme in Navarre just as they themselves were supreme in the two Biscayan provinces.

The Basque question thus resolved itself into a struggle between two ultra-Conservative Catholic parties, one of which hoped to satisfy its religious and social ideals by setting up a regime of its own in comparative isolation from the vicissitudes of Spanish politics, whilst the other, which had just the same ideals, preferred the more ambitious policy of assisting the Catholic parties of Castile to impose them by force upon the rest of the country. A glance at the map will show the reason for these differences of attitude. Vizcaya and Guipúzcoa are cut off from Spain by the Cantabrian Mountains and look out on the sea, whilst Navarre is cut off from France by the Pyrenees and faces the interior of the Peninsula. The former have developed strong links with Western Europe by their industry and commerce, whilst the latter is oriented towards Castile. These factors, not to mention other historical ones, account for wide differences of temperament and outlook—differences which one may observe even in their religion, for whereas the Basques have developed a Catholicism of the Belgian type with trade unions and social services, the Navarrese have retained their primitive crusading mentality. Under normal conditions this rivalry of the two branches of the Basque family would have remained a local issue, but as the tension in the rest of Spain between the parties of the Right and Left mounted up, it was natural that they should be drawn in and forced to take sides.

This, however, did not happen immediately. The first reaction of the Basque Nationalists to the Republic was not favourable. Outraged by the anti-clerical clauses in the Constitution, their deputies walked out of the Cortes. But the bait of an autonomy statute soon brought them back. Some time was spent in the discussion of the different drafts, partly because the Basques insisted on having full religious control with the right to appoint their own representatives at the Vatican, and partly because Álava, torn between the Biscay provinces and Navarre, was lukewarm. A suitable text had only just been agreed on when the Cortes was dissolved.

At the elections the Basques voted with the Ceda. But hardly were they over when they discovered that neither the Ceda nor the Radicals would allow the passage of their Autonomy Statute. This set them moving towards the Left. In the question of the Catalan *Ley de Cultivos*, they took sides with the Esquerra. At this moment the Government, which seemed to take pleasure in multiplying the number of its enemies, was unwise enough to impose a tax that was contrary to the provisions of the *Concierto Económico*.

The Basques decided to hold special elections in their municipalities as a protest against it. The Government forbade the elections and when they took place tried to prevent them. A few shots were fired and the Monarchist paper, the *A.B.C.*, came out with a leading article in which it said: 'We prefer the Communists to the Basques.' All the Basque municipalities resigned and their deputies followed the example of the Esquerra and again walked out of the Cortes. Thus by September the Spanish Government had managed to quarrel seriously with both the Basques and the Catalans.

Whilst the Radical Government had succeeded in revoking the majority of the acts of the First Republican Cortes and was now proceeding to threaten the remainder, Gil Robles' party, the Ceda, was preparing to take a step forwards. The composite nature of this party, continually at variance with itself, and the necessity for appearing to accept the Republican regime without outraging its Monarchist allies had led to a number of contradictory statements being made by its leader. But there was never any secret as to what its aims really were. Gil Robles' programme was conceived in the form of a series of steps: first he would form a coalition government with the Radicals: then he would hold power alone: then, having prepared the ground, he would hold elections which he would manage so as to secure an overwhelming victory: finally, he would return triumphant to the seat of glory and change the Constitution. Circumstances would decide whether a Corporative State on the Austrian model should be at once set up and whether the Monarchy should be restored.[1]

---

[1] At a speech to his followers just before the 1933 election Gil Robles spoke as follows: 'We must move towards a new state. What matters if it means shedding blood? We need an integral solution—that is what we are seeking. In order to realize that ideal we will not detain ourselves in archaic forms. Democracy is for us not an end, but a means to go to the conquest of a new state. When the moment comes either the Cortes will submit or we shall make it disappear.' (*El Debate*.)

At other times he insisted that rebellion against constituted authority was illegal and contrary to the teachings of the Church. Neither sedition nor conspiracy was permissible. It would certainly be true to say that he hoped to attain his ends by legal means. The Falangist writer, Giménez Caballero, makes the following comment: 'Apparently fascist, apparently nationalist, he has felt obliged to eliminate from his side every authentic nationalist and fascist element.' He and his party with their 'vatican policy of traditional jesuitism' were 'bastard souls, without genital force'.

The moment for carrying out the first step seemed now to have arrived and at a great rally of the Youth Organizations of his party at Covadonga in September, their leader made one of his typically equivocal and provocative speeches: 'The way is clear before us. Not one moment more! For ourselves we want nothing, but we will no longer suffer this state of things to continue.' These words were interpreted to mean that his party would no longer support the Radicals when the Cortes reassembled on 1 October. A week later he confirmed this in less oracular language.

The parties of the Left had watched the gradual sabotage of almost all the legislation of the Constituent Cortes without any protest more violent than a strike, but they did not, if they could help it, intend to see the Constitution destroyed altogether. They were ready, if necessary, to take up arms to prevent this. The only question was, when should that moment arise? The Republicans, bound to their parliamentary rules, did not think it had come yet. The Socialists were divided—the followers of Prieto being of the opinion that a revolution at this moment would fail, whilst those of Caballero were eager for it. It was a difficult decision to take: on the one hand the preparations for a rising were not sufficiently advanced and few arms were available: on the other hand, if this moment were not seized and the Ceda were allowed to enter the Government, the opportunity might never occur again. The memory of the destruction of the Socialists in Vienna by Dollfuss was still fresh in everyone's minds and Gil Robles was one of Dollfuss's disciples. A vote was taken, and a decisive majority gave their support to Caballero. The Esquerra, which controlled the Generalidad, were also ready to raise the standard of revolt in Catalonia.

On 1 October the Cortes met and the Government resigned. Gil Robles demanded a majority of the seats in the next cabinet for his followers. The parties of the Left warned the President that if any member of the Ceda entered the Government they would regard it as a declaration of war on themselves. They pressed him on the contrary to dissolve the Cortes. After long hesitation Don Niceto chose what seemed to him to be the correct constitutional course and instructed Lerroux to form a government which should include three minor members of the Ceda. Correct perhaps, but catastrophic in its results, when one remembers that all the disasters that have followed for Spain may be traced to this one unhappy decision. For the Socialists did not accept this compromise and on the following day (5 October) a general strike of the U.G.T. began all over the country. Azaña and the other members of the Republican parties, including even the Conservative Miguel Maura, were so disgusted with the President that they declared they would no longer sit in this Cortes nor have personal relations with him again.

The revolutionary movement that followed broke out simultaneously in three different centres—Barcelona, Madrid and the mining district of the Asturias. In the other provinces of Spain, wherever the U.G.T. was sufficiently strong, there were general strikes in the towns but no violent action. The country districts kept quiet because the *campesinos'* strike in June had exhausted them. Only in Extremadura did a few *yunteros* rise under the leadership of Margarita Nelken, a woman Socialist.

We will begin by describing what happened in Barcelona. The situation at this moment in Catalonia was extremely complex. The Esquerra controlled the Generalidad or Autonomous Catalan Government, but was far from being itself a homogeneous body. One may distinguish four separate groups in it.

(*a*) The Republican *petite bourgeoisie* led by Companys.

(*b*) A separatist group, the *Estat Catalá*, made up of young patriots, led by Dencás and Badiá.

(*c*) The Catalan Socialist party, a small group composed of workmen closely linked up with the co-operative movement.

(*d*) The *Rabassaires*, or Peasants' party.

For months (ever since Maciá's death) a struggle had been going on in the Esquerra between these groups, which finally became polarized in Companys and Dencás. Companys' wing, which was far more numerous than that of Dencás, was based on the view that the workers, like the middle classes, had Catalan sympathies and preferred the Esquerra to any party, whether Socialist or Monarchist, that took its orders from Madrid. It held out a hand to the Anarchists and believed that a *modus vivendi* could be reached with them. The *Estat Catalá*, on the other hand, was a Youth movement founded by Maciá and composed mostly of workmen and adventurers—men drawn from the same soil as the *sindicatos libres* of a dozen years before—with a violent antagonism to the Anarcho-Syndicalists. It had a small military organization, the *escamots*, who wore green uniforms. It represented Catalan Nationalism in its most intransigeant form: in fact it was Catalan Fascism. In spite of its small size it had acquired, partly through its military organization, a temporary ascendancy over the other groups in the Esquerra, and Companys felt obliged to yield to Dencás' demand that Catalonia should take this opportunity for breaking with Madrid. To have refused would have meant destroying his party and so, though full of qualms as to the possibility of success, he felt it better to lead the movement for independence himself.

The absurdity of a rising in Catalonia without the support of the C.N.T. must be only too evident. The only mass following on which the Esquerra could count were the forces of the *Alianza Obrera* (two Left Marxist groups and Peiró's *Sindicatos de Oposición*), whose numbers in Barcelona were insignificant, and the *Rabassaires*, whose forces must take several days to arrive. Companys, left to himself, could probably have persuaded the Anarcho-Syndicalists to join, but Dencás and Badiá, the Chief of Police, went out of their way to prevent this from happening. The offices of the C.N.T. were closed and daily broadcasts by Dencás against the F.A.I. continued up to the day of the rising. At the same time the chances of an immediate success lay all on the side of the insurgents. The Generalidad controlled 3400 armed *escamots* under Badiá and 3200 Assault Guards, who could be implicitly relied on. The garrison consisted of 5000 men, of whom very few were ready to fight. In fact their commander was only able to muster 500. The question of eventual success was a different matter: without the support of the masses, that is of the C.N.T., there was no possibility of this.

At 7.30 p.m. on 5 October Companys, speaking in a weak and hesitating voice, proclaimed from the balcony of the Generalidad the independence of the Catalan State within a Spanish Federal Republic. After that events moved rapidly. The sympathy of the commander of the garrison, General Batet, who was a Catalan, had been hoped for. However he stood firm. Soon after ten o'clock several companies of troops left the barracks and surrounded the Generalidad. Artillery was trained on it and towards midnight a few shells were fired. Before dawn next morning the building had been taken, Companys was a prisoner and the fight was over.

While this was going on, Dencás had remained at his office, refusing Companys' appeals for help. When everything was over he dismissed his *escamots*, who had not been allowed to leave their barracks, and sent them home: escaped by an underground sewer and crossed the frontier. Later he took refuge in Italy. Although Spain is a country where the strangest combinations of cowardice and fanaticism are possible, the only rational explanation of Dencás' conduct is that he was an *agent provocateur* in the pay of the Spanish Monarchists. After the rising was over Gil Robles declared in the Cortes that he had deliberately provoked it: that statement might seem a mere boast if Dencás' conduct did not appear to confirm it.

Meanwhile a general strike of the U.G.T. was going on all over Spain, the miners of the Asturias were battering their way into Oviedo and there was fighting in the streets of Madrid. Madrid was the capital of Spanish Socialism and also the headquarters of its revolutionary wing. Largo Caballero was personally in charge of the operations there. But all the arrangements had miscarried. In view of the strong garrisons commanding the exits from the city, it was especially important that the workers should have plenty of arms. But the greater part of the arms destined for Madrid had been seized a month earlier in Asturias and the others did not arrive. A plan to blow up the Home Office could not be carried out. The Madrid rising was therefore a complete fiasco.[1]

The failure of the risings in Barcelona and Madrid had been ignominious: that of the Asturian miners was an epic which terrified the bourgeoisie and fired all the working classes of Spain. One may regard it as the first battle of the Civil War. The position in Asturias was this. The miners and iron workers of Oviedo, Gijón and the surrounding towns and villages belonged to an old and long established community, which had been syndicated in the U.G.T. and C.N.T. since 1912. They had their own cultural institutions, newspapers and co-operatives and, though the working conditions in the

---

[1] The arms used in the October rising all came originally from the Government arsenals. The principal supply had been ordered by Echevarrieta, the well-known Basque financier and friend of Prieto, from the Consorcio de Fábricas Militares in 1932: nominally required for Abyssinia, they were really intended for Portuguese revolutionaries. They were paid for by him and delivered at Cadiz. Hidden first at Huelva, they were later taken back to Cadiz for fear the Anarchists should get hold of them. Then in August 1934, with the permission of the Radical Minister for War, they were embarked on the steamer *La Turquesa* bound for Bordeaux. On the way *La Turquesa* stopped off the Asturian coast and landed them there, but the police got wind of it and seized a considerable part, mostly cartridges. These were the arms intended for Madrid, but as the roads to the capital were now closely guarded, what remained had to be distributed in Asturias. This consisted of 500 Mauser rifles, 24 machine guns and several thousand hand grenades. To make up for the loss of ammunition seized, a whole train of ammunition from the Toledo Arsenal was diverted to Asturias by forging the papers, and stored there.

The story that the arms used in this rising came from Russia was an invention of Right-wing propagandists intended for foreign consumption. As the newspapers of every shade of opinion reported at the time, all the arms seized by the police had the stamp of the Toledo Arms Factory on them.

mines were bad, they were, as workmen go in Spain, well paid. They
had won these advantages through a series of tenacious strikes which
had developed their sense of solidarity. The great majority belonged
to the U.G.T. Gijón, however, the port, and La Felguera, a large iron
foundry, belonged to the C.N.T. and rivalry between Oviedo and
Gijón, Sama and La Felguera was the normal situation down to 1931.
Then the Communists captured one of the C.N.T. syndicates and the
two older parties combined together against the intruder. This new
alliance was facilitated by the fact that the C.N.T. in Asturias was
very little under the control of the F.A.I. Peiró was their chief
influence and, but for the danger of further Communist successes, the
C.N.T. in this province would probably have joined the *Sindicatos de
Oposición*.

Thus it happened that when the *Alianza Obrera* was created under
Largo Caballero's auspices, the Asturian branch of the C.N.T. joined
it. Then the policy of the Comintern changed suddenly to suit the
exigencies of the Franco-Russian alliance, and the Communist party,
which hitherto had execrated all contact with other parties, began to
preach the necessity for united fronts. A few days before the Asturian
rising broke out their party gave its adhesion to it and the *Alianza
Obrera* became the *Frente Unico*, the prototype of the Popular Front.
For once all the Spanish working-class parties were united.

On 5 October the rising began with the storming of the police
barracks at Sama with sticks of dynamite. On the 6th the miners
began to enter Oviedo. On the 8th the Small Arms Factory at La
Trubia was captured with 30,000 rifles and many machine guns.
By the 9th the whole of Oviedo had been occupied except for the
cathedral and the Governor's palace, in which the small garrison of
about a thousand soldiers and police took refuge. Without artillery
they could not be dislodged. All the towns and villages around except
Gijón had already been occupied.

Meanwhile three columns were converging on Asturias from the
east, west and south. On the 7th a considerable force of Moorish
troops (*Regulares*) and Foreign Legionaries (*Tercio*), hastily sent for
from Morocco, disembarked safely near Gijón and was joined by the
column from the east. On the 10th they occupied Gijón. On the 12th
the main column coming from the west, under the command of
General López Ochoa, effected its junction with the Moorish troops
and legionaries of Colonel Yagüe outside Oviedo. On the following
day they entered Oviedo. Three days of severe street fighting fol-

lowed, but by the 17th the game was evidently up and Belarmino Tomás, one of the miners' leaders, met López Ochoa and arranged the surrender on the following day. His only request was that the Moorish detachments should not enter the miners' villages first. Thus ended the unequal war.

From the moment that Barcelona capitulated and the rising in Madrid fizzled out, the miners were of course doomed. Their leaders had, however, kept up their spirits with false bulletins and they fought till the last with touching optimism, in the belief that the social revolution was within their grasp. At La Felguera and in the working-class quarters at Gijón *comunismo libertario* was proclaimed with its invariable accompaniment, abolition of money and property, and lasted for a few hours. Elsewhere the movement was managed by workers' committees on which four Socialists sat with two Anarcho-Syndicalists and two Communists. In the villages rationing was instituted and bonds for food were issued to shopkeepers.

The losses were serious—altogether 3000 dead and 7000 wounded, of whom the immense majority were workmen.[1] In Oviedo the centre of the city, including the university, was destroyed. The cathedral was badly damaged and its eighth-century chapel, the Cámara Santa, containing a treasure that dated from the tenth and eleventh centuries, was blown up by a mine. The artillery fire of the soldiers and the dynamite cartridges of the miners had between them done the damage.

The impression made throughout Spain by this rising was naturally tremendous. But one effect that could scarcely have been expected was the atrocity campaign that raged through all the press of the Right. The most incredible tales were solemnly told and vouched for. The nuns in the Convent of the Colegio de las Adoratrices at Oviedo were said to have been raped: the eyes of twenty children of the police at Trubia were said to have been put out: priests, monks and children had been burnt alive: whilst the priest of Sama de Langreo was declared to have been murdered and his body hung on a hook with the notice 'Pigs' meat sold here' suspended over it. Although the most careful search by independent journalists and Radical deputies—members, that is, of the party then in power—revealed no trace of any of these horrors, and although the considerable sums raised for the twenty blinded children had to be devoted to other purposes because

---

[1] About 70,000 workers rose. Of these 40,000 belonged to the U.G.T., 20,000 to the C.N.T. and 9000 to the Communists. According to the official statistics less than three hundred of the dead belonged to the armed forces.

none of these children could be found, these and other stories continued to be repeated in the Right-wing press for months afterwards. Making every allowance for the ease with which the Spanish upper classes fly into a panic and for the fact that atrocity stories make a strong pornographic appeal, one can only suppose that a deliberate intention lay behind the refusal of the Right-wing press to examine the evidence. They wished to produce an atmosphere in which a terrible vengeance could be taken.[1]

The greater part of the fighting had been borne by the *Tercio*, or Foreign Legion, and by the Moors. It was without precedent that these troops were used in Spain. In 1931, just before the fall of the Monarchy, a regiment of the *Tercio* had been brought over from Africa on the King's express wish to put down the expected republican rising. They had broken out and committed their usual depredations and Major Franco, the famous cross-Atlantic flyer, had protested against the barbarity of their being used on Spanish soil.[2] Now it was Major Franco's brother, General Francisco Franco, who had ordered their despatch and employment. The new War Minister, Diego Hidalgo, a prominent member of the Radical Party, had a couple of days before called the future Generalísimo to the War Office.

But if the despatch of the Foreign Legion to fight the miners

---

[1] *El Sol*, the leading Liberal newspaper, made an investigation into these atrocity stories and could not find a vestige of truth in one of them. A Radical deputy, Señora Clara Campoamor, who in 1937 published a book denouncing the mass shootings in Madrid, made a similar investigation with the same result. The Mother Superior of the Colegio de las Adoratrices indignantly denied that any of her nuns had been raped: they had merely, she said, been made to nurse the wounded. Other evidence by impartial and even hostile witnesses is given in *Revolución en Asturias* by Testigo Imparcial. Yet books continued to be brought out for the delectation of the middle classes in which the most fantastic and horrible atrocities were repeated without any attempt at proof. One must add, however, that exactly similar books were brought out to excite the feelings of the working classes upon the horrors supposed to be perpetrated by monks and nuns within their convent walls.

As to the real 'atrocities' of the Asturian miners, these were confined to the shooting in cold blood of about twenty persons, all men. Fourteen of these were shot at Turón and included a priest and six teachers of the Brothers of Christian Doctrine. The miners had been annoyed by the attempt of the management to introduce a new union on the Austrian Catholic model.

Several churches were burned. At La Felguera the Anarchists set fire to the church and all its images with great ceremony: at Portugalete they amused themselves by burning a museum of the Inquisition, with its display of instruments of torture. At Bembibre in Leon miners of the U.G.T. burned a church, but spared an image of the Sacred Heart because it wore a red dress. 'Red Christ,' they wrote on the pedestal, 'we will not hurt you because you are one of us.'

[2] See Note E on p. 296 at end of chapter.

shocked public opinion, what is one to say of that of the Moors? For eight hundred years the crusade against the Moors had been the central theme of Spanish history: they still continued to be the hereditary enemy—the only enemy, in fact, against which the Spanish armies ever fought. Their savagery in war was well known—only a dozen years before these same tribesmen had surrounded a Spanish army and massacred every man of them except the officers, whom they held to ransom. Yet they were now being brought to fight in Asturias, that one sacred corner of Spain where the Crescent had never flown. By this single act the Spanish Right showed that neither tradition nor religion—the two things for which they professed to stand—had any meaning for them. In the terror produced in them by the rebellion of 40,000 miners, they showed that they were ready to sacrifice all their principles.[1]

The surrender had hardly been made when the repression began. General López Ochoa, a humane man and a freemason, who had been appointed to command the expedition before General Franco took his seat at the War Office, was virtually superseded by the Minister for War.[2] The fate of the victims devolved on the Guardia Civil and the Foreign Legion. Thousands of arrests were made and the prisoners (except for those killed on the way) were brought to the Police barracks at Oviedo. Here they were taken out and shot without any trial at all in batches. Colonel Yagüe's Foreign Legionaries and Moors had already, as their custom was, shot all prisoners taken in the fighting. How many more fell in the execution squads of the Civil Guard it is impossible to say. The Spanish police are not tender-hearted and they were now avenging their comrades, who had fallen fighting because their tradition does not allow them to surrender. Various estimates have been given of the victims and all number thousands. But soon news of very much worse deeds than these began to be bruited abroad. The miners had captured large numbers of arms; many of these could not be found. It was evident that they had been hidden. To find out where, a torture squad was organized by a certain police major called Doval. All the devices of the worst German concentration camps were then resorted to. That this is not invention is shown by the investigations made separately by Fernando de los Ríos, Álvarez del Vayo and Gordón Ordás and presented to the Cortes with full particulars of names, dates and signatures. The

[1] See Note F on p. 297 at end of chapter.
[2] See Note G on p. 297 at end of chapter.

Government at first refused to believe that such things were happening, but in the end grew frightened, dismissed Doval, who had to leave the country, and set its face against further executions.[1]

Had the Ceda been in control of the Government at this moment, it is easy to see what would have happened. But they were not. Even Gil Robles was still out in the cold. A silent struggle therefore began between the Ceda on one side, and the President and the Radicals on the other. If the Ceda could not obtain power whilst the effect of the miners' rising was still fresh in people's memories and the Left lay crushed and speechless, they would lose their opportunity. The struggle took the form of a debate over the fate of the prisoners. There were some 40,000 of these. Many of them had been arrested merely on suspicion. The charges against them had been lost and no one knew why they were there.[2] Against the great majority no evidence could be produced because no witnesses would come forward. Still the courts martial went on relentlessly, awarding the usual long sentences of imprisonment which everyone knew would never be carried out. Then, at the end of March 1935, the expected crisis came. González Peña, the Socialist deputy for Oviedo, and nineteen others of the miners' leaders had been condemned to death by court martial. Gil Robles pressed for their execution. But he failed to obtain it. Their sentences were commuted by the President on the advice of Lerroux, and the ministers belonging to the Ceda together with the Agrarians resigned from the Government. Gil Robles had been de-

[1] The tortures most in use were twisting the scrotum, burning the sexual organs, squeezing the hands and toes with pincers, breaking the knees with hammers, the 'torture chair', pretending to execute, beating in the presence of mothers, wives and sisters. Some of them left marks which could be seen long afterwards. Mrs Leah Manning in her book quotes from various reports.

[2] Apart from the discomfort and overcrowding, the political prisoners in the State prisons (those in the Asturias were under police detention) were far from having a bad time. They were allowed to walk about the prison as they pleased. Their relations and comrades brought them food and cigarettes and there was often a prison library well stocked with the works of Lenin and Marx. As the prison governors did not know whether their charges might not within a year or two be at the head of the Government, they treated them as well as they could. The prisoners in the Model Prison at Madrid had however a high idea of what was due to them. They sent in a list of demands—in every cell there must be a reading lamp, a radio and comfortable chair. Charwomen must be provided and every prisoner be allowed a daily bath. If these terms were not complied with they threatened to open hostilities and prepare *la gran huida general revolucionaria*—'a grand general revolutionary escape'.

In other words the prisoners were in high spirits and quite undeterred by the long sentences that were being imposed by the courts martial. They got through the time in reading and in political discussions and, as one would expect, came out a good deal more revolutionary than they went in.

manding either elections or that he should be allowed to form a government, and again he was foiled.

The Radicals could not however govern alone, and in April a new arrangement was come to which was more favourable to the Ceda. Gil Robles and four others of his party sat with two Agrarians and three Radicals in the Cabinet: as the Agrarians were more or less a branch of the Ceda, Gil Robles must have felt that he was very near his goal. A project for the reform of the Constitution was drawn up. It included changes in the anti-clerical clauses, a modification of the statute of regional autonomy, a repeal of the divorce laws and of the clause in the Constitution allowing the State to confiscate private property on payment of compensation. But the Government had no legal power to modify the Constitution before the end of the year and it is doubtful whether Gil Robles would any longer have been satisfied with anything short of a corporative regime. The programme was therefore mainly a piece of window-dressing.

Some positive legislation, however, was demanded by everyone. The state of misery in the country districts was greater than it had ever been within living memory. There were a million more or less continually unemployed. Wages had fallen, all the Casas del Pueblo and Sindicatos were closed and the landlords paid wages and arranged rents as they pleased. Father Gafo, one of the leaders of the Catholic Syndical movement, was pressing on Gil Robles the necessity for doing something to keep the triumphant landlords in check. A small concession, he said, would ruin the Socialist party in Castile. Gil Robles listened, but knew that his power rested on the support of the landlords. A Catholic minister of the Ceda, Jiménez Fernández, a professor at Seville University who belonged to a small group called 'popular agrarians', brought in a bill to assist the *yunteros* of Extremadura. Owning ploughing mules or oxen but no land, they were dependent for employment upon the large landlords, and these had decided to leave a considerable part of their estates unploughed. The bill was thrown out. On his invoking Canon Law in the Cortes to defend the justice of more stable leases, a Monarchist deputy called out: 'If you try to take away our land with your encyclicals, we shall become schismatics.' When in July a project of agrarian reform was at last brought forward by the Government, it was so reactionary that even Jiménez Fernández declared it would be useless. The most sensational law of this Government was, however, the Law of Restrictions, an economy measure brought in by the independent and energetic Finance Minister, Chapaprieta. The finances of the country had declined gravely from the relatively healthy state in which the Azaña Government had left them. As a first step towards introducing a budget, Chapaprieta proposed some severe cuts in the Government service. Sinecures, which had greatly increased during the Radical term of office, were once again to be abolished and employees were to be compelled to work the hours assigned to them. The law was passed, but, as one would expect, it was never put into execution.

The parties of the Right spent this summer in a state of fervid exultation. Since Oviedo the Ceda had greatly increased its membership. Gil Robles had become a miraculous figure, a führer, a master of that machiavellian policy at which the Jesuits are reputed to be such adepts and which Spaniards of the Right often regard as the highest form of statesmanship. With consummate foresight he had provoked the Reds into a premature rising which had ruined them: in the same way he would lead the Church and the landlords to triumph without incurring the dangers of a civil war. It was the tactics of the bull fight—to provoke the animal to charge and charge again until he was worn out, and then to kill him. There was a long tradition among the Spanish governing classes of how to break a revolution. Indeed such arts contained for them the whole of politics.

Meanwhile the hero was busy pouring out speech after speech. In these he exalted the virtues of prudence, patience, guile and above all tactics. Tactics was the word that would lead his followers to the summit they desired, that would enable them to place their feet upon the necks of their enemies once again. He was never tired of pointing out that all the events of the past year, through which he had made such a tortuous progress, had been foreseen and even brought about by himself. To increase his popularity with his followers he rarely spoke now without insulting and defying the other side. The Republicans, he said, were assassins—thieves and criminals of the worst type. They were the people whose hands were dyed in the blood of innocent priests and children.

'Let us now', he said, addressing a monster meeting at Valencia in June, 'raise the walls of our city and set you outside them, for you are not worthy to defile what we are fortifying.' Such was the language in which a Spanish minister, engaged on a revision of the Constitution, addressed one-half of Spain.

But the Left were now recovering from their despondency. Largo Caballero, Azaña and Companys faced their trials that summer.

Caballero and Azaña were acquitted because no evidence could be produced against them. Caballero, it seemed, had acted with great caution and during the fighting in the streets of Madrid had not left his house. Azaña had been arrested in Barcelona in a friend's flat: as is now known he had gone there to dissuade the Esquerra, with which he had great influence, from committing any rash action. Companys drew particular sympathy. Although everyone knew that he had been opposed to the rising, he took all the blame for it himself and accused no one. He was tried by the Tribunal of Constitutional Guarantees and sentenced to thirty years' imprisonment, to be served in a convict prison. The Right had certainly played their cards as badly as possible. By the mass shootings after Oviedo and by the revolting tortures employed against the prisoners, a movement of sympathy in their favour had been created all over the country. The execution of the leaders had become impossible. At the same time the squabbles of the Radicals and the Ceda, the incessant shufflings of the ministers and the incapacity of any of them to produce any legislation whatever had disgusted that large mass of the people whose allegiance was not committed either to one side or the other. The Ceda, which had virtually held power all summer, had given a pitiful exhibition of its weakness and intransigence. Gil Robles' political manœuvres had not impressed anyone except his own followers. The result was a sudden and violent revival of popularity for the Left. Azaña, who had reorganized the Left Republican groups in a new party, *Izquierda Republicana*, held a monster meeting at Comillas, outside Madrid. It was the largest political meeting ever held in Spain—four hundred thousand people from all over the country attended—and it was a triumphant success.

Among the working classes the enthusiasm and expectation were even greater. The rebellion in Asturias, which from a military point of view had been such a fiasco, had, thanks to the stupidity of the Right, been turned into an enormous moral and political success. The entire proletariat and peasantry of Spain had been thrilled by the miners' heroism and roused to indignation by the vengeance taken against them. The Anarchists had been especially affected. They were jealous of the success of the despised Socialists and ashamed of the small part they had played in it themselves.

But the one fact about the Asturias rising that impressed itself on everyone was this: the miners had gained their rapid success because the three working-class parties had united and fought side by side.

U.H.P., Unite Proletarian Brothers, had been their watchword. From now on there rose from the ranks of the C.N.T. and the U.G.T. an insistent demand that the leaders should scrap their petty jealousies and stand side by side to make the revolution. It was this feeling that before the end of the year would create the Popular Front.

This return of the Left to activity had not passed unnoticed by Gil Robles. Although he expected before the end of the year to obtain power by political means, he did not neglect other precautions. Very significantly he had demanded and obtained from Lerroux the Ministry of War. With General Franco as his right-hand man he was reorganizing the Army and eliminating all officers whom he thought might have Left tendencies. It was at this time that those concrete trenches were dug on the Sierra Guadarrama overlooking Madrid that proved so useful to General Mola's levies in the Civil War. Gil Robles showed himself especially anxious to have the control of the Civil Guard transferred from the Home Office to the War Office, so that all the armed forces in the country should be in his hands. To this both Lerroux and the President of the Republic objected, but in the new Government formed in September he was able to replace the Home Secretary, Manuel Portela Valladares, a man of the Left Centre, by another more amenable to his purposes.

The new Government was led by Chapaprieta, the independent who had been Finance Minister in the summer. The object it set itself was the passage of a budget. But, whilst it held on its uneasy career, an event occurred which destroyed the Ceda-Radical coalition once and for all. This was the *straperlo* (or *estraperlo*) scandal. Several of the Radical ministers were proved to have taken bribes from a Dutch adventurer who wished, against the law, to set up gambling saloons in several Spanish cities. Lerroux's adopted son was involved, as well as Ricardo Samper, who a few months before had been Prime Minister, and it was evident that Lerroux himself must have known of it. Another scandal relating to embezzlements from the Colonial Treasury came to light at the same moment.

The truth is that the Radicals were a survival from the old parties of the Monarchy. The only party in Republican Spain to have no political ideals, all they wanted was that the country should jog along quietly. Lerroux personally had a shady history. These scandals showed that, in the critical and dangerous times through which Spain was passing, a group of ministers and deputies were calmly engaged in lining their own nests—or perhaps one should say, paying their gambling debts. Spanish opinion, outside a small class of political adventurers, is intensely sensitive to such things, and the Radical party lost all credit in the country. The majority of the ministers resigned.[1] But the actual event that brought the whole Government down was different. Chapaprieta at last had his budget ready. Great economies had been agreed to, the Civil Service had had its salaries cut by 10 to 15 per cent, all new expense on education had been abolished—but the Prime Minister ventured to impose a small tax on the landowners. Death duties were to be raised from 1 to $3\frac{1}{2}$ per cent. The Government split over this—the Ceda, on the insistence of the landlords, refusing to hear of it. It was December 1935.

Gil Robles' moment seemed at last to have arrived. The Radicals had destroyed themselves. Surely the President would now entrust his party with the task of forming a Government. The plan was this— once in power and having consolidated their position, they would pass a bill requesting the President to dissolve the Chamber and hold elections on the question of the reform of the Constitution. The President would have no option but to do so and the election would come at the moment chosen by themselves. Alcalá Zamora as a sincere Catholic also desired a reform of the Constitution, but the conversations he had held the previous summer with Gil Robles had convinced him that the latter wished to do away with parliamentary government altogether and substitute for it a corporative state on the Austrian model. He had also a personal grievance: Gil Robles, far from being the consummate diplomat he imagined himself to be, had made the mistake of treating the President with hauteur. Alcalá Zamora had secretly determined that he would never give him complete power. In his opinion the most urgent thing was to build up again a Centre party to take the place of the Radicals. He therefore handed the reins of government to Portela Valladares, the leader of a small independent group, on the understanding that, as soon as he had organized his forces sufficiently, there would be an appeal to the polls. He forgot that the election law did not favour the success of central parties, but on the contrary accentuated the normal swing of the pendulum from one side to another. Violently assailed both by the Right and the Left (Gil Robles' fury against the President now knew no bounds) Portela Valladares found it impossible to maintain a

[1] One reason for the frequent reshufflings of the Government during this Cortes was that anyone who had been a minister received a pension of 10,000 pesetas for life. During the space of two years thirty-eight different members of the Radical Party qualified for this pension.

majority in the Cortes and the President was therefore obliged to sign the order for its dissolution. The polling day was fixed for 16 February 1936.

FURTHER NOTES ON CHAPTER XII

A (p. 272). The Anarcho-Syndicalists accused the Socialists of *enchufismo*, which one might translate as the art of getting cushy jobs. Andrade, one of the leaders of the Left Marxists, has written a whole book upon it. But when one gets down to facts one sees that the U.G.T. was organized much like any other European trade union. The salaries were small compared to those paid in England and the number of officials not excessive—there was one to every thousand members. The Anarchists of course thought it a scandal that any salaries should be paid at all.

As regards union funds, these were large for a poor country like Spain and the fear of wasting them helped to keep strikes down to a minimum. It was considered to be another scandal that so little was paid out for the assistance of prisoners. In the Anarchist ranks the prisoners came first: they were regarded by them in the same light as were the martyrs in the Early Christian Church and a tremendous propaganda and agitation was built up around them.

When the Republic came in, the rapid expansion of the Socialist movement created new posts which there were not sufficient trained men to fill. Some Socialist leaders therefore adopted the practice of taking on several posts at once, with of course the corresponding pay. This certainly led to scandals: there were cases of well-known Socialists receiving as much as £1000 a year—a very high salary in Spain. Such things gave point to the Anarchists' campaign against voting in 1933. 'The Cortes', ran one of their posters, 'is a basket of rotten apples. If we send our deputies there, they will become rotten too.'

On the other hand the Socialists could point to the fact that very large sums passed through the hands of the C.N.T. and F.A.I. and that, incredible though it may seem, it was against their principles to keep accounts. Old-fashioned Anarchists regarded money as the source of all evil and abolished it whenever, in some village insurrection or other, they proclaimed *comunismo libertario*, and the others were too high-minded to insist on the usual safeguards. Besides it was felt that as a large part of the money raised went into buying arms, the less trace of it there was the better. But this system was open to abuse and in fact had often been abused. During the disturbed years that preceded the Dictatorship in Barcelona, membership of the C.N.T. and subscription to its funds had frequently been enforced at the point of the revolver and professional *pistoleros* had found the setting up of a new syndicate to be a profitable line of business.

B (p. 273). The official statistics of the U.G.T. are as follows:

	Syndicates	Affiliated workers
Dec. 1930	1734	277,011
Dec. 1931	4041	958,451
June 1932	5107	1,041,539

The last figures (for 1932) exclude 1091 syndicates which had not answered the questionnaire in time. Workers who were not affiliated to a syndicate, but who followed the movement, were also numerous. For example, in the Rio Tinto mining district, out of 8000 workmen, 4200 belonged to the U.G.T. and about 600 to the C.N.T. The remaining unorganized workers mostly followed the U.G.T. (G. and J. Picard-Moch, *op. cit.* p. 280).

As to the numbers of the C.N.T., in November 1934 Miguel Maura in a speech in the Cortes gave the statistics collected by the Dirección General de Seguridad—apparently during the previous year. They were:

U.G.T.	1,444,474 affiliated members
C.N.T.	1,577,547 ,, ,,

But the absurd exaggeration of the Communists' adherents (given as 133,236) shows that these police figures cannot be relied on.

The distribution by trades of the Socialists and Anarcho-Syndicalists is well seen in the case of Valencia. Here the dock workers, fishermen and more than half the builders and metal workers belonged to the C.N.T. The U.G.T. had all the shop employees and typographers and half the builders. It also shared with the Catholic Associations the peasants and workers on the land: the C.N.T. had none of these.

C (p. 274). The history of the small Left Marxist group in Catalonia is somewhat confusing. At the end of 1931 Nin and Maurín left the Communist party to found the Left Communist party. This new group split after the 1933 elections on the question of co-operating with the Socialists. Maurín with the great majority (in Catalonia they numbered some 25,000) who desired that co-operation founded the *Bloque Obrero y Campesino*, a loose confederation with a small subscription and little discipline, and the *Federación Comunista Ibérica*, a nucleus of 3000 militants with a stricter discipline.

It is amusing to note that their eagerness to initiate Popular Front tactics nine months before Stalin gave the word led to their being furiously attacked in the official Communist press as fascists and traitors. The remainder of the Left Communist party, numbering only some 5000, but containing most of the intellectuals— Nin, Gorkín, Andrade and so on—remained outside the *Alianza Obrera* until October 1934, when, like the Communist party, they joined it a few days before the rising.

Then in February 1936 the two branches of the old Left Communists reunited to form the P.O.U.M. Oddly enough all the members of this rigidly Marxist group syndicated with the C.N.T. and not with the U.G.T. The U.G.T. in Catalonia was too reformist.

D (p. 275). *Agrarismo*, by the Vizconde de Eza, 1936, p. 155. The British Embassy Reports, quoting the statistics issued monthly by the Ministry of Labour, give the figure of 220,000 wholly unemployed in agriculture in March 1934. In industry the figure was 180,000. But one has to remember that in Spain large numbers of the unemployed do not consider it worth while registering with the Labour bureaus. In agriculture too the immense extension of hunger and misery among landless labourers was caused by partial unemployment. No record exists of those who worked only fifty, a hundred or a hundred and fifty days in the year. There can be no doubt whatever that in agricultural districts unemployment increased steadily from 1932 to the outbreak of the Civil War. An olive crisis in 1929, due to a collapse of the foreign market, helped to bring down the Dictatorship and the bumper wheat crop of 1932 led to a fall of prices that ruined the small farmer.

E (p. 287). Nicolo Pascazio, an Italian fascist journalist, who was present in Spain at this time (i.e. in 1931), thus describes the behaviour of the *Tercio*: 'The intrusion of legionaries of every race under the sun upon the Spanish soil has provoked strong disapproval in the Army and has made a far from agreeable impression upon the public. At Aspe, near Alicante, they sacked houses, violated women and assassinated their husbands' (*La Rivoluzione di Spagna*, 1933, p. 99).

Major Ramón Franco, in an interview with André Germain, spoke of how deeply this violation of Spanish soil had shocked him. (*La Révolution Espagnole*, 1931.)

It may be remembered that the famous Kirke's Lambs of English history, who showed such savagery in liquidating Monmouth's rising, had, like these legionaries, learned their brutal methods in warfare against the Moors at Tangiers. Indeed one of the reasons for the British evacuation of Tangiers in 1684 had been the objection of Parliament to the maintenance of a garrison which was 'a hotbed of popery' and might be used by the King to subdue the nation. But for this Foreign Legion the Civil War of 1936 could never have taken place.

F (p. 288). The following anecdote will show in what way the Moors were till recently regarded in Spain. At the conclusion of the Moorish War of 1893–1895 the Sultan sent an ambassador to Madrid to conclude terms of peace. Meeting a Moor in the street not far from the Royal Palace, a certain General Fuentes was so indignant that a Moslem should venture to enter the capital of Spain that he struck him on the face. To make up for this there had to be a public apology and the ambassador was sent back in state to Tangiers on the cruiser *Reina Regente*. A somewhat doubtful honour, since on its return journey the cruiser, which was unaccustomed to leaving port, heeled over and sank with all hands. (Manuel Ciges Aparicio, *España bajo la Dinastía de los Borbones*, p. 337.)

Sr. Alfred Mendizábal, a witness by no means friendly to the miners since he is both a professor of law and a Catholic, but who was present in Oviedo at the time, describes the conduct of the *Tercio* and Moorish troops in these words: 'After hard fighting they conquered the insurgent zones by the most brutal violence and without any respect for the laws of war. Prisoners were executed, many without trial, from the first day of the pacification and in numbers out of all proportion to those of the victims fallen in battle' (*The Martyrdom of Spain*, 1937, p. 216).

It is surprising that Professor Allison Peers, in the long account of the Asturias rising which he gives in *The Spanish Tragedy*, should have forgotten to mention either the Moors or the Foreign Legion.

G (p. 288). The cruel predicaments offered by Spanish history are shown by the fact that General López Ochoa was shot by the Republicans during the Civil War for his responsibility for the repression at Oviedo, whilst General Batet, who had so successfully put down the Barcelona coup and had even been decorated for it, was shot by General Mola in January 1937 for refusing to join the Glorious Movement. Such was the reward of two soldiers who, in their different ways, remained true to their oath of allegiance.

Chapter XIII

THE POPULAR FRONT

España ha cansado á la historia. EMILIO CASTELAR.

The elections resulted in a victory, by a narrow margin, for the Popular Front. The Right (in which must now be included the Catalan Lliga) gained 3,997,000 votes, the Popular Front 4,700,000 and the Centre 449,000. To these must be added the Basque Nationalists, with 130,000 votes; this party, though Catholic and Conservative, was to give its adherence to the Popular Front just before the outbreak of the Civil War. But these figures were not reflected in the Cortes. In accordance with the electoral law of 1932 the Popular Front obtained 267 deputies and the Right only 132. The form of suffrage which in the previous election had favoured the Right now accentuated the swing of the balance towards the Left. It gave the Popular Front an overwhelming majority.

The first thing to notice about these elections is the great drop in the Centre vote. The Radicals, who had put up few candidates, were annihilated. Their temporizing policy, ending in the scandals of the *straperlo* and the Colonial Office, had disgusted their own followers who, alarmed by the Oviedo rising, voted mostly for the Right. The principal group in the Centre block was a new party formed by Manuel Portela Valladares, the leader of the Government which was responsible for the holding of the elections. He had not had time to build up a new party out of the ruin of the Radicals. After attempting at first to fight alone, he had been forced to realize the disadvantages which the electoral law gave to a minority party and in many provinces, at least, had made an electoral pact with the Right. This assisted them by giving them the police 'protection' which only a Government can give.[1]

It will be seen that for the first time the parties of the Right and of the Left were fighting on approximately equal terms: each, that is, had formed a combination which took full advantage of the electoral

---

[1] Portela Valladares went to unusual lengths in changing the Provincial Governors and municipalities before the election: this no doubt was intended as a step towards 'making' the elections in the old way, but the state of feeling in the country prevented it. The collapse of the Centre and Right Centre may be judged from the fact that neither Lerroux, Cambó, Melquíades Álvarez nor Martínez de Velasco (leader of the Agrarian Party) obtained seats.

law. The Ceda had at first had some difficulty in forming a league
which should include the Monarchists, who were disgusted by their
temporizing tactics, but this did not prevent them from organizing a
propaganda campaign on an unprecedented scale. Monster posters
displaying Gil Robles' uninspiring features decorated the Castilian
towns. The captions under them had a Fascist ring. 'Gil Robles
demands from the people the Ministry of War and all the power.'
'All power for the leader.' 'The leaders are never wrong.' His election
speeches were of extraordinary violence and consisted mainly of insults to his opponents. Only the vaguest electoral promises were given,
but most of his supporters understood that his victory would mean
the end of parliamentary government and the setting up of an authoritarian regime. During the past year they had become convinced that
they would never get the Spain they wanted under a freely elected
Cortes. Yet it should be noted that, in spite of failures in the Basque
provinces and in Galicia, where the Popular Front programme
promised statutes of autonomy, the Right polled considerably more
votes than it had done in 1933: its much smaller representation in the
Cortes was due to the fact that it was now a minority party.

As to the Popular Front, there is no means of knowing what votes
were cast for the various parties that made it up. The numbers of
deputies returned merely reflect the agreement made between them
before the election. Thus the Socialists were awarded 89 deputies, the
Republican Left (Azaña's party) 84 and the Republican Union
(Martínez Barrio's group which had seceded two years before from
the Radicals) 37. The Communists got 16. Most certainly both they
and the two Republican parties gained by this arrangement. What
turned the balance was the Anarcho-Syndicalists' vote. Although
neither the F.A.I. nor the C.N.T. nor even the Sindicatos de Oposición were represented in the Popular Front, the immense majority of
their members voted for it.[1] The reason they gave for this was that
some 30,000 workmen, many of them belonging to the C.N.T., were
in prison. Others were refugees in France: countless more had lost
their jobs for political reasons. The 1936 election, one may say, was
won by the Popular Front because it promised an amnesty. It did not
need any other propaganda.[2]

It might be thought then that the result of these polls showed with

---

[1] Ángel Pestaña, breaking with all Anarcho-Syndicalist traditions, was elected on
a Popular Front ticket as Syndicalist deputy for Valencia.
[2] See Note A on p. 314 at end of chapter.

fair accuracy the real strength of the Right and the Left at this critical
moment. Unfortunately the question of compulsion and vote-buying
complicates the matter. Although in most places the elections were
orderly, the Right could fairly claim that in working-class districts
many of their more timid supporters did not dare to vote. But what of
the pressure of caciques and landlords in the country districts? In the
villages round Granada, for example, where both parties were strong,
the police prevented anyone not wearing a collar from approaching
the polling booths. This was no doubt an extreme case, but all over
Spain, wherever the *Casas del Pueblo* were feebly organized, peasants
and workmen were voting according to the orders of the local estate
agent in order not to lose their jobs. The prolonged spell of bad
weather that winter, by increasing the amount of seasonal unemployment, had given the landlords a strong handle and they made it clear
that only those voting for the Right would be given work. To cite but
one example, Dr Borkenau, during the tour of investigation which he
made six weeks after the outbreak of the Civil War, found that the
villagers of Alía, a remote pueblo on the borders of Toledo and
Extremadura, were in a state of wild enthusiasm for the Socialist
cause.[1] Yet at the previous elections, under pressure of the landlord's
agent, they had all voted for the Right. Obviously hundreds of other
villages had behaved in the same way.

The victory of the Popular Front produced the greatest expectations
among the working-class supporters of the Left and a corresponding
consternation in the Right and Centre. Whatever the leaders of the
Ceda had expected, the rank and file of this party had been confident
that they would win. The result was at once seen to be much more
than a mere electoral victory: instead of, as they had hoped, undoing
everything that had been done since 1931, it inaugurated a new stage
in the revolutionary process.

A panic therefore followed the announcement of the election results.
Some thought that, in the state of excitement prevailing, the Socialists
and Anarchists would rise and seize arms. Others with more reason
feared a *coup d'état* from the Right. The Prime Minister, Portela
Valladares, later declared that Gil Robles and General Franco had
proposed to him a military coup before the Cortes could meet.[2] At all

---

[1] *The Spanish Cockpit*, by Franz Borkenau, p. 143.
[2] Three days after the Civil War started Portela Valladares wrote an enthusiastic
letter to Franco. Then, like so many others, he changed his mind. In the autumn of
1937 he gave his adherence to the Republic and attended the meeting of the Cortes
at Valencia. It was here that he divulged the proposals made to him by Franco and
Gil Robles.

events it was felt too unwise to prolong even by a day the life of the Government. Portela Valladares resigned without waiting for the new Cortes to assemble, and the President of the Republic called on Azaña to form a government. He at once issued a decree releasing the 15,000 or so prisoners that remained from the October rising. In many places the prisons had already been opened without the local authorities daring to oppose it.

The Popular Front pact in Spain had been an election agreement only. Prieto's original proposal that a Popular Front government should be formed had been turned down by his own party. Largo Caballero was resolved never to sit in the same cabinet with Republicans again: all that he had been ready to concede was a promise to support them in the Cortes whilst they carried out their programme. This programme was an almost ostentatiously modest one. No socialization whatever—not even that of the Bank of Spain—was included in it: its only positive feature was the pressing forward of agrarian reform. Azaña personally did everything possible to reassure moderate opinion. 'We want no dangerous innovations', he said in an interview to *Paris Soir*. 'We want peace and order. We are moderate.'

The first event of importance after the opening of the Cortes was the deposition of the President, Don Niceto Alcalá Zamora. His natural term was up at the end of the year: one might have supposed therefore that he could have been allowed to retain office till then. But the situation was felt to be too dangerous. The possibility of his throwing in his lot with the Right and organizing a *coup d'état* or attempting, with doubtful legality, to dissolve the Cortes was always there. He was besides not on speaking terms with any of the Popular Front ministers except Martínez Barrio. He was therefore declared to be guilty of having dissolved the last Cortes without necessity--an absurd charge for the Left to make, but the only one which under the Constitution could secure his dismissal. The Right, which had even stronger reasons for disliking him than the Left, abstained from voting. Thus fell Don Niceto, whose only fault was that he had behaved with the meticulous correctness of a peace-time President whilst Spain was going through a revolutionary period.

It now remained to choose his successor. To everyone's surprise Azaña allowed his name to be put forward. For if he were elected, who would take his place at the head of the Government during this critical year? The Republican parties were particularly short of men and contained no one who could even remotely be compared to him. There were various reasons for this. In the first place Azaña was no longer the man he had been. He was suffering from a great disillusionment with political life. The Republic which he had formed and on which he had set all his hopes had failed to satisfy more than a small number of Spaniards. The greater part of the Right was now definitely opposed to parliamentary government, whilst on the Left Largo Caballero had appeared as a formidable rival who was getting ready, with the support of the working-class masses, to step into his shoes. The followers of the Spanish Lenin, as he began to be called, were already prophesying for him the fate of a Kerensky. And then, by accepting the Presidency, he would be in a position to ensure that the Socialists should never be allowed to form a government alone. He would block their road to power in the same way that Alcalá Zamora had blocked that of Gil Robles. His antipathy for Largo Caballero and what he stood for being well known, his position at the head of the State would be a guarantee to all who feared revolution. He would also be a guarantee against a Fascist reaction and a rallying point for those who feared the spectre of Civil War. He was elected on 10 May by a huge majority with only five dissidents. The Right, to show that the Republic had ceased to exist for them, returned their papers blank.

The situation that spring and early summer could scarcely have looked more ominous to those (and they were still the great majority of the country) who desired peaceful solutions. Both on the Right and on the Left the leading factions were tired of half-measures and were ranging themselves under revolutionary banners. The Right kept quiet about their aims: they were organizing secretly, collecting arms, negotiating with foreign governments and keeping the country in a state of continual turmoil by their provocations and assassinations. The Falangists had not been too proud to borrow the tactics of the Anarchists and, in the matter of terrorism, to exceed them. The Socialists, on the other hand, were not arming nor planning an immediate revolution, but were preaching the necessity for a great transformation at some not far distant date. They aimed at taking over power peaceably from the Republicans, just as Gil Robles had aimed at doing from the Radicals in the previous year. The question which people asked themselves was, whether the situation in the country could disintegrate to such a point that they would be able to do so.

We have already described the division of opinion that took place in the Socialist ranks after the dissolution of the first Republican Cortes. Since the last elections it had become much deeper. Prieto, who was the leader of the moderate wing, held that if the present strikes and disorders went on the middle classes would be driven to fascism and armed rebellion. The Socialists must form a government in collaboration with the Republicans and introduce legislation which would 'make forever indestructible the power of the working classes'. By this he meant, among other things, a carefully organized and thorough agrarian reform combined with irrigation projects which would transform large areas of the country, absorb the excess of rural population and provide more work for the factories. If, he declared, the aspirations of the workers went beyond the capacity for capitalist economy, the structure would break down. Then one would merely have 'the socialization of poverty'. It was the old social democratic programme of Pablo Iglesias, but it required a security of power over many years and a peaceable, unrevolutionary atmosphere. The mass of the Socialist workers appeared to reject it. Prieto's only supporters were among the party officials, mostly older men, and the miners and iron workers of Bilbao and the Asturias, who had learned caution from their unsuccessful rising. Yet one should note that in Madrid, the stronghold of the Socialist vanguard, Besteiro, an extreme Right-wing Socialist, had obtained more votes at the February elections than Largo Caballero: if there had been a ballot in the U.G.T. on the question of whether the party should enter the Government, there is some doubt as to what the result would have been.

The leader of the other wing among the Socialists was of course Largo Caballero. His recent spell of prison had given him some leisure and he had employed it to read, apparently for the first time, at the age of sixty-seven, the works of Marx and Lenin. Then, as he said, 'of a sudden I saw things as they are'. The not very heroic part which he had played in the rising of 1934 and the complete failure of the operations which he had directed had done little to diminish his popularity. The Socialist masses needed a leader and Caballero with his striking personality, his fifty years of work in the party machine and his strict personal integrity (no one could forget that Prieto had become a comparatively rich man) was the only person cut out to play the part. Then, a few months before the election, the Communists took him up and an article appeared in *Pravda* hailing him as the Spanish Lenin. At once, all over the world, Socialists began to feel that a new star had risen in Spain.

The months of April, May and June saw then the decline of Azaña, the man of the 'bourgeois Republic', and the rise of Largo Caballero, the man who stood for a New Spain. In the Socialist party itself the feud between the Prietistas, who wished to collaborate with the Republicans, and the Caballeristas, who wished to supplant them, grew more and more bitter. On a propaganda tour through the country which Prieto made that summer with González Peña and Belarmino Tomás, they were received by the Socialist Youth with shouts and insults and in Cuenca and Ecija they barely got away with their lives. Yet Peña and Tomás were the heroes of the Oviedo rising who had been condemned to death by the military tribunals and had narrowly escaped the firing squad. Whilst this was going on the Falangists in Seville were mobbing and beating up the leaders of the Ceda. It was becoming a practice in Spanish politics to reserve the bitterest attacks, not for the open enemy, but for the groups regarded as lukewarm.

At the same time great efforts were being made by the Socialists who followed Caballero to secure an understanding with the Anarcho-Syndicalists. Caballero himself visited Saragossa, where they were holding a congress, and addressed a large meeting. But his efforts did not lead to any definite results. The C.N.T. and the F.A.I. were observing a waiting policy, keeping up the revolutionary tempo in the country by lightning strikes and closing their ranks (the *Trentistas* rejoined the C.N.T. in May), and they did not in the least trust Caballero. They knew well enough the fate which these Left-wing Socialists reserved for them if they ever brought off their revolution. In several towns the Socialist Youth and the Libertarian Youth had begun shooting at one another.

One must ask what were Caballero's plans for acquiring power. 'To wait till the Republicans have proved their inability to solve the problems of Spain and then to take over the Government' was the official answer. But this left out of account the fact that Azaña was President of the Republic and that he would never, under any circumstances, hand over the keys of the State to the Socialists. Caballero's position was therefore that of Gil Robles in 1934. It was in fact worse, for whereas Robles could always have seized power by force had he thought it expedient, Caballero could not make his revolution against the Army and the Civil Guard. But perhaps he banked upon such a general increase of the revolutionary feeling of the people as would lead to a disintegration of the whole State? To this one must reply that the condition of Spain in 1936 was in no way similar to that of Russia in 1917 and that as fast as disintegration occurred in certain milieux, nuclei of resistance were growing up in others. There was really only one chance of Caballero's attaining power and that was that the generals should rise, that the Government should distribute arms to the people and that the people should win. Consciously or unconsciously, he and his party were gambling on there being a military insurrection.

Meanwhile they were indulging in an orgy of optimistic dreams and wish-fulfilments. A new and brighter Spain was about to rise from the ashes of the old. Socialists from all over the world flocked to Madrid and Barcelona to be present at the inauguration ceremony. Caballero's paper, *Claridad*, brilliantly edited and written, proclaimed every day the great doctrine of Marxian predestination. The cause of the people must infallibly triumph because the laws of history had decreed it. And the moment of their triumph was fast approaching. No failure was possible. Those English people who were living in Spain at this time will agree that nothing contributed so much to terrify the Spanish bourgeoisie or to prepare the atmosphere for a military rising as these daily prophecies couched in severe and restrained language. Terrible images of Russian massacres and famines flitted through their minds. The calm assurances of *Claridad* were a thousand times more alarming to them than the inflammatory phrases to which a century of demagogic journalism had accustomed them.

But was the predestinarian frame of mind which the dialectic of materialism bestows upon its devotees altogether of advantage to them? It seems more likely that, in this case at least, it only served to put them to sleep and to blind them to the dangers of their situation. Spaniards are by nature all too prone to an easy optimism which encourages them in their desire to put off immediate action. They are inveterate procrastinators with sudden bouts of impatience. For whilst the Socialists were drawing up plans of what they would do when power fell into their hands, the Army officers and the Falangists were, almost publicly, preparing a rising and negotiating with Mussolini and Hitler for assistance. *Mucho sabe el rato, más el gato* is a Spanish proverb. The rat knows a lot, but the cat knows more. Had Caballero been indeed the Spanish Lenin, that is, a man with a sure instinct for power, he would have made terms with Azaña and allowed the Socialists to enter the Government. It was because he was at heart a social democrat playing at revolution that he did not.

The year 1936 saw the rise of two parties, the Communists and the Falangists, from very small beginnings to positions of power and influence in the country. First the Communists. During the Dictatorship of Primo de Rivera they had been so insignificant that the Government had not even troubled to suppress their newspaper, *Mundo Obrero*. When the Republic came in the Comintern was going through a period of Left extremism and the Communist party violently opposed all compromise with the bourgeois state. It was left to the dissident Communist group (the 'Trotskyists') under Maurín to advocate a democratic republic and a popular front. But in the summer of 1934 after the signing of the Franco-Russian pact, the policy of the Comintern changed and Communists took part in the Asturian rising. This greatly put up their stock. One of the heroines of the rising, Dolores Ibarruri, usually known as 'La Pasionaria', belonged to their party and their skilful propaganda took full advantage of this. So influential had they become by the end of the following year that in the Popular Front agreement they were allotted a representation that gave them sixteen deputies in the new Cortes. This was at least four times the figure to which their voting strength would have entitled them.

Their numerical weakness—in March 1936 their party membership was probably no more than 3000—was their chief handicap.[1] In all their fifteen years of existence they had only been able to acquire a solid proletarian following in two places—Asturias and Seville. In both these cases they had captured syndicates from the C.N.T. during the struggles and jealousies that had attended the first appearance of the F.A.I. Their main recruiting ground was Seville and to a certain extent Cadiz and Malaga. At Seville the more militant sections of the workers, the dock hands and the café waiters, belonged to them. The situation here was one of perpetual war with the C.N.T., with small sections of the U.G.T. looking on. One should note—for the coincidence can scarcely be accidental—that Seville and Cadiz were also the birthplaces of the Falange. Even allowing for the fact that the atmosphere of Seville, the city of *flamenco* singers and bull fighters, of taverns and brothels, was not propitious to the formation of a disciplined proletarian movement, it must be agreed that the Communist penetration had destroyed all possibility of working-class solidarity.

---

[1] They claimed to have at least 20,000 party members at the end of 1935, but nobody believed this. Or rather this figure should be taken to include all their sympathizers. In the partial biennial renovation of all municipalities in Spain in April 1932 only 26 communists were elected out of 16,031 *concejales* in all Spain. In the elections to the Cortes of 1933 they returned one deputy. General Krivitsky, who ought to know, gives the party membership as 3000 early in 1936 and 200,000 in January 1937 (*I was Stalin's Agent*, by W. G. Krivitsky, 1939). Dr Borkenau agrees with this.

The consequences of this were felt when in July General Queipo de Llano was able to capture the city—one of the key points of the Civil War—with a handful of men.[1]

During the months that followed the elections Communist policy was governed by two considerations—how to fit in with the requirements of Stalin's foreign policy and how to increase their following in Spain. As regards the first, they strongly supported the Popular Front pact and, unlike Caballero, wished to see it develop into a Popular Front government. Under a façade of revolutionary slogans they were moderate. 'Vote Communist to save Spain from Marxism' had been a Socialist joke during the elections. And after the elections they did their best to reassure the Republicans. 'We have still', said the secretary of the party in April, 'a long road to travel in their company.'

One may therefore dismiss the story that they were planning a revolution for that autumn as Fascist propaganda. A revolution would have alienated the Western Democracies whom Stalin was courting at this time. It would have put Largo Caballero and the Socialists into power. The Communist policy this spring was simply to take advantage of the revolutionary situation to increase their own influence and following. They would thus be in a position, whatever happened, to influence events.

The difficulty about this was that the Socialists and Anarcho-Syndicalists had already absorbed all the available land and factory workers and that trade-union loyalty was strong. They could not, as they had always done in the past, appeal to the more revolutionary elements among the masses because they were now less revolutionary than the trade-union leaders. Their appeal was therefore made on the grounds of their being more up to date, more European and more dynamic than the old Spanish parties. To the factory workers they pointed out that they alone had sufficient experience to lead a successful revolution. To the white-collar workers and to the professional classes they explained that they were the men of destiny, fated to rule the country after the Revolution and that anyone who threw in his lot with them would be sure of a good job. And behind them stood Russia. All that spring the shops were flooded with translations of Lenin, novels by obscure Russian authors and descriptions of life in the great Socialist paradise. Russia provided not only material assistance but a *mystique* which gave its votaries an energy and a devotion unequalled by any other party in Spain.

[1] See Note B on p. 315 at end of chapter.

Their tactics were of the kind first employed by the Jesuits in the seventeenth century and since carried to greater lengths by Hitler. There was the powerful propaganda machine, always well supplied with money. There were organizations such as *Socorro Rojo Internacional* which provided food and money for political prisoners whatever their party affiliations. There was the flattery of intellectuals and of anyone who might be useful to them. But their most characteristic method of adding to their forces was by infiltration into or union with other working-class organizations. They set themselves to capture in this way the Socialist trade union, the U.G.T. In Largo Caballero's lieutenant, Álvarez del Vayo, they found a sympathizer, who, without leaving the Socialist ranks, was ready to act in their interests. On his return from a visit to Russia in April he was able to persuade Caballero to agree to the merging of the Socialist Youth with the (much less numerous) Communist Youth. A few days after the Civil War broke out, the whole body under their Socialist secretary, Carillo Jr., went over to the Communist party. At one swoop Caballero lost some 200,000 of his most active supporters.

The rise to power of the Falange was very similar to that of the Communists, though more rapid and more successful. José Antonio Primo de Rivera, a son of the dictator, founded the *Falange Española*, or Spanish Phalanx, in 1932 and two years later merged it with other small Fascist groups as the *Juntas de Ofensiva Nacional-Sindicalista* or J.O.N.S. Down to the elections of February 1936 it remained a very small party which obstinately refused to grow. The Church gave it the cold shoulder and the landlords disliked it both for its 'socialism' and for its violence. It sent only one deputy, José Antonio himself, to the Cortes. More than half its numbers were university students and only one in five of the rest came from the working classes. These were usually disgruntled Anarcho-Syndicalists. Its chief breeding ground was Lower Andalusia, Seville, Jerez and Cadiz, where the *señorito* element was strong, and of course Madrid. In the Conservative and Carlist north and in industrial Catalonia it made no progress.

Its leader, José Antonio, as he is always called, was a young Andalusian of charm and imagination. Even his enemies, the Socialists, could not help having a certain liking for him. In café discussions he used to insist that he was closer to them than to the Conservatives. He blamed the Republic for not socializing the banks and the railways and for being afraid to tackle agrarian reform with energy. Where he disagreed with the Marxists was in their doctrine of class war, which he maintained was corrosive and dissolvent. His own solution was a 'harmony of classes and professions in one destiny'.

'If one starts off from a conception of unity of destiny, all errors are eliminated and one sees that the Patria is not territory, nor race, but only unity of destiny oriented towards its universal north.'

Translated into concrete terms, as the Falangist programme of twenty-six points makes clear, this was simply orthodox fascism, the only point on which it differed from the Italian model being in its attitude to the Church. A Falangist might at the bottom of his mind be an atheist, but he must hold the Catholic Church in respect because it represented the historic ideal for which Spain had always stood. In return for protection the State would control the Church and impose on it 'a new Catholicity'. In other words a Nationalist and Falangist character. Finally the 'destiny' which they held out for Spain was the creation of an empire, by which they meant the acquisition of further territory in Morocco and, though this was not said openly, the annexation of Portugal. Beyond this lay a still more dazzling prize, the spiritual and political suzerainty over South America. Hitler's approaching victory would make that possible.[1]

Fascism is, as is well known, the reply of the 'classes of order' to revolutionary situations which fail to come to a climax. Tired of the perpetual tug-of-war between opposing forces and of the resulting anarchy, the middle classes take refuge themselves in an extreme solution. But so long as there was any chance of Gil Robles coming peacefully into power the Spanish bourgeoisie turned its back on the Falangists. In the elections of February 1936 they polled only 5000 votes in Madrid out of a total Right-wing vote of 180,000. It was the Popular Front victory that made them. The Right had gone to the polls expecting to win and full of faith in their leader, and their defeat caused immense disillusion. Just as the Socialists had done in 1934, they abandoned all idea of peaceful and legal solutions and put their hopes in violent ones. Gil Robles found himself almost deserted. His followers either flocked into the ranks of the Monarchists, whose new leader, Calvo Sotelo, was known to favour a military rising, or they enrolled in the Falange. Among the latter were the *Joventudes Acción Popular*, Gil Robles' Youth Organization, which under its secretary Ramón Serrano Suñer joined the Falange in April, just as a few months later the Socialist Youth joined the Communists.

---

[1] See Note C on p. 315 at end of chapter.

From now onwards the Falange began to grow rapidly. As it was secretly organized in groups of three and no lists of its members were kept, it is impossible even to guess at its numbers. But it was especially strong in Andalusia. Its adherents belonged to just the same type of person, were drawn from the same class and province, as those who had flocked into the Masonic lodges in 1814–1820 and made the Liberal Revolution. Only the tactics were different. The Falangists believed in terrorism and violence. They treated the parties of the Right—the Ceda, for example—with insults, rotten eggs, broken windows and furniture: the Left were beaten up or murdered. In Madrid they had their cars of *escuadristas*, armed with machine guns, which went round the streets shooting down whoever opposed them. Judges who condemned Fascists to prison, journalists who attacked them in the press, were assassinated. But their particular vendetta was with the Socialists. All this spring and summer the streets of Madrid and of other Spanish cities were enlivened by shooting affrays between the two parties. The object of this was, of course, to increase the sense of disorder and confusion to the point when the 'passive classes' would rebel and call out for some change of government. One should note, however, that it was not the *señoritos* of the Falange who exposed their lives in these encounters. They employed professional *pistoleros* taken, or sometimes merely borrowed, from the C.N.T. Falangists often professed a certain sympathy for Anarcho-Syndicalism and claimed that several sections of the C.N.T. had a private understanding with them. It may be so, for if their ideologies were different, they had the same enemies and the same belief in violence.

The Falange was not the only party that was working for a counter-revolution in Spain. There was also a group of Army officers, the Carlists or Traditionalists, and the Monarchists. The officers belonged to the *Unión Militar Española* or U.M.E., a secret society which had taken the place of the old *Juntas de Defensa*. They were in touch with the Italian and German Governments and their preparations for a rising were already far advanced. The Traditionalists, under the leadership of Fal Conde, were drilling their militia in the mountains of Navarre. Owing to the practical extinction of Don Carlos' line (the last survivor, Don Alfonso Carlos, was now eighty-seven) and to the repudiation by the Monarchists of parliamentary government, the gulf that had once separated these two parties no longer existed.

The Monarchists had never ceased plotting since the Republic came in. Their chief, Antonio Goicoechea, had been in secret re-

lations with the Italian Government since 1933.[1] Not long after this
Calvo Sotelo, who had been Finance Minister during the Dictatorship, returned from exile and took over the general leadership of all
the forces of the Right which favoured a rebellion. He was a man of
active and violent temperament with a blind hatred for the Republic
and all its ways, and he was the only figure of political ability on the
extreme Right. The fact that he was not personally committed to a
restoration of the Monarchy made him a valuable link between Army
officers, Falangists and Conservative politicians. In the Cortes his
policy was directed to preventing any reconciliation between the
Ceda and the Republicans and to drawing as much of the Right as
possible over to the side of insurrection and civil war. Like the rest of
his party he was especially violent in his denunciation of the Generalidad and of the Basque and Galician autonomists. *Prefiero una
España roja a una España rota* he declared: 'I prefer a red Spain to a
broken Spain.' Yet it was a broken Spain which the rising organized
by him was to create.[2]

The spring and early summer of 1936 were passed in a continual
effervescence. Only in the north and in Catalonia was there comparative quiet. Lightning strikes by the C.N.T., Socialist and
Falangist shooting affrays in Madrid, occasional church burnings by
the F.A.I., were the rule elsewhere. In some places the Communists
and the C.N.T. had come to blows, and in other places it was the two
wings of the Socialist party. In almost every trade there were strikes
in which the workers demanded higher wages, shorter hours and
large sums in compensation for wages earned whilst they were in
prison. Businesses were everywhere losing money, capital was leaving
the country and a financial crash seemed imminent. Spain had often
before stood periods of anarchy far worse than this and had survived,
but her industrial organization was now more complex, so that the
effects were more deeply felt. The primitive psychology of the country,
with its periodic need of kicking over the traces, no longer fitted in
with modern conditions.

[1] In a speech made at San Sebastian, on 22 November 1937, Goicoechea stated
that as early as March 1934 he and other Right-wing parties had 'planned a *coup
d'état* backed by an insurrection of the Army, or, if necessary for the safety of Spain,
even a Civil War'. Previous to this, he declared, he and other Spanish Monarchists
had made a visit to Italy in order to secure 'not only the support of the Italian
Government but also of the Fascist Party in the event of the outbreak of civil war in
Spain' (reported in *Manchester Guardian*, 4 December 1937).

According to a document in Goicoechea's handwriting found later in the Spanish
Foreign Office and published, the help asked for was promised by the Italian
Government. The date of his visit to Italy is here given as March 1933.

[2] See Note D on p. 315 at end of chapter.

In the country districts the small peasants and landless labourers were clamouring for land. There had been a very rainy winter and the unemployment and hunger were more severe than ever. But the Government, which seemed to have learned nothing from past experience, was in no hurry to listen to them. Then in Extremadura the *yunteros* (owners of teams of ploughing mules or oxen) marched out and forcibly occupied stretches of untilled land belonging to the large estates. The Government was obliged to give way and sent down surveyors to legalize the situation. Then a few weeks later, at Yeste, a remote mountain village near the source of the Guadalquivir, occurred one of those battles between the peasants and the Civil Guard of which the annals of the Spanish countryside provide so many examples. Twenty-three villagers were killed and over a hundred wounded. After this the peasants began in many places to plough the land on the large estates and the Government did not dare to interfere with them.

These disturbances, not very important in themselves, provided a background for the drama that was going on behind the scenes. Everyone knew that the Army officers were preparing a rising and that a civil war was imminent. The Government was as weak as possible. Attacked daily in the Cortes by Calvo Sotelo, undermined by its allies the Socialists and harassed by the guerrilla tactics of the Anarchists and Falangists, it could do nothing but utter threats. The Prime Minister, Casares Quiroga, was a consumptive: he reacted to the danger of the situation by an optimism that would have to be considered insane if it were not a symptom of his disease. He took certain precautions: his bed was set up in his office and he slept and ate there: the garrisons were reduced to skeleton strength by sending most of the conscripts home. But his espionage system worked badly. General Queipo de Llano, for example, retained his confidence until the last moment—and, in spite of what had happened at Oviedo, he seems never to have foreseen the possibility of an invasion by the Foreign Legion and the Moorish troops. Had he done so, the key points of Seville and Cadiz could have been secured, tanks and modern aeroplanes could have been bought abroad and negotiations could have been opened with the Berber tribes of the Riff for granting them autonomy.

One must ask what Azaña was doing. He was anxious to form a government of National Union under Prieto which would allay the fears of the middle classes and would yet be strong enough to deal with any emergency. For this the consent of the Socialist party was necessary. Caballero saw that it was not given. He was pressed to form a temporary dictatorship to save the country from the dangers of civil war. The Mexican President Juárez, whom Azaña in many ways resembled, had been driven to this step. But again the opposition of the Socialists and of the Anarcho-Syndicalists made this unfeasible. In the face of these difficulties a kind of apathy seems to have come over him. He decided to play for time, in the hopes that the excitement of the working classes would subside and that the middle classes would be reassured by his repeated promises that no further advance towards Socialism would be tolerated. The error in this calculation was that the Army would certainly strike before things went much farther.

It is impossible not to place a certain share of the responsibility for what followed upon Largo Caballero. On the first of May he had led a huge procession through the streets of Madrid. More than 10,000 workmen, saluting with clenched fist, bore banners declaring: 'We want a Workers' Government. Long live the Red Army!' Intoxicated by the enthusiasm of his followers, entirely confident of success, he shut his eyes to the dangers of the course he was following. He was sixty-eight, an age when one must hurry if one wishes to see the Promised Land. Proud and stubborn by nature, not easily influenced by others, he had spent all his life within the framework of a trade union. He therefore lacked a wide political vision. Otherwise he would have seen that the disposition of forces in Europe—to consider nothing else—would never tolerate the creation of a dictatorship of the working classes in Spain. As it was, the only effect of the Socialist policy of undermining the Republican Government instead of collaborating with it was to render it too weak, morally and materially, to resist the blow that was about to fall upon it. It was the mistake which the *exaltados* had made in 1823 and the last Cortes of the First Republic in 1874. One may call it the national mistake, Spanish history being made up in large part of the ruins left by such acts of inebriation and over-confidence.

In June, when a military coup was believed to be imminent, Largo Caballero had an interview with Azaña. Pointing out the dangers of the situation, he asked that arms should be distributed to the workers. That would of course have meant handing over the power in the country to them. One wonders what answer Caballero can have expected. During the past few months he had been doing everything he could to make Azaña's acceptance of such advice impossible. The President of the Republic was as much pledged to prevent a dictatorship of the Left as of the Right. What reason was there for thinking that he would prove even feebler than Kerensky?

On 13 July the news became known that Calvo Sotelo had been assassinated by some Socialists disguised as police as a reprisal for the murder of one of their companions by the Falangists a few days before. He was, with General Sanjurjo and José Primo de Rivera, the most outstanding figure among the men who were about to raise the standard of revolt. The date of the rising was brought forward a little to take advantage of the shock produced by his death. On the 16th the Army in the Spanish Zone in Morocco rose and occupied Ceuta and Melilla. The Government still had time to act: the Army could have been dissolved and arms distributed to the people. Instead a proclamation was issued to the effect that 'nobody, absolutely nobody in Spain had taken part in this absurd plot'. That afternoon the officers of the garrisons rose in almost every Spanish city. It was not until midnight on Saturday the 18th that the order for distributing arms to the people was issued. Even then some of the Civil Governors refused to obey it.

FURTHER NOTES ON CHAPTER XIII

A (p. 299). Whilst no exact comparison of the number of votes cast in the 1933 and 1936 elections is possible, one may make the following observations:

In 1933 the Right vote totalled 3,385,000. In 1936 it totalled 3,996,931. But in 1933 the Basque Nationalists (130,000) voted for the Right whilst the Catalan Lliga (400,000) did not. What one may call the hard core of the Right was therefore 3,250,000 in 1933 and 3,600,000 in 1936. Its increase was chiefly due to the fact that the Oviedo rising had scared the middle classes. Most of the Radicals, who in 1933 had already begun to form local election agreements with the Right, now voted for them. On the other hand in some districts, such as Galicia, where the Right had formerly done well, it suffered a heavy defeat. This was because the Galicians had been promised a Statute of Autonomy.

As for the Centre, it only obtained 449,320 votes in 1936, whereas in 1933 one party alone, the Radicals, had obtained 700,000 in those constituencies in which they had fought alone. The total Centre vote in Spain, if one includes in it the Catalan Lliga, can be estimated as at least a million and a half.

The vote of the Left Republicans (including the Catalan Esquerra) and of the Socialists cannot be distinguished in 1936. In 1933 the former obtained 640,000 and the latter 1,722,000 where they fought separately. To these figures must be added the votes cast in those constituencies where they combined—a figure which might amount to three-quarters of a million. The membership of the U.G.T. in 1936 was about a million and a half and many workers who were not affiliated sympathized with it. Taking into account the female vote one might have expected the Socialists to poll nearly three millions. That they did not do so was partly due to the pressure of landlords in the country districts, but more, I think, to a reaction against the adventurous policy of the Socialist leaders.

In 1933 just over eight millions voted: in 1936 the poll was just over nine and a quarter. (The total number of voters in Spain was 12½ millions.) The increase of a million and a quarter can to a great extent be put down to the Anarchist vote.

B (p. 307). This situation first came to a head at the 1931 elections to the Cortes. The Radical Socialist candidates were Comandante Franco (brother of the general) and Balbontín. They were supported by the C.N.T. and its well-known Anarchist leader Dr Vallina. The Communist candidate was Adame, late secretary-general of the C.N.T., who a few months before had gone over to them after a quarrel with Vallina, taking with him the dock workers' and café waiters' unions. Thus two branches of the C.N.T. were fighting one another under other names and on the forbidden territory of the ballot box. This is not so surprising as one might think, for, of all the many parties in Spain, none showed a more intense and consistent interest in the game of politics than the Anarcho-Syndicalists. It had the same fascination for them that scandal has for spinsters. Incidentally Adame lost, getting only 5211 votes.

C (p. 309). The Falange has a kind of shadowy ancestor in Spanish history in the *Comuneros* or *Hijos de Padilla* who appeared in 1832, in the middle of the Liberal Revolution, in antagonism to the Masonic lodges and to their international, humanitarian character. They stressed the national side of the Revolution, called their lodges *torres* (towers) instead of *talleres* (workshops) and used a ceremonial derived from Spanish chivalry. As the Revolution was suppressed by a French army in the following year, their history was short-lived.

D (p. 311). This was one of the matters on which the Army and indeed all the Right felt strongly. Fal Conde, the Traditionalist leader, addressing the Catholic Union at Bilbao in February, had welcomed to his party 'all without exception, but not the Basque Nationalists. With them there can be no union.'

Thus the historic Carlist and Liberal roles were reversed: in the past the Carlists had been the defenders of the provincial *fueros*, and the Liberals, then associated with the Army, had been the upholders, or rather the creators, of Castilian centralism. The feud between the two leading Basque provinces—traditionalist Navarre and autonomist Guipúzcoa—which broke out this summer, led to one of the bitterest repressions of the Civil War.

Chapter XIV

EPILOGUE—THE CIVIL WAR

El vencido vencido y el vencedor perdido.

The history of the Civil War lies outside the scope of this book. Those two and a half years require a volume to themselves and in any case the time when an objective survey of them can be made has not yet arrived. However, to round off the events described in the last chapter, some observations upon the political developments brought about by the war seem to be called for.

The Military Junta and group of Right-wing politicians which rose against the Government in July expected to occupy the whole of Spain, except Barcelona and perhaps Madrid, within a few days. They had at their disposal the greater part of the armed forces of the country—the Civil Guard, the Foreign Legion, a division of Moorish troops from Spanish Morocco, four-fifths of the infantry and artillery officers and a certain number of regiments recruited in the north and therefore reliable. They had also the Carlist levies or *requetés* which had for some time been drilling secretly and the promise of Italian and German tanks and aeroplanes if necessary. Against these the Government had only the Republican Assault Guards and a small and badly armed air force. But the plans of the rebels were defeated by the tremendous courage and enthusiasm with which the people rose to defend themselves and by the loyalty of the naval ratings who at a critical moment deprived them of the command of the sea. Each side being then left in control of one half of Spain, a civil war became inevitable.

In the political sphere things did not follow quite the lines that might have been expected. After a period of violent social revolution the 'Reds' or 'Loyalists', as the parties supporting the Republic were variously called, began to move more and more to the Right, taking as their slogans 'Respect the property of the peasant', 'No interference with the small business man' and 'No socialization of industry'. At the same time they took up a national and patriotic attitude of defence of their country against the foreign invader. What seemed strange was that the chief advocates of this policy were the numerically feeble but actually very influential Communist party. The 'Nationalists', on the other hand, fell more and more deeply under German and Italian influence and, to give their own side something of a mass following, were obliged to hand over the greater part of the political power to the Falangists and to come out with a social programme that, if it were meant seriously, was more drastic than anything ever proposed by the Republic.

The result of the war was decided by the question of foreign help. Whilst there was little to choose between the political and military competence or incompetence of either side, almost all the mass support, the enthusiasm, the spirit of sacrifice was upon the Republican. The Falangists proved to be a mere Iron Guard, undisciplined and irresponsible: for a crusading spirit Franco could count only on the Carlists. But German and Italian help was enormously more powerful than Russia's, and for this reason the Franco forces won.

To consider first the Republican side, the rising of the masses that led to the defeat of the insurrection in Madrid and Barcelona carried everything before it. The Government, which to impress foreign opinion was composed of Liberal Republicans, led by Giral, a friend of Azaña's, lost all authority. The workers, through their party and trade-union organizations, became the real rulers of the country and the organizers of the war. This, one might say, was the Soviet phase of the Spanish Revolution. And yet it would, I think, be a mistake to regard it as a purely revolutionary phenomenon in the sense usually given to that word. On several occasions before in Spanish history the people have pushed aside their weak and clumsy governments and taken the conduct of affairs into their own hands. This happened notably in the war against Napoleon, when the local juntas, composed of men of all classes and opinions, but mainly of priests and artisans, were the really effective organs of resistance. That war had also been to a certain extent a civil war just as the 1936 war could likewise be regarded as a war of defence against a foreign aggressor.[1] It was thus natural that the juntas of 1808 should be reborn in the Workers' Committees of July–October 1936.

---

[1] The Dos de Mayo was followed in Madrid and all over Spain by attacks on the Governors, nobles and other members of the ruling classes who were thought to favour the French. A tract was printed with this title: 'List of the houses assaulted by *el Gran Pueblo Libertador* against the rascals who have ruined the nation of Spain, which is worthy of better governors and of honourable kings and of other things.' The church of San Juan de Dios in Madrid was burned by the mob because it contained a portrait of Godoy.

The function of these committees was triple. Through the militia, which they armed and organized, they carried on the war against the enemy forces. By terrorism they destroyed or intimidated the enemy in their midst. And they took over the factories and estates abandoned by their owners and in one way or another continued to work them. Where the committees were Anarchist, there was a definite policy of collectivization which was intended to prepare the way for a thorough-going social revolution.

A great deal has been written about the Red terror of the first two months. It was at bottom a spontaneous movement, corresponding to the necessities of a revolutionary war, where the enemy within may be as dangerous as the enemy outside, and in spite of many protests both public and private, it accorded for a time with both the policy and the sentiments of all the Popular Front parties except the Republicans. The victims were selected by Public Safety committees of the three working-class parties and the executions carried out by small groups of men, who took them from their homes in the dead hours of the night in motor lorries. In addition to these *paseos*, as they were called, there were the mass executions of Fascist suspects taken by mobs from the prisons in reprisal either for an air raid or for some report of Fascist atrocities. But the most typical acts of mass terrorism were those carried out by the Durruti column in Aragon or by the militia in Madrid on their way to the front. In their irresponsibility and ruth-lessness as well as in their psychological implications they were the counterpart of the September Massacres of 1792. The troops on the way to the war cleared the way for the revolution and made certain that there would be no surrender by the Government and no fifth-columnist rising behind their backs.

The reaction against this revolutionary terror began after 25 August, when the news of the massacre of Badajoz reached Madrid. The indignation caused by this was so great that a general massacre of the political prisoners was only averted by the setting up by the Govern-ment of a Revolutionary Tribunal. Although this tribunal only tried cases of open treason or rebellion, it provided a safety-valve for public opinion, which from this time began to condemn irregular executions. During September and October these fell off considerably, those that still took place being attributed to the 'uncontrollables', who usually turned out to be terrorist groups hailing from the ranks of the Anarcho-Syndicalists. They were gradually put down, the F.A.I. itself lending a hand, so that by the end of the year unauthorized 'eliminations' had practically ceased to occur. Their place was taken by a police terror which, under the increasing Communist influence, was exerted almost as much against the dissident members of the Left as against Fascist suspects. Although this caused comparatively few deaths—for whilst the prisons were filled, executions were rare—it did harm to the morale of the Republican side because it increased the atmosphere of mutual hatred and suspicion between the different anti-Fascist parties who should have been co-operating loyally.

The other important function of the committees was the taking over of the estates, factories and businesses whose owners had disappeared or who were regarded as reactionaries—that is to say, of almost all estates or factories of any size. There was no general rule as to how this was to be done: the procedure was left to the discretion of the local committees and even when a Popular Front Government headed by Largo Caballero came in on 4 September, it abstained from laying down any general policy In U.G.T. territory estates were, as a rule, simply taken over by the municipality or by the officials of the Institute for Agrarian Reform and the workers continued to be paid at the same rate as before. Often they were not even confiscated but merely administered in the name of the owner, who continued to live in his own house and to receive a small monthly payment. Only in those areas where the Land Workers' Federation of the U.G.T. had established collectives before the war was any real collectivization carried out: here the example spread, the small peasants and agricultural labourers took matters into their own hands and the Agrarian Reform officials then stepped in to legalize the position. This happened all over New Castile and La Mancha. What one never saw (except occasionally in Catalonia and Aragon) was the sharing out of the land among the peasants. That was because both the U.G T. and the C.N.T set their faces against it.

The Anarchists, on the other hand, had a policy of collectivizing both land and industry which they did their utmost to push through. For them it was the first and most important step in social revolution. Far from regarding the war as a mere war of defence against Fascism, they saw in it the opportunity for which they had long been waiting to create a new type of society and were perfectly aware that, if they failed to set up a *fait accompli* in the first days of the struggle, they would be overcome by events and defeated. Moreover, they believed that the war could only be waged successfully if it was accompanied by social revolution behind the lines. The side which could show most self-sacrifice and devotion to a cause would win, but if the workers were to rise to the heights demanded of them they must be given some tangible proof that a new and better world lay in store for them. If that were done, the military discipline and organization, about which the Communists made such a song, would follow automatically. They therefore, in the first days of the war, collectivized all the large and many of the small industries in Catalonia, urged the peasants to collectivize not only the estates which had been expropriated but their own plots as well and in some cases, though this was contrary to their declared policy, used force to compel them to do so. There was often a connection between the 'elimination' of factory owners and land-owners and these expropriations.

Were these collectives successful? There is a certain amount of evidence to show that they often were so to a surprising degree. Even so sceptical an observer as Dr Borkenau was struck by the effective-ness of some of the large industrial collectives in Barcelona, whilst most people are in agreement that those set up in the Catalan country-side worked admirably. One should remember, however, that here the Anarchists had the skill and good business sense of the Catalan people to build upon: we have seen how admirably the collectives set up in Catalonia before the war by the Co-operative Societies were managed. Outside this province Anarchist collectivization had less success, and in Andalusia was either taken up reluctantly by the C.N.T. and allowed to languish, or else pushed through by a small number of militants in a fanatical spirit. But then in Andalusia there was an almost complete lack of the necessary farm machinery.[1]

The later history of the large industrial collectives in Barcelona was

---

[1] The first act of the villagers in revolutionary villages was to abolish money, the symbol of all evil in their eyes. So deeply rooted was this in the Spanish conscience that sometimes U.G.T. villages did it as well. All the money in the village was 'voluntarily' collected and handed to the *comité*. Wages were paid in coupons: they were paid not according to the amount of work done, but according to the size of the family. The unemployed received the same amount as the employed. The *comités* judged, performed marriages, buried the dead, directed the collective and fixed salaries. They alone could buy or sell. Their members were changed often so that everyone should take their turn at sitting on them. There was a distinct leaning to asceticism and a disapproval of alcohol and other 'luxuries'. Whilst there is no doubt that in many villages this system worked well and was popular, it is also true that wherever property was much divided, the peasants were against collectivization and no revolution took place. Another reason in its favour was that the peasants were often afraid of dividing up the large estates themselves in case the rebels won. Collectivization would, they thought, prevent victimization.

In the towns there was of course no question of abolishing money: one must distinguish between urban anarchism which was an affair of modern syndicalist theories and village anarchism which was really a revival of old collectivist impulses.

not as happy as their beginning. The Central Government, and especially the Communist and Socialist members of it, desired to bring them under the direct control of the State: they therefore failed to provide them with the credit required for buying raw materials: as soon as the supply of raw cotton was exhausted the mills stopped working. Other industries that had been turned over to making munitions fared somewhat better, but even they were harassed by the new bureaucratic organs of the Ministry of Supply and had a perpetual struggle to maintain their independent existence. In spite of the support given them by the Catalan Generalidad, the end of the war saw them well on their way to being absorbed by the State. In other words, the fact that the Anarchists had not been strong enough in the first days of the war to abolish the State altogether inevitably meant the at least partial failure of their experiment of free collectivization. No government, least of all one that had come to birth in times of stress, could afford to allow the heavy industries of the country to rule themselves, even though it is true that the special position of Catalonia *vis-à-vis* Madrid allowed room for compromise.[1]

Meanwhile the insurgent forces, with the aid of a certain number of Italian tanks and aircraft, had advanced to the suburbs of Madrid and had there been held. On this side too there was a terror. It seems probable that the generals and politicians who had started the revolt had intended to employ a certain amount of terrorism, both to intimidate their opponents and to get rid of the more troublesome leaders of the working-class parties on the other side. But thanks to the failure of the *coup d'état* and to the eruption of the Falangist and Carlist militias, with their previously prepared lists of victims, the scale

---

[1] In a published correspondence between Companys and Prieto (*De Companys a Indalecio Prieto, Barcelona,* 1939) Companys declares that the workers in the arms factories in Barcelona had been working 56 hours and more each week and that no cases of sabotage or indiscipline had taken place. But since June 1937 production had fallen off owing to the prodigious bureaucratization set up by the Government. An army of inspectors and directors owing their appointment to political reasons (i.e. to their being members of the Communist party or of its dependants the P.S.U.C.) had descended on the factories, and the workers had been demoralized. Things had grown worse since the factories had been militarized by the decree of August 1938, i.e. after Prieto had left the Government.

Obviously the old triangle of Castile—Catalonia—and the Castilian party in Catalonia was reasserting itself in a new form. Just as Madrid had used the Radicals against the Lliga, and the Sindicato Libre against the C.N.T., and the Lliga against the Esquerra, and the F.A.I. and the Esquerra against one another, so the Valencia Government was now using the P.S.U.C. against the C.N.T.—but not (here is the difference) because the Catalan workers were giving trouble, but because the Communists wished to weaken them before destroying them.

on which these executions took place exceeded all precedent. Andalusia, where the supporters of Franco were a tiny minority and where the military commander, General Queipo de Llano, was a pathological figure recalling the Conde de España of the First Carlist War, was drenched in blood. The famous massacre of Badajoz was merely the culminating act of a ritual that had already been performed in every town and village in the South-West of Spain.[1]

The North did not escape either: here everyone connected with the Republican movement, unless he sought safety by entering the Falange, was ruthlessly shot—middle-class freemasons and liberals suffering as frequently as Communists and Socialists. Tales of atrocities on the other side were used to work up the hysteria. Unfortunately the Church, which might have played a moderating part, applauded all these horrors. Everything that its enemies had said about it seemed to come true when it was seen that scarcely a voice was raised on behalf of Christian charity to stem this flood of executions. How many died before the firing squads of one side and the other it is impossible to say, but both the accounts of eyewitnesses, who emphasize the prolonged and systematic nature of the purge, and the evidence of history, which shows that White Terrors are usually worse than Red ones, lead us to suppose that for every person executed in Government territory, two or three were executed in the Rebel zone during the first six months of the war. For Andalusia the proportion was probably even higher.

The method of execution was similar to that employed on the Republican side: the victims were taken from their houses in lorries driven by young Falangists and Carlists and shot before dawn outside the town. Nothing is so like a rising of Spanish revolutionaries, says Galdós, as a rising of Spanish reactionaries. But executions without trial also took place every day in the prisons and this continued for a considerable while, in fact until the prisons had several times been filled and emptied. If this did not happen to any great extent on the other side that was because the Republican authorities were strongly opposed to terrorism and put an end to it as soon as they were able,

---

[1] I have in my possession a file of cuttings from Portuguese newspapers which abundantly proves this. Every rebel column in Andalusia was accompanied by Portuguese journalists and their accounts made no effort to conceal the terrible savagery with which the war was being conducted. But when the reports of the culminating massacre at Badajoz got into the English and American press, the Portuguese censorship was tightened up and no more stories of this sort were published.

whereas on the Nationalist side the terrorists themselves—that is the Falangists and the Carlists—were in charge of the Home Front and remained so throughout the war. And though as time passed the position became regularized and the number of executions diminished, they broke out again whenever a new tract of territory was conquered. The will to exterminate their enemies never failed the Nationalists.[1]

The decisive factor in the war was, as has already been said, the foreign intervention. Germany and Italy supported the rebel generals from the start. Stalin only decided to intervene in September. It should be noted that there was a difference in their method of doing so. The Fascist dictators dealt directly with Franco and his generals and sent their war materials to them. Although they encouraged the Falangists, they never made them their representatives in Spain, but (as they have since done in Roumania) kept them as a lever for putting pressure on the Government. Stalin, on the other hand, saw to it that the arms which he supplied and the International Brigades which he organized should secure the predominance of the Communist party. They alone could be trusted to look after the Soviet interests.

The policy they were to follow in Spain is contained in a letter

---

[1] The great difference in the degree of humanity shown on the two sides may be judged from the fact that from the beginning of the Civil War to the end not a single protest appeared on the Nationalist radio or in its press or in the books published at Burgos and Salamanca against the atrocities that were taking place. The British Fascists and neo-Catholics visiting Franco denied that there had been any irregular executions, yet in private conversations the Falangists never concealed what was happening and during the first months bodies were exposed to view everywhere.

On the Government side, on the other hand, the radio almost every night during August and September contained strong denunciations of the executions that were going on: not only the Government authorities but members of the U.G.T., F.A.I. and Communist party spoke in this sense. Posters were put up ordering the summary execution of the gangsters who were engaged in these murders. How far the rank and file of the U.G.T., C.N.T. and F.A.I. supported these protests may be doubted: for a time humane opinion among them was silenced and it was dangerous for anyone to protest too much, but the leaders of the Left parties often protected people who were in danger and facilitated their escape. The Communists, who to annoy the Anarchists had adopted a protective attitude towards the Church, took on themselves the task of sheltering priests. And there were some outstanding exceptions to the general acceptance of the terror. Juan Peiró, the well-known Anarchist and editor of *Llibertat*, denounced almost every day in his paper the crimes of certain elements of the C.N.T. He did not stint his language. They were 'modern vampires', 'fascists in a latent state', 'thieves and assassins, guilty of a crime against the honour of revolutionaries'. His paper was not suppressed and he was not interfered with. Can one imagine even a tenth part of this outspokenness being possible on Franco's side? See *Perill a la reraguardia*, Mataró, 1936, where these articles are reprinted. Peiró is not only a courageous man but an intelligent one and his opinions on collectivization are worth reading.

written by Stalin to Largo Caballero and dated 21 September 1936.[1] He recommends him to attract the peasants by settling the agrarian question and by reducing taxes: to attract the middle and lower bourgeoisie by avoiding confiscations and furthering their trade: to draw the Republican leaders into the Government and to appease foreign capital. It must be agreed that from the point of view of winning the war this was extremely sensible advice. The support of the lower-middle classes, who had been deeply antagonized by Anarchist expropriations, was essential. The peasants, too, needed to be reassured and satisfied. And it was urgent to gain the sympathy of the Democracies, who had been shocked by the confiscations and the terrorism: as many at that time foresaw, the war would be won or lost in London. But it was also the policy most suited to the Communists themselves. Russia is a totalitarian regime ruled by a bureaucracy: the frame of mind of its leaders, who have come through the most terrible upheaval in history, is cynical and opportunist: the whole fabric of the state is dogmatic and authoritarian. To expect such men to lead a social revolution in a country like Spain, where the wildest idealism is combined with great independence of character, was out of the question. The Russians could, it is true, command plenty of idealism among their foreign admirers, but they could only harness it to the creation of a cast-iron bureaucratic state, where everyone thinks alike and obeys the orders of the chief above him.

Another factor which helped them to take up their position on the Right rather than on the Left of the Popular Front movement was their deep-seated dislike of all Spanish revolutionaries. No one is so severe on the excesses of the young as the reformed rake. The Communists felt an intense hatred and suspicion of what they called Trotskyism—a word which could be made to cover not merely the pedantic Marxism of the P.O.U.M., but the moral and revolutionary enthusiasm of the Anarcho-Syndicalists and of the Left-wing Socialists. As we have said, they were probably quite correct in their appreciation of the fact that the day of such parties is over. Even in Spain successful revolutions cannot be brought off by the proletariat and the landless labourers without the help of a large section of the more energetic and technically-minded middle classes. But such an admission involved a contradiction of everything they had ever said or done in the past. When they accused the Anarchists of 'Left-wing

---

[1] Published in the *New York Times* on 4 June 1939, with a photostat copy of the original.

infantilism', they forgot that only two years before they themselves had been the most extreme and intractable of all the revolutionary parties in the country.

As we have seen, the Russian intervention gave the Communists a position they could never otherwise have held in Spain. The power to distribute the arms that arrived put the Anarchists in their hands: the C.N.T. accepted the situation and broke the most sacred of its taboos by entering the Government. The prestige of the International Brigade, which had saved Madrid, was another factor. Besides, it seemed that Stalin had been correct in thinking that a moderate Left-wing-line was the one which held most future for his party. Unable to draw to themselves the manual workers, who remained firmly fixed in their unions, the Communists found themselves the refuge for all those who had suffered from the excesses of the Revolution or who feared where it might lead them. Well-to-do Catholic orange-growers in Valencia, peasants in Catalonia, small shopkeepers and business men, Army officers and Government officials enrolled in their ranks. Far better than the feeble Republicans, they could give protection or offer a career to anyone who joined them. In Catalonia, where fear and hatred of the Anarchists were very strong, they were able to combine the various Socialist groups (all of which were very much to the Right and contained few manual labourers) into a single party, the P.S.U.C., which was affiliated to the Comintern. Many of the Esquerra and of the *Rabassaires* joined it. There were even a few rich manufacturers who obtained important posts in it. Thus one had a strange and novel situation: on the one side stood the huge compact proletariat of Barcelona with its long revolutionary tradition, and on the other the white-collar workers and *petite bourgeoisie* of the city, organized and armed by the Communist party against it.

But it would be a mistake to suppose that the Communists owed their success merely to their control of Russian arms and to their dislike of social revolution. They had a dynamism that no other party in Government Spain possessed. In their discipline, their organizing capacity, their drive and above all in their understanding of modern military and political technique, they represented something new in Spanish history. With missionary fervour (for most of the young were on their side) they set out to conquer the traditional inertia and passivity of the Spanish bureaucratic temperament. And it must be admitted that with the relatively feeble means at their disposal they were very successful. They built up out of nothing a splendid army and staff which won victories against great odds. Their propaganda was skilful. For two years they were the heart and soul of the anti-Fascist resistance. Compared to the Falangists on the other side who never became more than a feeble imitation of their German and Italian masters, adept at mopping up the rearguard but chary of risking their lives in battle, their superiority is evident. But it was not easy for other parties to get on with them. They suffered from a fixed belief in their own superior knowledge and capacity. They were incapable of rational discussion. From every pore they exuded a rigid totalitarian spirit. Their appetite for power was insatiable and they were completely unscrupulous. To them winning the war meant winning it for the Communist party and they were always ready to sacrifice military advantage to prevent a rival party on their own side from strengthening its position. Thus they kept the Aragon front without arms to spite the Anarchists and prevented a very promising offensive in Extremadura from taking place because the credit for its success might have gone to Caballero.

But perhaps more serious than this in the long run was their lack of moral or political integrity. Their opportunism extended to everything. They seemed to have no programme that could not be reversed if its reversal promised them any advantage, and they were just as ready to use the middle classes against the proletariat as the proletariat against the middle classes. No doubt the historical method of Marxism lends itself to a good deal of stretching: even so their going back on so many of their past tenets recalled the feats of those Jesuit missionaries of the seventeenth century who, the better to convert the Chinese, suppressed the story of the Crucifixion. It is a comparison that is worth insisting on. By their devotion to an institution rather than to an ideal, to a foreign Pope rather than to a national community, they were following the road laid down by Loyola. And their impact on Spain was very similar. Just as the Jesuits from the time of Laínez had turned their backs on the great ascetic and mystical movements of their age and had worked to reduce everything to a dead level of obedience and devotion, so the Communists showed that the great release of feeling that accompanies revolution was distasteful to them. They frowned on all its impulses, both its cruel and its creative ones, and applied a severely practical spirit to its various manifestations. Thus not only did they disapprove of even such rural and industrial collectives as had arisen spontaneously and flood the country with police who, like the Russian Ogpu, acted on the orders of their party rather than of the Ministry of the Interior, but by their perpetual intrigues and machinations they helped to sap the fibre of the various Popular Front parties and of the two great trade unions, on whose firmness and solidarity the morale of the Republican forces depended.

The damping effect of this attitude of theirs can hardly be exaggerated. Revolutionary movements are movements which spring up from below and are fed by new desires and impulses. Spain is precisely a land where such impulses are perpetually bubbling up from underground. In no country of Europe is there so much spontaneity of speech or action, so much dislike of restraint and regimentation. Yet in the middle of a war of liberation the Communists appeared in the guise of professionals and experts and, not content with harmonizing such impulses and directing them towards the end of military victory, they proceeded as far as they could to suppress them altogether. For their whole nature and history made them distrust the local and spontaneous and put their faith in order, discipline and bureaucratic uniformity. It may be replied that this ordering impulse corresponds to an inevitable phase in all revolutions. But the Communists were not, as Robespierre or Bonaparte had been, the product of a native upheaval, but were a ready-made importation from outside, acting under the orders and in the interests of a foreign dictator. That is why, rapid as their progress was and responsive as is the Spanish soil to every kind of bureaucratic weed, they never succeeded in rooting themselves in it firmly.

We may now, in the light of these remarks, examine briefly the history of the war on the Republican side. By the end of 1936 the period of committees and of social revolution was over and the well-armed P.S.U.C. confronted the C.N.T. in Catalonia. A state of tension at once developed. The first crisis came in January. Communist pressure on the Government had become very great and for a moment it was thought that a *coup d'état* was imminent and that the International Brigade would march on Valencia. But there was a combination of all the other parties against them and they gave way. However, the question of an increase in their power was not the only issue involved. They stood for a regular army instead of party militias, for an end to all revolutionary measures, for greater centralization and a more efficient conduct of the war. In this Prieto and Negrín with about half the Socialists and all the Republicans supported them. On the other side stood the Prime Minister, Largo Caballero, with his group of Left-wing Socialists and the whole of the C.N.T. Matters came to a head in May when, as the result of a somewhat obscure incident, there were three days of street fighting in Barcelona. The bulk of the C.N.T. and F.A.I. remained at home and their leaders did everything possible to put an end to the conflict, but this did not prevent the Communist ministers from demanding the complete suppression of the trade unions in Catalonia and the placing of the Catalan press and police under what would in practice have amounted to Communist control. Caballero refused this request, but Communist insistence procured the suppression of the P.O.U.M., who as 'Trotskyist' heretics were especially hated by Stalin, and the prosecution of its leaders on the absurd charges of treason and collaboration with the enemy. Although the other members of the Government prevented any executions, Andrés Nin, the principal figure in the P.O.U.M. (Maurín was in Franco's hands), was secretly murdered in prison. Whilst few shed any tears over the fate of these Left-wing Marxists, the Anarchists could not help seeing that they were next on the list.[1]

The Barcelona affair led to the fall of Largo Caballero's government. Prieto as Defence Minister and Negrín as Finance Minister succeeded him with a cabinet that contained both Communists and Republicans, but no Anarcho-Syndicalists. But Prieto, brought in by the Communists, soon found himself in serious conflict with them. The main ground of their disagreement lay in the question of the control of the Army. The Communists were endeavouring to increase their hold on all the armed forces and Prieto was determined to resist this. Everyone remembered that after the last civil war the Army had ruled the country for a whole generation. If the Communists could win over the troops to their side, they would be able, as the Liberals had done in 1840, to impose a military dictatorship. The means by which they hoped to effect this was through the appointment of Communist officers and by propaganda carried on by the political commissars. Through the good offices of Álvarez del Vayo, who had been in charge of the War Commissariat since October 1936, almost all the commissars were Communists, but the allotment was only one per battalion and they now insisted that there should be one to every company. La Pasionaria is said to have threatened Prieto that if this

---

[1] The Russian press had never made any bones about this. 'So far as Catalonia is concerned', wrote *Pravda* on 17 December 1936, 'the cleaning up of the Trotskyist and Anarcho-Syndicalist elements has already begun, and it will be carried out with the same energy as in the U.S.S.R.'

were not done there would be no more help from Russia. Thanks to the Anglo-French policy of non-intervention they had in the Russian arms a lever which never failed, for whatever private inclinations the Socialist and Republican ministers might have, they knew that a breach with Stalin would mean the rapid loss of the war. Prieto bowed to the inevitable and left the Government (April 1938).[1]

After his resignation, which led to a reorganization of the cabinet, Communist influence reached its height. The Basque Minister for Justice, Irujo, and the minister from the Esquerra resigned in protest and the direction of the war centred in Negrín, del Vayo and the Communist Uribe. The Communists, in fact, were indispensable and Negrín, whose political opinions were ill-defined and who put the winning of the war above everything, was careful to maintain a close relation with them.

The last months of the struggle saw, however, a decline in their strength. Gradually during the last two years they had infiltered and penetrated, in Nazi fashion, into the various organs of the administration and of the Army till now they held many of its key positions. As we have seen, nearly all the political commissars in the Army were Communists and the Subsecretario de Propaganda, which was the Government department which directed propaganda, had also become a party organization. They controlled the Cypher Bureau and (except in Madrid) the new political police,[2] in addition to which they had of course their own police and prisons, run by the Ogpu. In the Army the best divisions were theirs. And although the rank and file of the U.G.T. (except for their Youth Organization, which had gone over to them in the first days of the war) had resisted incorporation, many of the union leaders leaned towards them. And yet in spite of all this, as soon as it became clear that Stalin was withdrawing from his Spanish adventure and would send no more arms, their influence began to diminish. In the Government the Socialists and Republicans were able to take a firmer line against them. The unsubstantial

---

[1] Actually few of the arms sent to Spain were Russian. They were bought in Europe and America by Comintern agents with gold paid in advance by the Spanish Government. When, owing to the pro-Franco sympathies of the French bankers, it became difficult to make payments in the ordinary way, the greater part of the gold reserve of the Bank of Spain, some 574 million dollars, was sent to Russia. From this time on the control of the Politburo over Valencia was greater than ever.

[2] The *Servicio de Investigación Militar* or S.I.M. It was composed mainly of the old political police, those Struldbrugs who survive all revolutions, and who had now become Communists. Its action, especially in Catalonia, was directed at least as much to suppressing the political enemies of the party as to unearthing those of the Republic. Like all the Spanish police it was extraordinarily incompetent.

nature of their power, dependent upon prestige and success, became obvious.

There is little that need be said of the political developments on Franco's side. The first six months passed without any trace of the revolutionary enthusiasm and exhilaration that was seen among the Republicans. The atmosphere at Burgos and Salamanca, as even ardent Fascist sympathizers have admitted, was heavy with suspicion and hatred.[1] The spring of 1937 saw a political crisis similar to that which occurred on the Republican side. The 'Old Shirts', as they were called, of the Falange, led by the Secretary of the Party, Manuel Hedilla, took José Antonio's social programme seriously and demanded that the Twenty-Six Points which contained it, and which had been adopted by Franco, should at once be put into execution. That alone, they said, would give the Nationalists the mass following they needed to win the war. It was a feeble reflection of the quarrel of the Left Socialists and the Communists, but Hedilla's following was small and the Franco administration felt strong enough to deal with it vigorously, especially as the Germans and Italians did not support it. Hedilla himself with his principal followers was arrested and imprisoned.

At the same time the Carlists or Traditionalists, who had recently merged with the Monarchists and the remnants of the Ceda, became restive. Franco dealt with them by a decree forcibly uniting them to the Falange and assumed himself the leadership of the new party, which was known as Falange Española Tradicionalista. At the same time he exiled their leader, Fal Conde. The death two months later of General Mola, the most intelligent of the military junta and a strong anti-Falangist, was a further blow to them, for they had always had hopes of his supplanting Franco. After this their influence, like that of their opposite number, the Anarcho-Syndicalists, declined. Both the Right and the Left wings of the Nationalists had been put in their place.

From now on the power was divided between the Army and the New Shirts, as those who had joined the movement since February 1936 were called. The latter were an amalgam of people of different kinds—Government clerks, *nouveaux riches*, second-rate intellectuals, lawyers and doctors with all that tribe of needy and ambitious people who in every country (but especially in a poor one such as Spain) join parties which have jobs to offer. The Andalusian bourgeoisie were

---

[1] See in particular Capt. Francis McCullagh, *In Franco's Spain*, 1936.

well represented and there was a strong youth movement—it will be remembered that the entire Youth Organization of the Ceda had gone over to the Falange just before the outbreak of the Civil War. A mass following was provided by ex-anarchists and socialists who had joined to save their skins—almost the same elements that on the other side made up the Communist party. There, however, the analogy ends: discipline was lax, for there was no real bond of union. They had no military feats to their credit, for the Army and the Carlists did all the fighting and the Old Shirts, who alone could have given it some cohesion, had been swamped by the new arrivals. There was not even a real führer, for Franco was merely one general among many who had come to power through an accident and who was singularly lacking in all führer-like qualities. Their own leader, José Antonio, had met his death in a Republican firing squad. Thus the Falange never succeeded in becoming a coherent Fascist party, but remained an amorphous flock of job hunters united to a disreputable but vociferous Iron Guard. But it had no rivals, for the Army, divided as it was between pro-Falangists and Monarchists, pro-Germans and those who were jealous of the foreigners, and taken up with the waging of the war, tended to withdraw from politics.

Once more, in the summer of 1938, trouble broke out in the Nationalist ranks. This time it was among the Army officers. General Yagüe made a speech in which he spoke of the Germans and Italians as beasts of prey and praised the courage of the Republican soldiers. There were mutinies in various places. Negrín then issued his Thirteen Points with a view to creating a movement favourable to reconciliation. This was the moment for the British Government to have repudiated the stupid and cynical farce of non-intervention and given the Germans a hint that further convoys of armaments would not be well looked on. Such action might well have led to an armistice. But the appeasement policy was in full swing and Mr Chamberlain saw nothing disturbing in the prospect of an Italian and German victory. Indeed he put special pressure on the French Government to close their frontier. Under these circumstances, for Russia withdrew her assistance, it is nothing less than a miracle that the Spanish Government was able to continue resisting until March 1939.

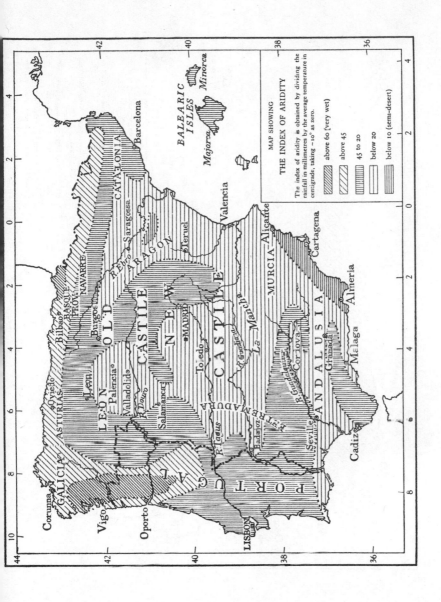

MAP SHOWING
THE INDEX OF ARIDITY

The index of aridity is obtained by dividing the
rainfall in millimetres by the average temperature in
centigrade, taking –10° as zero.

above 60 (very wet)

above 45

45 to 20

below 20

below 10 (semi-desert)

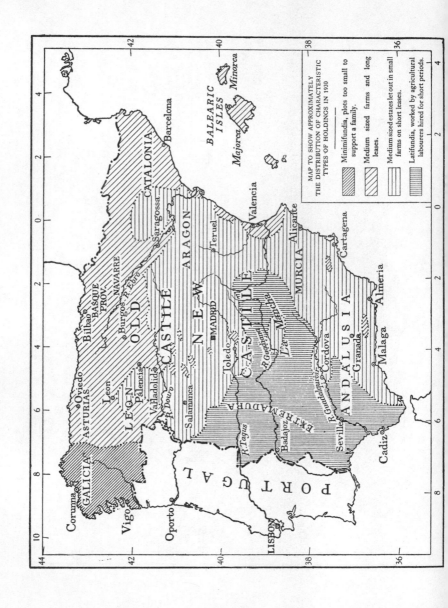

MAP TO SHOW APPROXIMATELY
THE DISTRIBUTION OF CHARACTERISTIC
TYPES OF HOLDINGS IN 1930

Minifundia, plots too small to
support a family.

Medium sized farms and long
leases.

Medium sized estates let out in small
farms on short leases.

Latifundia, worked by agricultural
labourers hired for short periods.

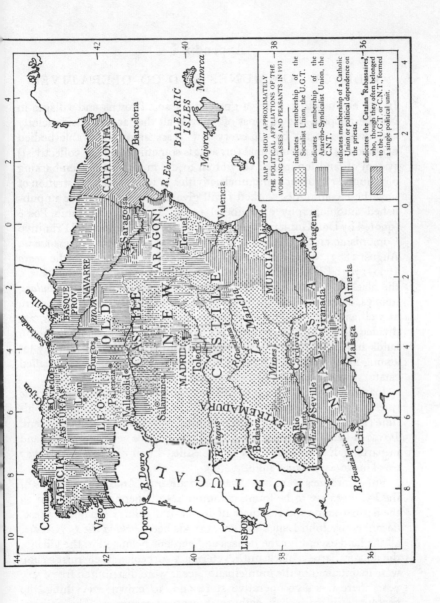

MAP TO SHOW APPROXIMATELY
THE POLITICAL AFFILIATIONS OF THE
WORKING CLASSES AND PEASANTS IN 1933

⣿⣿⣿ indicates membership of the
Socialist Union, the U.G.T.

▥▥▥ indicates membership of the
Anarcho-Syndicalist Union, the
C.N.T.

▤▤▤ indicates membership of a Catholic
Union or political dependence on
the priests.

▨▨▨ indicates the Catalan 'Rabassaires,'
who, though they often belonged
to the U.G.T. or C.N.T., formed
a single political unit.

Appendix I

VILLAGE COMMUNES AND CO-OPERATIVES

In the eighteenth century a great many small towns and villages in Northern Spain owned most of or even all the land in their vicinity and divided it up by lot every few years among the able-bodied neighbours. This communal (or, as it is sometimes called, collectivist) system of land tenure led very often to the municipalities embarking on a number of other communal activities as well. As an illustration of how these communes worked I will give an extract from the unpublished autobiography of a liberal priest, Don Juan Antonio Possé (quoted by Don Gumersindo de Azcárate in his 'Vestígios del Primitivo Comunismo en España', *Boletín de la Institución Libre de Enseñanza*, August 1883), describing the village of Llánabes in Leon in the years 1790–1793: 'The police is admirable. The surgeon, the shepherds, the blacksmith, the apothecaries' shop, the papal indulgences (*bulas*), litanies, etc. are all provided free by the municipality. Salt, seed-corn, as well as what remains over from renting the *bienes de propios*, are divided up in the village fairly and justly. All the lands are common lands and are shared out every ten years in equal portions and by lot among all the neighbours.... There is only one *mayorazgo* (entailed estate) in the village.'

Joaquín Costa, who copies this passage in his *Colectivismo Agrario* (pp. 348–9), adds that Llánabes still remained unchanged in his time (1898) and that other villages round it followed the same system. It was in fact a relic of a form of land tenure once general in Leon and in parts of Extremadura and Old Castile. Land divided in this way was known as *quiñones* (allotments).

But communes were not always agricultural. Among the valleys of the Pyrenees are to be found communities of shepherds who own all the pasture lands and run their affairs on similar lines. In one of these, described by John Langdon Davies in his book *Behind the Barricades*, all the land except for the houses and gardens belonged to the village: the doctor, barber, blacksmith, veterinary surgeon and chemist's shop were maintained by the municipality, seeds were distributed free every year, there was a co-operative store and, to crown everything, the peasants still wore their eighteenth-century costumes. The political colour of this village, whose name was Ansó, seems to have been neutral, but the priest was popular and the surrounding country was Carlist. Although Mr Langdon Davies asserts that the pasture lands belonged to a benevolent landlord, he was probably mistaken in this, for fifty years ago the pastures in this valley as in most of the other valleys of the Pyrenees were communal. Thus Ansó provides another example of a municipal co-operative grafted on to a system of communal ownership that dates from very early times, though whether this co-operative is of modern foundation or goes back like that of Llánabes to the eighteenth century or earlier, I cannot say.

These *comunidades de pasto* are not, however, confined to the Pyrenees; they exist in Cáceres and in the Asturian highlands. The village of Caso, for example, which has 15,000 inhabitants, has 20,000 head of cattle all owned collectively and no arable land at all. But one must go to Catalonia if one wishes to see the greatest extension of communal undertakings. Many of these are industrial, such as the very old one at Bagur for making nets. Others are fishing communities, and here I cannot do better than quote John Langdon Davies' description of one of these called Port de la Selva, in his book *Behind the Barricades*. His observations were made in 1936, shortly before the Civil War broke out, and he has kindly allowed me to read the little pamphlet which he brought back with him to England giving the rules of the community.

The village was run by a fishermen's co-operative. They owned the nets, the boats, the curing factory, the store house, the refrigerating plant, all the shops, the transport lorries, the olive groves and the oil refinery, the café, the theatre and the assembly rooms. They had developed the *pósito*, or municipal credit fund possessed by every village in Spain, into an insurance against death, accident and loss of boats. They coined their own money. They imposed fines for wrangling, for speaking badly of the Society, for insults, for any action opposed to morality and decorum. According to Article 6 of their rules the *diversión* of the members would consist in dances and their *expansión* in theatre and movie shows, in literary and scientific evenings and in lectures on farming and pisciculture.

Port de la Selva was in short a libertarian republic and had achieved the ideal of all those villages of Catalonia, Andalusia and even Castile which at different times during the past century have declared themselves independent and have proceeded to divide up lands and issue their own coinage. Mr Langdon Davies rather naturally assumed that it was the creation of the Anarchists. That, however, is not so. The present constitution of Port de la Selva was set up in 1929, just before the Republic came in, by the co-operative movement founded in the 1860's by the Fourierist, Fernando Garrido. This movement, which is unrevolutionary, has kept its distance both from Anarchism and from political Socialism and has succeeded in establishing in various parts of Spain productive co-operatives similar to that of Port de la Selva. What is interesting is to see how naturally these co-operatives have fitted into the Spanish scene. For Port de la Selva is one of the old fishermen's communes of Catalonia which have existed from time immemorial. Cadaqués, a few miles away, is shown by contemporary documents to have been organized in a similar manner early in the sixteenth century: other documents speak of the Port de la Selva community and its communal nets which were kept in the church. (See Costa, *Colectivismo Agrario*, pp. 579–582.) Another exactly similar fishing community at Tazones, near Villaviciosa in Asturias, is described by Professor Antonio Camacho in the *Revista Nacional de Economía.*

Here then we have a modern productive co-operative grafted on to an ancient communal organization and functioning perfectly. And what has been done at Port de la Selva in Anarchist surroundings has also been done at Ansó where the ambience is Carlist, whilst at Llánabes the co-operative organization dates from the eighteenth century and thus precedes the European co-operative movement by at least sixty years. So Llánabes provides one more example of the truth of St Augustine's remark: *Nolite foras ire, in interiore Hispaniae habitat veritas:* 'One need not look for outside influences; the source of everything Spanish lies in the interior of Spain.'

As to the origins of these agricultural and pastoral communities, it has been shown that they date back to the early Middle Ages (ninth to eleventh centuries) when the Kings and the nobles, anxious to re-populate the immense no man's land that lay between the Cantabrian Mountains and the Moslem territories, granted land to communities of liberated serfs (the so-called *familias de criación*) on easy terms. Two forms of charter were used—either a *carta puebla* (or *carta de población*, as it was also called), which was a simple contract made by the lord of the manor with the community, or else a *fuero municipal*, which carried with it certain jurisdictional and self-governing privileges that required the assent of the King. In both cases the usual custom was to give a *solar* (i.e. a house with its garden, threshing floor and barn) to each family and to hand over the land to the community, which would divide it up at fixed periods among its members. But the *villas* which received municipal charters were above everything else markets (it was for this reason that they obtained more extensive privileges) and they evolved differently from the smaller *aldeas* which had only *cartas de población*.

After the capture of Toledo in 1085 *cartas de población* ceased to be given. The new lands that were being conquered already had a Moslem population. The Military Orders and the nobles to whom the King granted estates worked them for the most part with Moorish slaves. The towns received municipal *fueros* and generous grants of land, but the Christian immigrants who settled in them formed only one element in a heterogeneous population: so far as one can tell from the occasional references in histories (for no research has been done upon the origins of the agrarian question in Southern Spain) the contact with Moorish slave labour proved demoralizing to the new settlers and the common lands were turned over to pasture and became in time the monopoly of the rich or well-to-do, who alone had herds. At any rate no trace of agricultural communes exists south of the Tagus.

As to the shepherd communities of the Pyrenees, it is uncertain whether they arose in the same way as the agricultural communities of Leon and Castile, out of the need for giving the inhabitants of the frontier districts something that was worth their while fighting for, or whether they go back to much earlier times. It is significant that several of the Celt-Iberian tribes are described by Strabo and Diodorus Siculus as having practised a precisely similar system of communal agriculture and pasturage. And there is evidence that all over Spain the villages (*vici*) kept their communal pastures intact through the Roman and Visigothic eras.

There is of course nothing very remarkable about this communal system of cultivating the land. It was once general—in Russia (the *mir*), in Germany (the *flurzwang*), in England (the open-field system). What is, however, remarkable is that in Spain the village communities spontaneously developed on this basis an extensive system of municipal services, to the point of their sometimes reaching an advanced stage of communism. As we have seen from the case of Port de la Selva, the municipality provided the villager with everything he required for his daily life and supported him in sickness and old age: at Llánabes he found his needs in the future world attended to as well.

One may ask what there is in the Spanish character or in the economic circumstances of the country that has led to this surprising development. It is clear that the peculiar agrarian conditions of the Peninsula, the great isolation of many villages and the delay in the growth of even an elementary capitalist system have all played their part. But they have not been the only factors at work. When one considers the number of guilds or confraternities (*cofradías*) that till recently owned land and worked it in common to provide old age and sickness insurance for their members: or such popular institutions as the Cort de la Seo at Valencia which regulated on a purely voluntary basis a complicated system of irrigation: or else the surprising development in recent years of productive co-operative societies in which peasants and fishermen acquired the instruments of their labour, the land they needed, the necessary installations and began to produce and sell in common: one has to recognize that the Spanish working classes show a spontaneous talent for co-operation that exceeds anything that can be found to-day in other European countries.

NOTE

For the origin of these communities and of the early municipalities see Eduardo de Hinojoso, *Origen del Régimen Municipal en Castilla y León*, 1903 and *El Régimen Señorial y la Cuestión Agraria en Cataluña durante la Edad Media*, 1905: also Henrique da Gama Barros, *Historia da Administraçao Publica em Portugal nos Seculos XII a XV*, Lisboa: Tomo I, 1885; Tomo II, 1896; Tomo III, 1904. There is a full bibliography in Ballesteros, *Historia de España*, Vol. II. See also the same book, Vol. IV, Part II, p. 152.

For further information on the modern Co-operative Movement see p. 226, also the short bibliography given at the end under Chapter x.

Also Joaquín Costa, *Colectivismo Agrario en España*, 1898 and J. Langdon Davies, *Behind the Barricades*, 1936, pp. 66–67 and 78–80 of the second edition.

Appendix II

SOCIALIST TENDENCIES IN SPAIN IN THE SEVENTEENTH CENTURY

The theoretical attitude of the Spanish Church of the sixteenth century to social questions is expressed by the great theologian Domingo del Soto when he laid it down (in 1545) that 'under pain of mortal sin the rich are obliged to give away in alms everything of which they do not have an absolute need'. Others used stronger language. For example Luís Vivés, tutor to the English Queen Mary, declared that everyone who did not divide up among the poor what was left over after satisfying the elementary needs (*usos necesarios*) of Nature, was a thief and that even though he was not punished by human laws, he certainly was by divine ones. And all the doctors and theologians agreed that the hungry had a right to steal from the rich if charity was refused them because 'the right to private property ceases when there are some who lack necessities'.

One must be careful, however, not to exaggerate the scope of these remarks. In spite of a certain emphasis, which was due to the new preoccupation with social questions, they are really nothing more than a restatement of the classic view of the Church—the old, ever repeated, never fulfilled hope that the rich would some day be generous. According to this view, as expressed by St Thomas Aquinas, the 'communication' of superfluous riches to the common use should be based on Christian feelings of love and generosity and not on compulsion. For compulsion took away the merit.

The end of the century brought a change in this way of thinking. The modern state had come into existence and with it the question of the State's responsibility in social matters. The continuing economic decline made it clear that the voluntary attitude of the Middle Ages could no longer be maintained. And so one finds a great historian such as Father Mariana declaring that the State ought to compel the rich to distribute their surplus lands or, where that was not possible, at least to rent them at a reasonable rate to persons who would cultivate them adequately. It is important to notice the change that these words mark. What for centuries had been a moral or religious question, to be decided according to the free conscience of each individual, had now become a question of compulsory action by the State.

Moreover this harsh attitude towards landed property was peculiar to Spain. For two reasons: the apparent inability of Spaniards to develop the resources of their country as other races were doing by individual enterprise, and the fact that Spain was the only European nation at this time to live for an idea. The Catholic Church had fused with the State and was endeavouring to impose its moral views upon it.

One of the chief distinctions between the social philosophy of the Middle Ages and that of modern times lies in its attitude towards utopias. The mediaeval utopia lay in the past. 'In the beginning', said Grotius, 'all things were common and indivisible: they were the patrimony of everyone.' The Biblical Eden and the classical Golden Age were merged, and the corruption of human nature made return impossible. The discovery of America did something to shake this view, partly because it opened to the mind such unimagined prospects, but also because it showed a civilized race, the Peruvians, living in a state of communism which seemed to be almost as perfect and as 'Christian' as that of the Golden Age. Perhaps indeed these Indians were survivors from that happy period! Certainly the missionaries, charmed by their simplicity and by the readiness with which they imbibed Christian doctrines, did not hide their opinion that they were less 'corrupted' than Europeans. Sir Thomas More's *Utopia*, which was widely read in Spain, and the new translations of Plato helped to provide the literary and philosophic background by which the State communism of the Incas might be interpreted.

It happened that at this time Spanish economy, and with it Spanish agriculture, was entering the second stage of its long agony. Trade and industry were falling off, the population was decreasing, large stretches of the country were ceasing to be tilled. No one understood the causes of this decline, but clearly something would have to be done to arrest it. A method must be devised for getting production going again. Individual enterprise had failed, those 'lazy Spaniards' refusing to take the road that was leading other nations to capitalism: perhaps some form of state collectivism would solve the problem. Thus the theological and poetical discussions upon communism and the golden age began to give way to practical suggestions. And so one has the rise of what Costa, with some exaggeration, perhaps, has called the 'Spanish School of Collectivist Economics'. It is a phenomenon to which there is no parallel at this time in the rest of Europe.

I can only cite a few particulars here. To begin with those ideas which had their origin in America, there is a Jesuit, Josef de Acosta, who in his *Historia Natural y Moral de las Indias* (Seville, 1590) described in detail the economic system of the Incas and declared that in his opinion it was superior in all respects to the regime of industrial competition and private property in vogue in Europe. 'Without being Christian', he said, 'the Indians had kept that high perfection of owning no private property and providing what was necessary for all and supporting on a magnificent scale their religion and their King' (Lib. VI, Cap. 15). The same view had already been expressed by a lawyer of Cuzco, Polo de Ondogardo, in 1561 and it was repeated by a Spanish lawyer, Murcia de la Llave, towards 1595, with the rider that to preserve Spain from the ruin and desolation that had befallen it, certain elements of Peruvian collectivism ought to be adopted there. The natural development of these ideas led to the famous Jesuit Reductions in Paraguay, which, for all their missionary character, are the first example in historical times of the organization of a Communist state by Europeans.

To return to Spain, we find early in the seventeenth century a humanist called Pedro de Valencia who presented an address to Philip III in which he expounded the theory of a sort of social contract to account for the existence of private property. Originally, he said, all land had been held in common, but for greater convenience it had at some later time been leased by the community to individuals so that they might cultivate it in their own way, but only on the condition that each attended to his own portion, which should not be larger than what he could maintain with his own hands. The consequences that Valencia drew from this were that no one was entitled to possess more land than he could work himself with his family, and that every man without exception had a right to as much as this. He therefore proposed that all land in Spain should be compulsorily nationalized (allowing out of charity a small indemnity in the form of an annual pension to the landlords who had been expropriated) and that this land should be let in lots to men who would cultivate it, with State supervision to see that they did so properly. In each district the land would be distributed by lot each year, as was the practice in the old collectivist communes (*El Almacén de Frutos Literarios*, Vol. IV, 1818–1819).

Another example of this way of thinking is provided by Martínez de la Mata, a brother of the Third Order of Franciscans, whose

Discursos were published in 1659. He started off from the axiom later made famous by Adam Smith that the only true wealth is industry. It will not be enough, he declared, to restore agriculture: commerce and manufacture must be restored too. After a lengthy discussion of the advantages and disadvantages of Socialism (*Comunismo*) he decided in favour of a mixed system, similar to what would to-day be called controlled capitalism. His chief principle was what he called *general harmony* between all members of the republic: unless that existed— and in his time, he declared, it did not exist—no serious revival could be expected. His most concrete suggestion was for the institution of an *Erario* or credit bank for agriculture, with branches in every town. Martínez de la Mata held his views so strongly that he devoted his life to publishing them, not only in his writings, but in lectures which he gave all over the South of Spain in the public squares. Calling himself the 'Slave of the poor afflicted', dressed in his Franciscan robes and surrounded by a few disciples he held forth to anyone who would listen to him. There is a record of his being prosecuted by the Municipality of Seville in 1660 for creating a disturbance. He was far from being a crank however. Campomanes, the great statesman and reformer of the eighteenth century, so admired his *Discursos* that he republished them in his *Apéndice a la Educación Popular*, Vol. 1, 1775.

Among all the many writers of the seventeenth century upon political economy who declared that no one had any right to live by rents and who recommended that the State should either expropriate or severely control large properties, I will select Miguel Caxa de Leruela, a high official of the Mesta or sheep-farmers' guild from 1623 to 1625, who believed that the decline of Spain was due to the deficiency of sheep and cattle among the peasants and small landowners. (The herds of the Mesta were migratory and, far from assisting to keep a certain balance in agricultural life, were detrimental to it, so that his theories were not a simple vindication of his profession.) He maintained that the natural employment of peasants and farmers in Spain should be sheep and cattle farming and not agriculture, which was distasteful to Spaniards 'because the bread of the ploughman is bitter and is kneaded with sweat'. No herdsman was ever seen to beg, and even when he was old he would still be able to carry on his business. He therefore held that the State should nationalize all pasturage and establish each peasant with sufficient head of sheep and cattle to support him. (*Restauración de la Abundancia de España*, Naples, 1631. Reprinted in 1713 and 1732 in Madrid.)

Far from these views being thought fantastic, two years later (in 1633) the King issued a pragmatic which went a considerable way towards putting into practice Caxa de Leruela's project. By this the Crown claimed a right to regulate the conditions on which all pasture land (i.e. six-sevenths of the surface of the country) should be let in Spain, fixed the rents in perpetuity, gave the tenants absolute right of access, made the leases irrevocable and hereditary, forbade the lands to be ploughed, limited the number of cattle to be grazed per acre and set up commissions to see that these regulations were carried out. Needless to say, owing to the weakness of the executive and to the resistance of the nobles, the *caciques* and the *poderosos*, all these ambitious provisions remained a dead letter.

This does not, however, exhaust the number of 'collectivist' schemes put forward during this century by projectors (*proyectistas*) with the object of saving the country. Much more sweeping proposals were made by some people—for example, by Álvarez Ossorio, who in 1686 suggested that the State should confiscate all money and landed property in Spain in order to found a 'Universal Company' which should have a monopoly of trade, manufacture and agriculture. Such schemes need not be taken very seriously: the pressing problem for Spain in the seventeenth century was the land. But there can be little doubt that if the State had possessed more energy at this time, if the bureaucracy had not been hopelessly corrupt and incompetent and the resistance of the landlords and local authorities had not made any decrees issued by the Government ineffective, the agrarian question would have been settled along collectivist, that is to say, Socialist lines. As it was, it was postponed and when an opportunity for settling it came up again in the late eighteenth and early nineteenth centuries, the conditions for a solution of this sort were no longer favourable. Spain therefore had a political revolution in place of the social revolution which would have suited her far better, and the Church, which stood to lose by the former, but would certainly have gained by the latter, allowed her opportunity to pass without seizing it.

BIBLIOGRAPHY

GENERAL

ANTONIO BALLESTEROS. *Historia de España*. 8 vols. Barcelona, 1919–1936.

RAFAEL ALTAMIRA Y CREVEA. *Historia de España y de la Civilización Española*. 4 vols. Barcelona, 1913–1914.

—— Spain, 1815–1845. *Cambridge Modern History*, vol. x.

ANTONIO PIRALA. *Historia Contemporánea* (1843 to 1879). 6 vols. Madrid, 1875–1880.
The most detailed history of this period.

GUSTAVE HUBBARD. *Histoire Contemporaine d'Espagne* (1814 to 1868). 6 vols. Paris, 1869–1883.
Written from a liberal and anti-clerical point of view.

G. DESDEVISES DU DEZERT. *L'Espagne de l'Ancien Régime*. 3 vols. Paris, 1897–1904.
The standard work on the eighteenth century.

ANGEL MARVAUD. *L'Espagne au XXième Siècle*. Paris, 1913.

H. B. CLARKE. *Modern Spain* (1815–1898). Cambridge, 1906.

G. F. WHITE. *A Century of Spain and Portugal*. 1798–1898. London, 1909.

F. CARAVACA and A. ORTS-RAMOS. *Historia Ilustrada de la Revolución Española*. 1870–1931. 2 parts. Barcelona, 1931.
Two large volumes, profusely illustrated and containing much odd information, drawn mostly from the press of the time.

KARL MARX and FREDERICK ENGELS. *Revolution in Spain*. London, 1939.
This contains 'Revolutionary Spain', a series of articles by Marx on the Napoleonic War: 'Articles and Notes', on the Revolution of 1854 by Marx and Engels: 'Revolution in Spain', an article by Marx on the end of the 1854–1856 Revolution: some articles on the Spanish Army and Moorish War of 1859 by Marx and Engels and 'The Bakuninists at Work' by Engels. All of these were first written in the form of articles for the *New York Daily Tribune*. Marx's essay on the Napoleonic War is one of the most penetrating things ever written upon Spanish history. It is strange however that in his articles upon the Liberal Revolution, the economic basis of that revolution, which was the acquisition of the estates of the Church and of the common lands by the new middle classes, entirely escaped him.

M. FERNÁNDEZ ALMAGRO. *Historia del Reinado de Alfonso XIII*. Barcelona, 1933.
Written from a conservative point of view.

MANUEL CIGES APARICIO. *España bajo la Dinastía de los Borbones*. Madrid, 1932.
A readable book written by a Republican.

SALVADOR DE MADARIAGA. *Spain.* London, 1930.
A useful handbook.

Sir GEORGE YOUNG. *The New Spain.* London, 1933.

J. B. TREND. *Origins of Modern Spain.* Cambridge, 1934.

J. P. OLIVEIRA MARTINS. *Historia da Civilizaçao Iberica.* Lisbon, 1885.
There is an English translation.

ANGEL GANIVET. *Ideárium Español.* Granada, 1897.

JOSÉ ORTEGA Y GASSET. *España Invertebrada.* Madrid, 1922.

Dr FRANZ BORKENAU. *The Spanish Cockpit.* London, 1937.
The introductory chapter contains a brilliant résumé of recent Spanish history. The rest of the book deals with the Civil War.

Bulletin of Spanish Studies, 1923–1940, Liverpool. Edited by Professor Allison Peers.

The following books of travel seem to me to throw a special light on recent events:

M. J. QUIN. *Visit to Spain in 1822 and 1823.* London, 1824.
Contains a vivid account of these two and a half years of Liberal regime.

A. J. M. DE ROCCA. *Mémoires sur la Guerre des Français en Espagne.* London, 1814; 2nd ed. Paris, 1814.
The memoirs of a young Swiss cavalry officer fighting in Napoleon's army, and one of the best books by foreigners on Spaniards. Rocca later married Madame de Staël.

CHAPTERS I AND II

There is no good life of Cánovas. The best portraits are given by:

CHARLES BENOIST. *Cánovas del Castillo. La Restauration Rénovatrice.* Paris, 1930.

BENITO PÉREZ GALDÓS. *Cánovas.* Madrid, 1912.
A novel.

A. M. FABIÉ. *Cánovas del Castillo.* Madrid, 1901.
The standard biography, by an intimate friend of Cánovas, but unrevealing.

For Cánovas' ideas one should read especially:

ANTONIO CÁNOVAS DEL CASTILLO. *Estudios del Reinado de Felipe IV.* 2 vols. Madrid, 1888–1889.
The best of his admirable historical books on this period of Spanish decadence.

—— *El Solitario y su Tiempo.* 2 vols. Madrid, 1883.
A biography of his uncle Serafín Estébanez Calderón, which contains his opinions on the Liberal Revolution.

ANTONIO CÁNOVAS DEL CASTILLO. *Discursos pronunciados en las Cortes...
durante la Discusión del Mensaje de Contestación al Discurso de la
Corona en la Legislatura de* 1876. Madrid, 1876.

—— *Problemas Contemporáneos.* 2 vols. Madrid, 1884.
Less informing.

Upon the Spanish administration and the cacique system there are:

JOAQUÍN COSTA. *Oligarquía y Caciquismo como la Forma Actual de Gobierno
en España.* Madrid, 1902.
Contains, besides a statement on the subject by the author, the contributions
of sixty distinguished members of the Ateneo belonging to all parties. Those
by Antonio Maura and Unamuno are especially interesting.

JOHN CHAMBERLAIN. *El Atraso de España.* Valencia, 1919.
John Chamberlain is the pseudonym for Tomás Jiménez Valdivieso.

ADOLFO GONZÁLEZ POSADA. *Estudios sobre el Régimen Parlamentario en
España.* Madrid, 1891.

—— *Evolución Legislativa del Régimen Local en España de* 1812 *a* 1909.
Madrid, 1910.

J. TANSKI. *L'Espagne en* 1842 *et* 1843. Paris, 1844.
Contains an account of the *cesantes* at the beginning of the Constitutional
period.

JULIÁN DE ZUGASTI Y SAENZ. *El Bandolerismo. Estudio Social y Memorias
Históricas.* 10 vols. Madrid, 1876.
By a governor of Cordova famous for his energy in putting down brigands.
It contains much information upon the Andalusian caciques of the period.

B. JARNÉS. *Castelar, Hombre de Sinai.* Madrid, 1935.
An excellent study of the Spanish Cicero.

Upon the Catalan question there is a mass of material. I select:

ANTON SIEBERER. *Katalonien gegen Kastilien.* Vienna, 1936.
An admirable book on the growth of Catalan Nationalism by an Austrian.

ANGEL MARVAUD. *Le Mouvement Catalan.* Paris, 1913.

G. DWELSHAUVERS. *La Catalogne et le Problème Catalan.* Paris, 1926.

MANUEL PUGÉS. *Como triunfó el Proteccionismo en España.* Barcelona,
1931.
This illustrates an important side of the Catalan national movement which is
often neglected.

VALENTI ALMIRALL. *Lo Catalanisme.* Barcelona, 1886.
The most famous and complete statement of the Catalan Nationalist claims.

ENRIQUE PRAT DE LA RIBA. *La Nacionalidad Catalana*. Barcelona, 1916. (The 1st edition in Catalan came out in 1906.)

ALBERTO Y ARTURO GARCÍA CARAFFA. *Prat de la Riba*. Madrid, 1917. (In the Españoles Ilustres series.)

Upon the political history of Spain from 1902 to 1914 I have used:

CONDE DE ROMANONES. *Notas de Una Vida*, 1868–1912. 2 vols. 2nd ed. 1934. Madrid.
These memoirs, written with some literary pretensions, are an important source in the political life of this period.

—— *Las Responsabilidades Políticas del Antiguo Régimen de 1875 a 1923*. Madrid, 1924.
Especially interesting for its account of Spanish foreign policy during the Great War.

J. RUIZ CASTILLO. *Antonio Maura. 35 Anos de Vida Pública*. 2 vols. Madrid, 1917.
Extracts from Maura's speeches pieced together with explanations. This is the best book for the understanding of Maura's ideas.

CÉSAR SILIÓ. *Maura*. Madrid, 1934.

LUIS ANTÓN DEL OLMET and ARTURO GARCÍA CARAFFA. *Maura*. Madrid, 1913.

JOSÉ FRANCOS RODRÍGUEZ. *La Vida de Canalejas*. Madrid, 1918.

ALBERTO Y ARTURO GARCÍA CARAFFA. *Francisco Cambó*. Madrid, 1917.

—— *Alejandro Lerroux*. Madrid, 1917. (Both in the Españoles Ilustres series.)

SALVADOR CANALS. *Los Sucesos de España de 1909. Crónica Documentada*. 2 vols. Madrid, 1910.
By a former under-secretary of the Presidencia de Ministros under Maura.

A. ORTS-RAMOS and F. CARAVACA. *Francisco Ferrer Guardia, Apóstol de la Razón*. Barcelona, 1932.
Dozens of books have been written upon Ferrer. This gives the facts.

RAFAEL SHAW. *Spain from Within*. London, 1910.
An interesting account by an English journalist of the working classes in Barcelona and their opinions, especially upon religious questions.

CHAPTER III

J. MARTÍN DE OLÍAS. *Influencia de la Religión Católica Apostólica Romana en la España Contemporánea*. Madrid, 1876.

LUÍS MOROTE. *Los Frailes en España*. Madrid, 1904.

P. ANTONIO VICENT. *Cooperatismo Católico. Cooperativas de Consumo, de Crédito y de Producción*. Valencia, 1905.
An account of his work by the pioneer of Catholic co-operatives in Spain.

Dr JUAN BARDINA. *Orígenes de la Tradición y Régimen Liberal.* 1916.

SEVERINO AZNAR. *El Catolicismo Social en España.* Saragossa, 1906.

—— *La Cruzada Sindical.* Barcelona, 1913.

P. FRANCISCO PEIRÓ. *El Problema Religioso-Social de España.* Madrid, 1936.

G. ROBINOT MARCY. *Ante la Apostasía de las Masas.* Madrid, 1935.

SISIMIO NEVARES. *El Porqué de la Sindicación Obrera Católica.* 1935.

VICTORINO FELIZ. *La Conquista de la Joventud Obrera.* Madrid, 1935.

—— *Jóvenes Campesinos de Acción Católica y Social.* Madrid, 1934.

Grupo de la Democracia Cristiana. *Problemas Sociales Candentes.* Barcelona, 1930.

CHAPTER IV

League of Nations Armament Year Book. From 1924 on.

CONDE DE ROMANONES. *El Ejército y la Política.* Madrid, 1920.

GONZALO DE REPARAZ. *Política Española en Africa.* Madrid, 1907.

—— *Alfonso XIII y sus Cómplices.* Madrid, 1931.

A severe indictment of the King by a journalist who was an authority on Moroccan questions and who had long advocated a policy of peaceful penetration similar to that practised by the French.

CORONEL MÁRQUEZ and J. M. CAPO. *Las Juntas Militares de Defensa.* 1923.

Colonel Márquez was one of the founders of these Juntas and a Republican.

EDUARDO ORTEGA Y GASSET. *Annual.* Madrid, 1923.

GABRIEL MAURA GAMAZO. *Recuerdos de mi Vida.* Madrid, 1934.

By the Conde de la Mortera, son of the great Maura. Contains much interesting information on the politics of the time.

MANUEL DE BURGOS Y MAZO. *Páginas Históricas de 1917.* Madrid, 1918.

—— *El Verano de 1919 en Gobernación.* Madrid, 1921.

Two books that throw considerable light on the Spanish administration by the Conservative Minister of the Interior during this period.

F. MADRID. *Ocho Meses y un Día en el Gobierno Civil de Barcelona. Confesiones y testimonios.* Barcelona, 1932.

Compiled by the Barcelona Correspondent of *El Sol* from the material of a Republican journalist of the Esquerra, Carlos Madrigal, who had ample sources of information upon events in Barcelona from 1917 onwards. It contains extracts from the official reports of two Civil Governors and speeches by Pestaña and Seguí. The first chapters of the book deal with the events of 1917–1923. The last chapters give a detailed account of the efforts of the first Civil Governors of the Republic in Barcelona to come to terms with the Anarcho-Syndicalists (April–October 1931).

R. PLÉ Y ARMENGOL. *Impresiones de la Huelga General de Barcelona del 24 Marzo al 7 Abril 1919.* Barcelona, 1930.

By a Left Republican, hostile to Anarchism.

PEDRO FOIX. *Los Archivos del Terrorismo Blanco.* Barcelona, 1931.

A collection of documents from the secret dossier of the political police attached to the Captain Generals of Catalonia during the period 1916–1924.

F. BARATECH ALFARO. *Los Sindicatos Libres de España. Su Origen, su Actuación, su ideario.* Barcelona, 1927.

By an ex-secretary of the Sindicatos Libres.

CHAPTER V

NICOLO PASCAZIO. *La Rivoluzione di Spagna.* Rome, 1933.

A lively and penetrating study of the Dictatorship and of the fall of the Monarchy by an Italian journalist of Fascist sympathies.

FRANCISCO CAMBÓ. *Las Dictaduras.* Madrid, 1929.

—— *Por la Concordia.* Madrid, 1930.

A penetrating analysis of the Catalan situation during the Dictatorship and of the causes of Primo de Rivera's failure.

GABRIEL MAURA GAMAZO. *Bosquejo Histórico de la Dictadura.* 2 vols. Madrid, 1930.

A detailed history of the Dictatorship by the Conde de la Mortera, son of the famous Maura. Although written from a strongly Conservative point of view, it is hostile to Primo de Rivera.

J. CALVO SOTELO. *Mis Servicios al Estado. Seis Años de Gestión.* Madrid, 1931.

An account of his work as finance minister, written from an objective point of view and free from the violent party feeling that characterized his later books. His attitude to Primo's policy is often critical.

EDUARDO ORTEGA Y GASSET. *La Verdad Sobre la Dictadura.* Madrid, 1925.

A bitter attack on the Dictatorship.

JOAQUÍN MAURÍN. *Los Hombres de la Dictadura.* Madrid, 1930.

Contains an interesting appreciation of the part played by Cambó and a criticism of the Socialists from a Left Marxist point of view.

—— *La Revolución Española. De la Monarquía Absoluta a la Revolución Socialista.* Madrid, 1932.

S. CÁNOVAS CERVANTES. *Solidaridad Obrera. Apuntes historicos.* Barcelona, 1937.

A collection of articles dealing with Spanish politics during the Dictatorship and Republic, first published in the Anarchist daily, *Solidaridad Obrera.* The author devotes a good deal of space to exposing the financial scandals and rackets of this period.

SALVADOR CANALS. *España, la Constitución y la Monarquía.* Madrid (no date).

ANDRÉ GERMAIN. *La Révolution Espagnole.* Paris, 1931.

JACINTO CAPELLA. *La Verdad de Primo de Rivera. Intimidades y Anecdotas del Dictador.* Madrid, 1933.

An interesting and sympathetic account of Primo de Rivera's life and character.

MIGUEL PRIMO DE RIVERA. *Epistolario del Dictador.* Madrid, 1930.

General E. LÓPEZ DE OCHOA. *De la Dictadura a la República.* Madrid, 1930.

López de Ochoa had helped to bring Primo de Rivera to power, but afterwards opposed the Dictatorship.

R. SALAZAR ALONSO. *La Justicia bajo la Dictadura.* Madrid, 1930.

CARLOS BLANCO. *La Dictadura y los Procesos Militares.* 1931.

General QUEIPO DE LLANO Y SIERRA. *El Movimiento Revindicativo de Cuatro Vientos.* Madrid, 1931.

COMANDANTE FRANCO. *Madrid bajo las Bombas.* Madrid, 1931.

These last two books describe the premature Republican rising at Cuatro Vientos aerodrome under the brother of the present Spanish Dictator and General Queipo de Llano.

CHAPTER VI

MAX SORRE. 'Espagne-Portugal.' In *Géographie Universelle,* vol. VII, Part I, Paris, 1934.

HISTORICAL

The Cambridge Economic History of Europe. Vol. I, The Agrarian Life of the Middle Ages. 1941.

JOAQUÍN COSTA. *Colectivismo Agrario en España.* Madrid, 1898.

Costa was the Spanish Cobbett, without his literary and journalistic genius, but with a talent for historical research instead. This is the fundamental book for the understanding of agrarian questions in Spain.

—— *La Fórmula de la Agricultura Española.* 2 vols. Biblioteca Costa. Madrid, 1911 and 1912.

—— *Estudios Ibéricos.* Madrid, 1891.

M. WILLKOMM. *Grundzüge der Pflanzenverbreitung auf der Iberischen Halbinsel.* Leipzig, 1896.

Gives interesting proofs of the decline of cultivation and spread of heath and palmetto in the Peninsula.

J. G. KLEIN. *The Mesta. A Study in Spanish Economic History* (1273–1836). Cambridge, Mass., 1920.

A serious piece of research upon the great sheep and cattle breeding guild.

EUGENIO DE LARRUGA. *Memorias Políticas y Económicas sobre los Frutos, Comercio, Fábricas y Minas de España.* 45 vols. Madrid, 1793.

A vast jumble of information good and bad upon economic and agrarian matters.

MANUEL DE COLMEIRO. *Historia de la Economía Política en España.* 2 vols. Madrid, 1863.

PEDRO RODRÍGUEZ, CONDE DE CAMPOMANES. *Memorial Ajustado del Expediente Consultivo para una ley agraria*. Madrid, 1784.

A summary of a series of reports upon the agrarian situation written between 1752 and 1769 by special Royal commissioners. These reports were collected in 1771 together with a project for an agrarian law drawn up or inspired by Campomanes. Since this collection was too bulky to be printed, the Junta de Ley Agraria made a summary of it and published it with the title of *Memorial Ajustado*.

—— *Discurso Sobre el Fomento de la Industria Popular. Discurso Sobre la Educación Popular de los Artesanos y su Fomento*. Con Apéndice. 6 vols. Madrid, 1774–1777.

The Memoir of Martínez de la Mata is contained in the fourth volume of this work (vol. 1 of Appendix).

—— *Cartas político-económicas escritas al Conde de Lérena, publicadas ahora por primera vez por Don Antonio Rodríguez Villa*. Madrid, 1878.

These admirably satirical letters, first discovered and published in 1878, throw a great deal of light on the condition of Spain in the eighteenth century.

—— *El Tratado de la Regalía de Amortización*. Madrid, 1765.

Written to show that the policy of the Crown both in Spain and in other Catholic countries had always been to restrict the landed property of the Church and, if necessary, to appropriate it.

FRANCISCO, CONDE DE CABARRÚS. *Cartas sobre los Obstáculos que la Naturaleza, la Opinión y las Leyes oponen a la Felicidad Pública*. Vitoria, 1808. Republished in Madrid in 1820.

Cabarrús, though born a Frenchman, was one of the group of enlightened men whom Charles III collected round him. Like Jovellanos, he was a disciple of Adam Smith. His daughter was the famous beauty of the Directory, Madame Tallien.

GASPAR MELCHOR DE JOVELLANOS. *Informe sobre la Ley Agraria*. Madrid, 1787.

A reply by the famous disciple of Adam Smith to the suggestions for an agrarian law made in the above cited *Memorial Ajustado*. These are the two key books for an understanding of Spanish agrarian problems at a moment when, by the destruction of the *mayorazgos* and common lands, they were about to enter an entirely new phase. Jovellanos' book marks the beginning of the Liberal era in agrarian questions.

FRANCISCO LUÍS LAPORTA. *Historia de la Agricultura Española. Su Origen, Progresos y Estado Actual*. Madrid, 1798.

FRANCISCO DE CÁRDENAS. *Ensayo sobre la Historia de la Propiedad Territorial en España*. 2 vols. Madrid, 1873–1875.

A history of the agrarian question in Spain from Roman times, written in defence of the interests of the landowners and emphasizing the juridical aspect.

JUAN ÁLVAREZ DE COLMENAR. *Délices de l'Espagne et du Portugal*. 5 vols. Leyden, 1707.

The Baedeker to eighteenth-century Spain.

G. Desdevises du Dezert. 'La Richesse et la Civilisation Espagnoles au xviiiième Siècle.' *Revue Hispanique*, Paris, June 1928.

An admirable study by the chief authority on Spain in this century.

Arthur Young. *Travels during the Years 1787, 1788 and 1789 in the Kingdom of France (and Spain)*. London, 1792.

—— 'Tour of Catalonia.' Published in the *Annals of Agriculture*, vol. viii, London, 1787.

Lucius Junius Moderatus Columella. *De Re Rustica*.

Columella was born at Gades during the time of Augustus and spent his youth on his uncle's latifundia there. Most of his book however is concerned with Italian agriculture.

Abu Zacaría...Ebn el Awam. *Libro de Agricultura*. Translated by José Banqueri, with a preface by Campomanes. Madrid, 1793. (There is a later edition with notes in 1878.)

Abu Zacaría was a Sevillian who lived towards the close of the twelfth century. His book is based on both Roman and Arab writers. The greater part of it is devoted to fruit culture and market gardening and to the breeding of birds and animals.

E. Lévi-Provençal. *L'Espagne Musulmane au Xième Siècle. Institutions et Vie Sociale*. Paris, 1932.

Gabriel Alonso de Herrera. *Obra de Agricultura Copilada de Diversos Auctores....* Logroño, 1513.

Reprinted several times and modernized under the titles of *Libro de Agricultura* and *La Labranza Española*.

Herrera was a Sevillian who lived and wrote at Talavera, chiefly for the benefit of Castilian agriculture. His book is based on ancient authors (both Latin and Arab, though not Abu Zacaría) and also on practical experience. It sums up all that was known on agriculture in Spain at the end of the Middle Ages and remained the classic book on the subject down to the end of the eighteenth century.

R. Altamira y Crevea. *Historia de la Propriedad Comunal*. (With a prologue by G. de Azcárate.) Madrid, 1890.

A survey of the history of communal property in Europe from the earliest times, but containing some interesting chapters on its origins in Spain.

Oliveira Martins. *Quadro das Instituição Primitivas*. Lisbon, 1883.

Boletín de la Institución Libre de Enseñanza. Madrid.

This review contains a number of interesting articles on primitive land tenure in Spain. For example:

'Vestigios del Primitivo Comunismo en España', by Gumersindo de Azcárate. 1883.

'Apuntes sobre el Derecho de Propriedad', by D. M. Pedregal. 1884.

'La Familia Rural en Asturias', by the same author. 1885.

'La Propriedad Comun en el Norte de España', by the Rev. Wentworth Webster. 1886.

Rev. WENTWORTH WEBSTER. *Les Loisirs d'un Étranger au Pays Basque.* Chalon-sur-Saône, 1901.

A collection of essays which first came out in the *Boletín de la Institución Libre de Enseñanza* in 1886 and 1888 on various points connected with Basque history. Two of them contain a discussion of their methods of land tenure.

C. BERNALDO DE QUIRÓS and F. RIVERA PASTOR. *El Problema de los Foros en el Noreste de España.* Published by the Instituto de Reformas Sociales. Madrid, 1923.

This is the classic work on the Galician Foros.

ÁLVARO FLÓREZ ESTRADA. *Curso de Economía Política.* 1st ed. Madrid, 1828; 5th ed. 1840.

By a Liberal deputy and landowner who saw the harm that would be done by the Liberal policy of selling the common lands. He later became a disciple of Fourier.

FERMÍN CABALLERO. *Fomento de la Población Rural.* Madrid, 1864.

Contains interesting information upon the havoc wrought to the peasantry by the sale of the common lands.

G. LINARES. *La Agricultura y la Administración Municipal.* Madrid, 1882.

Of the many books of travel, memoirs, ambassadors' reports, etc. which throw light on Spanish agrarian conditions in the sixteenth, seventeenth and eighteenth centuries, I give only these, which I have quoted from:

MARQUIS DE VILLARS. *Mémoires de la Cour d'Espagne de 1679 à 1681.* Edited by A. Morel-Fatio. Paris, 1893.

Relazioni degli Stati Europei lette agli Senato degli Ambasciatori Veneti nel sec. 17. Spagna. Rome, 1856.

JOSEPH TOWNSEND. *Journey through Spain in 1786–1787.* London, 1792.

FRANÇOIS VAN AERSSEN. *Voyage en Espagne.* Paris, 1665.

The real author of this book was van Aerssen's tutor, Antoine de Brunel, a French Protestant.

CONTEMPORARY PERIOD

PASCUAL CARRIÓN. *Los Latifundios en España.* Madrid, 1932.

This book, by the Secretary of the Junta Central de Reforma Agraria, provides by far the most comprehensive survey of this subject. It is based exclusively on statistics drawn from the new *Catastro* or Land Survey and as this was prepared carefully and impartially by a body of engineers specially trained in the work, the results can be relied on.

VIZCONDE DE EZA. *El Problema Agrario en España.* Madrid, 1915.

—— *Agrarismo.* Madrid, 1936.

By a well-known authority on Spanish agriculture who himself owns large estates in Andalusia and in Castile. Since 1910 he has been an advocate of breaking up the large estates and settling small farmers on them. He was a minister in several Conservative Governments before the Dictatorship.

ANONYMOUS. *El Problema Agrario en el Mediodía de España; Conclusiones para armonizar los intereses de proprietarios y obreros; Medio de aumentar la producción del suelo.* Published by the Instituto de Reformas Sociales under the title 'Memoria que la Comisión nombrada para ajúdicar el premio concedido por S. M. el Rey, presenta al Instituto de Reformas Sociales.' Madrid, 1904.

A study by an anonymous author which won a prize offered by the King. Within the limits imposed by its title it is the most serious contribution to agrarian reform published up to this time since the *Informe* of Jovellanos.

—— *Información sobre el Problema Agrario en la Provincia de Córdoba.* Published by the Instituto de Reformas Sociales. Madrid, 1919.

An admirable survey of the results of an enquiry into agrarian conditions in the province of Cordova during a time of great unrest. The president of the Instituto at this time was the Vizconde de Eza. Most of the material is incorporated by Díaz del Moral in his great book which figures in the bibliography of the next chapter.

M. LORENZO PARDO. *La Confederación del Ebro. Nueva Política Hidráulica.* Madrid, 1930.

JEAN BRUNHES. *L'Irrigation…dans la Péninsule Ibérique et dans l'Afrique du Nord.* Paris, 1904.

FERNANDO DE LOS RÍOS. 'Agrarian Problems in Spain.' Published in the *International Labour Review*, June 1925.

E. H. G. DOBBY. 'Agrarian Problems in Spain.' Published in the *Geographical Review of the American Geographical Society*, vol. XXVI, April, 1936.

—— 'Galicia: A Little Known Corner of Spain.' *Ibid.* October, 1936.

These monographs by a geographer who has spent two years in field work in Spain are very informative.

—— 'Beneath the Surface in Spain.' An article from *Time and Tide.* August, 1936.

J. LANGDON DAVIES. *Behind the Barricades.* London, 1936.

Contains, among other things, interesting descriptions of agricultural and fishing communes in the Pyrenees and in Catalonia.

Reglamento de la Sociedad Pósito Pescado de Puerto de la Selva. 1929.

A pamphlet containing the rules of this commune.

Professor ANTONIO CAMACHO. An article in a recent number of the *Revista Nacional de Economía.* Date (?).

Contains a description of the collectivized fishing village of Tazones, near Villaviciosa in Asturias.

CHAPTER VII

Upon the general history of the working-class movement in Spain there are:

ANGEL MARVAUD. *La Question Sociale en Espagne.* Paris, 1910.
This book, in spite of its many inaccuracies, forms the best introduction to the subject.

PRÁXEDES ZANCADA. *El Obrero en España.* (With a preface by Canalejas.) Barcelona, 1902.
Interesting but not at all accurate.

P. ANTONIO VICENT. *Socialismo y Anarquismo.* Valencia, 1893.
By the pioneer of Catholic co-operatives.

JUAN DÍAZ DEL MORAL. *Historia de las Agitaciones Campesinas Andaluzas. Antecedentes para una Reforma Agraria.—Córdoba.* Madrid, 1929.
This long and admirable book by a *notario* of Bujalance, who later became a Republican deputy for this province, is indispensable for an understanding of the conditions under which anarchism arose in Andalusia. Besides giving an interesting account of the early days of the International in Spain, it contains a detailed history of the progress of libertarian ideas in the province of Cordova and of their relation to agrarian factors and to the peculiar temperament of the Andalusian *campesino.* The author is exceptionally well-informed and impartial and there is a valuable bibliography. Volumes promised on the other Andalusian provinces never came out.

FERNANDO GARRIDO. *Historia de las Asociaciones Obreras en Europa.* 2 vols. Madrid, 1870.
The second volume of this book contains a mass of information upon the history of the working-class movement and the diffusion of socialism in Spain between 1812 and 1864. Garrido, a disciple of Fourier, was the leading Socialist of his time and the editor of the first Socialist paper to be published in Spain. Most of what has been written since upon working-class movements before 1864 is drawn from it.

—— *Historia del Reinado del Último Borbón de España.* 3 vols. Barcelona, 1868–1869.
This also contains much information upon the Socialist movement in Spain during the reign of Isabella.

RAMÓN DE LA SAGRA. *Les Partis en Espagne.* Paris, 1849.
By one of the first Spanish Socialists, with Proudhonist tendencies. Contains a brief account of the origins of Socialism in Spain.

MANUEL REVENTÓS. *Els Moviments Socials a Barcelona durant el Segle* XIX. Collecció d'Estudis Socials. Barcelona, 1925.
A serious study of the various phases of the trade-union movement in Barcelona during the nineteenth century with interesting chapters on the Anarchists and on the Co-operative movement.

GEORGES RENARD. *Sindicatos, Trade Unions y Corporaciones.* Madrid, 1916.
At the end of this translation from the French there is an appendix by Manuel Nuñez de Arenas, giving a sketch of the Spanish working-class movement from 1840 onwards. There is a good bibliography.

On the origins of federalism in Spain there are:

PIERRE JOSEPH PROUDHON. *Du Principe Fédératif et de la Nécessité de reconstituer le parti de la Révolution.* Paris, 1863.

This book was translated into Spanish by Pi y Margall in 1868 just before the September Revolution and had an immense influence.

FRANCISCO PI Y MARGALL. *La Reacción y la Revolución.* Madrid, 1854.

This book, which anticipated by several years the federal theories of Proudhon, has had a great influence both upon Catalan Nationalism and upon Spanish Anarchism. Pi y Margall, though not an anarchist, has always been regarded by Spanish Anarchists as one of their precursors and this book has been reprinted in the Anarchist series of La Revista Blanca and has circulated all over Spain. Its sources were Herbert Spencer's *Social Statics* (1850), Proudhon's *Idées Générales* (1851) and possibly Stephen Pearl Andrews, *The Science of Society* (New York, 1851).

—— *Las Nacionalidades.* Madrid, 1882.

The most complete statement of his federalist theories.

—— *La Federación.* Madrid, 1880.

—— *Lecciones de Federalismo.* (With a bibliography by Sánchez Pérez.) Madrid, 1931.

FRANCISCO CARAVACA. *Pi y Margall.* Editorial Joventud. Barcelona, 1935. (With many photographs.)

On Anarchism in general I have consulted the following:

MICHEL BAKUNIN. *Oeuvres.* 6 vols. Paris, 1895–1913.

—— *Correspondance de Michel Bakounine. Lettres à Herzen et à Ogareff* (1860–1874). Paris, 1896.

H. E. KAMINSKI. *Bakounine. La Vie d'un Révolutionnaire.* Paris, 1938. The best life of Bakunin.

E. CARR. *Michael Bakunin.* London, 1937.

Scholarly, but marred by a lack of sympathy with the subject. The relations of Bakunin with his followers in Italy, Spain and the Jura are very briefly dealt with.

PRINCE KROPOTKIN. *Field, Factories and Workshops.* London, 1899.

—— *The Conquest of Bread.* London, 1906. (1st edition in French, 1902.)

These last two books together with tracts by Malatesta, Grave, Malato, Reclus and Tolstoy have been reprinted again and again by the Anarchist press in Spain and have had an immense circulation among the working classes.

G. M. STEKLOFF. *History of the First International.* Translated by E. and C. Paul. London, 1938.

The best history of the First International. It contains the history of the Anarchist branch of the International down to 1881, but is written from a strongly Marxist point of view which sometimes affects its accuracy. There is a good bibliography.

The principal sources for the first years of the International in Spain (1869–1874) are:

ANSELMO LORENZO. *El Proletariado Militante*. Vol. I, 1901; vol. II, 1923. Barcelona.

The classic of Spanish Anarchism. The first volume presents a lucid and detailed account of the movement up to 1881. The second is less interesting. The author was one of Fanelli's first recruits and one of the leading Anarchist militants in Spain until his death in 1914.

FEDERICA MONTSENY. *Anselmo Lorenzo*. Barcelona, 1936. (In the series Los Precursores.)

A small monograph with curious photographs.

JAMES GUILLAUME. *L'Internationale, Documents et Souvenirs*. 1864–1878. 4 vols. Paris, 1905–1910.

A history of the International by the principal follower of Bakunin at this period. It is also the chief source of information upon the work of the International in Spain, containing, besides many original documents, the well-informed and accurate monthly reports sent by their Spanish correspondents to the *Bulletin de la Fédération Jurassienne*. The *F.J.* was a federation of watchmakers in the Swiss Jura which adhered to Bakunin and its *Bulletin* was the leading Anarchist paper of the time.

MAX NETTLAU. *Miguel Bakunin, la Internacional y la Alianza en España* (1868–1873). Buenos Aires, 1925.

An account of the origins of the International in Spain, the quarrel with the Marxists and Bakunin's relations with the movement.

—— *Documentos Inéditos sobre la Internacional y la Alianza en España*. Buenos Aires, 1930.

Contains interesting extracts from the letters of Paul Lafargue and other *autoritarios* to Engels in 1872 and 1873.

—— *La Revista Blanca*, May–June 1936. Barcelona.

These numbers contain extracts from letters by Bakunin to Morago in 1872–1873 with comments by Max Nettlau.

—— *Bakunin und die Internationale in Spanien*. 1868–1873. Leipzig, 1913. A study published in *Grünberg's Archiv*, largely superseded by the books named above.

Marx oder Bakunin, Democratie oder Diktatur. Stuttgart, 1920.

A translation with preface and notes by Wilhelm Blos of the report of a Committee of the International concerning relationships of the Alliance of S.D. and the I.W.M.A. and published in London on 21 July 1873.

FRIEDRICH ENGELS. *Die Bakunisten an der Arbeit*. First published in 1873 and reprinted in English in *Revolution in Spain* by Marx and Engels, London, 1939.

A withering attack on the Bakuninists in Spain.

JUAN JOSÉ MORATO. *Historia de la Sección Española de la Internacional*. 1868–1874. Madrid, 1930.

An objective account by a veteran Spanish Socialist who was one of the first members of the International in Spain.

ÉLIE RECLUS. A series of articles written from Barcelona, Andalusia and Madrid between November 1868 and January 1869 which appeared in the *Revue Politique et Littéraire* (Rédaction P. Challemel-Lacour), Paris. Tomes II and III.

Élie Reclus, the brother of the famous geographer, travelled in company of the Socialist Fernando Garrido, who was making a political tour.

ÉMILE DE LAVELEYE. *Le Socialisme Contemporain*. Paris, 1888.

An unreliable book, based in its Spanish chapters upon the information of Engels, Marx and Lafargue, but containing some direct observations of the Bakuninists made during a short visit to Barcelona in 1869.

JOSEPH A. BRANDT. *Toward the New Spain*. Chicago, 1933.

A lively but somewhat meandering account of the Revolution of 1868 and the First Republic, written from a Liberal point of view and giving copious extracts from the debates in the Cortes. There is a final chapter on the Second Republic and a useful bibliography.

FRANCISCO PI Y MARGALL. *La República de 1873. Apuntes para escribir su Historia*. Madrid, 1874.

A. PUIG CAMPILLO. *El Cantón Murciano*. Cartagena, 1932.

A detailed account of the Canton of Murcia and siege of Cartagena, using local sources.

SATURNINO GIMÉNEZ. *Cartagena. Recuerdos Cantonales*. Madrid and Barcelona, 1875.

A history of the Cantonalist rising in Cartagena.

RAMÓN SENDER. *Mr Witt among the Rebels*. English translation by Sir Peter Chalmers Mitchell. London, 1937.

A novel giving a good picture of the relations of the Internationalists to the Federal Republicans at Cartagena.

The real history of the Anarchist movement is contained not in books, but in its daily press and in the memories of living Anarchists. Except for some files of *Solidaridad Obrera* (the organ of the C.N.T.) and others of *Tierra y Libertad* I have not been able to consult any daily newspapers, but the two following reviews have been useful:

La Revista Blanca. A fortnightly review edited by Frederico Urales (Juan Montseny) at Barcelona. Barcelona, 1896–1906 and 1922–1936.

Many well known writers, including Unamuno, Manuel Cossío and Giner de los Ríos, contributed to it.

La Revista Social. A fortnightly review dedicated to Anarchist ideas that came out in Madrid between June 1881 and October 1885.

MAX NETTLAU. *Impresiones sobre el desarrollo del Socialismo en España*. Published in the form of articles in *La Revista Blanca* between 1 September 1928 and 1 May 1929.

Gives the best account of the movement between 1868 and 1888.

'Del Nacimiento de las Ideas Anarcho-Colectivistas en España.' A series of unsigned articles appearing in the *Revista Social* (Madrid) between 27 December 1883 and February 1884 and later. They are an important source for the early history of the movement. Nettlau (*op. cit.*) gives extracts.

GUSTAVO LA IGLESIA Y GARCÍA. *Carácteres del Anarquismo en la Actualidad.* Barcelona, 1907.
The book from which the middle classes of the time took their views on anarchism, but ill-informed and misleading.

S. DE MAGALHAES LIMA. *O Socialismo na Europa.* Lisbon, 1892.
The section based on the information of Juan Salas y Antón on the origins of the International in Barcelona is alone valuable. This has been summarized by Max Nettlau in *Miguel Bakunin, La Internacional y la Alianza en España.*

CONSTANCIO BERNALDO DE QUIRÓS. 'El Espartaquismo agrario Andaluz.' This is an article published in *La Revista General de Legislación y Jurisprudencia.* Madrid, April 1919.
The author was a sociologist who was sent by the Instituto de Reformas Sociales to investigate the Anarchist movement in Andalusia at the time of the Mano Negra.

—— *Bandolerismo y Delicuencia Subversiva en la Baja Andalucía.* Madrid, 1912.

—— 'La Expansión Libertaria.' An article published in the *Archivos de Psiquatría y Criminología*, Buenos Aires, July 1906.
On the revival of anarchism in the south of Spain after 1900.

ANON. *Los Procesos de la Mano Negra.* Barcelona, 1883.
An anonymous account of the trials, with long extracts from the press reports.

V. BLASCO IBÁÑEZ. *La Bodega.* Madrid, 1904.
A novel written upon the rising of the *campesinos* and their march on Jerez in 1892. It gives a fair picture of rural conditions. The anarchist apostle who is its hero is said to be a portrait of Fermín Salvochea. There is an English translation with the same title.

TARRIDA DEL MÁRMOL. *Les Inquisiteurs d'Espagne*, 1892–1897. Paris, 1897.
An account of the barbarous methods of the police by a distinguished acratic who was himself imprisoned by them. It was this book which led to the agitation in the French and British press which brought the white terror in Barcelona to an end. Tarrida was well known to English Socialists and contributed to the *Nineteenth Century*.

A. and C. ORTS-RAMOS. *Francisco Ferrer, Apóstol de la Razón.* Barcelona, 1932.
A great many books have been published on Ferrer. This gives the facts.

PÍO BAROJA. *Aurora Roja.* Madrid, 1910.
This novel, which is a *roman à clef*, presents a vivid picture of Spanish anarchism in Madrid in the first decade of this century.

MIGUEL SASTRE. *Las Huelgas en Barcelona durante los años* 1903, 1904, 1905, 1906. Barcelona, 1907.

— *Las Huelgas en Barcelona durante los años* 1910 *al* 1914. Barcelona, 1915.

Two books giving statistics of industries, trade unions and strikes by one of the organizers of the Catholic Associations.

CHAPTER VIII

Upon Syndicalism I have found the following books useful:

HUBERT LAGARDELLE. *Le Socialisme Ouvrier.* Paris, 1911.

LÉON JOUHAUX. *Le Syndicalisme et la C.G.T.* Paris, 1920.

PIERRE BESNARD. *Les Syndicats Ouvriers et la Révolution Sociale.* Édition de la C.G.T. Syndicaliste Révolutionnaire. Paris, 1930.

GEORGES SOREL. *Réflexions sur la Violence.* Paris, 1908.

—— *Les Illusions du Progrès.* 1909.

—— *La Décomposition du Marxisme.* 1908.

G. PIROU. *Georges Sorel.* Paris, 1927.

FERNAND PELLOUTIER. *Histoire des Bourses du Travail.* Paris, 1902. With an introduction by Georges Sorel.

Upon Spanish Anarcho-Syndicalism up to 1931 I have consulted the following:

MANUEL BUENACASA. *El Movimiento Obrero Español,* 1886–1926. Barcelona, 1928.

This book, by a former secretary of the C.N.T., is useful as a history of the Confederación between 1917 and 1923. The chapters on the period before 1917 are of no value. In the second part there are interesting monographs on the Anarchist movement in the different regions of Spain.

News Bulletins of the I.W.M.A. Madrid-Barcelona, 1933–1935.

Published by the so-called Syndicalist International, in Spanish A.I.T.

FRANCISCO MADRID. *Ocho Meses y un Día en el Gobierno Civil de Barcelona. Confesiones y Testimonios.* Barcelona, 1932.

Contains much information upon the Anarcho-Syndicalist movement in Barcelona between 1917 and 1923. See bibliography of Chapter IV.

PEDRO FOIX. *Los Archivos del Terrorismo Blanco.* Barcelona, 1931.

R. PLÉ Y ARMENGOL. *Impresiones de la Huelga General de Barcelona del 24 Marzo al 7 Abril* 1919. Barcelona, 1930.

EMILI SALUT. *Vivers de Revolucionaris.* Barcelona.

Short biographies of Seguí and others in Catalan.

F. BARATECH ALFARO. *Los Sindicatos Libres de España. Su Origen—su Actuación—su Ideario.* Barcelona, 1921.
By an ex-secretary of the reactionary Sindicatos Libres. It contains an interesting account of the Anarcho-Syndicalist movement in Barcelona from 1910 to 1923 from the point of view of a rival syndicate. The history of the years 1919–1922 is especially interesting.

C.N.T. *Memoria del Congreso de 1919...de Madrid.* Barcelona, 1932.
This gives the minutes of this important congress. The original papers had an adventurous history, having been moved from place to place to avoid discovery by the police and finally buried for ten years.

B. POU and J. R. MAGRIÑA. *Un Año de Conspiración.* Barcelona, 1933.
An account of the action of the C.N.T. in Catalonia during the year 1930 and of its action in bringing down the Dictatorship.

RAMÓN SENDER. *Seven Red Sundays.* Translated by Sir Peter Chalmers Mitchell. London, 1933.
A somewhat highly coloured novel upon the Anarchist movement in Madrid. Sender was Madrid correspondent for *Solidaridad Obrera* from 1930 on, till he went to Russia and was converted to Communism.

Other books dealing with the Anarcho-Syndicalist movement after 1931 are given in the bibliography of Chapters XI, XII and XIII.

CHAPTER IX

There is no single book that deals satisfactorily either with the Carlists or the Carlist Wars.

A. PIRALA. *Historia Contemporánea* (1843–1879). 6 vols. Madrid, 1875–1880.

D. BUENAVENTURA DE CÓRDOBA. *Vida Militar y Política de Cabrera.* 4 vols. Madrid, 1844–1845.
A lively portrait by a friend of his.

F. DE ONTAÑÓN. *El Cura Merino. Su Vida en Folletín.* Madrid, 1933.

MANUEL LASSALA. *Historia política del Partido Carlista.* 1841.

VICENTE DE MANTEROLA Y CASO. *El Espíritu Carlista.* 1871. A pamphlet republished in *Guerra Civil. Folletos,* 1870–1873, vol. v.
The author, a canon, had been Cabrera's secretary and was one of the leaders of the Carlist group in the Cortes of 1871. He gives an interesting exposition of Carlist ideology at this time. But all the *Folletos* contain interesting material.

—— *Don Carlos ó el Petroleo.* Madrid, 1871.
A famous pamphlet, written to show that the alternative to Carlism was the Paris Commune and later used against the Anarchists.

Biblioteca Popular Carlista. A monthly magazine published from 1895 to 1897 in Barcelona.

JULIO NOMBELA. *Detrás de la Trinchera: Páginas Íntimas de la Guerra y la Paz desde de 1868 hasta 1876.* Madrid, 1876.
An account by an eminent Carlist of the political intrigues that ruined his party.

JOAQUÍN DE BOLÓS Y SADERRA. *La Guerra Civil en Cataluña.* 1872–1876. Madrid, 1928.
A Carlist account, based on abundant documentary evidence.

JULIO URQUIJO É IBARRA. *La Cruz de Sangre. El Cura Santa Cruz.* 1928.

PÍO BAROJA. *El Cura de Santa Cruz y su Partida.* Madrid, 1918.
In addition to this Pío Baroja has written a number of novels and memoirs on Carlist subjects.

MIGUEL DE UNAMUNO. *Ensayos.* Madrid, 1916–1918. Especially the essay 'Sobre la Tumba de Costa' in Tomo VII.

J. DONOSO CORTÉS. *Ensayo sobre el Catolicismo, el Liberalismo y el Socialismo.* Madrid, 1851.
Donoso Cortés has been written up in Germany as the philosopher of Carlism. He is in reality a feeble imitation of le Maistre and his influence in Spain was inconsiderable.

JUAN VÁZQUEZ DE MELLA Y FANJUL. *Política Tradicionalista.* 2 vols. Barcelona, 1932.
A collection of speeches and articles from 1890 onwards. Of great importance for the recent development of Carlism.

—— *Ideario.* 3 vols. Barcelona and Madrid, 1930.
Extracts from articles and speeches.

For Spanish freemasonry one can consult, besides general histories such as Ballesteros and Altamira:

VICENTE DE LA FUENTE. *Historia de las Sociedades secretas antiguas y modernas en España, y especialmente la Franc-Masonería.* 3 vols. Lugo, 1870–1871. Last edition, 1933.
A famous book containing a vast amount of information, much of it inaccurate. It is written from a strongly clerical point of view.

BENITO PÉREZ GALDÓS. *El Grande Oriente.* Madrid, 1876.
This novel gives an admirable account of the masonic clubs of 1820–1823.

PÍO BAROJA. *Juan van Halen. El Oficial Aventurero.* Madrid and Barcelona, 1933.

ANTONIO ALCALÁ GALIANO. *Memorias.* 2 vols. Madrid, 1886.

CHAPTER X

JUAN JOSÉ MORATO. *El Partido Socialista.* Madrid, 1931.

—— *Pablo Iglesias.* Madrid, 1931.
These two books, admirably arranged and written, provide the best source for the history of Spanish Socialism.

FRANCISCO MORA. *Historia del Socialismo Obrero Español.* Madrid, 1902.
A useful but biased book by one of the first members of the International.

ADOLFO GONZÁLEZ POSADA. *El Socialismo y la Reforma Social.* Madrid, 1904.
By an eminent member of the Instituto de Reformas Sociales.

FIDEL. *Pablo Iglesias en el Partido Socialista.* Madrid, 1905.
An appreciation by the well known Socialist leader, García Quejido.

J. ZUGAZAGOITÍA. *Pablo Iglesias.* Madrid, 1935.

JAIME VERA LÓPEZ. *El Partido Socialista Obrero ante la Comisión de Informe sobre el estado y necesidades de la clase trabajadora y las relaciones entre el Capital y el Trabajo.* Madrid, 1895.
An admirable report by Dr Jaime Vera, a well-known scientist, who was one of the first members of the Socialist party.

On the Co-operative Movement I have consulted:

JOSÉ PIERNES HURTADO. *El Movimiento Cooperativo.* Madrid, 1890.

FERNANDO GARRIDO. *La Cooperación.*

RIVAS MORENO. *Biblioteca de la Cooperación.* Sevilla, 1913.
A series of tracts on the Co-operative Movement. That called 'Las Co-operativas de Producción' is especially interesting.

G. and J. PICARD-MOCH. *L'Espagne Républicaine.* Paris, 1933.

MANUEL REVENTÓS. *Els Moviments Socials a Barcelona durant el Segle XIX.* Barcelona, 1925. Chapter VII.

CHAPTERS XI, XII AND XIII

ANGEL MARVAUD. The following articles appeared in *Revue des Sciences Politiques*, a publication of the École Libre des Sciences Politiques.

—— 'La Seconde République Espagnole.' Oct.–Dec. 1931.

—— 'La Nouvelle Constitution Espagnole.' July–Sept. 1932.

—— 'Les Premières Cortes Ordinaires de la République Espagnole.' Jan.–March 1934.

—— 'La Guerre Civile en Espagne.' Oct.–Dec. 1936.

These four articles provide one of the best general accounts of the political history of the Republic. Marvaud writes from a conservative point of view and his knowledge of working-class movements since 1913 is insufficient.

G. and J. PICARD-MOCH. *L'Espagne Républicaine.* Paris, 1933.
This book, by two Socialists, gives what is probably the best account of the Republic at its height (September 1932) that has so far been written. It is especially valuable on the working-class movement. The authors made a journey of investigation to all the principal towns in Spain.

RHEA MARSH SMITH. *The Day of the Liberals in Spain.* Philadelphia, 1938.
Consists chiefly in a detailed account of the passage of the Republican Constitution through the Cortes. It ends with the resignation of the Provisional Government in December 1931.

ALLISON PEERS. *The Spanish Tragedy.* 1936.

This book gives a lucid account of the political events of the Dictatorship and Republic as seen through the eyes of the Catalan bourgeoisie, but shows little understanding of the deeper causes of discontent in Spain or of the aims and organizations of the great working-class parties.

HENRY BUCKLEY. *The Life and Death of the Spanish Republic.* 1940.

By a press correspondent who spent a good deal of time between 1930 and 1940 in Madrid. The chapters that deal with the period up to the outbreak of the Civil War give a good picture of events.

ANTON SIEBERER. *Katalonien gegen Kastilien.* Vienna, 1936.

An admirable book by an Austrian on the growth of Catalan Nationalism and on the events of 1934.

—— *Espagne contre Espagne.* Geneva, 1937.

Not so good as the previous book.

HENRI RABASSEIRE. *Espagne Creuset Politique.* Paris, 1938.

A mass of undigested but occasionally interesting facts.

S. CÁNOVAS CERVANTES. *Solidaridad Obrera.* Barcelona, 1937.

A collection of articles dealing with Spanish politics during the Dictatorship and Republic, first published in the Anarchist daily, *Solidaridad Obrera.* The author devotes a good deal of space to exposing the financial scandals and rackets of this period.

British Embassy Reports. *Spain.* 1931–1934.

Foreign Affairs, 1933–1934. New York.

Articles by L. A. Fernsworth in October 1933 and in April 1934. The latter throws light upon the 1933 elections.

H. R. G. GREAVES. *The Spanish Constitution.* London, 1923. (Day to Day Pamphlets, Hogarth Press.)

A short but clear description.

JUAN JIMÉNEZ DE ASÚA. *Proceso Histórico de la República Española.* Madrid, 1932.

M. SOLANA Y GUTIÉRREZ. *Miguel Maura y la Disolución de las Órdenes Religiosas en la Constitución Española.* Madrid, 1934.

An interesting account of the passing of the legislation on the Church from a Catholic point of view.

ÁLVARO DE ALBORNOZ. *La Política Religiosa de la República.* Madrid, 1935.

A collection of speeches made in the Cortes in 1932.

—— *Al Servicio de la República.* Madrid, 1936.

A collection of speeches made in 1936.

JOSÉ ORTEGA Y GASSET. *Rectificación de la República.* Madrid, 1931.

This includes a famous speech made in December 1931, criticizing the Republic.

General E. MOLA. *Memorias de mi paso por la Dirección de Seguridad.* In three volumes, entitled: 'Lo que yo supe'; 'Tempestad, Calma, Intriga y Crisis'; 'El Derrumbramiento de la Monarquía.' Madrid, 1931–1933.

J. CALVO SOTELO. *La Voz de un Perseguido.* (With an introduction by José María Pemán.) Madrid, 1933.
A collection of articles written in the violent and bitter tone characteristic of Calvo Sotelo after his return to Spain from exile.

JUAN DÍAZ DEL MORAL and JOSÉ ORTEGA Y GASSET. *La Reforma Agraria y el Estatuto Catalán.* Madrid, 1932.
Two speeches made in the Cortes and bound together in the same book. That by Díaz del Moral is a criticism of the projected law of Agrarian Reform.

MATEO AZPEITIA. *La Reforma Agraria en España.* Madrid, 1932.
A criticism of the project of agrarian reform written from a moderate conservative point of view.

Upon the working-class movement during this period there are:

JOAQUÍN MAURÍN. *Hacia la Segunda Revolución. El Fracaso de la República y la Insurrección de Octubre.* Barcelona, 1935.
An interesting book written from a Left Marxist point of view.

EDWARD CONZE. *Spain To-day.* London, 1936.
A short book based to a great extent upon the views of Maurín and Andrade, but containing some interesting first-hand observations.

JUAN ANDRADE. *La Burocracia Reformista en el Movimiento Obrero.* Madrid, 1935.
A bitter attack on the Socialists from a Left Marxist point of view.

E. VILLA. *Un Año de República en Sevilla.* Seville, 1932.

RAMÓN SENDER. *Viaje a la Aldea del Crimen. Documental de Casas Viejas.* Madrid, 1933.

FREDERICO URALES. *La Barbarie Gubernamental en Barcelona etc.* Barcelona, 1933.
Accounts by various authors of the beatings given by the police to Anarchists after a rising.

MANUEL BUENACASA. *La C.N.T., los Treinta y la F.A.I.* Barcelona, 1933.

Memoria del Congreso Extraordinario de la C.N.T. celebrada en Madrid los Dias 11 al 16 de Junio de 1931. Barcelona, 1931.

D. A. DE SANTILLÁN. *El Organismo Económico de la Revolución.* Barcelona, 1936.
The best exposition of the Anarcho-Syndicalist programme.

—— *After the Revolution.* New York, 1937.
A translation, with a final chapter on the Civil War, of the above.

FRANCISCO MADRID. *Ocho Meses y un Día en el Gobierno Civil de Barcelona.* Barcelona, 1932.
The last chapters give a detailed account of the efforts of the first Civil Governors of the Republic in Barcelona to come to terms with the Anarcho-Syndicalists.

F. BORKENAU. *The Communist International.* London, 1939.
The classic on the subject. It contains a short chapter on the Spanish Communists.

Upon the rising in 1934 there are:

MANUEL AZAÑA. *Mi Rebelión en Barcelona.* Madrid, 1935.

—— *Discursos en Campo Abierto.* Madrid, 1936.

ANTONIO RAMOS OLIVEIRA. *La Revolución Española de Octubre.* Madrid, 1935.
The best general account, by a Socialist.

MANUEL VILLAR. *El Anarquismo y la Insurrección de Asturias.* Buenos Aires, 1936.

—— *La Represión de Octubre.* Barcelona, 1936.
By the editor of *Solidaridad Obrera,* the Anarcho-Syndicalist daily.

ALFRED MENDIZÁBAL. *The Martyrdom of Spain.* 1937.
By a Catholic professor who was caught by the rising in Oviedo.

'Testigo Imparcial. *Revolución en Asturias.* 1935.

IGNACIO NUÑEZ. *La Revolución de Octubre de 1934.* 2 vols. Barcelona, 1935.
Very reactionary and clerical.

LEAH MANNING. *What I saw in Spain.* London, 1935.
Written mainly on material provided by the Socialist party.

Upon the rise of the Falange there are:

Hacia la Historia de la Falange. Primera Contribución de Sevilla. 2 vols. 1937.
A detailed and interesting account of the early history of the Falangist Movement in Lower Andalusia.

RAMIRO LEDESMA RAMOS. *Discurso a las Joventudes de España.* First published in May 1935, reprinted in 1938.
An interesting book by one of the first members of the Falange.

E. GIMÉNEZ CABALLERO. *Genio de España.* Madrid, 1932.

—— *La Nueva Catolicidad.* Madrid, 1933.
The author is a journalist who aspired to be the Rosenberg of the Spanish Falangist movement. His principal thesis is the identity of Catholicism and Fascism. Mussolini is the new St Ignatius. Though of some importance in Spain to-day, his ideas are such a farrago of nonsense that they can scarcely be taken seriously.

For the general ideas of Falange I have consulted:

José Pemartín. *Qué es 'lo Nuevo'. Consideraciones sobre el Momento Español presente.* Salamanca, 1938.

The Falangist *Mein Kampf.*

W. G. Oliveros. *Falange y Requeté.* Valladolid, 1937.

A propagandist work by a doctor at law in Salamanca University on the need for uniting the Requetés and the Falange.

Fe. The monthly magazine of the Falange, published from 1937 onwards.

CHAPTER XIV

Apart from the brief summaries in the Survey of International Affairs no objective history of the Spanish Civil War has yet come out. But the bibliography on these two and a half years is enormous. I shall not attempt to select from it here, but will mention only one book which I have found invaluable. This is *The Spanish Cockpit*, by Dr Franz Borkenau (1937). Its introductory chapter contains a brilliant essay on Spanish history and the rest of the book is a model of what field work by a social historian ought to be. Many of its conclusions are borne out by George Orwell's *Homage to Catalonia* (1938) and H. E. Kaminski's *Ceux de Barcelone* (Paris, 1937).

A good bibliography is given in the last number of *The Voice of Spain*, 14 June 1941.

INDEX

376